THE CHANGING VOIC
ABORTION MOVEMEN

The Rise of "Pro-Woman" Rhetoric in Canada and the United States

When journalists, academics, and politicians describe the North American anti-abortion movement, they often describe a campaign that is male-dominated, aggressive and even violent in its tactics, religious in motivation, anti-woman in tone, and fetal-centric in its arguments and rhetoric. Are they correct?

In *The Changing Voice of the Anti-abortion Movement*, Paul Saurette and Kelly Gordon suggest that the reality is far more complicated, particularly in Canada. Today, anti-abortion activism increasingly presents itself as "pro-woman": using female spokespersons, adopting medical and scientific language to claim that abortion harms women, and employing a wide range of more subtle framing and narrative rhetorical tactics that use traditionally progressive themes to present the anti-abortion position as more feminist than pro-choice feminism.

Following a succinct but comprehensive overview of the two-hundred-year history of North American debate and legislation on abortion, Saurette and Gordon present the results of their systematic, five-year quantitative and qualitative discourse analysis, supplemented by extensive first-person observations, and outline the implications that flow from these findings. Their discoveries are a challenge to our current assumptions about the abortion debate today, and their conclusions will be compelling for both scholars and activists alike.

PAUL SAURETTE is a professor in the School of Political Studies at the University of Ottawa.

KELLY GORDON is a PhD candidate in the School of Political Studies at the University of Ottawa.

The Changing Voice of the Anti-abortion Movement

The Rise of "Pro-Woman" Rhetoric in Canada and the United States

PAUL SAURETTE AND KELLY GORDON

UNIVERSITY OF TORONTO PRESS
Toronto Buffalo London

ISBN 978-1-4426-4761-9 (cloth)   ISBN 978-1-4426-1569-4 (paper)

♾ Printed on acid-free, 100% post-consumer recycled paper with vegetable-based inks.

Library and Archives Canada Cataloguing in Publication

Saurette, Paul, author
The changing voice of the anti-abortion movement: the rise of
"pro-woman" rhetoric in Canada and the United States / Paul
Saurette and Kelly Gordon.

Includes bibliographical references and index.
ISBN 978-1-4426-4761-9 (cloth). – ISBN 978-1-4426-1569-4 (paper)

1. Pro-life movement – Canada – History.   2. Pro-life movement – United
States – History.   I. Gordon, Kelly, 1984–, author   II. Title.

HQ767.5.C3S29 2015   363.460971   C2015-907240-9

This book has been published with the help of a grant from the Federation
for the Humanities and Social Sciences, through the Awards to Scholarly
Publications Program, using funds provided by the Social Sciences and
Humanities Research Council of Canada.

University of Toronto Press acknowledges the financial assistance to its
publishing program of the Canada Council for the Arts and the Ontario
Arts Council, an agency of the Government of Ontario.

 Canada Council **Conseil des Arts**
for the Arts **du Canada**

 ONTARIO ARTS COUNCIL
CONSEIL DES ARTS DE L'ONTARIO
an Ontario government agency
un organisme du gouvernement de l'Ontario

Funded by the   Financé par le
Government   gouvernement
of Canada   du Canada

Contents

Preface   xi

1   Introduction   3
   1.1   Abortion Politics in North America Today   4
   1.2   Why Study Abortion Politics?   11
   1.3   The Traditional Portrait: Male, Religious, Legislative,
       Anti-woman, Fetal-centric   12
   1.4   Theoretical Framework: Words Matter   17
   1.5   Methodology and Research Design   21
   1.6   Methodological Reliability   27
   1.7   Chapter Overview   31

Part I: Historicizing the Abortion Debate in North America

2   The History of the Abortion Debate in the United States   37
   2.1   Abortion before 1840   37
   2.2   The AMA's Crusade against Abortion: Medicalizing
       and (Im)moralizing Abortion   39
   2.3   Criminalizing Abortion, 1840–1900   43
   2.4   Liberalizing Birth Control, 1900–1940   47
   2.5   Legal Reform: Therapeutic Abortion Committees,
       1950s–1960s   51
   2.6   Setting the Stage for the Rise of the Abortion Rights
       Movement, 1960–1965   52
   2.7   The Rise of Rights before *Roe v. Wade*, 1965–1972   55
   2.8   The *Roe v. Wade* Decision, 1973   59
   2.9   Conclusion   62

3 The Abortion Debate in the United States after *Roe v. Wade*   65
   3.1   The Rise of the Contemporary American Anti-abortion
       Movement and the Hyde Amendment   66
   3.2   The Rising Influence of the Religious Right   68
   3.3   Operation Rescue   71
   3.4   The Rise of Anti-abortion Violence and the Decline of Operation
       Rescue   77
   3.5   The Backtrack: *Webster v. Reproductive Health Services*, 1989   79
   3.6   *Planned Parenthood of Southeastern Pennsylvania v.*
       Robert P. Casey et al., 1992   81
   3.7   Partial Birth Abortion Bans: *Stenberg v. Carhart* and *Gonzales v.*
       Carhart   83
   3.8   Contemporary Abortion Legislation   84
   3.9   Conclusion   90

4 The History of the Early Abortion Debate in Canada   92
   4.1   Criminalizing Abortion in Britain and Colonial Canada   93
   4.2   Abortion Reform in the United Kingdom   96
   4.3   The Birth Control Movement in Canada   99
   4.4   Abortion Reform in Canada   101
   4.5   The Decriminalization of Abortion: Section 251   105
   4.6   The Fallout over Section 251   106
   4.7   The Emergence of the Canadian Anti-abortion Movement   108
   4.8   The Intensification of the Anti-abortion Movement
       in Canada   110
   4.9   The Christian Right in Canada   111
   4.10 The Discourse of the Early Canadian Anti-abortion Movement   113
   4.11 Conclusion   116

5 The Abortion Debate in Canada: *Morgentaler* and Beyond   118
   5.1   Abortion in the Courts, Round 1: *Morgentaler v. The Queen*,
       1976   118
   5.2   A Transforming Political and Legal Context   120
   5.3   Abortion in the Courts, Round 2: *R. v. Morgentaler*, 1988   123
   5.4   Establishing a "Sense of the House": The Parliamentary
       Abortion Debate of 1988   126
   5.5   Abortion in the Courts, Round 3: Borowski's Attempt to
       Establish Fetal Rights   129
   5.6   Abortion in the Courts, the Final Round:
       Tremblay v. Daigle   130
   5.7   Drafting a New Abortion Law: Abortion in the
       Political Realm   132
   5.8   Anti-abortion Violence   134

5.9   Recent Anti-abortion Legislative Efforts   136
5.10   Conclusion   143

6 Intermezzo: The History of the Abortion Debate in
North America   145
6.1   Abortion Politics in the United States and Canada: Historical
Similarities and Differences   145
6.2   The Historical Abortion Debate and the Traditional Portrait   152

Part II: The Changing Voice of the Contemporary
Anti-abortion Movement

7 Shifting Strategies: A Little Old, a Lot New, a Bit of Both   159
7.1   Failing to Plan Is Planning to Fail: Results-Oriented
Strategizing   162
7.2   The Terrain of Contestation: Law and/or Culture   166
7.3   To the Web! The New Anti-abortion Network   170
7.4   Communications, Communications, Communications   173
7.5   Persuasion in the Streets: Reason, Rhetoric, and
Respect   178
7.6   Conclusion   188

8 Women Up Front, God Out Back: The Changing Anti-abortion
Arguments   189
8.1   God and the Public Sphere   191
8.2   Think about the Women: The "Abortion-Harms-Women"
Argument   198
8.3   Framing Harm: Discursive Medicalization, Progressive
Cooptation, Repetition   206
8.4   Visual Signalling: The Changing Face of the Movement   211
8.5   Fetal Personhood Renewed   216
8.6   Conclusion   220

9 We're All Progressives Now: Rebranding the Movement   222
9.1   Essentially Contested Concepts, Networks of Association,
and Framing   222
9.2   Identity/Brand Frame Extension: Progressives against
Abortion   231
9.3   Historical Progressivism   234
9.4   Contemporary Progressivism   237
9.5   Seekers of Truth, Defenders of Free Speech   240
9.6   Conclusion   243

10 Anti-abortionism as the New Feminism: Reframing the
    Position   245
       10.1 Values Framing: Equality and Choice   245
       10.2 Issue Framing: Anti-abortionism as a Women's Issue   253
       10.3 Epistemological Framing: Standpoint Anti-abortionism   264
       10.4 Conclusion   270

11 From Jezebel to Snow White: Moralizing through
    Narrativizing   271
       11.1 Metaphorical Tone: Strict Father or Nurturant Parent?   271
       11.2 From Jezebel to Snow White: Narratives in Action   277
       11.3 Conclusion   291

12 "Pro-woman" Discourse in the United States   292
       12.1 The Enduring Relevance of the Traditional Portrait in the
             United States   292
       12.2 The Emergence of Woman-Protective Anti-abortion
             Arguments   296
       12.3 The Prevalence of Woman-Protective Anti-abortion Arguments
             in American Anti-abortion Discourse   301
       12.4 Conclusion: Comparing the United States and Canada   308

Part III: Conclusions and Implications

13 Theoretical Implications   315
       13.1 Our Findings   316
       13.2 Implications for the Study of Canadian Politics   320
       13.3 Implications for the Study of Political Movements,
             Communication, and Ideology   321
       13.4 Implications for the Study of Religion and Politics in Canada   323
       13.5 Explaining the Shape of Contemporary Anti-abortion
             Discourse in Canada   327
       13.6 Implications for Gender Studies   331
       13.7 Methodological Implications   334

14 Where to Now? Practical Implications for Abortion Rights
    Advocates   337
       14.1 A Reproductive Justice Frame?   339
       14.2 Organizational and Tactical Implications   345

Acknowledgments   361

*Appendix A: Glossary of Key Legal and Political Events,
Organizations, and Individuals*   367
    A1. Legislation, Policy, Legal Decisions   367
    A2. Civil Society Organizations and Campaigns   373
    A3. Individuals   379

*Appendix B: Historical Timeline – Abortion Politics in the United Kingdom,
Canada, and the United States*   384

*Appendix C: Historical Timeline – Abortion Discourse in Canada and the
United States*   388

References   393

Index   423

Preface

In 2003, Canada's Parliament Hill witnessed the sixth March for Life – the annual anti-abortion[1] rally organized by the Campaign Life Coalition (CLC), one of Canada's most prominent and traditional national anti-abortion organizations. According to a report by LifeSiteNews (2003), the march drew 3,300 attendees[2] and was characterized by speeches from anti-abortion parliamentarians, activists, and religious leaders "demanding an end to the discrimination against unborn babies" – the fetal-centric refrain that is often taken to be the heart of the North American anti-abortion movement's discourse.

True to form, this refrain was also taken up by the keynote speaker at the post-march banquet, Dr. John Willke. An M.D., author of several anti-abortion books, and influential leader in the American anti-abortion movement,[3] Willke was also an adviser to 2012 Republican presidential candidate Mitt Romney (Atlantic Wire 2012). Willke is perhaps most infamous, however, for being one of the foremost proponents

---

1 Given the diversity of discursive and philosophical grounds employed by contemporary anti-abortion activists and organizations, we have chosen to refer to them as "anti-abortion" (which simply describes their policy position) rather than "pro-life" (which implies a certain discursive and philosophical foundation that is not necessarily an accurate description) (see Cuneo 1989). We have done the same with the other side of the debate, describing them as "abortion rights" activists – or the abortion rights movement. That said, we sometimes use "pro-choice" or "pro-life" when it is more historically accurate or is necessary for another reason.

2 This figure may well be a significant exaggeration, as their estimates are routinely much higher than police and media estimates.

3 Dr. John Willke was president of National Right to Life from 1984 to 1991 and was the founder and president of the International Right to Life Federation.

of the discredited theory that pregnancy almost never results from rape[4] and for using his theory to support the belief that abortion should be prohibited without any exception (Atlantic Wire 2012). In fact, Willke's "legitimate rape" theory came to play a pivotal role in the 2012 US elections when Todd Akin, a Republican member of the House of Representatives, justified his belief that there should be no "rape exception" in abortion laws by stating that, "from what I understand from doctors, that's [pregnancy resulting from a rape] really rare. If it's a legitimate rape, the female body has ways to try to shut that whole thing down. But let's assume that maybe that didn't work or something. I think there should be some punishment, but the punishment ought to be on the rapist and not attacking the child" (Jaco 2012). In the wake of the resulting controversy, Willke defended Akin's comments, arguing that rape "is a traumatic thing – she's, shall we say, she's uptight. She is frightened, tight, and so on. And sperm, if deposited in the vagina, are less likely to be able to fertilize. The tubes are spastic" (Atlantic Wire 2012).

These comments, and the controversy they engendered, received widespread media attention, generating political commentary not only across the US but in Canada as well (the *Globe and Mail*, Canada's national newspaper, published no fewer than seven articles on the issue). Given that for the past twenty-five years, most of the media coverage of abortion politics in North America has focused (even in Canada) on the American context, it is perhaps unsurprising that many Canadians and Americans assume that Willke and Akin are representative of the contemporary anti-abortion movement and their strategies of persuasion. Male-led, conservative, politically uncompromising, fixated on criminalizing abortion through legislation, fetal-centric in its argumentation, religious in its philosophical justification, and "anti-woman" in its tone and orientation – this "traditional portrait" of the anti-abortion movement in North America is the dominant characterization accepted by most popular observers, citizens, and scholars.

But how accurate is this portrait? This book is an attempt to answer that question by analysing the nature of the contemporary North American anti-abortion movement (in particular, its rhetorical and communication strategies) and comparing them to the essential characteristics

---

4 Willke claimed that no more than 200 rape-related pregnancies occur annually in the United States, despite strong evidence suggesting that 5 per cent of rapes – or 32,000 annually in the United States – result in pregnancy (Holmes et al. 1996).

of anti-abortion activism and discourse in previous eras (in Canada, the US, and the UK since the 1800s). What are the key characteristics of the contemporary North American anti-abortion movement (particularly the understudied Canadian movement) and the rhetorical strategies of persuasion it uses? Does the traditional portrait accurately convey the core nature of the anti-abortion movement today? Or has the contemporary anti-abortion movement developed important characteristics and practices that are largely unrecognized by the traditional portrait?

The answers to these questions are far from obvious. Take the Canadian context, for example. Ten years after Willke's keynote in 2003, the March for Life and the movement that organized it look quite different. To begin with, they both appear to be better organized and much more effective. In contrast to the three thousand or so protestors estimated to have been in attendance in 2003, the anti-abortion website LifeSite-News claimed that 25,000 attended the 2013 March for Life – which, if accurate, would be a 750 per cent increase (Craine 2012). Even if we use the much lower estimates offered by neutral organizations (the police, for example, estimated that the 2013 march attracted approximately 12,000–15,000), attendance has quadrupled in ten years (Stone 2013a).

Even more notable than the increase in numbers, however, is the contrast between the main themes and tones of the two marches. In 2003, the posters, arguments, and core demands were tightly focused on fetal rights ("an end to discrimination against unborn babies"). In contrast, the mission of the 2013 march was expressed in language that could easily be mistaken for the slogan of any number of feminist activist groups: "Stop Gendercide: Protect Girls." This "pro-woman,"[5]

---

5 Throughout this book, we use terms like "pro-woman" and "anti-woman" to describe the overall tone and general orientation of a given discourse. Lest this create misunderstandings and unnecessary controversy, let us be clear. When we speak of "pro-woman" or "anti-woman," we are not using these terms to make a normative value judgment. When we use these terms, we are not claiming that, in their effects or in their motivation/intention, a given discourse, policy, organization, or actor is actually "pro-woman" or "anti-woman" in the evaluative sense of the term. We are not, in other words, using this term normatively to evaluate the actual content of the motivation, intention, or effect. Rather, we are simply using "pro-woman" or "anti-woman" to describe the overall "positioning" of a given discourse/policy – i.e., the way it would sound to an average Canadian citizen (the "average Canadian citizen" is obviously a simplified fictitious construct, but a useful one in this case). We use the term "pro-woman" if it seems that a given discourse is seeking to convince its audience to support its point of view by appearing supportive, respectful, and

feminist-sounding messaging characterized other 2013 March for Life events, as well. The 2013 banquet keynote speech, for example, was delivered by Reggie Littlejohn, the founder and president of an organization called Women's Rights without Frontiers. Her speech was a perfect reflection of the March for Life's "Stop Gendercide" thematic and drew heavily on the language of feminism. According to Littlejohn, on the issue of forced abortion in China and India, "it doesn't matter if you are pro-life or pro-choice" (Brown 2012). Rather, in her view the real question is not whether you believe a fetus has a right to live. The real question is whether you support women's and girls' rights.

Littlejohn reiterated these themes forcefully the next day as well when addressing a room of almost 1,000 high school students at the annual March for Life Youth Conference – a conference designed to educate youth on anti-abortion activism so they can bring the "pro-life message back to their schools, communities and churches." Drawing on feminist tropes that would seem at home in any gender studies course, Littlejohn opened her talk by asking the teens, "Do you ever feel like boys have it better than girls?" and highlighted her own personal childhood experience fighting sexism ("when the boys wouldn't let me play kickball, I started an all-girls kickball team … Girls can do anything boys can do"). She then closed with a passionate critique against the practice of sex-selection abortion in China by calling it "China's War on Women" (2013 March for Life Youth Conference, authors' observation).

The contrast between the stances of Littlejohn and Willke is extraordinary. Willke's views were explicitly grounded in religious appeals and gave a central role to fetal-centric arguments. In contrast, Littlejohn explicitly assured the audience that both her politics and her organization were resolutely non-religious (although she did acknowledge the importance of faith in her own "personal journey"). Where Willke's

---

positively oriented towards women and women's interests – and that many Canadian citizens would hear it in that way. Similarly, we use the term "anti-woman" if it seems like the given discourse or policy is seeking to convince its audience to support its point of view in terms that would appear to either ignore or dismiss women's perspectives and interests and would thus seem patriarchal and controlling to many Canadians. Admittedly, these are fuzzy terms, and even the simple, descriptive, and non-normative way we are trying to use them involves a series of judgment calls. At the end of the day, however, we believe that they are useful heuristics that help us capture an absolutely crucial element of what is at play in the Canadian abortion debate (as well as many others) today.

politics reflected a punitive and controlling attitude towards female sexuality and his language displayed a dismissive attitude towards women and gender issues (see, e.g., Willke 1978), Littlejohn lamented the violence and abuse faced by women as a result of traditional patriarchal attitudes towards female sexuality in ways that strongly paralleled feminist analyses (2013 March for Life Youth Conference, authors' observation).

Not everything has changed, of course, and the characteristics of the two marches also suggest that some important continuities exist between the older anti-abortion movement and the contemporary one. For example, some actors in the Canadian anti-abortion movement, such as the Canadian Centre for Bio-ethical Reform (CCBR), continue to rely on fetal-centric arguments and have even introduced much more aggressive and graphic fetal imagery in their public demonstrations. Moreover, the fact that only two of the twenty-two politicians who spoke or were officially recognized at the 2013 march were women says much about the important role that men continue to play in the movement.

However, even these apparent continuities should not be overstated. Despite the fact that the CCBR has launched campaigns across the country using graphic imagery and fetal-centric slogans, such themes and images were surprisingly absent from the 2013 march. Instead, most placards and speeches conveyed "compassionate" and pro-woman-sounding messages. By our estimate, at least half of the signs on display were variations on these themes – for example, "I regret my abortion," "ProWomanProLife," or "Women deserve better than abortion" (2013 March for Life, authors' observation).

Moreover, even the gender disparity of the official speakers was counter-balanced in several ways. The official speeches on the Hill, for example, reflected an increasingly "pro-woman" tone, with many speakers stressing the pain and suffering abortion causes *women*. The organizers of the march also took pains to highlight the twenty-five women who had walked from Montreal to Ottawa to attend the march (each symbolizing one of the twenty-five years of legal abortion in Canada). The presence of these women was emphasized throughout the March for Life – through their visual presence on the steps of Parliament (as a backdrop for the other official speakers), at post-march events and speeches, and in terms of media availability. The message from each woman was essentially the same: abortion harms women. Couched in a tone of sympathetic understanding and empathy, each spoke at length about the emotional trauma of their abortions while stressing that it was the "pro-woman" compassion of the anti-abortion movement that ultimately helped them overcome the damage done to them as a result of abortion (2013 March for Life, authors' observation).

To what degree do the many differences (and some continuities) between the two rallies reflect a broader shift in the public discourse and communication strategies used by the anti-abortion movement in Canada, and throughout North America? Was the 2013 March for Life simply an outlier in a relatively static and homogeneous anti-abortion movement? Or has the Canadian anti-abortion movement shifted its public image and arguments? How is the contemporary anti-abortion movement seeking to persuade the public to accept its policy stance? What are the main rhetorical techniques it is using? How do these techniques function? How widely are they used? To what degree do these contemporary strategies parallel and diverge from those used in previous eras of anti-abortion activism? And to what degree do the strategies of the contemporary Canadian movement mirror and/or differ from those employed by contemporary American activists? These are some of the key questions we address in this book.

Rather than assuming that the answers to these questions are self-evident, we have sought to explore them through rigorous empirical analysis. Over the past five years, we have systematically investigated the rhetorical and communication strategies employed in the public discourse of the anti-abortion movement in North America. Our contemporary analysis has focused particularly on the Canadian anti-abortion movement because the Canadian context has been understudied, compared to its American counterpart.

What did we find? Our analysis reveals that the thematic, tonal, and visual differences between the 2003 and 2013 Marches for Life are neither random nor outliers. Rather, they are emblematic of a considerable transformation in the communications strategy of the anti-abortion movement in Canada – a shift that has made the movement's political discourse quite distinct from that of earlier Canadian and American anti-abortion activists, and even from the dominant strains of the contemporary American movement (although, as we discuss in chapters 6 and 12, some of the core arguments of the "pro-woman" framing first emerged in the US, and there is some evidence that it is starting to become increasingly popular in the contemporary US anti-abortion movement as well).

We have found, for example, that over the past decade the Canadian anti-abortion movement has increasingly employed a public discourse that serves to distance itself from the stereotypical image of the movement as male-led, religiously grounded, focused on criminalizing abortion, fetal-centric, and aggressively anti-woman in its tone. Instead, the movement is increasingly using a variety of rhetorical techniques (including arguments, visuals, frames, and narratives) to present a profoundly different public face and voice to Canadians – one that portrays the anti-abortion position as modern, non-religious, open, sympathetic, and, above all, "pro-woman" and progressive.

This transformation can be seen in many different dimensions of the contemporary anti-abortion movement and its discourse. We have found, for example, that the anti-abortion movement in Canada in 2015 seems to be a movement in resurgence. Its main actors and organizations are increasingly networked and are self-consciously strategic in their vision. It has adopted sophisticated and innovative approaches to strategic communications, including carefully managing how, why, and when its supporters engage in public debate. It has increasingly foregrounded a highly visible core of young, female activists as its primary spokespersons. And it has largely eliminated the raw public expressions of anger and violence that were associated with the movement in previous decades.

We have also found that the thematic and rhetorical content of contemporary Canadian anti-abortion discourse is quite different from that suggested by the traditional portrait of anti-abortion activism. When directed to audiences outside the movement, contemporary discourse in Canada largely avoids public appeals to religion as a philosophical ground and justification. It increasingly employs a new "pro-woman" argument (the "abortion-harms-women" argument) in its public discourse. And it has reduced its reliance on traditional fetal-centric arguments and refined its remaining fetal-centric arguments so as to infuse them with "pro-woman" themes and tones.

The public discourse of the anti-abortion movement is also employing a variety of more subtle rhetorical strategies of persuasion that parallel and reinforce these more explicit "pro-woman" arguments. Contemporary Canadian anti-abortion discourse is seeking to transform the traditional image of the movement as a regressive, conservative attempt to control women by rebranding its public identity as an heir to many other progressive/social justice movements. It has taken up, redefined, and redeployed feminist values such as equality and choice in surprising ways. It has adopted a version of female stand-point epistemology and reframed its cause as a women's issue, arguing that the anti-abortion position is both aligned and consistent with other feminist goals such as the struggle against domestic violence. The movement has adopted a new, more compassionate metaphorical tone, and has even developed new narratives (in which women are no longer villains but are instead victims of abortion) to present the anti-abortion position as consistent with the progressive, "pro-woman" beliefs and attitudes that many Canadians hold.

Overall, then, our historical and comparative analysis suggests that, while there are some important continuities between the contemporary Canadian movement and that of previous historical eras in North America, the strategies of persuasion employed by the contemporary Canadian movement are quite distinctive insofar as they include a wide variety of new techniques, some older techniques, and some hybridized techniques that combine both old and new elements. Interestingly, our comparative historical analysis shows that the traditional portrait accurately describes only a very narrow sliver of anti-abortion activism in North America (essentially the period between the 1970s and the late 1990s in Canada and between the 1970s and the present day in the US) and that anti-abortion discourse has gone through a variety of shifts since the mid-nineteenth century.

Exploring the various questions outlined above has resulted in a much more expansive and comprehensive book than we had imagined. What we originally envisioned as a short book on contemporary anti-abortion discourse in Canada became a much longer work that traces the historical and contemporary nature of abortion politics in North America. As a scholarly work, the research design, analyses, and findings of our study are supported by all the methodological and evidential rigour required of academic studies. However, our goal has been to ensure that this book is accessible to both non-academic and academic readers alike. Given this goal, we have done a number of things to make it as user-friendly as possible.

First, we have sought to avoid academic jargon as much as possible and have attempted to explain and concretize our theoretical concepts and methods using everyday examples so that our readers don't need to be experts in discourse analysis to understand our findings.

Second, we have also tried to structure the book in a way that will allow readers, should they so desire, to focus on the themes they are most interested in. Part I of the book is historical, tracing the history of the abortion debate and the anti-abortion movement in Canada (and, as context for the debate in colonial Canada, the United Kingdom) and the United States. The second part looks at the contemporary anti-abortion movement in North America, with a particular focus on Canada. Part III contains two concluding chapters (a more scholarly consideration of the theoretical and academic implications of our findings; and a more concrete discussion of the practical implications of our study). In essence, then, this book comprises two distinct, but closely related and complementary, studies, with a concluding third part that explores their shared implications.

We have therefore organized this book to ensure that, while linked, each part and each chapter offers a clear and concise story on its own. The historical chapters in Part I, for example, are structured in such a way that they flow into and set the context for Part II. But they can also be used on their own by readers who are looking for a succinct synthesis of the main legal decisions, political events, and discursive trends that have characterized the history of the abortion debate in North America over the last two hundred years.

Parts II and III will be much richer for the reader who knows the comparative historical context outlined in Part I. However, readers who are solely interested in the contemporary context and who choose to read only Part II and Part III will nonetheless be able to follow our analysis of the contemporary context. (In such cases, however, we would recommend that readers consult chapter 6 and Appendices B and C, as these components briefly summarize and synthesize some of the main findings of Part I.) To ensure that our analysis in Part II is as clear as possible, each chapter in Part II is organized around clusters of related rhetorical techniques of persuasion. This ensures that each chapter not only contributes to demonstrating how anti-abortion discourse functions as a whole, but also gives the reader a detailed sense of how specific rhetorical techniques are used in public political discourse.

Finally, we have included three appendices to help readers keep track of the many dates, organizations, and events that have characterized the abortion debate in North America. Appendix A briefly describes key events, organizations, and individuals in the anti-abortion movement. Appendices B and C consist of historical timelines of the main political and legal events – as well as the key discursive trends – related to the movement over the last several hundred years. Collectively, the appendices may come in handy for those moments when the forest might seem lost for the trees, or for when the trees seem to disappear into the forest.

Our hope, then, is that this book speaks to as many different readers as possible, offering them an interesting and engaging view of the way the political world of words functions – particularly in relation to the abortion debate in North America.

THE CHANGING VOICE OF THE ANTI-ABORTION MOVEMENT

The Rise of "Pro-Woman" Rhetoric in Canada and the United States

Chapter 1

Introduction

This is a book about the way that words and politics intersect. At a theoretical level, it is about how we "talk" in politics and why it matters. It is about the different rhetorical techniques that political actors and movements use to persuade their fellow citizens to agree with them and how these techniques actually function to change people's minds and build support. At a more concrete level, it is about how we talk about abortion and what we might call the specific discursive politics of the abortion debate in North America today. It is about which rhetorical techniques of persuasion and communication strategies are being used by the contemporary anti-abortion movement, how these techniques function, how widely they are used, whether they differ from those used by previous waves of Canadian and American anti-abortion activism, and why all of this matters.

While it might be tempting to dismiss all the "talk" of contemporary politics as sound and fury, this could not be further from reality. In the media- and communications-saturated universe of North American politics, it is more important than ever for citizens to be able to identify, unpack, and evaluate the sophisticated and often subtle techniques of persuasion that various social, economic, and political actors employ to convince us of what to think and how to behave. At this level, our hope is that the theoretical frameworks and empirical analyses of specific techniques contained in this book will help readers navigate and proactively engage with the world of political persuasion. Because abortion policy remains an important political issue in North America – and may be re-emerging as an important site of contestation in Canada – we also hope that this book sheds light on both the historical context and the contemporary nature of the rhetorical and organizational tools that are being used to try to convince the public to support one vision or another.

1.1 Abortion Politics in North America Today

Few would question the relevance of examining abortion politics in the United States today. In fact, given the intensity of the American debate over abortion – and the degree to which it is covered in the media even in Canada – it is virtually impossible for Canadians to think about abortion politics without invariably, even if subconsciously, importing assumptions and comparisons from the battle over abortion in the US. The stark visibility of a fairly extreme American anti-abortion movement combined with the relatively quiet Canadian context has encouraged many observers to make one of two assumptions: either that the anti-abortion movement in Canada must be basically the same as it is in the US, or that because we don't see much of the extreme, American-style anti-abortion politics in Canada, there must not be much happening in Canada when it comes to abortion politics. Yet, neither of these assumptions is particularly well grounded. As such, it is important to start with some discussion of the abortion debate in both the US and Canada.

Over the past forty years, North Americans have spent an immense amount of energy talking and politicking about abortion. In the US, the issue has been on heavy rotation during most electoral cycles since the US Supreme Court established (basic) access to abortion in its famous *Roe v. Wade* decision in 1973. Today the question remains a staple of US politics; indeed, legal abortion is as intensely contested today as it ever has been. It has long been the case that one cannot become the Republican candidate for president without being explicitly anti-abortion. The last Republican presidential candidate who was openly in favour of abortion rights was the libertarian Barry Goldwater in 1964. Richard Nixon and Gerald Ford essentially dodged the issue in the late 1960s and early 1970s by claiming that it was the prerogative of states. Since then, the Republican Party has been staunchly anti-abortion. Ronald Reagan explicitly highlighted his anti-abortion beliefs as both a candidate and as president and during the late 1970s and early 1980s and the Republican Party itself adopted a strong anti-abortion position as its official policy in the early 1980s. Since then, even "moderate" Republican candidates, such as George H.W. Bush in 1988 and 1992, have found it necessary to assert an anti-abortion position. Mitt Romney, who had supported a women's right to choose in his 2002 bid for the governorship of Massachusetts, was forced to pivot sharply to the right and adopt a much more explicit and rigid anti-abortion position to win the Republican nomination for the 2012 presidential election (this included promising to nominate Supreme Court justices who would overturn *Roe v. Wade*).

Moreover, since 1973, abortion has often been a key issue to mobilize the base and get out the vote in US elections, and the anti-abortion movement has achieved significant success in the electoral and legislative realms. More than twenty-nine of the fifty governors in office at the beginning of 2011 were considered staunchly anti-abortion (Eckholm 2011). And despite the fact that *Roe v. Wade* struck down absolute bans on abortion as unconstitutional, many states have since passed legislation that has dramatically limited access to abortion, even if they have not been able to ban it completely. For example, in 2011 and 2012, nineteen states introduced bills prohibiting abortion later than 20 weeks post-fertilization, with Arizona declaring that pregnancy legally begins two weeks *before* physical conception, reducing the available window down to 18 weeks after fertilization (Gold and Nash 2013). In total, forty-two states now prohibit abortions after a certain point – most frequently the 20–24 week mark (Guttmacher Institute 2015). Many states also impose additional requirements on doctors and women before abortions can be performed – impositions that have forced many clinics to shut down and that create serious obstacles for women who have to travel long distances to find a doctor who will perform abortions. In 2012, for example, Wisconsin passed a law that requires doctors to have three meetings with the patient before prescribing the medical abortion pill (Mifepristone). In Louisiana – where existing legislation already forces women seeking an abortion to view an ultrasound of the fetus – lawmakers have proposed a bill that would also require women to listen to the embryonic heartbeat before being allowed to have an abortion.

In the US, these examples are not outliers. They are increasingly the norm. The Guttmacher Institute analyses every state's existing legislation and policy regarding abortion and then identifies them as either "hostile," "middle-ground," or "supportive" of abortion rights. Between 2000 and 2011, fifteen states became more hostile; none became more supportive (Guttmacher Institute 2013a). Moreover, the frequency of new anti-abortion legislation in the US has increased substantially: both 2011 and 2012 were unprecedented years for anti-abortion legislation, with more than 1,100 bills that regulated reproductive rights introduced in state legislatures in 2011. Of these, 135 were successfully passed, of which 92 were aimed at restricting abortion access in various ways. Given that the previous high was 37 successful bills restricting abortion in 2005, this meant that the 2011 total was 250 per cent more than the previous record (Guttmacher Institute 2013a). Although the 2012 number was down from 2011, its 43 successful laws still vastly outstripped the earlier 2005 high-water mark.

In contrast, the political contest over abortion in Canada has seemed to be in deep hibernation since the early 1990s. Canada's sitting Conservative prime minister, Stephen Harper, has explicitly stated on several occasions that he will not reopen the abortion debate (CBC News 2011a). Even with a majority government and a political structure that gave him policy control that American conservative politicians can only dream about, throughout his tenure as prime minister, Harper consistently took active steps to shut down debate on anti-abortion motions, despite the fact that this approach has caused tension within his caucus and core supporters (see, for example, the discussion of Mark Warawa's Motion 408 below). Since 1988, when the Supreme Court of Canada's decision in *Morgentaler* declared federal abortion law unconstitutional, there has been no torrent of federal or provincial laws designed to re-regulate abortion (although abortion was nearly recriminalized in 1991). Moreover, even the Abortion Rights Coalition of Canada (ARCC) has concluded that anti-abortion "protest activity has been relatively low and sporadic at most [abortion] clinics since the mid-1990s" (Wu and Arthur 2010, 31) and that many clinics that do experience such activity have been largely able to take "effective measures" to reduce the impact of the protests (10–11).

Recently, however, the abortion debate has become much more visible. For example, despite the *Morgentaler* decision, Prince Edward Island and New Brunswick have imposed a variety of policies that were designed to significantly limit abortion access. PEI has resolutely disallowed every attempt to have abortions performed in the province (it does cover the medical cost of abortions performed outside the province but does not cover women's travel costs). This situation appeared to be poised to change in 2013, when a new initiative was proposed that even the province's own Department of Health and Wellness stated would save the province money and improve patient outcomes. However, it was scuttled after the Minister of Health and Wellness instructed the department that there was no chance that the government would support the initiative (CBC News 2014). Given the mobilization of both anti-abortion and abortion rights groups around this decision, it seems likely that this issue will reappear and become an ongoing and actively contested issue in PEI for the foreseeable future.

In New Brunswick, abortion access became a major political issue in 2014. Despite the *Morgentaler* decision, New Brunswick had long refused to reimburse women for abortions performed outside hospitals. Moreover, its Regulation 84-20 had required that all abortions performed within hospitals had to be authorized by two doctors, a policy that closely resembled the pre-*Morgentaler* status quo. In April 2014, the Morgentaler Clinic, the only stand-alone abortion clinic in New Brunswick (which was also one of the primary providers to PEI residents and one of the few stand-alone clinics in Atlantic Canada), announced that it was shutting down, primarily due to the fact that the New Brunswick government refuses to fund abortions performed in private clinics. This announcement created significant political mobilization on both sides of the issue. A successful online funding campaign in support of the clinic raised over $128,000 from individual donors by August 2014 (CTV News 2014), and a new health clinic (which provides a wide range of health services, including abortion) is now operating from the same location as the previous Morgentaler Clinic (CBC News 2015). Moreover, the issue of abortion access became central to the October 2014 provincial election in New Brunswick when Liberal Party leader Brian Gallant pledged to review barriers to abortion access in the province. Gallant's Liberals won the election and, in November 2014, he announced the elimination of Regulation 84-20 effective 1 January 2015. At the time of writing, his government had not addressed the question of New Brunswick's refusal to fund abortions performed outside hospitals, so it seems that the issue will continue to be the subject of some debate.

Abortion policy also became the topic of much more discussion on the federal scene in 2014 than it had been for many years. In May 2014, for example, the leader of the federal Liberal Party, Justin Trudeau, announced that, under his leadership, votes on abortion would no longer be considered so-called free votes of conscience (as had been the historical norm in the party). Rather, he stated that – as is the practice for almost all issues voted on in Parliament – Liberal members of Parliament (MPs) would henceforth be expected to vote in line with party policy, and that policy would now be explicitly pro-choice. The announcement led various anti-abortion advocates to attack Trudeau's judgment and the legitimacy of his decision and to argue that a new debate about abortion was required. It also inspired a surprisingly robust and highly visible debate in the mainstream media, with the vast majority of pundits criticizing Trudeau as being "undemocratic," with many of them echoing questions about whether the status quo abortion policy needed to be revisited (Saurette 2014). For many commentators, abortion was now closer to being on the mainstream political agenda than it had been since the early 1990s.

Those who follow the subject closely, however, know that over the past several decades, the issue has not been quite as settled in Canada as many have assumed. Since the *Morgentaler* decision in 1988, the anti-abortion movement has consistently contested the status quo. Protesters continue to demonstrate outside many abortion clinics (Wu and Arthur 2010, 9). The 40 Days for Life campaign, which was imported to Canada from the US, has led to more protests at several clinics over the past several years. Reliable estimates suggest that the last several national anti-abortion March for Life rallies attracted up to 15,000 marchers to Parliament Hill – more than four times the size of the 2003 march (CBC News 2012). There have also been, and continue to be, a variety of ongoing provincial campaigns to "defund" abortion. In 2010, the federal Conservative government announced that its G8 child and maternal health care initiative for developing countries would not fund abortion under any circumstances (CBC News 2010). Moreover, the reality of accessibility means that abortion rights in Canada remain complicated – as of 2006, less than 16 per cent of hospitals across the country offered abortion services (Shaw 2006, 30). And as we will discuss in chapter 5, there are major differences in access depending on geographic location, especially in regard to First Nations populations (Health Canada 2012). Further, as we will demonstrate throughout this book, at the level of discursive politics the anti-abortion movement has been making significant changes to its communications and persuasion strategies.

The abortion question has also been the subject of more political debate over the last several decades than most Canadians would suspect. In response to the *Morgentaler* decision, for example, Brian Mulroney's Progressive Conservative government introduced Bill C-43 in 1991 (a bill that essentially sought to recriminalize abortion except in cases where it was necessary to save a women's life or protect her health). It was was passed by the House of Commons but failed to become the law of the land only because it was defeated in the Senate at the last minute by the narrowest of margins – the only tie vote in the history of the Senate. Since that time, at least forty-four private members' bills with anti-abortion implications have been introduced in the House of Commons (although none have passed). Between 2007 and 2013, there have been three anti-abortion bills – Bill C-484 (the Unborn Victims of Crime Act allowing for separate homicide charges if an act of violence to a pregnant woman causes the death of a fetus) in 2007, Bill C-537 (preventing medical personnel from being "coerced" into performing abortions) in 2008, and Bill C-510 (banning "coerced abortions") in 2010 – as well as several motions.

Even before the events of 2014, Parliament witnessed a particularly interesting uptick in abortion politics. In 2012, Conservative MP Stephen Woodworth's private member's bill, Motion 312, clearly sought to revisit the abortion question, although in a very Canadian way. It was politely worded. It did not propose a law banning abortion. It simply sought a study of, and discussion about, "modernizing" the definition of *human being* in the Criminal Code. Woodworth himself, however, admitted publicly that it would have direct implications for the question of abortion. In an attempt to keep his previous election promise not to reopen the abortion issue, while at the same time not entirely alienating anti-abortion MPs, Prime Minister Harper urged his cabinet to vote against the motion but did not whip the vote. Although the motion was defeated, it was notable that ninety-one MPs – almost 30 per cent – voted for it, including ten cabinet ministers – most notably Peter Van Loen (Government House Leader at the time), Jason Kenney (who held several cabinet posts in the Harper government and is widely perceived as a serious contender to replace Harper as leader), and Rona Ambrose (the Minister for the Status of Women at the time and the current interim leader of the Conservative Party of Canada).

Perhaps even more notable for its political effect was Conservative MP Mark Warawa's follow-up attempt to introduce a private member's bill, Motion 408, in 2012. This motion, which called on Parliament to condemn sex-selective abortion, caused significant debate in both Parliament and in the media. When the motion was eventually deemed technically "non-votable"[1] by a Conservative-dominated committee, there was a revolt by Conservative backbenchers who believed that then Prime Minister Harper was using his influence to quash the motion.

---

1 This is a technical and rarely used procedural decision that disallows a motion or bill from reaching the floor and being debated by the House of Commons.

More surprising was that the mainstream media also engaged on this issue in an intense and sustained way, with the vast majority of the commentary arguing in favour of allowing the motion to go forward (not necessarily because pundits supported the content, but because most felt it was a serious matter worthy of parliamentary debate that had been quashed by backroom technicalities for political expediency).

The fact that so many MPs and high-profile cabinet ministers were willing to ignore the prime minister's preference and vote in favour of Motion 312 (as well as kick up a fuss about Warawa's motion) suggests that, under different Conservative leadership, abortion might once again become an issue in mainstream politics. In an interview with the *Vancouver Observer*, Woodworth not so subtly suggested that he believed this to be the case: "As you have probably heard me say, I always keep private conversations private, but I know enough of Minister Kenney's character, background, and beliefs to know that he, like me, would be an advocate for enshrining in Canadian law the equality and dignity and worth of every human being" (Wong 2012).

In the wake of the 2015 election and the debate over the strategic future of the Conservative Party of Canada, to suggest that a new Conservative leader might reopen the abortion question – and to note that many mainstream pundits seem willing to give the issue coverage that is at least partially sympathetic – is not to engage in "the sky is falling" hyperbole. Nor does it assume that the conservative movement and Conservative Party of Canada have a hidden agenda and that the party is simply biding its time for the opportunity to recriminalize abortion. It seems quite clear that many influential actors in the conservative movement worry that reopening this issue would deeply harm efforts at solidifying the Conservative platform for long-term electoral success. Thus, they want to avoid the issue becoming repoliticized. Moreover, there is little evidence to suggest that the bulk of conservative opinion leaders and decision makers want to recriminalize abortion. For instance, at the 2014 Manning Centre Networking Conference – one of the largest annual conservative events, whose intent is to bring together conservative-minded thinkers, activists, and politicians – not a single panel directly or indirectly addressed the abortion issue (2014 Manning Centre Networking Conference, authors' observations). Moreover, even the anti-abortion groups who were at the conference presented themselves as conservative outsiders. When offering his organization's pamphlets, for example, the exhibitor working at the Campaign Life Coalition table warned us that we might want to hide their graphic materials because they were considered too "extreme" by the event (2014 Manning Centre Networking Conference, authors' observations).

That said, there are clearly some influential actors in the federal Conservative Party and the conservative movement more generally who would be willing to facilitate the resurrection of abortion as an actively contested political issue should the right political circumstances arise. As we see it, those circumstances would include the federal Conservatives choosing a new leader who is more of a social conservative than Harper and a belief among influential political advisers that public opinion surrounding abortion could be shifted, perhaps as a result of new types of anti-abortion bills and framing that might hold broader public appeal. Thus, while abortion may not currently be an issue that is boiling away visibly on the front burner in Canada, that does not mean that it might not feature prominently on some future political menu.

1.2 Why Study Abortion Politics?

While there has been significant analysis of the abortion debate in the US, there is surprisingly little academic work on the contemporary abortion debate in Canada. More specifically, there are virtually no studies on the strategies of persuasion and communication tactics used by the contemporary Canadian anti-abortion movement. The bulk of the academic work on the politics of abortion in Canada emerged in the 1980s and 1990s in response to the political battle over abortion law, which culminated in the 1988 Supreme Court of Canada's *Morgentaler* decision striking down the federal laws regulating abortion (see Cuneo 1989; Dubinsky 1985; Brodie, Gavigan, and Jenson 1992; Morton 1992; Perrault and Cardinal 1996; Tatalovich 1997; McLaren and McLaren 1997). Since that time, the little scholarly work that has appeared on abortion politics has largely focused either on contextualizing Canada's policy in a comparative setting or on the challenges of real access to abortion in Canada (e.g., Boucher 2004; Haussman 2005; Erdman 2006; Halfmann 2011; Kaposy 2010; Sethna and Doull 2013; Shaw 2013). None of these studies, however, have examined the contemporary anti-abortion movement or its discourse in detail. In fact, the subject of abortion politics is notably absent from mainstream Canadian political science more generally. For example, before we published some of our findings in it in 2013, the *Canadian Journal of Political Science* had, in its entire history, published exactly one research article that focused on the topic sufficiently to include the word "abortion" in its title or list of keywords (Perrault and Cardinal 1996) and only a few others in which abortion policy is examined as a minor case study (Mathie 1986; Mendelsohn and Nadeau 1997; Morton and Allen 2001).

Interestingly, a scan of the most influential American political science journals reveals a similar pattern. In its 100 years, neither the flagship journal of the American Political Science Association (the *American Political Science Review*) nor its more topical cousin *Perspectives on Politics* have published a single article focused primarily on abortion – a finding that is also true of *Political Science Quarterly* (with its 128 year history of publication), *Political Theory* (the seminal journal in political thought), and *Theory & Event* (a more critical and applied journal of political theory).[2] Perhaps even more surprising, however, is the relative silence of even some of the best-known feminist journals. *Politics and Gender*, for example, has not published a single article focusing on abortion, and the *International Feminist Journal of Politics* has published only three articles with "abortion" in the title or keywords. Even *Signs*, the pre-eminent North American feminist journal, has published only four articles on abortion in its forty-year history (and none of these investigate the discursive strategies of the contemporary anti-abortion movement). It is thus not surprising that, in their systematic overview of the extensive literature examining the causes of public attitudes towards abortion, Jelen and Wilcox note that the discursive dimension of abortion politics remains surprisingly under-researched in contemporary scholarship (even in regard to the US context). According to them, "one area of research which will likely become extremely important is the development of new frames covering abortion and related issues as populations, environments, and (perhaps especially) technologies change" (Jelen and Wilcox 2003, 497). Our analysis of the shifting and diverse rhetorical strategies of persuasion employed by the anti-abortion movement is one attempt to address this important gap in the literature.

1.3 The Traditional Portrait: Male, Religious, Legislative, Anti-woman, Fetal-centric

Despite (or, perhaps, because of) the fact that the contemporary abortion debate has been relatively understudied in Canada, there is a widely shared image of the nature of the anti-abortion movement and the type of

---

2 As measured by the use of the word "abortion" in either the title or list of keywords. The *American Political Science Review* did publish one article in 1989 that uses abortion as a case study in its analysis of the impact of the Supreme Court. However, it did not centrally engage the politics of abortion. Rather, it simply used it as a case study to test other theories.

communication strategies it uses. In many ways, this dominant portrait of the anti-abortion movement (which we will call the "traditional" portrait) is rooted in studies of the rise of the American anti-abortion movement in the late 1970s and 1980s. The image sketched by Susan Faludi in her famous book *Backlash: The Undeclared War against Women* is, in many ways, a concise (if slightly intense) distillation of the traditional portrait of the anti-abortion movement. Faludi tells the story of "the many 'warriors' of Operation Rescue," men "clutching a crucifix shouting, 'Don't kill me mommy'" (1991, 409). In her telling, the words of this movement may "praise the lord, but they also curse the women; mingled among the 'amens,' the words 'whore' and 'dyke' can be heard more than once" (409). Risen and Thomas agree on the centrality of the Operation Rescue modus operandi, arguing that it transformed the movement from "a small, ragtop group of easily ignored protesters into a genuine movement, an aggressive national campaign that put the anti-abortion cause back onto America's Page One" (Risen and Thomas 1998, 220). Other observers, such as Blanchard, underline the fact that the aggressiveness and confrontational approach of groups like Operation Rescue increasingly "appeared to characterize, to the public, the anti-abortion movement from 1987 – the date of Operation Rescue's founding – until the present" (Blanchard 1994, 54). This image was further cemented with the rise of anti-abortion extremist terrorism in the 1990s and early 2000s.

The portrait that arises from such studies and continues to define much of the popular imaginary of, and academic scholarship about, the anti-abortion movement can be summarized as follows. The anti-abortion movement and its discourse: (a) has a largely male-dominated public face; (b) aims primarily at limiting/banning abortion by using legal challenges, political mobilization, legislation, and even intimidation and violence; (c) publicly and explicitly defends its policy position with reference to explicitly stated religious principles; (d) often embodies an angry, aggressive, sometimes violent, and "anti-woman" tone; and (e) employs heavily fetal-centric arguments to buttress its position.

As we discuss in chapter 12, there have been a few studies that have examined new currents in anti-abortion discourse in the US (see Hopkins, Reicher, and Saleem 1996; Siegel and Blustain 2006; Siegel 2007; Rose 2011). Despite such work, most studies of the abortion debate in the US tend to represent the anti-abortion movement in ways consistent with the traditional portrait (see Dworkin 1983; Faludi 1991; Muldoon 1991; Blanchard 1994; Jelen and Chandler 1994, especially chapters 3, 6, 7; Cassidy 1996; Herring 2003, especially chapter 5; Steiner 2006).

The traditional portrait also dominates almost all accounts of the anti-abortion movement in Canada. For example, while some political scientists have examined less "formal" realms of contestation regarding abortion (see Halfmann 2011), most academic studies have focused on describing and analysing the legislative and judicial battles around this policy issue and thus give the impression that abortion politics largely takes place in the political, legislative, and legal spheres (see Morton 1992; Brodie, Gavigan, and Jenson 1992; Tatalovich 1997; McLaren and McLaren 1997). Religion has frequently been presented as a key element of both the motivation and the philosophical justification for the anti-abortion movement in Canada (see, in different ways, Cuneo 1989; Brodie, Gavigan, and Jenson 1992, 78; Jelen and Chandler 1994; Bowen 2004). In fact, Brodie's recounting of an anti-abortion protest outside a Morgentaler clinic on 28 January 1988 (the day that the Supreme Court struck down Canada's abortion laws) echoes Faludi's portrait almost point by point: "The pro-life group, decidedly older and more male, kept its vigil waving its familiar placards of mutilated foetuses and chanting 'Give Life a Chance.' The pro-choice supporters, almost all women, relished their apparent victory with embraces and cheers" (Brodie, Gavigan, and Jenson 1992, 58). In this portrait, the battle over abortion is the struggle between old, religious men and young, vibrant women.

Virtually all of the major academic accounts also suggest that the core arguments of the anti-abortion movement's public discourse have been intensely fetal-centric. These studies argue, for example, that the core of the anti-abortion position rests on claims that "the right to life of the fetus takes legal and moral precedence over women's rights to self-determination" (Brodie, Gavigan, and Jenson 1992, 5), bolstered by narratives that "depict the knowing foetus being torn limb by limb" and "photographic images of the foetus which arouse public identification with it and obscure the pregnant woman's body" (77).

Given this emphasis on the fetus, a wide variety of scholars have asserted that the Canadian anti-abortion movement and its public discourse embody a profoundly anti-woman tone and orientation. Shelley Gavigan, for example, argues not only that the fetal argument is the dominant anti-abortion frame, but that the effect of "the imagery of the foetal personhood campaign [is] to render women invisible" (Brodie, Gavigan, and Jenson 1992, 146). Her co-author Brodie agrees, suggesting that "control of the womb is of primary importance" to the anti-abortion movement and that it wages a "discursive campaign against women" (81–2) in which the construction of the fetus as fully autonomous and human requires anti-abortion discourse to "render the woman's body invisible and irrelevant to fetal personhood" and reduce women to the status of a "mechanical incubator" (80–1). In this framework, women who choose abortion are represented as being "governed by their irrational subjectivity" and "pursuing their own selfish ends at the cost of another's life," and as "morally bankrupt ... self-centered and hedonistic" (84).[3]

1.3.1 The Traditional Portrait Today

As we will see in the comparative historical analysis of Part I, the traditional portrait is a relatively accurate overview of many of the key characteristics of the anti-abortion movements in Canada and the US between the 1970s and 1990s (and perhaps even later, in the case of the US). However, the traditional portrait does not merely exist as an historical representation of the anti-abortion movement during that period. Rather, it continues to shape the way much of the public – and many academic and journalistic observers – imagines the anti-abortion movement and its public discourse both well before the 1970s and well after the 1990s. A recent *Salon* article, for example, encourages us to conceptualize the anti-abortion movement in the US as an even more extreme version of the traditional portrait. Focusing on the extreme and violent elements in the movement, the author argues that the broader, more mainstream anti-abortion movement shares many of these traits. According to the author, "anti-abortion activists in Albuquerque are using the same rhetoric and tactics that led to Dr. Tiller's killing" (Dr. George Tiller was assassinated in 2009 by an extremist member of the anti-abortion movement), and there is a close and intrinsic connection between extremist violence and the broader mainstream movement: "Th[is] is the anti-abortion ecosystem. It gives the more mainstream players plausible deniability when violence occurs, while allowing the radical actors to keep pro-choice activists and clinic workers in a state of fear. It's a multi-pronged onslaught that dismantles abortion rights

---

3 Brodie does note in passing that some anti-abortion discourse argued that women themselves were being harmed by abortion and a "selfish abortion-oriented society" (Brodie, Gavigan, and Jenson 1992, 84), but this is presented as a very minor, ad hoc, argument.

and terrorizes providers out of working. It's not a handful of crazies shooting doctors, bombing clinics and blocking healthcare access. Shooting doctors, bombing clinics and blocking healthcare access are all necessary parts of the bigger picture" (Filipovic 2013). Other prominent commentators – for example, the *New York Times* columnist Thomas L. Friedman (hardly a left-winger) – have also recently described the anti-abortion movement in similar tones, as the "voices of an ever-more-assertive far-right Republican base that is intent on using uncompromising positions on abortion to not only unseat more centrist Republicans … but to overturn the mainstream consensus in America on this issue" (Friedman 2012).

Many observers in Canada, including some of the most engaged and knowledgeable, continue to suggest that the traditional portrait still accurately conveys the main characteristics of the contemporary Canadian anti-abortion movement and its discourse. In 2003 Joyce Arthur, founder and president of Abortion Rights Coalition Canada (ARCC), offered a portrait of "who comprises the [anti-abortion] movement and … their underlying motivations and worldview" (Arthur 2003, 1). Her report offers a picture that is remarkably in line with the traditional portrait – one in which the anti-abortion movement is viewed as a male-dominated, extremist, religious, and anti-woman movement that opposes abortion because of fundamentalist belief that abortion kills a human being. According to Arthur, "the vast bulk of anti-choicers … are *religious fundamentalists*" consisting of "Evangelical Protestants, Papal Catholics, Other Religious [sic], and Far Right" (8; emphasis in original). "Anti-choice literature is often completely suffused with religious language" and often has the goal of "try[ing] to convert women to Christianity" (7). Arthur also argues that the movement is largely motivated by an anti-woman "sexist paternalism that requires control of women and their sexuality" (5) and suggests that this orientation is reflected in, and reinforced by, public discourse that essentially sanctifies the status of the fetus while it "completely excludes and negates women's fundamental right to bodily integrity – and even their right to life" (24).

Arthur's perspective is reflected in recent scholarship as well as the popular imaginary. In the first three months of 2013 alone, Arthur's account was cited favourably and employed by at least two academic articles when describing current anti-abortion strategies (Sethna and Doull 2013; Shaw 2013). It has not been surprising, therefore, that virtually all of the diverse audiences with whom we have discussed our findings (including university students, medical practitioners, feminist and legal scholars, political scientists, political activists and organizers, and journalists) recounted all of the key elements of the traditional portrait when asked to describe their initial assumptions about the nature of the anti-abortion movement.

How accurate are these assumptions about anti-abortion activism? What are the essential characteristics of historical and contemporary anti-abortion movements and their discourse in Canada? In the United States? Does the traditional portrait accurately capture these characteristics or do we need a different understanding? These are the key questions answered in the first two parts of this book.

Before we turn to our findings, some readers will want to know how, exactly, we conducted our analysis. Therefore, in section 1.4, we outline our overall theoretical framework, discussing how we conceive of political discourse and why we think it is important to investigate it. In section 1.5, we explain the specific methodology and research design we have employed. In section 1.6, we discuss the overall reliability of our methodology before closing with a chapter-by-chapter overview of the book.

1.4 Theoretical Framework: Words Matter

From a very young age, we are taught some paradoxical lessons about the importance of words. On one hand, we're told that words matter. We should mind our p's and q's. Not yell at our brothers and sisters. Say please and thank you. And at some point, we've all learned that these are important lessons. For how we speak can have significant impact on our success in life.

Often, however, we're also told that words don't really matter. "Sticks and stones may break your bones but words can never hurt you" – even though every child knows how untrue this is. "Don't be scared by stories, they're just make-believe" – even though every child knows how real that sick feeling in his or her stomach can be. "I didn't mean what I said; I was just angry" – even though everyone knows that some words can't be taken back, can't be unheard, and can shift our deepest feelings about others in ways that cannot be undone. Is it any surprise that the colloquialisms of adulthood take this basic denial of the importance of words and intensify it with a healthy dose of cynicism – talk is cheap; you talk the talk but can you walk the walk; don't be so sensitive, it was just a joke?

Many political observers follow suit and denigrate political speech as mere idle chatter, suggesting that the real substance and key drivers of politics are to be found elsewhere. Scholars and observers who take this view often suggest that discourse is merely window dressing, post-facto justification at best, and thus not worthy of sustained examination on its own. Other perspectives assume that the rhetorical content of public, political debate is largely irrelevant and that the only issues worth examining are ones that focus on the material factors that are assumed to explain "why" a given discourse emerges and transforms.

But words do matter. And how we talk in politics matters a great deal. Hannah Arendt famously argued that the very foundation of democratic politics is speech. According to her, the most basic, unquestioned assumption of the progenitors of our modern democracy (the ancient Greeks) was that "to be political, to live in a *polis* meant that everything was decided through words and persuasion and not through force and violence" (Arendt 1958, 26). In fact, the belief that broad trends in private, public, and political discourse are important factors influencing many political phenomenon (whether persuading key constituencies to vote for a specific party or policy, or the much longer-term impact of reinforcing and making "commonsensical" certain patterns of argumentation, sets of values, emotional responses, and other ideological structures and practices) is shared by a diverse group of historical and contemporary thinkers. Political theorists such as Aristotle (1992), Cicero (2001), Antonio Gramsci (1971), Leo Strauss (2002), Catharine MacKinnon (1987), Judith Butler (2004), William Connolly (2002, 2008) and Sherene Razack (2004) all defend this view, as do cognitive scientists such as George Lakoff (1996; 2009), political psychologists such as Drew Westen (2007), scholars who study public relations (Ewen 1996; Hoggan 2009), and highly influential marketers and political advisers such as Edward Bernays (2005) and Frank Luntz (2007). Even legal scholars argue that trends in how we conceptualize and talk about political and legal values can have immense impact on what laws are passed, how they are interpreted, and which are upheld or struck down (see Dworkin 1986 and 1996; Ackerman 1991; Sunstein 1993). Many of these theorists thus believe that the task of identifying the specific rhetorical strategies used in a given political debate, decoding how they persuade their audiences, and tracking how they vary over time and space are crucial tasks for social scientists interested in politics. Indeed, even many of the founders of social movement theory have rejected the simplistic idea that the content of words are unimportant in explaining the success and nature of a given political movement.

Thus, they have increasingly explored ways to investigate and measure the various strategies of persuasion employed by political and social movements (see McAdam, Tarrow, and Tilly 2001; Snow and Benford 1992; and Snow and Benford 2000 on the importance of framing, for example).

The reason why it is sometimes necessary to study, in detail, the ways in which a given discourse functions is because political discourse is not merely a transparent medium of communication or simply an epiphenomenal by-product of other factors. Language – and particularly political language – is itself an important tool of politics. In fact, many theorists argue that the struggle over the definition and use of words and concepts lies at the very foundation of much modern politics (e.g., Connolly 1993, 6). Understanding how this struggle of words and rhetorical strategies of persuasion works – that is, identifying which words, concepts, arguments, narratives, and so on are used by different social and political movements and analysing how each of these techniques attempts to persuade the audience – is crucial to understanding the nature and success of a given political movement.

An understanding of the use of words and rhetorical strategies is particularly important in a highly contentious area of policy debate like abortion. As political science Janine Brodie has argued about the abortion debate in particular, public rhetoric is such an important site of analysis because it is "part of the process through which underlying interests of differently empowered social groups struggle with each other for particular outcomes through the negotiation of persuasive meanings" (Brodie, Gavigan, and Jenson 1992, 70). If certain discursive representations become dominant, it "increases the likelihood that this particular set of social meanings will be reflected in public policy" (70). In other words, discourse matters because it can have very material impacts on what type of policy is imagined, pursued, and implemented. Understanding precisely how it works, therefore, is a crucial task for political analysis.

To use an analogy: the public discourse used by a given political movement might be imagined as a car – an instrumental vehicle that plays a crucial role in getting the movement (or a policy) from one place (usually out of favour) to another (into power or law or policy). If we want to understand the nature of that car, how it relates to other cars, how fast it goes, how reliable it is, and how likely it is to successfully take a movement towards its destination – then we need to not simply investigate material questions about how the car was funded, who built it, and why they chose this particular car.[4] Rather, if we want to know how likely the car is to win its discursive race, we need to investigate very precisely how the car itself works.

Most of us, of course, know how to very capably use a car on one level – we know that if we hit the accelerator the car will move and that tapping the brakes will slow and eventually stop it. However, few of us actually understand the details of how an internal combustion engine functions. And even fewer of us understand exactly how a particular variant of a specific engine, combined with all of the other technology of the car, functions, how it might be tweaked to improve its performance, and how fast and responsive it is in relation to other engines. If we don't understand these elements, however, we can't evaluate the car's relative strengths and weaknesses, and thus we won't be able to determine how strong a contender it will be in a race with other cars.

This is also the case with language. Most people have a very strong unconscious competence in using language to persuade others. We can hit the accelerator, use the brakes, and veer left and right in conversation to try to find different routes that might convince people to agree with us. But few of us take the time to step back, consciously pop the discursive hood, understand precisely how the internal engine of our language functions, and figure out how to fine-tune it in relation to other discursive competitors. If we don't understand how that linguistic engine functions, however, we won't actually know what gives a specific discourse its persuasive force or how it helps mobilize supporters and resources, nor will we be able estimate or improve how successful a given discourse is likely to be in persuading its intended audience.

To understand these things, we need to go beyond knowing that pressing the accelerator will move the car forward. Instead, we need to understand how the linguistic engine works. In other words, we need to minutely trace and analyse the rhetorical strategies of a given discourse, reconstruct how they work, and systematically track how

---

4 These are all important questions that would be raised by resource mobilization, political economy, and actor motivation theory: How did the movement raise the funds to construct/publicize their discourse? Who did they raise it from? Why did these donors support it? Which of their attitudes influenced the design of the discourse? Who are the people that actually build and then publicize the discourse? What are their motivations for doing what they do? Examining theses questions would tell us certain things about how the movement ended up with the discourse it did. But these are not the only, nor even the most important, questions to ask. For our purposes, the questions answered by our method of discourse analysis are much more relevant.

broadly and widely they are employed. This work is particularly important when the discourse of a given political movement relies heavily on subtle, semi-submerged rhetorical techniques such as narratives and framing. This is why we have not, in this book, merely traced the more explicit strategies of persuasion (e.g., clear cut assertions, exhortations, logical argumentation, and the offering of studies and data), but have also engaged deeply in an analysis of implicit rhetorical strategies of persuasion.

To give a concrete example, in chapter 11 we analyse how narratives about villains, victims, and heroes function to subtly and almost unconsciously reinforce the explicit arguments and implicit perceptions crucial to the success of a given discourse. In doing so, we both explain the theory of why it is important to take the time to investigate in detail the less obvious techniques of persuasion used by anti-abortion movement and we offer empirical illustrations of this importance. For if we don't understand that the contemporary Canadian anti-abortion movement uses a "nurturant parent" tone (as opposed to a "strict father" tone) and we don't see that the movement's narrative structures tell a story that sounds a lot like progressive feminist structural arguments about informal modes of influence/coercion, we won't understand how the discourse of the movement is actually seeking to convince people. And we will likely badly underestimate its persuasive force.

1.5 Methodology and Research Design

For the reasons discussed above, our approach is grounded in the widely held theoretical contention that how we talk about politics matters. But what does this approach mean concretely, in terms of methodology? How, practically, does one study political discourse?

For this book, we employed multiple methodologies. This is not only because the book encompasses at least two distinct (though related) projects (i.e., a historical contextualization as well as a detailed contemporary analysis). It is also because, as we will discuss in more detail in the next section, using multiple methods is often a useful way to test the findings of one methodology and improve their accuracy.

The historical part of the book is based primarily on a critical analysis of the secondary literature devoted to the history of abortion politics in North America over the past two hundred years or so. This approach allowed us to reconstruct a relatively concise overview of the most important events, trends, and discursive tendencies of the political abortion debate in North America since the early nineteenth century – an overview that offers an important context for our findings about the key characteristics of the persuasion strategies of the contemporary anti-abortion movement.

The second part of the book posed more substantial methodological challenges. The first methodological issue facing any attempt to undertake a systematic analysis of new discursive terrain is to identify the "raw data" (i.e., the sample of discourse) to be analysed. Where should we be looking? Whose words should we analyse? In what media? Over what period of time?

In Part II, our main focus is on determining how the contemporary anti-abortion movement (particularly in Canada) is making its case in public. To achieve this goal, we selected three main sites of discourse that together capture a diverse and representative cross-section of some of the most influential contemporary anti-abortion discourse in Canada – blogs, websites, and the discourse of some key anti-abortion members of Parliament.[5]

Because blogging is an increasingly influential mode of activist communication (both within a movement and to the broader public) and a mode that allows individuals to express their views without an organizational "spin," the first site of discourse we chose was the most prominent anti-abortion blog in Canada: ProWomanProLife (PWPL). PWPL first appeared in December 2007 to mark the twentieth anniversary of

---

5 It is important to note that, when we refer to Canada in this book, we are essentially referring to *English* Canada. The reason for this is that Canada's anti-abortion movement is based almost exclusively outside of Quebec, no doubt largely because support for abortion rights in Quebec today is virtually unequivocal – in clear contrast to the rest of Canada. In 2010, for example, when Quebec Cardinal Marc Ouellet stated that abortion is a moral crime, there was a near unanimous backlash. A poll taken immediately after found that 94 per cent of Quebeckers rejected Ouellet's views. Quebec's National Assembly unanimously passed a motion supporting "the right of women to free choice and free and accessible abortion" in response. And many commentators noted that Ouellet was the "only vocal anti-abortion supporter [even] in the Quebec Catholic hierarchy" (Gagnon 2010). More generally, there are no Quebec MPs of any party that hold outspokenly anti-abortion positions (indeed, Campaign Life Coalition does not list any Quebec MP as holding views or having voting records that indicate support for the anti-abortion position – see CLC, Find Your MP, at http://www.campaignlifecoalition.com/index.php?p=Find_Your_MP,ViewList). Therefore, although some of the bloggers we analysed on PWPL are Québécois, we chose not to examine any Quebec-specific organizations, as the very few that exist are largely irrelevant in comparison to their English counterparts.

the *Morgentaler* decision. Claiming to represent "a spectrum of nuanced pro-woman and pro-life views," the blog states that its posts are written by nine Canadian women from "different walks of life (medicine, psychology, actuarial science, journalism, and public policy), [and] different religions (or no religion at all), [who] have never been vocal or activist on abortion before, do not represent any larger group, and do not currently receive funding from any larger group" (PWPL 2007). It won the "best new blog" from the 2008 Canadian Blog Awards; it placed fifth in the overall "politics" category in the 2009 Canadian Blog Awards; its bloggers are regularly referenced and/or published in the *Ottawa Citizen*, the *Globe and Mail*, and the *National Post*; and it has a large set of blog entries (as of October 2013, it held almost 3,850 entries). One of its founders (Andrea Mrozek) is also the executive director of the Institute of Marriage and Family Canada (Canada's pre-eminent socially conservative think tank, funded by Focus on the Family Canada). Another of its bloggers, Faye Sonier, is a visible anti-abortion advocate as well as legal counsel for the Evangelical Fellowship of Canada, the national association of evangelicals that conducts research and advocates on a wide range of issues, including abortion. A third, Brigitte Pellerin, was a reporter in the parliamentary bureau of Sun News Network for several years. Given its contributors, the blog is both an important site of Canadian anti-abortion discourse in its own right and a reliably representative (and often surprisingly candid) exemplar of the discourse of influential anti-abortion activists and opinion leaders.

The websites of Canadian anti-abortion organizations are our second source of anti-abortion discourse. The language used at an organizational level provides an important site of analysis that is quite distinct from that of blogs, as its discourse is officially vetted by formal organizations whose primary aim is anti-abortion advocacy and who are the main actors instigating a variety of other anti-abortion organizations and campaigns. We examined the public websites of four of the most influential anti-abortion organizations across English-speaking Canada – Alliance for Life Ontario, LifeCanada, Toronto Right to Life, and Signal Hill). The entirety of each of these websites was analysed, including mission statements, advertising campaigns, video postings, newsletters, press releases, and links provided for women who need information about how to deal with unplanned pregnancies.

Finally, while the blogs and organizational websites allowed us to sample the discourse of both individuals and civil society organizations, we also analysed the overtly political realm by examining the discourse of four anti-abortion members of Parliament who have consistently been outspoken on this issue and whose views can be found in multiple media over the time period of our study. We selected Maurice Vellacott, Rod Bruinooge, Ken Epp, and Paul Szabo as representative of anti-abortion discourse in Parliament. These four MPs allowed us to tap different regions of the country (they represent, or represented, ridings in Saskatoon, Winnipeg, Edmonton, and Mississauga, respectively) and two of the three main federal political parties (Vellacott, Epp, and Bruinooge from the Conservative Party and Szabo from the Liberal Party).

For our study, then, we examined all the material contained on each of the four anti-abortion organizations' websites (as of May 2010) and all abortion-related blog postings at PWPL published between December 2007 and January 2011. This three-year period is particularly rich, as it includes not only the twentieth anniversary of the Supreme Court of Canada's decision in *Morgentaler*, but also Morgentaler's Order of Canada award (July 2008). In addition, we analysed the tabling of two abortion-related private members' bills in Parliament (Bill C-484, the Unborn Victims of Crime Act, and Bill C-510, Roxanne's Law). With these parameters, we collected 401 discrete documents,[6] which together created an exceptionally interesting and diverse discursive data set containing a wide variety of distinct types of actors, interests, and types of media, over a significant period of time.

Beyond this, we examined a variety of other sources to round out our analysis. Although we didn't include them in the formal quantitative data set outlined above, we also analysed in detail the websites, twitter accounts, promotional materials, and campaigns of many other anti-abortion organizations and actors – including Campaign Life Coalition (CLC), the Canadian Centre for Bio-ethical Reform (CCBR), the Association for Reformed Political Action (ARPA), the Evangelical Fellowship of Canada (EFC), the National Campus Life Network (NCLN), We Need a Law, and the Institute of Marriage and Family Canada (IMFC). We also examined the blogs, MPs' communications, and organizational websites in our data set from 2011 to 2014 and qualitatively analysed

---

6 Technically, we identified 430 cases from our initial data collection. However, 30 of those cases were identical petitions regarding Bill C-484 submitted to the House of Commons. Given that these did not represent discrete and different cases but simply repetitions as a reaction to the procedural context, we treated these 30 identical submissions as a single case, leaving us with 401 discrete cases.

them to ensure that there were no substantial differences between those years and what we found from 2007 to 2011.

To further supplement our discursive data set, we used naturalistic observation techniques to analyse a variety of anti-abortion talks, conferences, rallies, and other events we attended (including the 2011–14 March For Life rallies and related church services, talks, vigils and conferences). The qualitative analysis of these events was as crucial as the qualitative/quantitative analysis we performed on the 2007–11 data set, as it allowed us to pursue a variety of additional nuances that were apparent, but not fully developed, in the data set analysis itself but which became increasingly important after 2011.

It is also important to note that for reasons that we discuss in chapter 7 (largely pertaining to the fact that we are interested in *what* the movement is doing, discursively speaking, rather than *why* they are doing this or *what they think* they are doing), we decided not to interview individual activists and to instead allow their public discursive actions speak for themselves. Finally, with respect to our discussion in chapter 12 on the US context in comparison to Canada, our data set also included a select sample of US sources of anti-abortion discourse, as well as a wide variety of secondary literature on abortion politics and debate in that country.

How exactly did we analyse all these sources? What was our interpretive method? This is the second methodological challenge to solve when undertaking discourse analysis. Our specific methodological approach in this study follows the tradition of critical discourse analysis (CDA) and the work of theorists such as Fairclough (2001) and Wodak and Meyer (2009). They suggest that a discourse can employ a wide variety of mechanisms to persuade its audience (e.g., from explicitly stating an objective, to story telling, to priming and mobilizing network associations) and that researchers must undertake close qualitative interpretations of well-chosen samples of relevant discourses to identify the discursive patterns that are often impossible to identify through automated content analysis.

Our approach therefore insists on the importance of close qualitative readings of the relevant discourse. However, we also appreciate the value that quantitative analysis can provide. For, although it cannot replace qualitative methods, quantitatively measuring the frequency of various rhetorical strategies (as well as relationships between them) can also help establish the relative importance of these strategies. As such, in our study, we employed multiple interpretive strategies.

In regard to our data set of documents, we employed a rigorous "mixed method" critical discourse analysis approach that allowed us to systematically analyse the explicit arguments of anti-abortion discourse in Canada both qualitatively and quantitatively. Unlike traditional quantitative content analysis/data-mining approaches (which automatically count specific *words* and therefore are not able to identify complex rhetorical formations such as types of arguments, narratives, framing devices, and so on), a mixed method approach requires a detailed, holistic, and manual qualitative interpretation and coding of every document before it is quantitatively analysed. Because it does incorporate a quantitative element, however, unlike purely qualitative approaches (which are less able to empirically establish how broadly a given technique is used), a mixed method approach allows us to test how widely, and how intensively, certain rhetorical strategies are employed across a given discourse. In our study, we thus first developed a detailed coding system designed to guide our qualitative interpretation and quantitative coding of a variety of rhetorical strategies. We then used this framework to qualitatively code all 401 cases (each case was analysed and the coding checked at least three times to ensure consistency), using the software system QDA Miner to help us keep track of, and then quantitatively analyse, the overall results.

We discuss each of the relevant coding systems and interpretive metrics as we outline the results of our analyses in chapters 7–11. However, at a general level, we constructed our coding dictionary to track a variety of strategic discussion and rhetorical techniques of persuasion, including types of philosophical justifications, appeals to religion, explicit argumentation, various types of framing devices (brand-identity framing, values framing, issue framing, epistemological framing), metaphorical tone, and narrative structure (particularly the key character roles of villain, victim, and hero). These coding categories were designed in response to three considerations. First, some were designed to allow us to test whether the characteristics of the traditional portrait remained central to the discourse of the contemporary anti-abortion movement. Second, some were designed to allow us to test hypotheses that emerged from a variety of theoretical academic literature about the nature of political (and especially conservative) discourse more broadly. And third, all were designed and honed through an iterative process (undertaken before we started the systematic coding) in which we qualitatively analysed representative samples of anti-abortion discourse in order to generate inductive hypotheses, which were then translated

into coding questions and were further tested and honed through iterative additional analyses of representative samples. The end result – our
finalized coding dictionary – thus reflects a series of analytic questions
and categories derived from theoretical sources, previous analyses of
abortion politics, and considerable inductive pilot analyses.

In addition to the coding itself, we undertook close qualitative readings of all the documents to track and interpret a variety of other themes
and strategies of persuasion. We broadly employed both the coding categories and these additional themes when we qualitatively analysed a
diverse set of additional discourse that supplemented the original data
set. We kept these themes in mind as we analysed the events (and the
discourse used at these events) that we examined using a method of
in-person naturalistic observation. We also used these close qualitative
interpretation and naturalistic observation methods with respect to
some of the US sources.

1.6 Methodological Reliability

As intimated above, there are many advantages to using the multiple
types of triangulation that our multi-method, multi-data set approach
allows. Combining historical and contemporary modes of analysis, for
example, allowed us to better understand and contextualize both the
distinctiveness, but also the continuity, over time of the anti-abortion
movement and its discourse. Constructing extremely wide, diverse,
and representative data sets greatly increased our confidence in gen-
eralizing the findings of our study. Incorporating naturalistic observation and an analysis of sources outside of our primary textual data set
brought to light insights that helped put into perspective and gave
nuance to some of our most important quantitative findings – for
example, with respect to the surprising lack of appeals to religion in
contemporary Canadian anti-abortion discourse. Without the insights
gained from naturalistic observation (and, for that matter, our historical analysis of the Canadian anti-abortion movement), the story we
would have told about the role of religion on the basis of our discourse
analysis would have been incomplete.

Perhaps the greatest advantage is that our use of multiple methodologies is a crucial tool in ensuring that our analytic results are as
accurate and free from subjective influences as possible. This is not an
insignificant issue in the social sciences. Whenever political scientists
undertake research on topics with contemporary relevance, there is

always the question of how to manage one's own political views to ensure that they do not taint the findings. In fact, some of the most persuasive methodological accounts of the social sciences argue that it is precisely this "embedded" nature that makes social scientific inquiry valuable, reliable, and socially relevant (Flyvbjerg 2001).

So, how have social scientists – and how have we – taken into account and addressed this dimension of social science research? One important practice is for authors to clearly raise the issue and outline their own subjective views. Doing so means that the reader won't be left guessing. It also gives researchers an incentive to keep their own subject position in mind and work hard to avoid importing value judgments into the work, precisely because they know that the audience will be on the lookout for such judgments.

In our case, neither of us could be characterized as holding an anti-abortion perspective. In fact, although we may disagree with each other on certain issues, we are both supporters of abortion rights. Is this a problem? Wouldn't an insider who agrees with the anti-abortion position be a better candidate to write a book like this?

The short answer is no. First, it is by no means obvious that insiders are better placed to understand and explain their own movement than are outsiders. For one thing, because insiders are so familiar with the movement, many core assumptions, ideas, practices, behaviours, arguments, and strategies of persuasion would appear to insiders as things that are unremarkable and natural, and thus not worthy of examination or discussion. As the truism goes, no one knows who first discovered water, but it probably wasn't a fish. In contrast, those same dimensions might strike an outsider as unusual and thus worthy of analysis and commentary. Often, an outsider's study and reconstruction can produce a more insightful portrait than those offered by insiders. After all, it's pretty hard to miss the importance and distinctiveness of water if you're a land-based animal. So while outsiders may not be the most skilled in unconsciously navigating in water, they may be far better at investigating, exploring, and explaining its nature. Thus, if your goal is to understand an aquatic ecosystem, rather than swim within it, being an outsider can be a crucial strength. At the very minimum, it certainly isn't a weakness in the case of this study.

Moreover, insiders face the challenge of managing their own subjective views and interests just as much as outsiders do. In fact, the political commitments and self-interest of insiders can make it infinitely more difficult and complicated for them to report accurately on their own movement. Insiders often have a strong interest in presenting the movement and its arguments in the most favourable light. They also frequently have deep sets of relationships with the people and organizations they are examining – a context that can invariably lead to a variety of complex dynamics, pressures, and interests that can badly distort the research. In contrast, sometimes outsiders (especially those whose academic vocation ensures their work is judged on the accuracy of its representations) actually have the strongest self-interest in accurately understanding and representing the opposing position.

This is not to say that it is impossible for insiders to offer accurate portraits despite those pressures, or that outsiders can't offer up a biased hatchet job. In our line of work (like many), the success of a project isn't predetermined by the incoming inside/outside position of the researcher. Rather, if done properly, the accuracy of the results is a function of the rigour and reliability of the methodological design and the execution of the analysis. This is why we invested heavily in creating and employing an extremely robust and systematic methodology, in particular in relation to our analysis of the contemporary movement (since this is the part of our project that is most likely to be perceived as relevant to our current political context). In fact, our methodology was intentionally designed to help insulate our findings from any influence our own positions could have. For example, our choice to construct very broad and deep data sets ensured that there was no chance that we inadvertently cherry-picked a few minor actors in the movement and incorrectly presented them as representative of the entire movement. In addition, the fact that we employed quantitative macro-analyses that empirically tracked the relative weight of different rhetorical techniques ensures that our study avoids the possibility that any pre-existing assumptions or hypotheses would lead us to over-emphasize the importance of certain characteristics and rhetorical strategies. We also intentionally began our project without rigid assumptions and hypotheses; we coded every document separately and individually *before* undertaking any quantitative macro-analyses, and we had several different individuals coding the material. All of these techniques ensured that our coding and meta-analyses were not influenced by expectations about what we had already found, or wanted to find.

As suggested above, the use of multiple methods also allowed us to limit the impact of any potential subjectivity (while also reducing other inaccuracies intrinsic to any single method) by triangulating our research findings in a number of ways. Triangulation is a method used by qualitative researchers from a wide variety of disciplines in order to establish validity in their studies by analysing a research question using multiple perspectives. The benefits of triangulation include "increasing confidence in research data, creating innovative ways of understanding a phenomenon, revealing unique findings, challenging or integrating theories, and providing a clearer understanding of the problem" (Guion, Diehl, and McDonald 2002, 2). Ultimately, triangulation can increase both the validity and the utility of research findings.

We triangulated our findings in several different ways. First, our methodological approach incorporated "actor triangulation" – meaning that we analysed different *sources* of information, building our data set of anti-abortion discourse from a wide-ranging assortment of different anti-abortion activists, organizations, politicians, events, types of media, and stakeholders from across Canada that represented many different dimensions of the movement. Second, we employed "category triangulation" – meaning that we analysed different *types* of discourse that were intended for very different audiences (some oriented towards the general public, others directed at elite policymakers, opinion leaders, or actors internal to the movement). Third, by supplementing our coded discourse analysis with additional methodological approaches, we also engaged in a more robust form of "methodological triangulation." We did this by (a) employing many different modes of interpretation (approaches ranging from classical philosophical analysis and affective theories to rhetorical literacy, discourse, and narrative analysis); (b) using both qualitative and quantitative analytic approaches; and (c) supplementing these approaches with naturalistic observation of a wide set of events and discussions.

Ultimately, of course, the proof is in the pudding. This study aims at identifying the primary communication and rhetorical strategies employed by the historical and contemporary anti-abortion movement and explaining how they function. This is not the same thing as saying that our study seeks to describe these strategies in the same ways that insiders might. For while insiders may be very skilled at using various strategies of persuasion, they may not be able to self-consciously and analytically describe them particularly well. As such, the question is not whether anti-abortion activists would necessarily recognize themselves in our portrait. Rather, the question is whether this book provides enough theoretical and empirical evidence to convince readers that anti-abortion discourse functions in the way that we have mapped it. Do we sufficiently and convincingly explain how these rhetorical strategies function and why they matter? And do we provide compelling evidence that the anti-abortion movement employs the strategies in the ways and to the degree that we suggest? Given the representativeness of our data set, the rigour of our interpretive methods, and the multiple forms of triangulation we employed to corroborate and confirm our findings, we are confident that we have.

1.7 Chapter Overview

So, how does this book communicate our findings? Part I, "Historicizing the Abortion Debate in North America," is designed to set the stage for the contemporary analysis that follows, and to address the fact that there are no existing concise and up-to-date comparative accounts of the history of abortion politics in Canada and the United States. As such, Part I offers an in-depth history of the main political and legal events, as well as an overview of the main patterns of discourse that have characterized the abortion debate in Canada and the United States over the past 200 years.

The first two chapters of Part I focus on the American context and trace the historical shifts in abortion policy. Stages include the relatively permissive common law regulation of abortion in the early 1800s; the emergence and rapid spread of campaigns to criminalize and prohibit abortion in the mid- to late 1800s; the tentative emergence of attempts to liberalize birth control (from the 1920s) and abortion access (from the 1960s); the opening up of abortion access significantly (in the 1970s); and the clawing back many of those liberalizing reforms (1980s–today). Throughout both these chapters, we outline the major discursive trends of each stage of the abortion debate. In a similar fashion, chapters 4 and 5 outline the political, legal, and discursive history of Canada's abortion debate, including the shift away from the more relaxed common law tradition towards a much harsher statutory prohibition of abortion in the early/mid-1800s; the initial move towards liberalization in the 1960s; the intensification of the legal and political battles of the 1970s, 1980s, and early 1990s; and the less actively contested debate that has characterized the abortion issue in Canada since the early 1990s. Chapter 6 acts as a mini-summary of Part I, synthesizing the key similarities and differences between the political, legal, and discursive history of the abortion debate in the US and Canada and evaluating the degree to which the image sketched by the "traditional portrait" accurately captures this history. For readers who are interested primarily in the contemporary story and who do not have time to read the entirety of Part I, this chapter (and Appendices B and C) offers quick access to an overview of some of the historical dimensions that are most important for an understanding and evaluation of the distinctiveness of contemporary anti-abortion discourse.

With the comparative historical context clearly established, Part II outlines the results of our detailed study of the contemporary anti-abortion movement in Canada (and, more briefly, of the United States). Chapter 7 begins by demonstrating that, over the past decade, there has been a vigorous conversation between influential actors in the Canadian anti-abortion movement about the need to revise and renew its overall vision, organizational structure, and strategies of persuasion. Having demonstrated that important organizations and individuals in the movement have been actively considering the use of new and updated strategies of persuasion, chapters 8 through 11 investigate whether the Canadian movement actually walks the walk in its (public) talk. That is to say, we ask whether the movement has actually changed its rhetorical strategies of persuasion. In each chapter, we identify the specific set of strategies of persuasion to be examined and theoretically explain how these strategies function. We then report our empirical findings about how frequently, widely, and intensely they are employed by contemporary anti-abortion discourse and we analyse to what degree they are similar to and different from previous modes of anti-abortion discourse.

Chapter 8 investigates what are perhaps the most well-known and easily recognizable strategies of persuasion – philosophical appeals and explicit argumentation – as well as the slightly less explicit technique of "visual signaling." We examine, among other issues, the extent to which contemporary anti-abortion discourse employs both traditional arguments (e.g., religious and/or fetal-centric arguments) and newer, much more "pro-woman"-sounding arguments and techniques (e.g., the "abortion-harms-women" argument and/or gendered visual signaling) to persuade external audiences to adopt an anti-abortion position.

Chapter 9 examines a slightly more subtle rhetorical technique: that of framing and frame extension. This chapter focuses on one specific type of framing (brand-identity framing) and examines the extent to which contemporary anti-abortion discourse is attempting to rebrand the movement. Chapter 10 extends this frame analysis by examining three related techniques, "values framing," "issue framing," and "epistemological framing." We examine the extent to which anti-abortion discourse has appropriated, redefined, and redeployed a variety of classic feminist values, issues, and epistemological tropes in order to appeal to a different, more "progressive," demographic of Canadians. Chapter 11 then concludes our analysis of the contemporary Canadian context by investigating the dominant metaphorical tone and narrative structures that characterize contemporary anti-abortion discourse. Using a revised version of George Lakoff's theory of political metaphor, we test whether contemporary anti-abortion discourse embodies the harsh, punitive "strict father" ethos (as portrayed by the traditional portrait) or whether the more "pro-woman" themes uncovered in previous chapters is further supplemented by a "nurturant parent" tone. We then examine the narratives of contemporary discourse and ask whether they tend to embody the traditional approach (of portraying women as immoral villains who must be shamed into virtue) or represent women in ways that are aligned with a more "pro-woman" orientation.

Although it is beyond the scope of this book to offer a fully systematic comparison, we close Part II with a preliminary comparative analysis of contemporary Canadian and American anti-abortion discourse. In chapter 12, we examine the contemporary US anti-abortion movement, analyse the similarities and differences between the dominant tendencies in the US and Canada (focusing particularly on whether a new "pro-woman" anti-abortion perspective is emerging in the US), and discuss what this might suggest for future research.

The findings in Part II hold a variety of important comparative, theoretical, and practical implications, which we outline in the two concluding chapters of Part III. Chapter 13 is a primarily scholarly and academic conclusion. It begins with a concise summary of the key findings of Part II before delving more deeply into the empirical, theoretical, and methodological implications of our findings. We close the book with chapter 14, a concrete discussion of the practical implications of our findings for readers who have a more active political interest in this issue. In particular, we ask what implications our analysis holds for actors on the other side of the abortion debate. What do changes in anti-abortion discursive strategies imply for organizations and individuals who are committed to defending abortion rights? What lessons and challenges does a newly rejuvenated anti-abortion movement and "pro-woman" anti-abortion discourse embody for abortion rights defenders?

Finally, we have included three appendices to help readers keep track of all the moving parts. Appendix A is a glossary of the key political and legal events, organizations, and individuals in the abortion debate in North America. With entries organized by category and country, if you find yourself forgetting what PWPL or the Hyde Amendment are, you can get a quick reminder here. Appendix B synthesizes, in chronological form, the main political and legal events in Canada, the UK, and the US from 1800 to today, while Appendix C does the same thing in regard to the main characteristics of, and shifts in, anti-abortion discourse. Together, they give the reader a concise bird's eye view of the last two hundred years of the politics and debate about abortion in North America.

And with that said, it is to Part I that we now turn.

PART I

Historicizing the Abortion Debate in North America

The History of the Abortion Debate in the United States

Abortion has a long history in the United States – much of it very different from the highly contested, pro-life versus pro-choice framing that we are so familiar with. Accounts suggest that many Aboriginal nations used a variety of practices to induce abortion in certain situations. And abortion was a fact of life in colonial America, practised in settler colonies as it had been in their European countries of origin (Acevedo 1979, 160). Over the past two hundred years, however, American views about abortion have shifted – from viewing it as an accepted practice largely regulated by medical expertise rather than by law, to a rigidly criminalized and prohibited act, and then to an intensely moralized political contest with strong voices both in favour of and against access to abortion. How was abortion transformed from an accepted practice into the moral and political battle that it is today? This chapter outlines the various twists and turns of the political, legal, and discursive history of abortion in the United States, taking us from the early 1800s (when abortion first became a salient political issue viewed worthy of medical and legal intervention) to the 1970s (when the US Supreme Court would eventually legalize abortion), and tracing the different language and arguments that have been used for and against abortion access.

2.1 Abortion before 1840

Prior to the 1820s, the reproductive health of American women was seen largely as an issue left to the knowledge and discretion of midwives, the medical practitioners who handled most women's health issues at the time. This meant that issues surrounding female sexuality and reproduction were rarely discussed in public forums and that procedures related to women's health (including abortions) were seldom politicized broadly or even debated in formal political settings. In this context, drugs that purported to induce an abortion were widely and publicly available in the market (Rose 2008, 1). To the extent that abortion was subject to legal regulation, the standards were relatively permissive and what law existed was difficult to implement and thus rarely enforced. Prior to independence, residents of the colonies that would become the United States were usually bound by the laws of their country of origin, which, for the most part, was Britain – a situation that was formalized after the revolution as the newly independent states based most of their laws on the precedents of British common law (Acevedo 1979, 161). In the case of abortion, this meant that in the early US, as was the case in the United Kingdom, abortion was subject to relatively loose legal regulation only after the moment of "quickening" (understood as the moment when a woman is able to feel the fetus move in her womb, usually occurring around the fourth month of pregnancy) (Reed 1978, 25).

The first American judicial decision regarding abortion – the 1812 Massachusetts case *Commonwealth v. Isaiah Bangs* – explicitly acknowledged this norm. The case concerned a young woman named Lucy Hollman who willingly took a substance that induced a miscarriage. Given the nature of the laws (which focused on persons who abetted an abortion, not women who procured one), the case centred on her partner, Isaiah Bangs, who was accused of giving her this substance against her will and committing an abortion. The court found Bangs not guilty, however, because, according to British common law, miscarriage could not be considered abortion before the point of quickening: "If an abortion had been alleged and proved to have ensued the averment that the woman was quick with child at the time is a necessary part of the indictment" (quoted in Rose 2008, 5).

While this legal context covered the white residents of the American republic, it is important to note that it did not apply to the large population of African-American slaves. While it seems that slave communities clandestinely used a variety of birth control and abortion methods, they were not accorded the same rights as free settlers (Acevedo 1979, 163). Legally reduced to the status of property, slaves were not covered by common law and thus had few, if any, of the legal rights and protections afforded to free settlers. Rather, they were largely subject to the whims of the slave owner. Since they profited when slaves gave birth, slave owners largely prohibited abortion, and violations were punished harshly if discovered (163).

Beginning in the 1820s, states slowly began to pass increasingly restrictive anti-abortion statutes. In 1821, Connecticut became the first state to pass an explicit statute legally regulating abortion. However, this law (and similar ones elsewhere) merely codified earlier common law norms that permitted abortion until "quickening." Moreover, most early laws did not punish women for inducing abortions. "Marriage manuals" published and distributed in the 1830s continued to provide advice to couples on how to avoid unwanted pregnancies (Reed 1978, 26). Clearly, these early laws were very different from the anti-abortion legislation that would be passed later in the century, which would criminalize virtually all abortions, at every stage (Reagan 1996, 10).

From a discursive perspective, what is perhaps most notable in this early period is that debate over abortion was virtually non-existent (Reagan 1996, 81). Moreover, even where they did exist, arguments about abortion largely reflected the reproductive norms of the time and accepted the entrenching of common medical practice into law. To the extent that it did exist, opposition to abortion was not primarily grounded in moral or religious arguments about the value of fetal life. Rather, when early anti-abortion statutes were passed, they were largely justified on the ground that women needed to be protected from the "unscrupulous practitioners and the use of poisons, and the fetus from post-quickening abortions" (Marmon and Palley 1986, 182). Rather than employing anti-woman tones or women-shaming rhetoric, early anti-abortion discourse framed (white) women as innocent victims, the targets of dangerous abortionists and midwives. Moreover, the direct targets of these early anti-abortion laws were not women, as most legislation opted to criminalize those individuals who were found guilty of *inducing* the abortion, rather than the pregnant woman herself. While these early arguments might be seen as infantilizing women – as beings incapable of making reproductive decision of their own – it is very clear that they did not embody the fetal-centric and anti-woman tone and moral rhetoric that would emerge at later stages of abortion history. Ultimately, the practice of abortion (especially pre-quickening) was widespread in the US and was not subject to significant debate until well into the 1840s.

2.2 The AMA's Crusade against Abortion:
Medicalizing and (Im)moralizing Abortion

By the mid-1800s, a number of elements were changing in American society that would have consequences for the practice of abortion.

Abortion became one of the first medical specializations, with practitioners increasingly advertising their services publicly. The press was also beginning to demonstrate a new willingness to cover sensationalist trials involving allegedly botched abortions and professional abortion providers (Mohr 1978, 46). Combined, these two factors contributed to a growing social awareness of the reality of the widespread practice of abortion in the US, ultimately leading to the emergence of new critical questions about the legality and morality of abortion. By the mid-1800s, abortion was increasingly viewed by elites and the broader public as an issue worthy of their political and professional concern (ibid.).

Other social realities would also help transform the practice of abortion into a moralized and politicized issue during this period. The spread of much more rigid Victorian societal norms, including those relating to sexuality, meant that women who attempted to procure an abortion were increasingly portrayed as unmarried women of loose morals or victims of male lust (Reed 1978, 25). This portrait was far from accurate: aspiring upwardly mobile couples were some of the most frequent users of various forms of contraception and family planning. Regardless, this current of Victorian moralization fused with other ideological trends (particularly moral panics about the supposed falling birthrates of native-born white Americans and threats from "fast-reproducing" immigrants) and led to the emergence for the first time of an explicit debate around abortion. Increasingly, elites framed the issue of abortion in relationship to motherhood, asking what proper women should do to live up to their place as "true wives" and fulfil their maternal duties in the name of their gender, nation, and race (Reagan 1996, 12).

As is so often the case in politics, however, it was only once an influential and politically mobilized group began pushing for systematic change that abortion became a contested political and moral issue in the US. In what is an excellent historical lesson in the profound effects that a determined interest group with social and intellectual capital can have, the politicization and criminalization of abortion in the US is inextricably linked to the efforts of a small group of physicians and the self-interest and ambition of the newly formed American Medical Association (AMA) (Reed 1978, 27; Rose 2008).

Founded in 1847, the AMA sought to represent certain health care providers, consolidating them under its membership while excluding others (including midwives) (Haussman, 2005, 25). While the majority of physicians involved in the AMA did not oppose abortion, a small but very vocal group organized within the association to make the prohibition of this practice a key issue on the AMA's agenda (25). The primary mover behind this group was Dr. Horatio Storer, who was a recently graduated physician when he founded the Physicians' Crusade Against Abortion in 1857. Until this time, male physicians had had very little role in women's health. Until the mid-1800s, gynaecological practice was generally the providence of women, especially female midwives (as female physicians were rare) (Acevedo 1979, 162). By the mid-1800s, however, male physicians and the AMA were increasingly expanding into these areas. In this context, Storer was a pioneer and innovator in obstetrics and gynaecology in the formal field of medicine, teaching one of the first courses on women's diseases to be offered as distinct from midwifery in a university.

In 1857, Storer petitioned the AMA to create a Committee on Criminal Abortion. The AMA agreed, made him chairman, and gave the committee the mandate to prepare a report on the issue. Storer led this process, publishing no fewer than nine articles on abortion for physicians in 1859, and authoring the committee's *Report on Criminal Abortion*. Interestingly, Storer's texts did not use the religious and highly moralized language that would eventually come to characterize anti-abortion activism in the latter half of the twentieth century. Instead, he focused on redefining, on the basis of a scientific perspective, the pre-quickening period as fundamentally the same as post-quickening and post-birth. In 1868, for instance, Storer advocated that physicians

> set aside all the speculations of the metaphysicians regarding moral accountability of the foetus, the "potential man" and its "inanimate vitalities," as useless as they are bewildering. If there be life, then also the existence, however undeveloped, of an intellectual, moral and spiritual nature, the inalienable attribute of humanity, is implied. If we have proved the existence of foetal life before quickening has taken place or can take place, and by all analogy and a close and conclusive process of induction, its commencement at the very beginning, at conception itself, we are compelled to believe unjustifiable abortion always a crime. (Storer 1868, 14)

Storer's report to the AMA concluded that "while physicians have long been united in condemning the act of procuring an abortion, at every period of gestation, except as necessary for preserving the life of either the mother or child, it has become the duty of the association, in the view of the prevalence and increasing frequency of the crime, publicly to enter into an earnest and solemn protest against such unwarranted destruction of human life" (quoted in Rose 2008, 10). The report went much further, encouraging the AMA to formally petition governors and legislatures of states, as well as the president and Congress, to revise statutory and common law to ensure that they prohibited abortion, although usually with one exception: that physicians alone had the right to induce abortions when they deemed them necessary (Tatalovich 1997, 37; Reagan 1996, 13). In 1859, the AMA unanimously adopted the report, and this remained its official policy on abortion until 1967.

While this early history might appear to suggest that abortion was already a profoundly polarized moral and political issue in the US over 150 years ago, historians have instead suggested that the main reasons why this report gained wide support within the AMA were not particularly ideological, political, or even medical. Rather, they suggest that most doctors supported this move for reasons of professional self-interest. By using abortion as a wedge issue and publicly opposing it, the AMA was able to portray itself as morally and professionally superior to the practice of midwifery; this allowed the AMA to undercut the influence of midwives over the crucial realm of female reproductive health (Haussman 2005, 24; Rose 2008, 10). Physicians were sometimes quite explicit about their financial motives in this struggle (Sanger 2004; Mohr 1978). In 1875, for example, the Southern Michigan Medical Society was reminded by one of its members that "regular physicians are still losing patients, even long-time patients, to competitors willing to 'prevent an increase in their families' by performing abortions" (quoted in Sanger 2004, 26). As historian Leslie Reagan has shown, the AMA's move against abortion also benefited its members in other important ways – for example, it increased their overall intellectual and social capital by elevating the scientific authority of doctors above the moral authority of religious leaders (Reagan 1996, 13). The push to criminalize birth control and abortion also was largely successful at eliminating midwives as legitimate medical practitioners. Over the latter half of the nineteenth century, physicians thus effectively took control of the domains of reproduction and women's health, including moving childbirth from midwife-supervised home births to (male) physician-supervised hospital births (Sanger 2004, 26).

Not surprisingly, the AMA's official discursive justifications for opposing abortion rarely made reference to the lucrative and self-interested underpinnings of its anti-abortion position. Instead, its public argumentation was grounded in scientific, medical, and (sometimes) moral rationales. In some ways, these early AMA arguments and efforts seem consistent with the "traditional image" of the anti-abortion movement. Storer and his colleagues were a group of white men who claimed to warrant control over women's bodies and reproductive lives on the basis of a variety of gendered and moralized norms. For example, using what would become a dominant anti-abortion strategy, Storer and the AMA's public discourse opposed abortion on the basis that it was analogous with murder. Physicians and religious leaders increasingly argued in tandem that there should be no difference in the treatment of a pre- or post-quickening fetus and that abortion should not be legally permissible except for therapeutic reasons (Sanger 2004, 26). With this shift, then, we can see the emergence of the early stages of the "fetal personhood" argument that would come to dominate the abortion debate in the 1970s and 1980s.

However, in many other ways, the AMA's anti-abortion position was very different from the dominant anti-abortion discourse of the late twentieth and early twenty-first century in the US. First, as did the anti-abortion lawmakers of the first half of the 1800s, the AMA often claimed to set morality aside and deal with abortion on strictly scientific, medical, and biological terms. This strategy was further substantiated by claims that new biological discoveries revealed pregnancy to be a "continuum from conception to birth"; accordingly, physicians declared the quickening distinction to have no medical legitimacy (Sanger 2004, 26). The AMA's opposition to abortion, then, most often drew on highly medicalized language, and not on a religious or moralized rhetoric of good and evil. Second, by framing abortion in medical terms, the AMA's anti-abortion position avoided the aggressive anti-woman tones and arguments that would emerge in later forms of anti-abortion discourse. This is not to say that the effects of the AMA's abortion policy did not reduce women's ability to control their reproductive lives. It most certainly did. However, by positioning physicians as the only legitimate authority on women's health, the AMA was able to frame its position against abortion as being a benefit to women. Moreover, by increasingly representing women as weak and naive, the medical and legal treatment of women reflected a distinctly patronizing tone, one that infantilized pregnant women by suggesting that a pregnant woman, left to her own devices, would never purposefully seek out an abortion.

2.3 Criminalizing Abortion, 1840–1900

Although the AMA was not the only actor pushing for the criminalization of abortion, its discourse had a substantial effect on framing the debate over abortion in the US for the next sixty years. The group also played a very active role in inspiring, aiding, and intensifying legislative efforts to enact further anti-abortion laws. And as the century progressed, federal and state governments increasingly began to enact laws in line with the AMA's views on the illegality of abortion and the immorality of contraception.

In fact, in the mid- to late 1800s, the US witnessed an explosion of new and far more restrictive legislation that sought to fully outlaw abortion at the state level. According to historian James C. Mohr, the campaign against abortion reached its climax between 1860 and 1880, with a surge of at least forty anti-abortion statutes being enacted into law. In the period between 1866 and 1877 alone, over thirty anti-abortion pieces of legislation came into law, many completely outlawing the practice. A total of thirteen state jurisdictions entirely banned abortion for the first time, while twenty-one others revisited and further restricted their existing statutes regarding the permissibility of abortion (Mohr 1978, 200). These new and updated laws "regarded abortion in an entirely different light from common laws and statutes regulating abortifacients" that had existed in the first half of the century (Reagan 1996, 13). In particular, most of these new laws included two innovations: first, they eliminated the concept of quickening altogether, prohibiting abortion at any point of pregnancy; and second, many also introduced punishments for women who had abortions, something unheard of in the early part of the century (Reagan 1996, 10).

Connecticut's 1860 anti-abortion legislation is an excellent exemplar of this trend. Directly influenced by Storer and the AMA, and establishing a highly restrictive benchmark that would shape many of the future anti-abortion statutes introduced in state legislatures across the country, the Connecticut statute contained four sections. The first eliminated the quickening distinction and made the practice of performing an abortion at any stage of pregnancy a crime punishable by a $1,000 fine (an extraordinary amount at that time) and a maximum five-year prison sentence. The second part extended the felony range to include a possible charge for anyone found aiding in the performance of an abortion. Significantly, sections 3 and 4 criminalized the behaviour of any woman soliciting an abortion. This meant that, for the first time in American history, women who had an abortion were subject to criminal charges.

Interestingly, the punishment was much more severe for abortionists than for the women (Mohr 1978, 201–2). The justification for this legal distinction was defended in the name of protecting naive and weak women. As one legislator explained, "the public policy which underlies this legislation is based largely on protection due to the woman, protection against her own weakness as well as the criminal lust and greed of others. The criminal intent and moral turpitude involved in the violation, by a woman, of the restraint put upon her control over her own person, is widely different from that which attends the man who, in clear violation of law and for pay or gain or any kind, inflicts an injury on the body of a woman, endangering health and perhaps life" (quoted in Mohr 1978, 201).

With the enactment of this legislation, Connecticut became the first state to eliminate the doctrine of quickening and render all types of abortion illegal. But it certainly wasn't the last. Forty years later, abortion was illegal in every American state. During this period, the federal government also passed legislation that limited abortion access, most notably the Comstock Act – a law that prohibited the distribution of lewd materials, abortifacients, and contraceptive devices through the US Postal Service (the major components of which continued to be in force until the 1930s) (Critchlow 1995, 4).

While the years between 1840 and 1880 "produced the most important burst of anti-abortion legislation in the nation's history," one exception continued to exist in many of the new anti-abortion laws (Mohr 1978, 200). Most of the legislation included a number of provisions that allowed for very restricted abortion access to protect the life and/or health of the woman, usually only in cases where it was authorized by more than one doctor. The inclusion of these life and health exceptions would prove to be notable for two reasons. First, the fact that physicians had both "won the criminalization of abortion and retained to themselves alone the right to induce abortion when they determined it necessary" underlines the degree to which control over women's reproductive decisions had been captured by the medical community (Reagan 1996, 13). Second, and even more importantly politically, although no one could have predicted it at the time, these exceptions created a legal context that would eventually allow doctors who were sympathetic to legalizing abortion to push for the reform and liberalization of abortion laws in the 1960s.

Although this time period was dominated by the creation of stringent anti-abortion legislation, many historians suggest that the practice and regulation of abortion remained far more complicated than it might appear. Leslie Reagan, for instance, contends that, even during this period, "the meaning of the law and the legality and illegality of abortion changed over time ... Because laws governing abortion did not precisely define what was criminal and what was not, this had to be worked out in practice, in policing, and in the courts" (Reagan 1996, 4–5). Reagan also has shown that the role of physicians in the criminalization of abortion was also more complicated than it might appear, given the aggressive role of the AMA (3). On the one hand, it would have been nearly impossible to enforce anti-abortion laws without the cooperation of physicians who, in many instances, acted as "an arm of the state" (3). On the other hand, many physicians displayed great sympathy for women who, for a wide variety of reasons, found themselves facing unplanned pregnancy. In this regard, "sympathy for their female patients drew physicians into the world of abortion in spite of legal and professional prohibitions" (3).

While there is no question that the AMA's influence and public discourse was a major factor in the growth of anti-abortion legislation, it is important to note that this surge was not simply the result of the medical profession's position against abortion. Nor was it the accomplishment of a unified, organized, and politically embedded anti-abortion movement. In reality, the campaign to ban abortion in the nineteenth century included many different groups, and anti-abortion discourse was itself quite diverse. Given the AMA's influence, its "scientific" perspectives on fetal life and arguments about women's health and well-being had an enormous impact on public opposition to abortion and defined the anti-abortion position in significant ways. However, historians insist that the move to ban "abortion was not solely based on a respect for unborn life at its earliest stages" but was rather part of a larger campaign that viewed women's reproductive freedom as "a threat to the power structure of nineteenth century America" on demographic, racial, and moral grounds (Sanger 2004, 25).

The AMA's medicalized anti-abortion discourse was joined in the public sphere by a number of other discourses. There was, for example, a highly nativist discourse that suggested that Protestant women's relatively easy access to birth control and abortion "threatened Anglo-Saxon Protestants who wanted to maintain control over American society" (Sanger 2004, 25). Fearing that, given the influx of Irish Catholic immigrants (largely between the years 1820 and 1880), native-born Protestants would soon be outnumbered – and outvoted – nativists grounded their opposition to abortion in the larger "goal to preserve the primacy of the Anglo-Saxon, Protestant religion, culture, and political power" in America (27). This argument was further buttressed by a distinctly racialized discourse, which represented an America under a larger threat from "non-white" immigrants. This heavily racialized discourse largely revolved around the falling birthrates of native-born white Americans and stoked racial and ethnic fears as an impetus to control women's reproduction. As one physician argued in 1874, "the annual destruction of fetuses has become so truly appalling among native American women that the Puritanic blood of '76 will be but sparingly represented in the approaching centenary" (27).

Finally, it is important to note that, while men were at the forefront of the opposition to abortion, some women also joined in, challenging the legality of abortion on moral grounds. Many of these women were part of the "social purity" campaigns that came to prominence after the Civil War, seeking to prohibit many "immoral" activities, such as gambling, drinking, and prostitution. For these women, any expression of sexuality outside the home was deemed a threat to marriage and decency, with access to birth control and abortion viewed as something that "enabled husbands to consort more freely with 'other women'" (Sanger 2004, 27–28). For social purists, then, periods of abstinence and self-control were the only acceptable ways for a woman to control her reproduction.

2.4 Liberalizing Birth Control, 1900–1940

Beginning in the 1890s, a related political battle regarding the medical and moral condemnation of contraception would emerge – something that would eventually set the stage for future attempts to liberalize abortion access. The push for the liberalization of laws regulating contraceptives came largely from women in the socialist movement, who felt that the ability of working-class women to access birth control should be an important goal of the larger socialist cause as a way of giving lower-income women more control over their lives (Critchlow 1995, 2). Early proponents of access to legal contraceptives thus largely framed their support for birth control as a fundamentally working-class issue. The most prominent among these early supporters was Margaret Sanger – a nurse, activist, and the founder of the organization that would eventually become Planned Parenthood.

Sanger, who was active in the socialist movement beginning early in the second decade of the twentieth century, became concerned about the challenges of child rearing and self-induced abortions, both of which she saw as endemic problems among the working class (Critch-low 1995, 3). Sanger and others knew that while some methods of birth control such as diaphragms and condoms were already used in high levels among the upper class, the lack of access to these devices meant that many women of lower socio-economic status had to rely on dangerous "back-alley" abortions (Rose 2008, 37). Beginning in 1914, Sanger therefore fought for broad access to birth control and began to publish and disperse handbooks that educated women about contraceptive use (Critchlow 1995, 2).

Sanger was prosecuted several times for distributed pamphlets with information about contraception and was jailed for starting an illegal birth control clinic in Brooklyn (McLaren and McLaren 1997, 56). However, her trial and appeal raised significant awareness for the birth control movement, and, in the 1920s, Sanger formed the American Birth Control League (ABCL), which campaigned to reform restrictive contraception laws and opened medically supervised reproductive health clinics for the poor (McLaren and McLaren 1997, 57; Critchlow, 1995, 3).

The advocacy efforts of the ABCL were ignored by policymakers so, in 1936, Sanger took more direct action and intentionally violated the Comstock law by ordering a package of pessaries from a Japanese physician. When the case went to trial (*United States v. One Package of Japanese Pessaries*, 1936), the presiding judge, Augustus Hand, ruled that it was unconstitutional to prevent the delivery of an object prescribed by a physician. From that point on, contraception devices and information could be distributed through the mail (Critchlow 1995, 4). However, even following the *One Package* ruling – and despite some state court rulings that affirmed the legality of contraception in some circumstances – the Supreme Court refused to strike down contraception bans in Massachusetts (*Gardner v. Massachusetts*,[7] 1938) and Connecticut (*Tileston v. Ullman*, 1943) (Critchlow 1995, 4). It would not be until the 1965 *Griswold* decision that these bans would be effectively overturned.

At the discursive level, the majority of early discourse around liberalizing contraception framed birth control not as a women's rights issue, but as a working-class issue. Largely preceding the rights-based argument that would arise in the 1960s, proponents tended instead to stick

---

7 For example, the ban on contraception was not completely thrown out in Massachusetts. In fact, the research ban on it meant that the pharmaceutical manufacturer Searle was not able to fund research on the birth control pill at its base in Worcester, Massachusetts in the 1950s (see Haussman 2013).

with the less radical language of "family planning." Their discourse insisted that birth control was an effective poverty fighter that allowed poor women the much-needed ability to space their children (Valenza 1985, 46). Indeed, the benefits of birth control were most often framed as being economic and financial. Moreover, the birth control movement, including Sanger herself, remained largely opposed to legal abortion, arguing that abortion was wrong on moral grounds and that illegal abortions were dangerous for women's health (Sanger 2004). While many within the movement acknowledged that abortion was perhaps a necessity in some cases, they hoped that it would become unnecessary when effective contraception became widely available.

Sanger also employed arguments that we would view as explicitly feminist today. For instance, she often supplemented sanitized arguments about family planning and economic stability with arguments about women's equality, choices, and health that condemned the discrepancies between rich and poor women's ability to access birth control (Sanger 2004, 30). Thus equality arguments were an important part of early pro–birth control discourse. In fact, Sanger sometimes forwarded even more radical arguments about women needing to have control over their bodies. In an editorial piece written in 1914, for example, she wrote, "a woman's body is hers alone. It does not belong to the Church. It does not belong to the United States of American or any other government on the face of the earth. The first step towards getting life, liberty or the pursuit of happiness for any woman is her decision whether or not she shall become a mother" (33). While this argument was not common for the period, many consider Sanger's defiant arguments about the importance of women's bodily integrity to be the discursive foundation of the "right-to-choose" argument that would be so influential in the emergence of the modern-day reproductive rights movement (33).

Overall, however, Sanger believed that emphasizing the class and feminist dynamics of birth control would be an ineffective strategy and would limit the birth control movement's efforts to influence US public opinion and the legal and political institutions of the era. As a result, Sanger and the birth control movement mirrored the approach taken by the AMA and used mostly scientific and medical arguments to contest the Comstock law. The overall message of Sanger and the birth control movement was that "birth control is necessary for the survival and health of humanity: government had to get out of the way" (Sanger 2004, 38). As Alexander Sanger (the grandson of Margaret) suggests, "in making these arguments, my grand-mother soft-pedaled her often strident feminism and used the argument that the ability of a woman to control and limit her childbearing was good for women, her children, and the rest of her family, but was also good for the public health, society, and the economy. Birth control became family planning" (30). In this sense, Margaret Sanger's approach was an early example of using "sanitized" strategic public discourse (something we will discuss more fully in chapter 8) to appeal to a broader constituency than would be possible with a public discourse that transparently expressed activists' core motivations and principles.

During this same period, other much darker strands of discourse emerged in the public realm to argue for the liberalization of birth control. Some were pitched in a highly racialized language that, paradoxically, echoed past anti-abortion arguments about the downfall of the white Protestant family. While this discourse had been previously mobilized by individuals opposed to the legality of contraceptives and abortion in an attempt to ensure that Protestants would not be overwhelmed by Catholics, now similar actors were promoting a deeply racialized and sometimes eugenicist view that sought to encourage birth control as a way of limiting the growth of certain racial and socio-economic groups (sometimes going as far as advocating forced sterilization). Groups targeted included certain racial groups (particularly African-American and indigenous women), individuals suffering from mental illness, prostitutes, and criminals (Critchlow 1995, 1; McLaren and McLaren 1997, 54).

Nor were these views entirely absent from the socialist strand of the pro–birth control movement. While Sanger never condoned practices like euthanasia, like many of her contemporaries, she expressed support for the use of birth control and even coercion to stop procreation by those who were considered "unfit." She even went as far as to argue that the "most urgent problem today is how to limit and discourage the over-fertility of the mentally and physically defective" (Sanger 1921).

In this discursive context, abortion remained stigmatized, although in a new way. Women who sought abortions were no longer framed as naive victims of dangerous abortionists. Instead, abortion was increasingly represented as a barbaric practice perpetuated and perpetrated by immigrant and marginalized communities (Haussman 2005, 26). Ultimately, while the availability and legality of contraception increased during this period (which would prove crucial for future abortion reform), abortion remained illegal across the US and was not politically contested in a significant way.

2.5 Legal Reform: Therapeutic Abortion Committees, 1950s–1960s

By the 1940s and 1950s, a variety of arguments and factors in favour of the liberalization of abortion began to emerge. While the relaxation of abortion laws at both the state and federal levels would not come to fruition until the mid-1960s and 1970s, anti-abortion laws were increasingly contested beginning in the 1940s.

As Leslie Reagan suggests, Americans have a long history of accepting abortion as a necessity in certain situations. Even during the first of the twentieth century – when abortion was illegal in every American state – women (especially those of the upper classes) regularly accessed abortion services (Reagan 1996, 48). Thus, there was a significant gap between the laws and actual (popular) morality when it came to the practice of abortion. In accordance with this popular morality, many physicians "responded to women's requests for abortion and participated in its illegal practice" (48).

Given the risks to doctors engaging in illegal procedures, it was not surprising that at some point, movement on the abortion front would come from within the medical profession. In the 1950s, then, sympathetic physicians began to form therapeutic abortion committees (TACs) in hospitals in order to use narrow medical exceptions that had been built into many state laws to increase access to abortion. TACs were physician-constituted committees designed to determine in which cases abortions were deemed medically necessary, on a case-by-case basis. The existence and size of such committees varied by state. In theory, in states that allowed TACs, any pregnant woman could be referred to a committee by her doctor, at which point the committee would review her case and make a decision about whether or not to authorize an abortion based on medical merit. In practice, it was mostly well-connected, upper-middle-class, white women who were likely to receive approval from the committees (Haussman 2005, 29). The TAC system did not always protect physicians from prosecution, however. Accordingly, doctors began to push for a universal abortion law to replace the patchwork system that existed from state to state (31).

In this context, the American Law Institute (ALI) – using a highly medicalized discourse to support arguments in favour of legal abortion – began to play an important role in the debate surrounding the TAC system. The mission of the ALI, which was founded in 1923, was to reduce uncertainty about and the complexity of US common law by promoting "the clarification and simplification of the law and its better adaptation to social needs" (Amerian Law Institute, n.d.). Although the ALI initially employed certain elements of the dominant discourse about abortion (e.g., that it was ultimately a morally ambiguous act), it nonetheless proposed replacing the TAC system with a national legal standard that better reflected the needs of pregnant women (Haussman 2005, 31). In doing so, it argued for a unified federal law and published a reformed "model penal code" in 1959 (which it suggested could form the basis of actual legislation) that relaxed the existing limitations on women seeking abortions (Francome 2004, 70). It proposed a much broader list of reasons under which a woman should be able to obtain a legal abortion (e.g., a threat to the physical or mental health of the woman; any pregnancy that was the result of a felonious sexual act such as rape or incest) (see Rose 2008, 38–39). Harkening back to earlier legislation that did not regulate miscarriages that took place before quickening, the proposed code held that fetal life was developmental and suggested relative leniency for illegal abortions performed during the earlier trimesters. The proposed code continued to require two physicians to authorize an abortion, but it offered a greater level of protection and flexibility for doctors to respond to their patients' needs (Francome 2004, 70). Soon after it was published, Colorado, North Carolina, and California passed bills based the ALI model, which made abortion legal in cases of rape, incest, and threats to mental or physical health (Haussman 2005, 31–32).

Significant differences of interpretation regarding what counted as a legitimate reason to grant an abortion continued to exist, creating considerable risks for doctors, especially in states that had not adopted the ALI model. Finally, in June 1967, the AMA released an updated policy in response to the ALI's pressure for legal reform. This time, the AMA began to lobby lawmakers to liberalize access to abortion (Tatalovich 1997, 38). By 1969, ten states had approved legal reforms based on the wording of the ALI model penal code (Haussman 2005, 33).

2.6 Setting the Stage for the Rise of the Abortion Rights Movement, 1960–1965

It was not only the legal standing of abortion that was being contested by medical and legal pro-reform discourse. Both the public face of illegal abortion and the discourse surrounding abortion policy were also undergoing profound changes. Prior to 1960, there was very little public discussion of the realities of underground abortions, either in terms of their frequency or their potential health risks. With the increase of medical and legal discussions around the necessity of safe access to abortion, the story of illegal abortion began to makes its way into popular discourse. Political scientist Celeste Condit argues that, in order to breach the long silence on the realities of illegal abortion in the US, "a special discursive form was needed – a form that could weave a compelling understanding of the abortion problem without engaging the powerful value set that surrounded it. The rhetorical form suited to the task was narrative" (Condit 1990, 23–24).

As we will discuss at length in chapter 11, story telling is a particularly powerful rhetorical tool that can profoundly reshape our understanding and interpretation of a given reality. Most social and political contexts have a variety of dominant narratives that heavily influence the political judgment and behaviour of many of the individuals in those contexts. This is partially because narratives can very effectively activate various "networks of association" – "bundles of thoughts, feelings, images and ideas that have become connected over time" – that can act as powerful motivations for political behaviour (Westen 2007, 3). According to Condit, the archetypal narrative about the dangers and injustices of illegal abortion was particularly persuasive because it was a "story of a good, ordinary person faced by social (not natural) circumstances that led her into evil scenes of self-destruction, magnified by gory details of the methods and sciences she was required to face" (Condit 1990, 28).

The archetypal story of illegal abortion was first popularized in public discourse through a series of exposés, the most dramatic of which was carried in the *Saturday Evening Post* in May 1961 (Condit 1990, 24). These largely journalistic accounts of clandestine abortion worked to construct a distinctive and dramatic tale. It was the story of "ordinary" women who, because of a series of "extraordinary" events, were forced to turn to the dangerous world of illegal abortion. Most public accounts of illegal abortion avoided dealing with subtle cases, opting instead to tell of the most extreme and culturally potent examples of dangerous underground abortions (26). The majority of the women cast in these stories were depicted as being "emotionally ill (had threatened suicide), had been raped, or were young girls of fourteen or fifteen who had been seduced by other men (even their father) and deserted" (26). By highlighting the extreme examples, the narrative of illegal abortion was more persuasive, encouraging audiences to see themselves in the narrative and identify more deeply with the social dimensions of abortion.

Although these early exposés largely avoided commenting on normative policy recommendations, they opened up discursive space for "a torrent of increasingly strident articles, many by female reporters" in support of the legalization of abortion (Condit 1990, 24). This second wave of coverage was much more critical of abortion policy in the US, "gradually recasting the issue from a general problem of law enforcement to a problem *for women*, deriving from the law itself" (24, emphasis in original).

Notably, the explicit arguments adopted by this second stream of coverage largely followed the contours of the reforms suggested by the ALI (Condit 1990, 24). These accounts argued that women should be able to access safe and legal abortions in circumstances where the continuation of pregnancy posed physical and psychological risk. Most of these accounts also argued for more leniency for physicians in referring and performing abortions, especially in cases of rape and incest. While the women in these dramatic abortion horror stories were represented sympathetically, the discourse remained largely medicalized, rarely making explicitly moral and feminist arguments about women's rights and choices.

The narrative also limited the types of solutions that could be proposed in response. First, by depicting women primarily as casualties of illegal abortion, women seeking abortions were still cast as helpless victims with limited agency. The idea that an intelligent, "rational" pregnant woman would actively *choose* abortion over motherhood was absent. In many ways, this abortion-reform discourse continued to characterize pregnant women as victims, unable to make their own reproductive decisions. Moreover, it also supported a conflicted "good" versus "bad" abortion patient dichotomy that paradoxically viewed abortion as most necessary for unmarried women (as a way of avoiding the stigma of being an unwed mother) but represented a woman as a "good" and worthy recipient of an abortion only if she were a a married mother (Condit 1990, 32).

Despite its limits, the narrative of illegal abortion proved effective in bringing the reality of clandestine abortions to the surface of public discourse. Unsurprisingly, the introduction of the abortion issue into public discourse through the narrative of illegal abortion did not go unnoticed by those who opposed abortion. Accordingly, anti-abortion advocates soon began to contest the legitimacy of the narrative of illegal abortion by introducing their own "pro-life heritage tale" (Condit 1990). This story argued that legal abortion went against an American heritage that correctly viewed abortion as both morally and legally wrong (43). Through the heritage tale, opposition to abortion was grounded not only in its "identity with murder" but also through a "selective and coherent account portraying a specific strand of white, Western, Christian history as the authoritative and legitimate American heritage" (45). This framing encouraged Americans to view the anti-abortion position as religiously, morally, and culturally superior by placing their opposition to abortion in the language of "moral progress." According to Celeste Condit, opponents of legal abortion contended that there had been a clear path of "moral improvement" through history and that "prohibition against abortion had become more and more restrictive through time, as humankind became increasingly aware of the fact that abortion represented the killing of a human being" (44). This story often rested on analogies between slavery, the Holocaust, and abortion. It also gave a particular place of pride to Christianity and its role in ushering in moral progress more generally. This discourse allowed advocates to introduce moralized and religiously righteous language into larger anti-abortion discourse – a strategy that would come to dominate the anti-abortion movement in the coming decades (49).

With the introduction of these two competing narratives – one decrying the dangers of illegal abortion, the other asserting the historical righteousness of the anti-abortion position – the stage was set for the emergence of a hyperpolarized battle over both the legality and the morality of abortion in the United States.

2.7 The Rise of Rights before *Roe v. Wade*, 1965–1972

Despite the existence of an anti-abortion counternarrative, by the mid-1960s, the powerful abortion rights narrative about the dangers of illegal abortion – in combination with a more formal medicalized and legal discourse – had strongly influenced the public language of the abortion debate. This changing discourse was matched by action, as official legal and medical attempts to moderately liberalize abortion law were being successfully undertaken in many individual states.

At the same time, there was an emerging discourse that sought to expand and radicalize, if not directly challenge, this "moderate" pro-abortion discourse. Increasingly, feminist activists began to engage on the abortion issue, believing that the mainstream arguments being made by pro-reform advocates were profoundly insufficient. For growing feminist circles, the medicalized narrative regarding the dangers of illegal abortion – and its recommendation that the (predominantly male) medical community be granted even more control over women's reproduction – was highly problematic. Feminists also believed that the arguments used by "moderate" abortion reformers largely failed to challenge the central values of "motherhood" and "traditional family" that, feminists argued, constrained women's real ability to exercise substantive reproductive freedom.

In the wake of the civil rights movement, discourses of "rights" and "equality" were gaining political salience and, increasingly, the concept of "equality" was used in arguments about discrimination in American political life. It is not surprising, then, that the first explicitly "feminist" argument about abortion capitalized on the language of equality and discrimination, arguing that illegal, unsafe abortions were "an unjustified discrimination" due to "socioeconomic disparity" (Condit 1990, 60). Echoing some of the earlier radical arguments put forward by Margaret Sanger about birth control, abortion reformers, "by employing the term *equality* as central to the meaning surrounding abortion," were finally able to create a way for more assertive feminist demands to be introduced in the public vocabulary (64, emphasis in original).

The introduction of the language of equality into mainstream abortion discourse "turned the *desire* for an end to illegal abortion into a constitutional *demand* for the repeal of all abortion laws"; "equality thus gained a hearing for abortion *as a right*" (ibid., 64, emphasis in original). However, the equality argument had clear limits. For instance, one of the most common anti-abortion responses to the equality argument was that it had no basis in law (66). Rich women, just like poor women, were not legally allowed to have an abortion. Therefore, even if there were some inequality in real access, that phenomenon had no basis in abortion laws (which were formally applicable to all citizens). Thus, those laws were not unconstitutional. This argument was often taken even further by some of the more militant anti-abortion lawmakers, who went as far as to argue that abortion law in fact favoured the poor, suggesting that "it is the unborn children of the middle class and the rich who are discriminated against ... [when] we have no way to limit their abortions" (66).

The answer to the shortcomings of the "equality" frame would come in the form of "choice." While "respecting women's choices" was always the key stake for some early abortion rights activists, "these voices did not become the most audible ones until the seventies," when a public discourse "gradually developed which framed the [abortion] controversy as a 'woman's choice'" (ibid., 67). In many ways, "choice" was a principle through which women could support concrete and material demands that would address the relative dearth of options they had to regulate and control their reproductive lives. It emerged out of the early stories of illegal abortion, where women felt they had "no choice." However, it ran much deeper. Choice soon became linked to larger critiques of dominant ideologies of motherhood, gender, and women's place within American society. Choice became a persuasive frame through which women could express all "those things which were fundamentally necessary for them to experience equality with men and freedom as human agents" (68). Ultimately, women would come to publicly express their political and reproductive needs through the language of choice. In many ways, then, the modern reproductive rights movement began to emerge during the 1960s as the values of equality and choice became the defining lens through which reproductive issues – including abortion access – were viewed and the public debate over abortion increasingly began to take the form of a battle between rights: the right to choose of the women and the right to life of fetuses.

The 1960s also witnessed the emergence and growth of more explicitly feminist abortion rights activist organizations. For instance, in 1963, the Society for Humane Abortion (SHA) was created (it had been founded a year earlier under the name the Citizens Committee for Humane Abortion Laws) and became one of the first groups to openly use women's rights discourse to argue for legal abortion. Even before the abortion controversy had reached mainstream America, the SHA rejected the ALI reforms, arguing that they gave physicians a disproportionate control over women's reproductive decisions. Instead, the SHA's activism focused on putting women's interests and self-determination at the centre of abortion law reform (Haussman 2005, 34). Its discourse challenged the medicalized language that had previously dominated abortion reform.

The SHA also engaged in direct action – referring women to reputable providers who would perform safe, if illegal, abortions. Other groups began to undertake similar initiatives. In Chicago, the Jane Collective was created by women who were concerned with the scarcity of doctors willing to perform abortions. Faced with the reality that women were often forced to obtain abortions from unlicensed providers who often had little training, the members of the collective learned how to perform abortions and began offering the service themselves.

Scholars estimate that they performed 12,000 underground abortions between 1969 and 1973 (Haussman 2005, 35).

Alongside these radical feminist groups, a variety of other new civil society advocacy organizations emerged to support liberalized abortion access and contest anti-abortion laws on largely medical grounds. Founded in 1964, the Association for the Study of Abortion (ASA) was composed mostly of legal and medical professionals. Its primary role was to educate the public on the topic of abortion by providing knowledgeable speakers for community events, television shows, and radio interviews (Francome 2004, 70). The ASA was limited in the scope of its political activism because of its tax-exempt status, but it provided the meeting place for two activists – Larry Lader and Lonny Myers – who believed it was possible to bring about a sweeping legislative change and repeal abortion laws. In 1969, Lader and Myers organized a conference on the topic, and from this the National Association for the Repeal of Abortion Laws (NARAL) was created (Haussman 2005, 36).

NARAL and the National Organization for Women (NOW) were the first feminist groups to explicitly demand the repeal of abortion legislation in the United States (Haussman 2005, 36; Rose 2008, 53). In 1968, NOW released the "NOW Bill of Rights," which demanded "the right of women to control their reproductive lives by removing from penal codes the laws limiting access to contraceptive information and devices and laws governing abortion" (quoted in Rose 2008, 53). The NOW Bill of Rights, which was structured to mimic the androcentric bias of the American Bill of Rights, highlighted equality differences between men and women as an underlying justification for legal access to adequate reproductive services.

These organizational efforts – combined with the shifting and expanding discourse around abortion reform – had significant effects. Public support for abortion reform began to grow. During the 1960s, polls showed that a majority of Americans supported the idea that abortion should be legal to preserve the woman's health and in the cases where significant genetic issues had been found in the fetus (Tatalovich 1997, 109). Polls also showed that, although support for abortion on demand was much lower than support in qualified circumstances, it was growing rapidly (109).

By the mid-1960s, several legal and legislative developments also began to have important consequences. In 1965, with the *Griswold v. Connecticut* decision, the US Supreme Court struck down the Connecticut law that had led to the arrest of Margaret Sanger in the 1930s.

Griswold also found that "married persons have a constitutionally protected right to privacy" – a right that was later extended to non-married persons in the 1972 case *Eisenstadt v. Baird* (Critchlow 1995, 4). This was a key precedent, and *Griswold* and *Eisenstadt* set the judicial stage for the "right to privacy" argument that would eventually be adopted in *Roe v. Wade*.

At the same time, some states were liberalizing their own abortion laws. As already noted, Colorado, California, and North Carolina legalized abortion in cases of rape or incest or where the continuation of a pregnancy would lead to permanent physical disability of a woman. Oregon soon followed suit. In 1970, Hawaii became the first state to legalize abortion on demand. In the same year, New York repealed its own law, which dated from the 1830s, legalizing abortion up until the twenty-fourth week of pregnancy. Similar laws were passed in Alaska and Washington (Tietze and Henshaw 1986).

Anti-abortion advocates did not accept these new laws, of course, and sought to challenge them in the courts. The abortion issue would first land in the US Supreme Court in 1971, when physician Milan Vuitch was indicted for performing abortions in violation of the District of Columbia's abortion statute. The Washington DC law allowed for abortions to be performed if the procedure was necessary to protect the life and health of the woman. In *United States v. Vuitch*, the Supreme Court overturned Vuitch's indictment, deeming "health" to refer to both psychological and physical well-being. Following this decision, liberalized abortion laws were introduced across the country. By 1973, just before the Supreme Court decided *Roe v. Wade*, abortion was legal in one third of the American states (Tietze and Henshaw 1986).

2.8 The *Roe v. Wade* Decision, 1973

With the US Supreme Court's acknowledgment, in *Griswold v. Connecticut*, of the "right to privacy" with respect to reproductive rights, the abortion issue had become politically salient at the federal level. In this context, abortion rights activists put forward a series of legal challenges that contested the constitutionality of state anti-abortion laws across the country. The most famous of these are the two companion decisions released on 22 January 1973: *Roe v. Wade* and *Doe v. Bolton*. These two decisions struck down abortion laws in Texas and Georgia as unconstitutional (largely under a right to privacy that the majority of justices found embedded in the Constitution, including in the due process clause of the Fourteenth Amendment). They have come to serve as "landmarks in the abortion controversy, with important implications in practice" (Muldoon 1991, 160).

In the case of *Doe v. Bolton*, the plaintiff Mary Doe (a pseudonym used to protect the anonymity of the woman who would later be revealed as Sandra Cano) sued the Attorney General of Georgia, Anthony Bolton, when she was denied an abortion in 1970. At the time, abortion law in Georgia permitted abortion only in cases of rape, severe fetal deformity, or the possibility of severe or fatal damage to the pregnant woman (Muldoon 1991 161). Moreover, in order for a woman to procure a legal abortion in Georgia she had to be a state resident and present her case for the approval of a TAC composed of three physicians. If two of the three physicians approved a woman's request for an abortion as being lawful under the Georgia law, then a woman could procure an abortion, as long as it was performed in an accredited hospital (Wood and Hawkins 1980).

After being denied an abortion by a TAC in Georgia, Doe took her case to the District Court, arguing that the TAC's denial infringed her constitutional right to privacy. While the three-judge panel ruled the conditional restriction portion of the Georgia abortion law unconstitutional, it upheld both the TAC approval process and the residential requirement sections of the law. Moreover, the District Court refused to grant Doe an injunction against the enforcement of the law. Doe decided to appeal the decision to the US Supreme Court (Wood and Hawkins 1980).

The case of *Roe v. Wade* also began in 1970. A pregnant Texas woman, Jane Roe (a pseudonym for Norma McCorvey), sued Dallas county prosecutor Henry Wade in an attempt to prevent him from enforcing the state's abortion law. At the time, Texas's abortion law was even more restrictive than that of Georgia, banning all abortions except to save the life of a pregnant woman. Like in *Doe v. Bolton*, the District Court of Texas found the abortion law to be unconstitutional. But it also refused to grant an injunction against the enforcement of the law. Like Doe, Roe appealed to the US Supreme Court. That court heard the case in December 1971, even though, by that time, Roe had carried her pregnancy to term and subsequently giving the baby up for adoption (Rose 2008, 93).

The Supreme Court found in favour of the plaintiffs in both decisions, ruling that the abortion laws in Texas and Georgia – as well as in most American states – violated a woman's inherent right to privacy and liberty. In *Doe*, the Supreme Court not only upheld the unconstitutionality of the conditional restriction portion of the law in Georgia, but also deemed both the TAC process and the residential portions of the law unconstitutional. In its 7–2 decision regarding *Roe v. Wade*, the Supreme Court argued that the "penumbras of the Bill of Rights" as set out in *Griswold v. Connecticut*, as well as the Ninth Amendment analysis in that case and "the concept of liberty guaranteed by the first section of the Fourteenth Amendment" that the court had recognized in *Meyer v. Nebraska* (1923), were fundamentally relevant in determining their judgment (Finkelman and Urofsky 2003).

The Supreme Court, however, did not rule that women had an unlimited right to abortion, arguing instead that this right must be balanced against two legitimate state interests: protecting prenatal life and protecting women's health. The *Roe* decision presented a three-stage standard for when abortion could be restricted at the state level. This standard largely followed the trimester system, arguing that a state's interest in regulating abortion increases over the course of a woman's pregnancy (Wood and Hawkins 1980, 400).

The court stated that, in the first trimester, a woman's decision to have an abortion was entirely between her and her physician, thus outlawing any state restrictions on abortion throughout the first trimester of pregnancy. State regulation over the second trimester of pregnancy, the court ruled, had to be limited to restrictions that are necessary to protect the health and safety of pregnant women. According to the court, it was only in the third trimester of pregnancy that states could constitutionally prevent abortion. The reason given was that "the fetus then presumably has the capability of meaningful life outside the mother's womb" (quoted in Wood and Hawkins 1980, 401). The court ruled that states may limit access to abortion throughout the third trimester, "except when it is necessary to preserve the life or health of the mother" (401).

Together, the decisions in *Roe v. Wade* and *Doe v. Bolton* recognized "a constitutional right to abortion." In doing so, they led to the nullification of nearly every law against abortion across the country and profoundly altered the landscape and delivery of abortion in the US. However, it was not just at the practical level that *Roe* and *Doe* changed abortion politics. The joint decisions also had a massive effect on the way that abortion rights advocates would shape the arguments and broader public discourse in support of abortion. Ultimately, *Roe* and *Doe* not only changed how abortion was legally regulated in the US, they also changed how Americans *talked* about abortion.

In what way did the Supreme Court shift public discourse about abortion? On the one hand, two Supreme Court justices – Byron White and William Rehnquist – vehemently opposed the legalization of abortion, writing emphatic dissents in both cases. Adhering closely to the traditional image of the anti-abortion position, this dissent described abortion and motherhood within the prevailing ideology of conservative America, describing women's reason for procuring abortion as "convenience, whim, or caprice of the putative mother." Justice White also opposed abortion for any reason of "family planning, economics, dislike of children, [or] the embarrassment of illegitimacy," further arguing that "the fetus had a right to life that outweighed the woman's right to privacy" (quoted in Condit 1990, 106–108). This representation of abortion as a decision taken by "capricious" women for irresponsible reasons would ultimately emerge as a major argument in anti-abortion discourse in the coming decades.

Perhaps the biggest discursive shift we see post-*Roe* is a change in the argumentation of abortion rights activists. Increasingly, proponents of legal abortion moved away from arguments about women's health and towards rights-based arguments. The biological, medical, and social arguments that had been made by previous generation of birth control and abortion proponents were largely sidelined by a right-based approach to the public debate over abortion (Sanger 2004, 44). This was particularly true once the majority decision in *Roe* essentially entrenched the pro-"choice" vocabulary of the abortion rights movement into US law. In the elaboration of the decision, Justice Harry Blackmun repeatedly cites women's "fundamental right to choose" and "freedom of choice" (42). While the "choice" frame had previously been largely a public – not legal – term, Blackmun legitimized the "right to choose" by demonstrating its link to women's "right to privacy," which had already been employed in *Griswold*.

In many ways, then, *Roe* and *Doe* fundamentally changed the US abortion landscape and proved to be a significant victory in the fight for women's rights in the US. Yet, far from settling the issue, these rulings were merely the starting bell in what has become a highly polarized and hyper-politicized battle that has taken place at every political and legal level from school boards to the Supreme Court.

2.9 Conclusion

This overview of the history of the abortion debate in the US from the early nineteenth until the late twentieth century reminds us that, while abortion is currently one of the most politically salient issues in the US, this has not always been the case. Prior to 1840, abortion was largely viewed as an acceptable and non-political issue – part of the lived reality of American women. Abortion – and women's reproductive health more generally – was mostly left to the knowledge and discretion of midwives. There was little public discourse that commented on women's reproductive lives. Moreover, what legal regulation did surround abortion was permissive of abortions occurring before quickening. The quickening doctrine – which regarded abortion as morally and legally permissible before the fourth month of pregnancy – was reflected in both popular morality and the legal realm.

Starting in the mid-nineteenth century, abortion increasingly came under scrutiny, led, in large part, by a small group of male physicians in the AMA who opposed the role that midwives were playing in the field of women's health. Following the lead of Dr. Horatio Storer, the AMA adopted a militantly anti-abortion position that would heavily influence medical and legal attitudes about the permissibility and morality of abortion. Somewhat surprisingly, the anti-abortion discourse employed by Storer and the AMA was not the heavily moralized and religious discourse that dominates American politics today. Instead, anti-abortion advocates of the nineteenth century framed their position mostly in scientific and medical discourses about fetal life and in paternalistic arguments about the need to protect women from "dangerous" abortionists. This framing and the efforts of the AMA and others were largely effective, and between 1840 and 1880, the US witnessed a major surge in anti-abortion legislation. By the beginning of the twentieth century, abortion was illegal in every American state.

By the twentieth century, however, there were also voices emerging in favour of allowing women more control over their reproductive choices. By the 1960s, an increasing number of actors were involved in the political struggle over reproductive rights in general – and increasingly about abortion specifically. Judicial judgments started to create significant legal openings for the abortion rights movement. Interestingly, while the pro-reform arguments of this decade hinted at the privacy rights and choice-based arguments that would become dominant, in the 1960s the main arguments were largely medicalized, framing both birth control and abortion as fundamental parts of women's health care.

This pro-reform discourse culminated in the 1973 *Doe v. Bolton* and *Roe v. Wade* decisions by the US Supreme Court, which recognized a constitutional right to abortion. Not only did *Roe* and *Doe* profoundly change the delivery and legality of abortion in the US, but they also changed the language used by abortion advocates opening the door for the use of rights-based argument in the judicial realm. As we will see in the next chapter, *Doe* and *Roe* not only greatly influenced the language and arguments taken up by the abortion rights movement, they also profoundly influenced the anti-abortion movement and its discourse.

Chapter 3

The Abortion Debate in the United States after *Roe v. Wade*

Roe v. Wade was a decisive victory for legal abortion in the United States. It made abortion legal throughout the US and framed the abortion debate in terms that were favourable to the growing abortion rights movement, both in the public sphere and in legal settings. This success, however, would be short-lived, as almost immediately after *Roe* the anti-abortion movement would become increasingly successful at popularizing counter-frames including in legal and political settings. In many ways, then, "the strategy and rhetoric of both the pro-life movement, as well as the pro-choice movement, were set by the terms of the *Roe* decision" (Sanger 2004, 50).

This chapter will examine the rise of the increasingly religious American anti-abortion movement in reaction to *Roe v. Wade*. As we saw in the previous chapter, although religion played some role in historical anti-abortion organization and activism, the movement's public discourse did not primarily frame itself through religious appeals before *Roe*. However, the rise of an explicitly Christian right as a politically significant movement in US politics (a phenomenon enabled not only by *Roe* but a variety of other factors as well) had an enormous impact on the contours of the US anti-abortion movement, its political and legal strategies, and its public discourse. In this chapter we chart this intertwined history; the anti-abortion movement's political, legal, and discursive victories; and the many ways in which these events have incrementally and continuously eroded the right to abortion originally laid out in *Roe* and *Doe*.

3.1 The Rise of the Contemporary American Anti-abortion Movement and the Hyde Amendment

Many argue that the seeds of the contemporary anti-abortion movement lay in the rapid success of the abortion rights movement throughout the 1960s and early 1970s and the fact that abortion became one of the most visible issues in the American's women's movement (Sanger 2004; Blanchard 1994; Ferree et al. 2002). Americans who opposed abortion were largely caught off guard by the 1973 abortion rights victory. Prior to *Roe*, "there was no reason to energetically fight abortion when, for nearly a century, abortion was a crime and no social movement suggested otherwise" (Blanchard 1994, 22). Moreover, prior to 1973, organized religion had little interest in abortion, and there existed no unified anti-abortion organization to coordinate efforts at a national level (ibid.).

Immediately following *Roe*, this quickly changed. The first post-*Roe* anti-abortion responses included organizing right-to-life groups at the state level and coordinating letter-writing campaigns to members of Congress and the Supreme Court itself. These early efforts were crucial, creating not only infrastructure but also early strategic models that focused on achieving the legislative and legal rollbacks that have occurred over the past forty years.

The first major legislative victory of the post-*Roe* anti-abortion movement was the Hyde Amendment, which prohibited the use of any federal money to fund abortion care. But it was far from the last, as the US would see a surge of federal and state bills aimed at restricting abortion access across the country in the following decades. Whereas the decade leading up to *Roe* saw only ten anti-abortion bills tabled (but not necessarily passed) in Congress, the fifteen years from 1973 to 1988 saw 571 abortion-related bills introduced in Congress, with 94 per cent advancing the anti-abortion agenda (Tatalovich 1997, 95–96).

Passed by the House of Representatives in 1976 and named after its main sponsor, Republican Congressman Henry Hyde, the original version of the Hyde Amendment stipulated that federal funds could not be spent on abortion under any circumstances. The Senate, however, blocked the Amendment, forcing the bill into conference committee (whose mandate is to resolve differences between bills passed by the House and Senate). The committee eventually struck a compromise whereby the bill would ban abortion funding "except where the life of the mother would be endangered if the fetus were carried to term" (quoted in Tatalovich 1997, 97). Because the Hyde Amendment is a "rider bill" (meaning it is attached to the appropriations bills funding the Department of Health and Human Services and thus must annually be re-enacted by Congress), it has been altered a number of times. Over the years, it has vacillated between a complete ban on federal abortion funding and the use of limited federal funds to cover abortions in cases of rape, incest, or where the continuation of the pregnancy threatens the life of the woman (97).

Banning and/or radically limiting public funding for abortion has been a very effective strategy for the anti-abortion movement since the late 1970s, with the Hyde Amendment being but one example. At the federal level, one version or another of the Hyde Amendment has been in effect since 1976. And at the state level, thirty-three states have legislation or policies that disallow the funding of any abortion procedures except when the continuation of a pregnancy directly places the woman's life in danger (Guttmacher Institute 2013c).

During this period, the major discursive strategy of the anti-abortion movement increasingly centred on the argument that the fetus was a person under the Constitution and thus could not be deprived of its right to life. Such arguments were often accompanied by concomitant representations of women seeking abortions as either too selfish or not morally capable enough to make decisions about their reproductive lives. Thus, by the mid-1970s, several of the core characteristics captured by the traditional portrait – a focus on legislative means, the wide-spread use of fetal-centric arguments, and a highly judgmental anti-woman tone – began to dominate anti-abortion strategy and discourse.

One of the advantages of fetal-centric and anti-woman arguments was that they could anchor many different types of legislative attempts to regulate abortion. They could justify legislation that sought to ban abortions outright. As with Hyde and other bills, they could also underpin demands to defund abortion (which was viewed as an incremental step that reduced the number of abortions). These arguments could also easily be married with other supplementary claims. For example, anti-abortion discourse began to combine fetal-centric arguments with "choice" arguments. Anti-abortion advocates argued that although *Roe* granted women the "choice" to terminate their pregnancies, taxpayers must have the "choice" not to fund those abortions – compelling taxpayers to pay for abortion was effectively "discrimination against the taxpayer" (Condit 1990, 114). These were effective strategies of persuasion – especially when combined with attacks on the legal logic of *Roe* and the argument that there "was no right to privacy at all, or at least not one that gives the right to women to have an abortion" (Sanger 2004, 50).

Abortion rights activists sought to counter these arguments largely by focusing on the unequal effects of defunding abortion, arguing that defunding was particularly dangerous for low-income women, who, unlike their more affluent counterparts, might not be able to pay for their own abortion. Many advocates further asserted that defunding abortion violated the "equal protection" clause of the Fourteenth Amendment by preventing poor women from exercising their constitutional right to abortion. To buttress this argument, abortion rights activists and lawmakers often invoked the image of coat hangers and back-alley abortions, drawing on the narrative of illegal abortion that was so successful in the early stages of abortion reform (see chapter 2 and Condit 1990, 52). This equality/discrimination argument was also often reinforced by claims about the social and economic costs of defunding abortion (Condit 1990, 52).

3.2 The Rising Influence of the Religious Right

The language used by the anti-abortion movement in relation to the Hyde Amendment was much less religious than one might imagine, given the central role of religion in US anti-abortion language today. This is due to several reasons. First, while religious appeals are prominent in both the organizational and public discourse of the anti-abortion movement, in legislative and legal settings the movement has tended to frame their discursive rationales most typically around fetal personhood. Second, in the mid-1970s, the Christian right had not yet coalesced into the very powerful movement it would become in the 1980s. It was still a relatively new social movement and, accordingly, its impact was limited.

Despite the fact that it did not play a key role in the debate around the Hyde Amendment, there is little doubt that the emergence of the Christian right throughout the 1970s and 1980s has been the most significant factor affecting the organizational nature and public discourse of the American anti-abortion movement over the past forty years. Prior to *Roe,* the anti-abortion movement was not a unified and organized political force, and its judicial and legislative efforts had not been particularly intense. Anti-abortion groups tended to be "local groups of professionals, physicians, attorneys, and social workers who had contact with individuals caught in the abortion issue" (Blanchard 1994, 51). They were also predominantly Catholic. Largely drawing on the "pro-life heritage narrative" discussed in chapter 2, their discourse was designed to "awaken what they assumed was the 'natural' public opposition to abortion" (52). As states increasingly started to liberalize their abortion laws, these relatively small religious anti-abortion groups began to move from the local level to the national arena. At the centre of this move was a religious discourse that represented abortion as a moral evil.

In the early 1970s, it was far from clear that this perspective would become a major component of anti-abortion discourse. In the immediate aftermath of *Roe*, even major actors within the American anti-abortion movement seemed cautious about the potential effectiveness of religious discourse in garnering mainstream appeal (Ferree et al. 2002, 161–62). There was great diversity within religious discourse on the moral acceptability of abortion. While many Protestants opposed abortion – historically viewing it as an attack on the Protestant family – certain elements in other religions recognized the necessity of abortion in some cases. For instance, in forming "Catholics for Free Choice," some "social justice Catholics" (Cuneo 1989) went as far as to "affirm both the right and responsibility of a Catholic to follow his or her conscience on moral matters," arguing that "women can be trusted to make decisions that support the well-being of their children, families, and society, and that enhance their own integrity and health" (quoted in Ferree et al. 2002, 162). Moreover, as Duane Oldfield observes, well into the mid-1970s "when Americans thought of religiously based political activism, the images that came to mind were likely to be those of figures on the left: Martin Luther King, Jr., or anti-war priests such as Daniel Berrigan" (1996, 3). Consequently, when founding its first national organizations, the American anti-abortion movement was cautious about seeming too overtly religious. For example, despite the fact that the National Right to Life Committee (which was created in 1968 and would eventually become the largest national anti-abortion organization in the US) was founded and underwritten by the National Conference of Catholic Bishops, its leaders downplayed its Catholicism and even its religiosity, attempting instead to market the organization to multiple religious, and even non-religious, factions (Oldfield 1996).

This caution began to disappear, however, when much to the surprise of most political observers, the Christian right arose as a significant and politically salient movement in the late 1970s (Ferree et al. 2002, 162). While religious beliefs and organizations had always had an impact on politics in the US, the rise of the Christian right meant that religious discourse and leaders increasingly played a different, and much more assertive and explicit, role. The Christian right systematically took its opposition to abortion "out of the church and into the public domain" of American politics in organized ways (162–63). In the 1980s, under the guidance and leadership of evangelicals such as Pat Robertson, Ralph Reed, and Jerry Falwell, the Christian right became an increasing influence within the Republican Party.

Daniel Williams suggests that the alliance of the Christian right and the Republican Party arose in two stages. The first, from the 1940s through to the 1960s, was based primarily on an increasing number of conservative Protestants who "began to identify the GOP as the party of anticommunism and a Protestant-based moral order" (Williams 2010, 3). A shared anti-communist orientation led to the development of close relationships between religious conservatives and a number of influential Republican leaders in the 1950s, most notably President Dwight Eisenhower and Vice-President Richard Nixon. At this stage, however, evangelical Protestants did not exercise a controlling influence in the "Grand Old Party" (GOP), and their success was often limited by their lack of political skills and by religious divisions within their own movement (ibid.).

It would not be until the second stage, beginning in the late 1960s, that conservative Protestants would prove successful in asserting substantial influence on the agenda of the Republican Party. Throughout this second stage, evangelicals "focused more on the culture wars than the Cold War" (ibid., 3). By presenting themselves as a united front – combined with their growing alliances with Republican politicians – conservative Protestants and evangelicals began mobilizing against a number of new issues, including feminism, abortion, pornography, and gay rights. By the beginning of the 1980s, under the leadership of Ronald Reagan, these social issues would also find themselves on the GOP agenda.

Emboldened by their success, religious groups increasingly framed their positions as a function of their religious beliefs and justified policy platforms through direct appeals to religious authority and scripture. The more that religious discourse was introduced into the realm of formal politics, the more that religiosity gained acceptance and salience in the political arena, profoundly affecting both the structure and content of

American political discourse more generally. By 1994, the Christian right had become so politically powerful that *Campaign and Elections* magazine estimated that the movement's influence in "state and local Republican Party organizations grew to a point that it was dominant in 18 state parties and a substantial force in 13 more" (Ferree et al. 2002, 163).

Most significant for our discussion is the fact that abortion played a critical role within the discourse of the Christian right. In fact, many historians argue that *Roe v. Wade* acted as a catalyst for the movement's rise to prominence (Blanchard 1994; Williams 2010; Sanger 2004; Ferree et al. 2002). With the rising public profile of the American abortion debate, the Christian right used abortion as a mobilizing issue, which, in turn, transformed the organizational and discursive orientation of the anti-abortion movement. Opposition to abortion on explicitly religious ground began to emerge as a prominent anti-abortion strategy.

Moreover, the Christian right's success in influencing the GOP and making abortion a central issue ensured that this position has come to be viewed as an essential part of the conservative movement's basic world view. Through its opposition to abortion, the Christian right has been able to articulate and publicize its larger position on "distinctive gender roles, opposition to feminism, and opposition to sex outside marriage" (Ferree et al. 2002, 163). While the battle over school prayer, textbooks, and gay civil rights were all aspects of a larger struggle to reclaim "traditional values," abortion often stood out as both central to and representative of such values. Accordingly, not only did the Christian right have an enormous impact on anti-abortion discourse, but the abortion issue also had a huge effect on the mobilization and organization of the Christian right.

3.3 Operation Rescue

Prior to the mid-1970s, the anti-abortion movement largely "sought to cast its motivation and goals in broad, inclusive terms," downplaying the religious orientation and motivations of many of its members (Steiner 2006, 96). However, the rising influence of religious politicians and lawmakers and the greater visibility of explicitly religious discourse in the political realm encouraged many anti-abortion activists to rely more heavily on religious justifications and arguments. By the 1980s, the discourse of the anti-abortion movement had become not just more religious, but also much more fundamentalist. Political scientist Dallas Blanchard points to the importance of the Christian right's adoption of an overarching ideology or "ethos of fundamentalism" that minimized specific doctrinal differences (between Catholics, Protestants, Baptists, Mormons, and so on) and worked to unite all religious groups against "secularism" and the social ills it was visiting upon America (Blanchard 1994, 230).

This fundamentalist ethos – and its rejection of incrementalism and political compromise – would have profound implications for the strategic orientation of the anti-abortion movement, especially over the first two decades following *Roe*. Perhaps somewhat ironically, as the role of religion within anti-abortion activism grew, the movement itself became increasingly diverse, with multiple contending visions and motivations. On the one hand, the mainstream anti-abortion movement – which comprised organizations such as the National Right to Life Committee – seemed content to continue to focus on pregnancy counselling, anti-abortion education, and legal lobbying (King and Husting 2003, 300). However, other than the Hyde Amendment, anti-abortion efforts had proven largely unfruitful at the legislative level in the years immediately following *Roe*. Abortion rates had also remained static (at about 1.5 million a year) and public opinion continued to support (at least some) abortion rights for American women (Blanchard 1994, 53).

With sustained public support for legal abortion, many anti-abortion activists began to feel increasingly frustrated. One result of the mix of a fundamentalist ethos and political frustration was the emergence of an increasingly radical and militant anti-abortion movement in the late 1970s and early 1980s. More and more, anti-abortion groups began supporting direct action strategies that "engaged in picketing clinics and physicians offices and appealing to women entering them not to 'kill' their babies" (Blanchard 1994, 53). This intensification of anti-abortion activism was further exacerbated by the creation of Operation Rescue, a new anti-abortion organization. While beginning as a relatively small activist group, Operation Rescue would eventually become a prototype for ultra-aggressive anti-abortion activism and, in doing so, profoundly impact the contours of abortion politics in the US.

Operation Rescue, prominent between 1988 and 1992, has largely been credited with pioneering and popularizing highly confrontational social protest and direct action in the anti-abortion movement (Steiner 2006, 5). Founded in 1986 by twenty-six-year-old used-car salesman Randall Terry, the group was launched in order to "padlock the doors of the nation's family planning clinics" (quoted in Faludi 1991, 401). Somewhat surprisingly, Terry had been raised at the "knee of feminists" (401).

He was the eldest son in a family that had produced three generations of strong women, including a maternal aunt who wrote and spoke on university campuses across the country in support of safe and legal abortion. However, Terry himself was the result of an unplanned pregnancy before abortion was legal in the US, and this fact became a driving rhetorical force behind the righteousness of his anti-abortion position. In Terry's words, "I was conceived out of wedlock. I could've been aborted. I hope and think that my parents wouldn't have, but I'm just really glad they didn't even have the choice" (401).

Terry and Operation Rescue soon began to gain local, and increasingly national, attention. According to feminist scholar Susan Faludi, "Operation Rescue attracted thousands of young men who, one way or another, felt locked out themselves from a world that no longer seemed to have a productive place for them" (Faludi 1991, 401). In this respect, the organization had a "catalytic effect on a new generation of activists, part of a rising tide of conservative Christian activism" (Ginsberg 1989, 225). No longer was anti-abortion activism the purview of a group of "grizzled Christian elders." Increasingly, the members of Operation Rescue – and the larger, increasingly militant, anti-abortion movement – were angry young men, the majority belonging to lower socio-economic brackets (Faludi 1991, 401).

Operation Rescue first highlighted its confrontational approach in 1986 in Binghamton, New York. After gaining entry to a local abortion clinic, Randall Terry and six other protestors chained themselves to furniture in the procedure room. Just a year later, an Operation Recue demonstration in New York would draw thousands of protestors and led to over 1,600 arrests. After a series of demonstrations at the 1988 Democratic National Convention in Atlanta, Georgia, which received extensive media attention, Operation Rescue cemented itself as at the leading front of American anti-abortion activism (King and Husting 2003, 300). Operation Rescue was successful in finalizing the transformation of "anti-abortion activism from a movement of scattered and easily ignored pockets of local protest into a national phenomenon" (Risen and Thomas 1998, 21).

This shift from local to national activism was also accompanied by an ideological shift away from peaceful demonstration towards a more aggressive and quasi-violent strategy of "rescuing unborn children" (King and Husting 2003, 300). While Operation Rescue started its activism with sit-ins – largely mirroring the strategies of civil right activists such as Martin Luther King Jr. – by the late-1980s its strategies had fundamentally changed. Its protests began to draw hundreds, sometimes even thousands, of anti-abortion protestors, who staged aggressive blockades in front of abortion clinics across the US. This besiegement of abortion clinics often lasted weeks, or in some cases even months – the "Summer of Mercy" in Wichita, Kansas, lasted over two months and resulted in 2,661 arrests (Ginsburg 1989; Risen and Thomas 1998; King and Husting 2003).

Operation Rescue introduced the notion of a "rescue mission" to anti-abortion activism. A "rescue" occurred when protestors would block the entrance to an abortion clinic in order to "prevent the slaughter of innocent lives" (quoted in Steiner 2006, 7). The use of the term "rescue" largely "conveyed the message that their actions were not symbolic ... but were designed to impede clinic access and thus stop individual abortions – to 'rescue the unborn'" (Risen and Thomas 1998, 168). As one anti-abortion activist explained, "those who engage in rescue understand the urgent situation that cannot tolerate the slowness of [legal] reform. It is here and now that killing occurs, these babies and not those of the next century; it is every day in the abortion centers that we must ... stop the massacre" (quoted in King and Husting 2003, 302).

In terms of public discourse, Operation Rescue defended the righteousness of its position and extremist strategies by mobilizing three main discourses: one religious, one fetal-centric, and the last anti-woman. At the very core of its rhetoric was the construction of the anti-abortion position as a Christian duty. According to Terry himself, "the only reason for doing a rescue is to save children in obedience to God's world" (quoted in Steiner 2006, 8). Not surprisingly, the organization's slogan espoused, "If you believe abortion is murder, you have to act like it's murder" (quoted in ibid., 8).

A fundamentalist reading of the Bible shaped both the discourse and strategic orientation of Operation Rescue. Terry's public rationales made heavy use of biblical text (Steiner 2006). According to Risen and Thomas, it was through these religious claims that Terry was able to win over "his fellow Evangelicals by translating anti-abortion protest into their own Bible-based language of judgment and wrath" (1998, 220). While religious pluralism was permitted (and in some cases, even encouraged) in earlier forms of anti-abortion activism, it became less and less permissible in the movement as Operation Rescue's evangelical arguments rose to prominence and gained discursive and doctrinal dominance. For Terry and other "rescuers," the acceptance of diversity became little more than the condoning of immoral behaviour (Steiner 2006).

The righteousness of Christian opposition to abortion became increasingly expressed through what Nicole Youngman (2003) calls "Christian reconstructionism." Reconstructionism was the belief that the US was a fundamentally Christian nation being taken over by evil forces (529). Citing Francis Schaeffer's "Christian Manesfesto" as his inspiration, Terry clearly followed this doctrine, claiming that Operation Rescue was a response to the fact that Western secular culture was a "seedbed of moral decay" that threatened the moral righteousness of Christian Americans (532). By framing the fight against abortion as a fight against secularism and secular moral decay, Terry gave fundamentalists a way to unite against a common enemy, encouraging all evangelicals to focus less on their internal doctrinal differences and more on their opposition to legal abortion. In essence, Operation Rescue's discourse united anti-abortion evangelicals by encouraging them to see each other as comrades in arms, joined by the fact that they were following "God's Law, not man's" in publicly and politically opposing abortion (532).

While explicit Biblical references and a rigid interpretation of "Christian duty" underscored much of Operation Rescue's discourse, the Christian right also had a major impact on both the discourse of Operation Rescue and American anti-abortion discourse more broadly. In many respects, then, "the political imagery of the '80s antiabortion movement bore all the hallmarks of the New Right ideology that had preceded it. In its war-torn psychological landscape, the enemy was feminism, the weapon was aggressively moralistic rhetoric, and the strategy for reclaiming the offensive was largely semantic" (Faludi 1991, 405). However, according to Mark Steiner (an evangelical Protestant himself), founder Randall Terry's reading of the Bible also included a confluence of errors that advanced the notion that there is one, and only one, way to be authentically Christian (Steiner 2006). Terry argued that faith is antithetical to analysis of interpretation; that theological deconstruction of texts is both irrelevant and elitist; and that the Bible should be read in a literal way (ibid., chap. 5). These beliefs, argues Steiner, made it easy for Terry's followers to accept a language that merged abortion with murder, driving the emergence of a militant and aggressive US anti-abortion movement.

The second discourse mobilized by Operation Rescue, as well as the larger anti-abortion movement, was to emphasize the humanity of the fetus. Fetal personhood has always been, and continues to be, a predominant anti-abortion strategy. Not surprisingly, then, Operation

Rescue underscored the importance of using anti-abortion language that emphasized fetal personhood. For instance, in *Closed: 99 Ways to Stop Abortion* – a primary text of the militant anti-abortion movement – Joseph Scheidler advises his fellow anti-abortionists to, "rarely use the word 'fetus.' Use 'baby' or 'unborn child.'… You don't have to surrender to their vocabulary … They will start using your terms if you use them" (quoted in Faludi 1991, 405). Anti-abortion literature stressed that activists should carefully emphasize the humanity of the fetus through their use of language, encouraging the use of terms like "this little guy" to describe the fetus, and "place of residence" to describe the pregnant woman (421). In an even more extreme example, one militant right-to-life committee went as far as to draft an "unborn child's diary" in which a fetus "ruminat[ed] about flowers and confided, 'I want to be called Kathy'" (421). This fetal-centric discourse was also married, at times, with graphic imagery that featured the fetus but never the pregnant woman. The movement literature and signage most often featured photos of "the whole 'unborn child' float[ing] in a disembodied womb" (421).

Perhaps the most distinct element of this new evangelical, fetal-centric discourse was that it often merged fetal-personhood arguments with intensely anti-woman tones and arguments. According to many scholars, "as resentment over women's increasing levels of professional progress became mixed with anxiety over the sexual freedoms women had begun to exercise, [anti-abortion activists] developed a rhetoric of puritanical outrage to castigate their opponents" (Faludi 1991, 402; see also, Dworkin 1983; Blanchard 1994; Sanger 2004). Operation Rescue protestors would often hurl insults not only at abortion rights activists, charging them with being "feminazis" and "hating God," but also at pregnant women themselves (Steiner 2006, 9). One Operation Rescue activist went as far as to frame abortion as women's way of getting even: "In a subliminal way, [abortion is] revenge against men. Men have treated women shabbily and now the women's movement has struck back in overkill" (quoted in Faludi 1991, 401).

Operation Rescue was certainly not the only faction of the anti-abortion movement to mobilize anti-woman tones and argument. This brand of aggressive anti-abortion discourse would also permeate more "mainstream" areas of anti-abortion activism. John Willke, the former president of the National Right to Life Committee, for instance, argued that supporting abortion "do[es] violence to marriage [by] remov[ing] the right of a husband to protect the life of the child he has fathered in his wife's womb" (quoted in Faludi 1991, 402). Anger at women's ability to make reproductive choices without consulting their partners and husbands also emerged in the movement's public discourse, becoming particularly explicit in the many "father's rights" lawsuits filed across the US to stop women from obtaining abortion without the consent of the biological father of the child (402–3).

Ultimately, Operation Rescue and the militant and aggressive generation of anti-abortion activists it cultivated were not successful in stopping, or even diminishing the number of, abortions (King and Husting 2003). They did, however, have a profound and long-lasting effect on the strategic and discursive orientation of the anti-abortion movement in at least three ways. First, they transformed the types of tactics used by anti-abortion activists. Rescue-oriented tactics emerged as the most popular kind of anti-abortion protests nationwide and continue to shape contemporary anti-abortion activism throughout the US. Second, Operation Rescue was incredibly successful at mobilizing evangelical Christians and increasing the relevance, power, and media coverage not only of the American anti-abortion movement but also of the larger Christian right (ibid.). And lastly, Operation Rescue was perhaps most successful in bringing national political attention to the abortion issue. Because its extremist strategies typically garnered intense media coverage, it was an important actor in helping to make abortion a defining issue in American politics, especially within the GOP (ibid.). In doing so, it cemented the enduring portrait of the American abortion war as one of "evangelical fury crashing against feminist certitude" (Steiner 2006, 9) – something that has been both a boon and a burden to the larger anti-abortion movement.

3.4 The Rise of Anti-abortion Violence and the Decline of Operation Rescue

The emergence and popularization of groups like Operation Rescue were not the only ways in which the anti-abortion movement expressed its growing extremism and dissatisfaction during this period. The US also witnessed an explosion of anti-abortion violence in the late 1980s and early 1990s, largely as a result of "building frustration with the Reagan administration's lack of effectiveness in counteracting *Roe* and *Doe*" (Blanchard 1994, 55). While Reagan had campaigned partly on an anti-abortion platform and expressed great sympathy for the anti-abortion cause, he proved ineffective in overturning *Roe*, something that had been one of the primary goals of the anti-abortion movement throughout the 1980s. Bill Clinton's 1992 Democratic victory only added to the growing anti-abortion frustration and contributed to the "classic conditions for an increase in violence" and radicalism (58).

By the late 1980s and early 1990s, ever more aggressive anti-abortion tactics were being employed – and were being covered by the mainstream American media. Between 1985 and 1991, hate mail and harassing phone calls directed at abortion clinics peaked, as did the aggressive picketing and blockades that were the staple of Operation Rescue (see Blanchard 1994, chap. 5). Bomb threats also became increasingly common. Between 1977 and 1992, there were 161 recorded incidences of bombing and arson at abortion clinics (peaking in 1992). Even more violent methods followed, as extremist anti-abortion activists began assassinating doctors. The 1993 murder of Dr. David Gunn in Pensacola and the shooting the same year of Dr. George Tiller,[8] coupled with open statements by some activists supporting murder as a tactic, all pointed to the increased role that violence began to play in anti-abortion activism. To date, eight people – four doctors, two clinic employees, one security guard, and one clinic escort – have been killed by anti-abortion terrorists for their involvement in facilitating access to legal abortion. Moreover, since 1992, anti-abortion extremists have attempted to murder fourteen other abortion providers.

As the violence escalated, the anti-abortion movement became perceived as a violent, extremist, and fanatical movement by more and more of the American public, creating a significant public relations challenge for the movement. This perception, along with a series of lawsuits against extremist groups by abortion providers and patients, the election of a "pro-choice" president (Bill Clinton), and the 1994 Freedom of Access to Clinic Entrances (FACE) Act all helped to discredit groups like Operation Rescue and some of their more extreme tactics (Steiner 2006, 10). The FACE Act, in particular, curbed the effectiveness of Operation Rescue tactics by making it a criminal offence to block a clinic's door. Given the significant punishment for violating the

---

8 Tiller's clinic was firebombed in 1986; in 1993 he was shot five times by an anti-abortion activist but survived; in 2009 he was assassinated by another anti-abortion activist while Tiller was acting as an usher at his church. For a full breakdown of anti-abortion violence in North America see, "Violence Statistics and History" on the National Abortion Federation's website, at http://prochoice.org/education-and-advocacy/violence/violence-statistics-and-history/.

law (up to a year in prison and a $10,000 fine), it effectively deterred all but the most extreme anti-abortion activists from engaging in rescue-type protests. Fines incurred by Operation Rescue would soon force it into bankruptcy and, although it was eventually relaunched under the name Operation Save America, the damage had largely been done. Its extremism had become counterproductive and its direct influence over American anti-abortion activism was over (ibid., 10).

By the mid-1990s, both mainstream and even more fringe anti-abortion activism was forced to change. Increasingly, mainstream activists began to distance themselves from the militant, aggressive, and violent elements of the movement. By the late 1990s, assassination attempts of abortion providers had virtually ceased. When Dr. George Tiller was shot and killed in 2009, virtually every mainstream anti-abortion organization strongly condemned the murder. And yet there is no question that Operation Rescue and the extremist activists who employed violence have had a significant influence on and provided an enduring legacy for contemporary anti-abortion activism in the US. Republican politicians continue to appeal to the religious language of the Christian right when discussing abortion – a discourse largely popularized by Randall Terry and Operation Rescue. Moreover, the Christian right remains an influential political movement, contributing to the two-term presidency of George W. Bush and the subsequent rise of the Tea Party. As such, there is no question that Operation Rescue helped to cement the framing of abortion as a religious issue, a framing that continues to dominate mainstream American politics today.

3.5 The Backtrack: *Webster v. Reproductive Health Services*, 1989

Although militant anti-abortion organizations like Operation Rescue felt that legislative and judicial means were slow and ineffective, the anti-abortion movement began to achieve a series of victories in these areas as the 1980s and 1990s progressed. In particular, the US Supreme Court decision in *Webster v. Reproductive Health Services* (1989) is generally viewed as the most important political and legal turning point in the abortion debate after *Roe* and the passing of the Hyde Amendment. *Webster* has its roots in the 1986 Missouri state law that restricted abortion in ways that seemed to directly challenge the standards outlined in *Roe v. Wade*. The Missouri statute – the preamble to which affirmed that life begins at conception – sought to "amend existing state law concerning unborn children and abortion" (Rose 2008, 136). It banned the use of any public facilities, employees, or funds for the purpose of performing any abortion in circumstances that were not thought to directly threaten the life of a pregnant woman. Further, prior to an abortion, it required physicians to perform a viability test on the fetus if the pregnancy had advanced more than twenty weeks (136, 167).

Both the District Court for the Western District of Missouri and the Court of Appeal for the Eighth Circuit struck down the provisions of the statute, maintaining that the Missouri law directly contradicted the tenets set out in *Roe v. Wade*. The lower courts thus prohibited its enforcement. The Supreme Court, however, chose to hear the case and on 3 July 1989, the US Supreme Court ruled against the two lower courts and upheld the Missouri law in a 5–4 decision. While the decision fell short of an outright overturning of *Roe*, it was a "retraction from *Roe*'s holding that abortion is a fundamental right to privacy" (Rose 2008, 167).

In the aftermath, both sides of the abortion debate claimed victory. On the one hand, *Roe* was not overturned, something that many within the American abortion rights movement believed to be almost inevitable. On the other hand, the *Webster* decision did chip away at one of the core elements of the *Roe v. Wade*, the trimester system. The court ruled that the elaboration of a woman's right to privacy in *Roe* "erect[ed] too high a hurdle for states choosing to limit abortion access" (Rose 2008, 167). Overturning the tenets outlined in *Roe*, the *Webster* decision ruled that abortion could be more fully regulated as long as that regulation does not create an "undue burden" on women – a standard that gave states much more latitude to introduce restrictions and that would, as it became more precisely defined by the courts over the following years, represent a significant victory for the anti-abortion cause.

In this ruling, the Supreme Court "embraced a new era of abortion restriction," and its impact was felt almost immediately. Notably, while the *Webster* decision was fundamentally based on a fetal-right-to-life discourse, it also opened up discursive space for anti-abortion activists to oppose abortion on the grounds of protecting women's health and safety. Within a year, several hundred laws seeking to restrict abortion were introduced in state legislatures across the United States, many framed within the discursive rationale that women needed to be protected from dangerous and unsafe abortion. Waiting periods, consent requirements, and public facility bans all become popular strategies of the anti-abortion movement (the particularities of which we will return to at the end of this chapter). Thus, while it didn't overturn *Roe*, *Webster* definitively marked the beginning of a new era of anti-abortion politics at the state level.

3.6 *Planned Parenthood of Southeastern Pennsylvania v. Robert P. Casey et al.,* 1992

Unsurprisingly, this new wave of anti-abortion legislation led to legal challenges that sought to determine the scope that the Supreme Court was willing to grant states on this issue. The court's first major ruling on this question was the 1992 decision in *Planned Parenthood of Southeastern Pennsylvania v. Robert P. Casey et al.,* which answered many of the questions raised by *Webster.* The case concerned the Informed Consent Act in Pennsylvania, which included four main provisions. First, it required abortion providers to give women state-scripted counselling and information about the health risks of abortion and childbirth, the probable gestational age of the fetus, the available medical assistance for childbirth, child support required by state law, and agencies that provided adoption and other alternatives to abortion. Following this initial session, the statute also required women to wait at least twenty-four hours before having an abortion. Second, it required anyone under the age of eighteen to secure the consent of at least one parent before being able to obtain an abortion. Third – and most controversially – it required written spousal consent for married women (previously, a married woman had been required by law to prove that her husband was aware of her intention, but did not require the husband's permission). Finally, it required abortion providers to submit detailed information to the state regarding each abortion provided (including women's age, any prior pregnancies and abortions, and the weight of the fetus) (Richardson and Nash 2006).

The *Casey* decision presented what many observers believed to be the first realistic opportunity for the court to overturn *Roe.* In the three years since *Webster,* two liberal Supreme Court judges had been replaced by Republican-appointed judges David Souter and Clarence Thomas, leading many to believe that the complete reversal of *Roe* was inevitable. However, in a 5–4 decision, the court upheld *Roe* while once again allowing for greater restrictions at the state level. The court ruled that three of the four provisions set out in the Pennsylvania law were constitutional, choosing to repeal only the provision that required married women to obtain spousal consent.

The *Casey* decision is widely credited with creating a new standard for the adjudication of abortion restrictions (Rose 2008, 201). Its elaboration of the "undue burden" clause – which was first referenced with respect to abortion in *Webster* – became the guiding principle for future court rulings on the constitutionality of state abortion laws, making it much easier for states to enact restrictions on abortion in at least two noteworthy ways. First, *Casey* challenged the notion that state interest in the fetus does not begin until the third trimester of pregnancy, arguing that *Roe's* trimester model did not properly acknowledge state interest in early fetal life. Thus *Casey* allowed for fuller state restrictions on abortion at the earliest stages of pregnancy. Second, *Casey* opened the door for states to articulate a preference for birth over abortion (202). This meant that states could use state policy to persuade women not to terminate their pregnancies. While these state policies could not preclude the option of abortion, they could be used to strongly influence and "incentivize" a woman's decision about her pregnancy (203).

The implications of *Casey* were profound and continue to reverberate even today. A host of new state laws in the form of informed consent laws, ultrasound viewings, fetal personhood laws, and mandatory waiting periods have emerged throughout the country as a direct result of *Casey* (a point to which we will return later in this chapter). Equally important for our discussion, however, is the many ways in which *Casey* affected the types of discursive rationales advanced by anti-abortion lawmakers.

First, as was the case with *Webster*, *Casey* allowed states to restrict abortion on the basis of fetal viability, intensifying the anti-abortion movement's focus on fetal-personhood arguments. It also ensured that advancements in ultrasound technology would affect the shape of future anti-abortion arguments, both practically (by allowing the anti-abortion movement to try to pass legislation that would force women to obtain and view ultrasounds prior to procuring an abortion) and discursively (as a means of substantiating and defending claims of fetal personhood). Second, by permitting states to explicitly *persuade* women not to terminate their pregnancies, *Casey* encouraged anti-abortion activists to develop and employ arguments that frame women as not willingly choosing, or being coerced into, abortion. Further, by representing abortion as inherently unsafe, anti-abortion lawmakers have been able to enact legislation that places burdensome clinic regulations on facilities that perform abortions in the name of women's health and safety (Sanger 2004, 51).

Webster and *Casey* also had important effects on abortion rights discourse. Most notably, as neoliberal themes, policy ideas, and language became increasingly dominant in US politics (Brown 2006) and the protections of *Roe* were increasingly eroded, abortion rights defenders began to downplay the language of "women's rights" and increasingly framed their arguments as a case of resisting illegitimate government intervention and overreach (Saletan 2004). Instead of talking about equality and women's rights to privacy (as was commonplace prior to and during the *Roe v. Wade* period), activists increasingly "portrayed abortion restrictions as an encroachment by big government on tradition, family and property" (Sanger 2004, 52). This discourse, however, was largely ineffective, especially because anti-abortion activists used the same argument more effectively to argue against public funding of abortion and to justify fathers' rights cases. Accordingly, the tide continued to shift in favour of the anti-abortion movement, with states nationwide enacting increasingly strict anti-abortion laws (Saletan 2004).

3.7 Partial Birth Abortion Bans: *Stenberg v. Carhart* and *Gonzales v. Carhart*

Since the mid-1990s, another area of significant legal contestation at the federal level has been so-called partial birth abortions. "Partial birth abortion" is a term coined by the National Right to Life Committee in the mid-1990s that refers to a particular medical procedure, whose technical name is "dilation and extraction," used in late-term abortions and after late-term miscarriage (Rose 2008, 241). The procedure is almost exclusively used in extreme cases when the life or health of a pregnant woman is in danger.

The Partial Birth Abortion (PBA) Ban is legislation that prohibits physicians from performing the procedure. It was passed by Congress in 1995 and 1997 only to be vetoed by Democratic president Bill Clinton. In 2003, it was once again passed, and this time it was signed into law by Republican president George W. Bush (Rose 2008, 241). The constitutionality of the ban was immediately called into question. The passing of the PBA Ban was especially contentious because only three years earlier – in the 2000 Supreme Court decision in *Stenberg v. Carhart* – a state-level PBA ban in Nebraska was deemed to be unconstitutional in its violation of the due process clause, as outlined in the *Roe* and *Casey* decisions. The Nebraska ban was overturned in 2000 both because of its lack of exemption with regard to the woman's health and because of the lack of clarity as to whether or not the ban could be applied to abortion procedures other than the dilation and extraction method (Dailard 2004).

In a surprising move, and in opposition to three separate district court decisions and one Supreme Court decision that ruled PBA bans unconstitutional, on 18 April 2007 the Supreme Court in a 5–4 decision upheld the constitutionality of the 2003 PBA Ban in *Gonzales v. Carhart*. Although many political observers believed that the PBA Ban would not significantly alter the number of abortions performed in the US, it has two noteworthy implications. First, for the first time in the history of American abortion jurisprudence, the PBA Ban did not require an exemption to protect women's health. Many court observers argue that, as a result of this omission, "future legislation will attempt similar restrictions, as the court has stepped away from nearly four decades of commitment to women's health as the central concept of abortion policy" (Rose 2008, 242). Second – and somewhat paradoxically – the *Gonzales v. Carhart* ruling alluded to another form of anti-abortion discourse, one that laments abortion as not only harming fetuses but also as being harmful for women. In this respect, Justice Alito argued that "it seems unexceptionable to conclude that some women come to regret their choice to abort the infant life they once created and sustained … [and] severe depression and loss of esteem can follow" (242). His comments foreshadowed new types of, and justifications for, emerging anti-abortion legislation. In 2006, for instance, South Dakota passed one of the most restrictive pieces of anti-abortion legislation in American history, prohibiting all abortions except where it would prevent the immediate death of a pregnant woman. The measure was justified on the grounds that "abortions are coerced and subject women to physical and emotional harms" (Siegel 2007, 992). Although the South Dakota law was eventually overturned by way of referendum in November of the same year, the rhetorical framing of the abortion law is noteworthy as it "reflects a shift from fetal-focused to gender-based justifications for abortion regulation" (992).

3.8 Contemporary Abortion Legislation

While the federal legislation and the Supreme Court decisions discussed above have been a crucial part of the struggle over abortion politics in the US, in many ways it is the state-level legislation introduced over the past thirty years or so that has had a far more important and concrete impact on the lived reality of abortion rights in the US. While the specifics of state legislation vary greatly, there are certain dominant trends in these laws, and the nature of these state laws can be broken down into four categories:[9] (1) legislation that explicitly seeks to ban abortion, (2) requirements with respect to physicians and hospitals, (3) funding regulations, and (4) additional barriers placed directly on women themselves. The following sections will explain the ways in which each type of provision limits women's ability to legally and safely access abortion services.

3.8.1 Provisions that Seek to Directly Ban Abortion

Provisions that seek to directly ban abortion are perhaps the most straightforward way in which anti-abortion lawmakers have attempted to limit the number of abortions performed throughout the US. These provisions can take different forms, but all generally prohibit abortions after a specified point in pregnancy, most often fetal viability.

Since 1973, forty-one states have prohibited some types of abortions after a certain point in pregnancy. Twenty-one states ban abortion after fetal viability (usually understood to be at 24 weeks), sixteen states impose prohibition after a predetermined number of weeks (generally around 24–28 weeks), four states impose state regulations in the third trimester (after 28 weeks), and eight states prohibit abortion starting at 20 weeks post-fertilization, arguing that this is the point at which the fetus can start to feel pain (Guttmacher Institute 2013b). Attempting to legislatively ban abortion as early as possible (particularly in ways that seek to reduce even further the "first trimester" protection of abortion rights as outlined in *Roe*) remains a popular strategy for the movement today (Guttmacher Institute, 2013d). In March 2013, for example Arkansas and North Dakota passed laws that sought to ban abortion after 12 weeks and 6 weeks, respectively. While both laws have been blocked by judge-mandated injunctions pending legal challenge, they remain representative of the surge of anti-abortion bills that seek to challenge the very heart of *Roe v. Wade*.

3.8.2 TRAP Bills: Physician and Hospital Requirements

Bills concerned with the targeted regulation of abortion providers (TRAP bills) are another means by which women's ability to access abortion is

---

9 This typology draws on the research done at the Guttmacher Institute (2013b). This overview of American abortion laws is accurate as of October 2013.

seriously limited by a large number of American states. Because states hold the authority to regulate health care professionals and enforce certain health and safety standards, anti-abortion lawmakers began to use this power immediately after *Roe* to pass additional requirements that would shut down abortion clinics. In the late-1970s and early 1980s, these bills were repeatedly struck down by federal courts, and they fell out of favour the 1980s (Gold and Nash 2013). Beginning in the early 1990s in the aftermath of *Casey*, however, TRAP bills began to reappear as a central anti-abortion legislative strategy, and they once again are a popular legislative strategy. The justifications for these bills often reference the desire to protect women's rights and health, even though most observers argue that, both in intent and design, they do nothing to protect women and are explicitly aimed at shutting down abortion providers (ibid.).

At a general level, there are two main types of TRAP bills. The first type enacts barriers that target individual abortion providers. These types of laws typically require physicians to have admitting privileges at local hospitals or hold certain extraordinary certifications. These requirements may sound innocuous, but the burdens placed on abortion providers are far greater than those placed on other health care providers – something that can significantly increase the overhead costs of abortion clinics and even make it functionally impossible for them to remain open. For example, it is often difficult, and sometimes simply not possible, for abortion providers to secure admitting privileges at local hospitals, either because of the ideological leanings of the administration or because the hospital requires minimum admitting quotas, which most abortion providers do not meet.

The second type of TRAP bill places structural regulations on abortion clinics. Most often these types of regulations require abortion clinics to: (1) be equivalent to other surgical centers (even when abortion clinics only provide medication abortions), (2) adhere to strict procedure-room specifications, and (3) adhere to arbitrary physical specifications (e.g., having corridors that are much wider than those in most clinics and other buildings). This brand of TRAP bill has proven to be the most effective at shutting down clinics, as most of them target structural elements that, despite being tenuously related to health outcomes, are often impossible for clinics to meet (Guttmacher Institute 2013b).

As of March 2013, twenty-seven American states have enacted one or more TRAP bills. In fifteen states, these regulations also apply to private practices where physicians might provide abortion services as part of a larger family practice, and eighteen states apply TRAP regulations even to clinics that offer only medication abortions (which means these clinics never perform surgical abortions). Twenty-one states require that physicians hold connections to a local hospital, with three of those requiring that abortion providers hold admitting privileges in at least one of the local hospitals (Guttmacher Institute 2013b).

TRAP bills can be highly effective in reducing the number of facilities performing abortions. For example, a TRAP bill in Texas requires that all abortion clinics become ambulatory surgical centres, even if they do not provide surgical abortions, and that all abortion providers have admitting privileges at a hospital within thirty miles of the facility. In 2008, there were sixty-seven abortion providers in Texas (Grimes 2013). By 2013, the passage of various bills requiring mandatory transvaginal ultrasounds and pre-abortion waiting periods had reduced that number to forty-one. Less than a year after the passage of the TRAP bill, only twenty-four clinics remained open. At time of writing, the ultimate impact is unclear. Most estimates suggest that, if the law is upheld, only six to ten abortion clinics would remain open in the entire state, despite its being the second most populous state in the US (Fernandez 2014). The law was upheld by a federal appellate court in June 2015. However, it was appealed to the Supreme Court, which voted 5–4 to grant a temporary hold on the appellate court's ruling (meaning that the law will not come into force until the Supreme Court rules on its constitutionality).

3.8.3 Funding Regulations

Another area where the anti-abortion movement has experienced a great deal of success has been in the defunding of abortion nationwide. Funding restrictions in the US have been effective at the federal level, the state level, and at the level of private insurance companies.

First, and most obviously, abortion has been almost completely defunded at the federal level. As laid out by the tenets of the Hyde Amendment, no federal money can be used to fund abortion, except where the life of the mother would be endangered if the fetus were carried to term. In 1980, the US Supreme Court upheld the Hyde Amendment as constitutional in *Harris v. McRae*, ruling that a pregnant woman's right to privacy did not mean that Medicaid had to fund abortion. As a result, the Hyde Amendment has been in effect ever since its implementation in 1977, albeit in varying forms (Rose 2008, 119).

While the Hyde Amendment prohibits the use of federal money to fund abortion, it does not ban states from funding abortion. And many states do fund abortions, often for health reasons (e.g., Hawaii, New York, and Washington) and fetal abnormalities (e.g., Maryland) (Guttmacher Institute 2013c). However, because the Hyde Amendment is tied to Medicaid – the program that provides low-income individuals and families with access to health care – the effects of the bill are almost exclusively felt by low-income women and families. According to Guttmacher Institute, 20 to 35 per cent of Medicaid-eligible women who carry their pregnancies to term would choose abortion if the procedure were publicly funded. Moreover, the lack of federal spending on abortion can force low-income women to delay their abortion procedure while they try to gather funds, postponing their abortion to a time "when the costs and health risks can be higher" (Guttmacher Institute 2013c).

In 2009, the premise of the Hyde Amendment was used by Congressman Bart Stupak (D-Michigan) and Joseph Pitts (R-Pennsylvania) in their proposed Stupak-Pitts Amendment to President Barack Obama's Affordable Health Care for America Act (AHCAA). The Stupak-Pitts Amendment stipulated that the "public option" of the AHCAA (commonly referred to as Obamacare) – a new health insurance option through which Americans could buy subsidized health insurance from a federal agency – would not fund abortions. In exchange for their votes in passing AHCAA through Congress, President Obama agreed to the amendment. Although the amendment was not originally in the Senate version of AHCAA (which was ultimately passed as the Patient Protection and Affordable Care Act in March 2010), Obama issued an executive order banning the use of federal money to fund abortion under this new health care act (Annas 2010).

The second way in which the American anti-abortion movement has successfully defunded abortion has been to restrict the use of government money to fund abortion at the state level. Only seventeen states use their own funds to pay for all or most medically necessary abortion for those low-income individuals who qualify for Medicaid (only thirteen of which are legally required to do so). The rest of the states refuse to fund any abortion procedures, except when the continuation of a pregnancy directly places the woman's life in danger.

Finally, although the majority of American states allow for the purchase of additional abortion coverage through their private insurance companies, eight states restrict the coverage of abortion by private insurance companies, except in cases where the woman's life is in danger.

3.8.4 State Barriers Placed Directly on Women

Finally, the anti-abortion movement has also been very effective in restricting abortion access across the country through the implementation of state laws requiring women to fulfil certain requirements before being eligible for a legal abortion. Since the introduction and elaboration of the "undue burden standard" in *Webster* and *Casey*, the ability of states to impose these types of barriers has grown tremendously.

At a general level, the undue burden standard is a constitutional test created and used by the US Supreme Court to judge the constitutional acceptability of legislation and the restrictions it poses for individuals. Under the tenet of undue burden, a restriction is considered unconstitutional if it is "too severe or because it lacks legitimate, rational justification," as subjectively determined by US courts (*Planned Parenthood v. Casey* 1992, 920). By using this standard to evaluate whether a legislative restriction on abortion is justified, the court created a much lower justificatory bar, which made it easier for states to successfully argue that their restrictions on abortion were constitutionally legitimate. In practice, this has meant that states have been able to enact a wide range of regulations that negatively affect women's ability to access abortion throughout all stages of pregnancy, starting at conception.

There are four main types of restrictions. The first type has been the implementation of mandatory waiting periods for women seeking abortion. Twenty-six states mandate that women wait a specific amount of time between their initial counselling appointment and the actual abortion procedure. While the norm for mandatory waiting times is twenty-four hours, some states are more draconian. Both South Dakota and Utah, for instance, mandate that women wait at least seventy-two hours between their initial appointment and the abortion procedure. Moreover, in South Dakota this wait period excludes weekends and holidays, meaning that, more often than not, women are forced to wait for even longer periods. It is difficult to precisely measure the impact of such laws. However, one Mississippi study suggests that abortion rates fell after the new law came into effect and that the number of women going out of state to access abortion increased, as did the proportion of second trimester abortions (both of which suggest that women were forced to delay their abortions while gathering the additional financial and child care resources required due to the wait times and additional visits the law mandated) (Joyce et al. 2009).

The second type of state restriction is mandatory counselling. Thirty-five states require that women receive counselling before an abortion is performed. In twenty-seven of these states, government health agencies develop the written materials that must be used for abortion counselling. All twenty-seven of these states mandate that information about fetal development throughout pregnancy must be included in these materials. Twelve states include information on fetal pain, and in five states a woman must be told that personhood begins at conception (Guttmacher Institute 2013b). Ten states require that counselling be provided in person and that it take place before the waiting period begins, effectively necessitating two separate trips to the abortion clinic – a significant barrier for women, especially in states where TRAP bills and other factors have made clinics scarce (Guttmacher Institute 2013b).

The third way in which states have enacted barriers has been by requiring parental consent or notification if the procedure is for a minor. The majority of states (thirty-nine) require some type of parental involvement in a minor's decision to terminate her pregnancy. Twenty-one states require that one or both parents consent to the procedure; another thirteen require that at least one parent be notified. In eight states, the parental consent document must be notarized. Most of the states that require parental consent or notification also require that it occur at least twenty-four or forty-eight hours before the abortion takes place, although most of these states also include some form of court-approved judicial bypass (which is not, however, an easy process to navigate) (Guttmacher Institute 2013b).

Lastly, states have also regulated abortion access by introducing legislation that forces women to have an ultrasound prior to procuring an abortion. Since the mid-1990s, an increasing number of states have introduced mandatory ultrasounds and ultrasound viewing. Because such procedures are not considered medically necessary during the first trimester, critics have characterized them as little more than "a veiled attempt to personify the fetus and dissuade a woman from obtaining an abortion" (Guttmacher Institute 2013b). Of the twenty-two states that require an ultrasound, three mandate that the provider show and describe the ultrasound image.

3.9 Conclusion

This chapter has shown that the victory of the American abortion rights movement (in the form of *Roe v. Wade*) was short-lived. The anti-abortion backlash against it was fierce and immediate, even if its legal and political victories would take years to achieve. Moreover, many suggest that the rise of a unified and politically active American anti-abortion movement was, in many ways, a direct result of the *Roe* and *Doe* decisions.

Prior to *Roe*, anti-abortion activism was largely limited to local groups, and while religion (particularly Catholicism) was a mobilizing factor in the formation and organization of many of these early anti-abortion groups, it was not a defining feature of anti-abortion discourse. By the late-1970s, however, Americans began to witness the rise of the Christian right, a phenomenon that would ultimately change the trajectory of both American politics generally and the anti-abortion movement in particular.

By the 1980s, following the lead of newly founded groups like Operation Rescue, the anti-abortion movement would increasingly fuse the discourse of the Christian right with a more explicit, and intense, opposition to abortion. Operation Rescue and similar groups fundamentally changed the contours, strategies, and discourse of American anti-abortion activism. However, the rise of anti-abortion violence compromised the sustainability of Operation Rescue and its related, extremist anti-abortion tactics and arguments. Operation Rescue fell out of public favour by the mid-1990s, but it profoundly marked the US anti-abortion movement and its discourse. Religious, fetal-centric, and anti-woman arguments popularized by Operation Rescue and other militant sects have remained very powerful currents in contemporary anti-abortion discourse. What emerged in the wake of *Roe* was a movement that used highly moralized and heavily religious discourse and a focus on legislation and legal challenges to reassert anti-abortion policy and laws. Moreover, the Hyde Amendment, *Webster v. Reproductive Health Services*, and *Planned Parenthood v. Casey* have all worked to chip away at the fundamental tenets of *Roe v. Wade* and have ushered in a wide variety of anti-abortion legislation at the state level.

The success of the American anti-abortion movement has meant that even many Canadians assume that it is the archetype of anti-abortion activism. While the Canadian history has certain historical similarities, it is also characterized by profound differences. Therefore, we will now turn to that story.

Chapter 4

The History of the Early Abortion Debate in Canada

In comparison to the very public, hyper-moralized, highly partisan contemporary battle over abortion in the US, many assume that the abortion question in Canada has been far less controversial and long since settled. This comparative portrait is accurate, to some degree. Although actual access to abortion varies across Canada (currently there are no abortion services offered in Prince Edward Island; New Brunswick still does not pay for abortions outside hospitals; women outside major centres may have limited access), there is no criminal prohibition of abortion in Canada. Since 1988, abortion has been regulated by provincial medical policies and standards rather than by criminal law. It is therefore legal to provide and receive abortion services throughout Canada as long as they are undertaken according to the relevant professional medical standards and provincial health regulations.

Where the history of abortion in the US has been marked by a seemingly perpetual series of legislative and court battles, a mere handful of major decisions have shaped Canada's abortion history and there has been no legal or political backtracking from the Supreme Court of Canada's 1988 *Morgentaler* decision striking down the statutes criminalizing abortion or the court's 1989 conclusion in *Daigle* that the fetus is not a legal "person" until birth. Moreover, since 1991, no federal Canadian government has officially introduced new legislation seeking to regulate abortion (although there have been many private members' bills introduced to this effect). And, given Canada's different constitutional structure and division of responsibilities, provincial legislatures have not been major sites of contestation and of legislation on this issue.

The full story of how we got here, however, is far more interesting than we might assume.

4.1 Criminalizing Abortion in Britain and Colonial Canada

The story of abortion politics and discourse in Canada begins in the debates about abortion in the United Kingdom. Because Canada remained a colony long after the American states declared independence, the Canadian legal framework has closely reflected British common law. Throughout the eighteenth century, in both the UK and Canada (and, as we have seen, in the US), it was accepted practice that a pregnancy could be terminated prior to quickening, which was generally understood to be when the first fetal movement could be felt (around 4 months).

Before the nineteenth century, abortion in the UK had been loosely regulated by common law precedents rather than by a specific act of law of Parliament. The UK and Canada, however, began to codify and tighten the restrictions on abortion much earlier than did the US. In 1803, the British Parliament passed Lord Ellenborough's Act, which claimed to clarify, but also significantly intensified, the historical common law restrictions on abortion. Notably, the act not only formally codified that performing an abortion of a fetus after quickening was a capital offence, it also, for the first time, identified pre-quickening abortion as an offence (although with less serious punishments) (Keown 2002, 18). While it is not entirely clear why this change was championed at precisely this moment, Keown (2002, 12) argues that it was likely a combination three factors: the general trend towards greater clarity and codification of common law, the religious and moral commitments of certain key lawmakers, and an increasing perception of abortion as a social problem. Historians also suggest that, as was the case in the US, the interests and views of physicians and apothecaries seeking increased recognition and control over the medical sphere were key factors spurring on this type of legislation (24). In particular, the physician community sought to reject the popular distinction between pre- and post-quickening, as this was viewed as a far too subjective and unscientific mode of judgment (30–32).

The primary discursive justification for Lord Ellenborough's Act itself, as well as the later amendments to the act, rested on the idea that the existing common law approach to abortion was largely inadequate and vague (Keown 2002, 13). In this respect, the act was part of a much broader movement towards systematizing and explicitly legislating what had previously been more "implicit" norms embodied in centuries of common law judicial decisions. However, the discourse justifying

Lord Ellenborough's Act also drew on and furthered new views about the consequences of abortion on fetal life and women's health. On one hand, one of the central justifications for the act was based on the idea of fetal personhood and the consequent claim that abortion was murder. This idea of fetal personhood was not based on religious sources, but rather on what Keown has called the "scientific extension of legal principle" (22). Prohibiting abortion on pain of death was therefore presented as "medical man's concern that fetal life should be protected by the law at all stages of gestation" (22). As Dr. Samuel Farr argued at the time, since "life begins immediately after conception … there is no doubt that the destruction of [a fetus] ought to be considered a capital crime" (23). Interestingly, this medical discourse was supplemented by increasing representations of pregnant women as naive, ignorant, and unprepared to make autonomous reproductive decisions themselves. According to Dr. Farr, "It is to be lamented … that whilst this crime, which is practised generally by the most abandoned, escapes punished, a poor deluded creature, in the case of infant murder, whose shame highly extenuates her guilt, should suffer death" (21).

As the century progressed, the movement against abortion gained steam and the UK began to introduce increasingly restrictive legislation. In 1828, Parliament passed the Offences against the Person Act (OAPA, also known as Lord Lansdowne's Act), which closed certain perceived loopholes of the 1803 act and limited abortion access even more restrictively. In 1837, an updated OAPA was passed. While this act eliminated the death penalty for abortion, it added and intensified many other types of punishment. Significantly, the 1837 amendments also eliminated the quickening distinction: for the first time, pre- and post-quickening abortions were deemed to be equivalent and were similarly punishable (Keown 2002, 27). When the OAPA was next updated, in 1861, the maximum punishment for performing an abortion became life imprisonment. Also, rather than limiting criminal prosecution to the medical practitioners who performed an abortion, the 1861 version of the act established, for the first time, that any pregnant woman who procured her own abortion was also guilty of a crime (Grubb 1990, 493).

Although the above acts and amendments did not strictly apply in British North America, they did have significant influence. Following Lord Ellenborough's Act, several of the British North American colonies enacted legislation aimed at restricting abortion. New Brunswick was first, in 1810, followed by PEI in 1836. While early legislation maintained the traditional distinction between an abortion before and after quickening, by 1841 this too began to change. Four years after the UK eliminated the traditional quickening distinction in the 1837 amendments to the OAPA, the colony of Upper Canada adopted a similar law as its first abortion act. New Brunswick followed suit in 1842.

Up to this point, these laws did not hold women who were seeking abortions liable. Instead, following the norms of the day, the legal focus was exclusively on the medical practitioners who performed the procedure (Mitchinson 1998, 135). In 1849, however, amendments to the New Brunswick act eliminated the legal protection of pregnant women, as did Nova Scotia's first abortion law, passed in 1851. Such changes meant that the "full weight of criminal law could now be brought to bear against the woman" (135). This became the case across the country when the new federal government took on the responsibility for criminal law in 1869. In fact, the 1849 New Brunswick abortion law was used as a template in the drafting of the federal abortion law in 1869 (135). In keeping with the laws in most of the British North American colonies as well as Britain's 1861 amendments to the OAPA, the new Canadian law made any type of abortion illegal, with a maximum penalty of life in prison (Canada 1998).

The discursive and social rationales for these increasingly restrictive anti-abortion laws in the UK and Canada largely parallel the criminalization of abortion in the US during the same time period. While there is little evidence of public debate regarding abortion in Canada at this time, the discourse that did exist was largely driven by debates occurring in the UK during the same time period.

There were three main discourses opposing abortion. First, a discourse espousing medical concerns over maternal mortality was a common way for physicians and policymakers to publicly justify their opposition to abortion. Accordingly, "the hazards of attempted abortion were continually stressed by medical and medico-legal authorities from before the enactment of Ellenborough's Act" (Keown 2002, 35).

Second, criminalization was driven by medical concerns about fetal life, and thus the primary aim of the new laws was the protection of the fetus (Keown 2002, 38). It is noteworthy, however, that, unlike early American anti-abortion laws, which rarely targeted the pregnant woman, laws in Britain and colonial Canada treated women seeking an abortion much more harshly, framing them as active and complicit actors in the proliferation of abortion. Throughout this period, anti-abortion physicians and lawmakers in both the UK and Canada continued to "berate abortion as an evil indistinguishable from infanticide and calling for severe punishment" of all parties involved in an abortion (38). Sometimes abortion was treated even more severely than infanticide in the eyes of the law (see Backhouse 1991, chap. 4 and 5). As one anti-abortion proponent argued, "the mother most frequently is involved in the ruin, and falls a miserable victim to her own execrable and heartless depravity" (quoted in Keown 2002, 36). Clandestine abortions were framed as "a detestable species of murder," with some physicians going as far as to argue that "every woman who attempts to promote abortion, does it at the hazard of her life; if this were generally known it would in all probability deter them from such a proceeding, except that they are in a state of consummate depravity" (36).

Finally, professional concern about unprofessional practice was also a key discursive and motivational foundation for the drive to criminalize abortion in both the UK and Canada. As was the case with the US, there is also substantial evidence that in Canada members of the "regular" medical community were not only concerned about the welfare of the fetus but were also focused on establishing and consolidating their status as a profession (Keown 2002, 40).

4.2 Abortion Reform in the United Kingdom

As has been repeatedly proven throughout history, laws prohibiting abortion almost never eliminate, or even reduce, abortion. Historically, these laws have primarily had the effect of driving abortion underground, with predictable consequences – including the creation of significant gaps between popular morality and the formal law. Canada and the UK were no different in this regard, and as the medical community increasingly mobilized against abortion, many women continued to view abortion as a necessary and morally acceptable reproductive practice. In this sense, the historical contest over abortion was part of a larger battle over the medical community's increasing attempt to regulate, police, and influence the sexual and reproductive behaviour of women.

Despite its illegality, abortion continued to be common throughout the nineteenth and twentieth centuries. Although statistics are understandably scarce, one estimate suggests that, between 1923 and 1933, 15 per cent of all maternal deaths in the UK were a result of illegal abortion (Abortion Rights 2013). In the US, estimates suggest that, by the early 1960s, one million illegal abortions were being performed annually, resulting in five thousand maternal deaths each year (Leavy and

Kummer 1962, 124). These estimates are likely low, since deaths due to abortion were often "disguised on the death certificates as puerperal sepsis or some other cause in order to save the reputation of the family" (Chamberlain 2006, 559). And, contrary to stereotypes, it was not only unmarried women who resorted to illegal abortion. Older, affluent, married women who had already had their children – and for whom contraception was unreliable – also relied on underground abortion services (159).

In the decades following the adoption of highly restrictive abortion laws, women's groups and some within the medical and legal communities began to highlight the problems with illegal abortion and publicly question the value of these laws. In 1934, for example, a congress of the Co-operative Women's Guild in England passed a resolution in favour of legalizing abortion. Two years later, the Abortion Law Reform Association (ALRA) was established in the UK as a response of to "high maternal mortality resulting from criminal abortion" and with the aim of campaigning for abortion reform (Hindell and Simms 1968, 270). In 1938, a high-profile trial in the UK that resulted in a jury acquitting Dr. Aleck Bourne for having performed an abortion on a fourteen-year-old girl who had been gang raped by soldiers increased public debate around the nature and desirability of the laws that prohibited abortion (Tatalovich 1997, 31). In particular, the medicalized discourse that surrounded the *Bourne* decision revolved around the conditions under which a therapeutic abortion might be considered legally, and morally, acceptable. Dr. Bourne's testimony highlighted the possible risks pregnancy can have on women's health. He testified that his decision to operate was based mainly on the threat of "mental and nervous injury ... which was extremely difficult to cure" and argued that, in cases like this, the threat to a women's mental health could be so serious so as to be understood as a threat to her life (quoted in Keown 2002, 50). In advising the jury, the judge largely supported Bourne's medicalized testimonial, advising that, "if the doctor is of opinion, on reasonable grounds and with adequate knowledge, that the probable consequence of the continuation of the pregnancy will be to make the woman a physical or mental wreck, the jury are quite entitled to take the view of the doctor" (51).

The medicalized language of the trial reflected several themes that would come to characterize the abortion debate and policy of the following decades. On one hand, this discourse argued for legal flexibility regarding abortion on medical grounds – something that clearly represented a liberalization of existing abortion law. However, this medicalized discourse also affirmed that decisions over when an abortion was to be permitted lay exclusively with medical professionals, and not with the pregnant woman herself. Moreover, the judge was clear that fetal life was also worthy of legal and social respect: "the law of this land has always held human life to be sacred, and the protection that the law gives to human life extends to the child in the womb. The unborn child in the womb must not be destroyed unless the destruction of that child is for the purpose of preserving the yet more precious life of the mother" (quoted in Keown 2002, 51). As evident by the judge's statement, legal discourse around abortion reform alluded to the fact that abortion law had to carefully balance two sets of rights: those of the pregnant woman and those of the fetus.

The *Bourne* decision – combined with a growing public awareness around abortion – led the government to set up the Inter-Departmental Committee on Abortion to study the issue. In 1939, what became known as the Birkett Commission recommended that the law be modified to ensure that a doctor could perform an abortion in order to save a woman's life. The newly formed ALRA played a large role in the Committee on Abortion, testifying that over 90,000 women had illegal abortions each year. While the abortion issue disappeared from the political radar with the outbreak of the Second World War that year, after the war, support continued to build for revamping abortion legislation. Yet no sitting government would initiate such reform, and it took a private member's bill, supported by various medical organizations and mainstream Protestant churches, to convince the government to appoint a medical advisory committee on the issue (Steel 2004). The committee (the members of whom represented strong proponents of both sides of the issue) recommended the passing of revised legislation, and Parliament passed the Abortion Act of 1967.

This act significantly liberalized abortion access in the UK up until twenty-eight weeks. The new act legalized abortion if two medical practitioners agreed that (1) the "continuance of the pregnancy would involve risk ... of injury to the physical or mental health of the woman or any existing children in her family" or (2) "there is a substantial risk that if a child were born it would suffer from such physical or mental abnormalities as to be seriously handicapped" (Abortion Act 1967). For the first time, British statute law specifically made abortion legal on grounds other than to save the life of the woman. Moreover, the act allowed doctors "a great deal of discretion although not the total discretion which they enjoy with virtually all other operations" (Hindell and Simms 1968). In 1990, this act was revised, reducing the time limit to twenty-four weeks and including several clarifications of the conditions under which abortions could be provided. However, for all intents and purposes, outside of Northern Ireland (which has different laws), since 1967 the United Kingdom has had highly accessible access to abortion, virtually on demand, until twenty-eight, and ultimately twenty-four, weeks of pregnancy.

4.3 The Birth Control Movement in Canada

If abortion criminalization in Canada followed the footsteps of its imperial parent, abortion law reform in Canada also took place in the shadow of Britain. Like Britain, the reality in Canada was that laws prohibiting abortion were far from effective and largely had the effect of creating high numbers of unsafe illegal abortions and ineffective legal prosecution (Backhouse 1991). By the early 1900s, the issue of abortion was increasingly coming into public view. Newspaper advertisements became a popular and public way through which women were able to access abortion services. Newspapers often ran advertisements for the sale of abortifacients as well as abortionists' "offers of aid" (McLaren and McLaren 1997, 33). Women could self-induce miscarriage by drinking "an infusion of one of the traditional abortifacients." If these failed, women would also try "bleedings, hot baths, violent exercises, and consumption of large quantities of gin," after which would come more risky dilation techniques (most often performed by physicians or abortionists, but sometimes self-induced) (34).

Women seeking an abortion usually had to do so covertly, often foregoing the kind of supports that are important for any medical procedure (Cross 2009, 2). The cost for an illegal abortion was also often very high. As there was no way to regulate the qualifications of illegal practitioners, many providers did not have proper medical training. This, combined with the conditions in the locations in which these procedures were often conducted, meant that the risks of infection, incomplete abortions, and unintended sterilization were very high. Thus, women who procured an illegal abortion put themselves in considerable danger. Although no official records were kept and precise figures do not exist, it is estimated that between 4,000 and 6,000 Canadian women died from illegal abortions from 1926 to 1947 (Cross 2009, 2).

Although the problems surrounding illegal abortion were increasingly coming into public view, there was little explicit public debate around the issue in early twentieth-century Canada. However, Canadian women, like their American counterparts, were beginning to mobilize around a related issue: contraception. Prior to 1969, the use of contraception was illegal under the 1892 Criminal Code, unless it could be justified as being for the public good. However, by the 1920s, as couples were increasingly trying to limit their family size, mobilization in favour of contraception was beginning to take shape. In fact, the pioneer in the American birth control movement, Margaret Sanger, also helped initiate the birth control movement in Canada. Canadians often wrote to Sanger for advice, inquiring about how to go about limiting their family size (McLaren and McLaren 1997, 55). Consequently, Sanger's discourse – which stressed both the economic, social, and feminist dimensions of birth control reform – permeated north of the border. In July 1923, Sanger visited Canada and gave her first public lecture north of the border.

Sponsored and promoted by the Women's International League for Peace and Freedom and held in Vancouver, Sanger's visit to Canada was "very much a leftist women's affair" (McLaren and McLaren 1997, 60). Throughout her lecture, Sanger employed a profoundly feminist discourse, centring her talk on the "depiction of the bright future that lay in store once effective contraception was available for all" (61). Sanger highlighted the fact that, as was also the case in the US, middle-class Canadian women were able to access contraception but lower-classes women could not. By making contraception available for all, Sanger argued, "children would be healthy, and motherhood made 'glorious'" (61).

Sanger's talk had profound effects not only on the organization of the Canadian birth control movement, but also on its discourse and arguments. In the months following Sanger's talk, Canada's first birth control advocacy organization, the Canadian Birth Control League, was founded. Activists increasingly took up many of Sanger's points while advancing distinctly Canadian arguments for liberalized birth control access. Alexander Maitland Stephen demanded that birth control clinics become part of the larger socialist platform in Canada, and other activists argued that the decision to bear children must be a woman's decision alone, claiming that the "woman must become mistress of herself and her first duty shall be to herself" (quoted in McLaren and McLaren 1997, 63). However, the most common language that emerged from Canada's birth control movement centred largely on the notion of family planning. The goal of birth controllers was "not childlessness, but wanted children, better marriage, freedom for women, and race improvements" (65). Unsurprisingly, early birth control advocacy in Canada was inextricably linked to the eugenics movement, as it was in the United States. Historian Linda Revie (2006) has shown how birth control proponents such as A.R. Kaufman – founder of Canada's first birth control information centre – had deep ties to the Canadian eugenics movement.

Also much like its American counterpart, the goals and discourse of the early birth control movement in Canada centred on better family planning and did not often comment on the legality or morality of abortion. When abortion was raised, Canadian advocates often treated it as an issue that birth control could help solve (Brodie, Gavigan, and Jenson 1992, 22). While the American birth control movement achieved success in liberalizing the laws around contraceptives as early as the 1930s, the Canadian movement, in comparison, proved relatively ineffective. In fact, it would not be until Pierre Trudeau's omnibus bill in 1969 (the same bill that would also eventually decriminalize abortion) that contraception would become legal in Canada.

4.4 Abortion Reform in Canada

Many argue that it was the women's magazine *Chatelaine* that first placed abortion on the Canadian public agenda when, in 1959, it published an article calling for the liberalization of abortion (a story that was subsequently taken up by the *Globe and Mail*) (Stettner 2012; Halfmann 2011, 47; Brodie, Gavigan, and Jenson 1992, 23). The *Chatelaine* piece, in a number of ways, mirrored the narrative of illegal abortion that was being popularized in American public discourse of the era. It began with the story of a fourteen-year-old rape victim who could not procure an abortion, arguing that, when thinking about abortion, Canadians should consider that "quality of life, for the mother and other members of the family, counted more than that of the foetus." It further argued that children should be wanted and that "sociopaths were likely to begin as 'unwanted children'" (Brodie, Gavigan, and Jenson 1992, 23).

Chatelaine's central arguments, however, were that abortion reform was most necessary for "under-privileged" women and that society as a whole would benefit from abortion reform. While arguments focusing on the social and economic advantages of legal abortion were relatively common in the US throughout the 1960s, they would prove much less widespread in Canada (Brodie, Gavigan, and Jenson 1992, 23).

In fact, the *Chatelaine* article was one of the very few in Canada of this genre. Instead, the primary actor driving abortion reform and the discourse about abortion in Canada was the medical community, which was increasingly championing more liberal abortion access. As in the US, Canadian doctors had been a driving force in criminalization in the nineteenth century. However, by the mid-twentieth century, many doctors were unable to ignore women's lived experiences with failing birth control and the reality that, for many women, abortion was an essential method of fertility control (McLaren and McLaren 1997, 39).

Influenced by the seriousness of these realities, as well as the debates that were taking place in the UK (and to some degree in the US) various groups in Canada began substantial discussions regarding abortion reform in the early 1960s. At this point, the most influential actors were not women's groups (Brodie, Gavigan, and Jenson 1992, chap. 3). Rather, the first mainstream discussions began in the more technical and professional arenas of medicine and law, and demands for abortion reform came from the somewhat "unlikely coalition" between the Canadian Medical Association (CMA) and the Canadian Bar Association (CBA) (Morton 1992, 19). In Morton's analysis, the principal motivation for abortion law reform in Canada in the 1960s appears to have been "neither sexual equality nor social engineering" (as was partially the case in the US) but was instead "professional self-interest: to protect doctors against the legal uncertainties of the current law" (19).

This is not to say that women's voices were entirely absent from the abortion debate. Historian Shannon Stettner has demonstrated that, while lawyers and doctors undoubtedly set the political agenda for abortion reform in Canada, scholars have underplayed the various ways in which women had strong and well-framed perspectives on the issue. In particular, women directly contributed to the public debate over abortion through submissions to the 1970 Royal Commission on the Status of Women (RCSW) (Stettner 2012). Nonetheless, the public debate over abortion reform remained dominated largely by male intellectuals, doctors, lawyers, and clergy. Jane Jenson argues that this is not overly surprising, given that these groups held the most power in Canadian society and that neither women nor a progressive left was particularly well represented or influential in public institutions or political discourse (Brodie, Gavigan, and Jenson 1992, 26).

Given this context, it is not surprising that the early abortion reform discourse rarely argued that access to abortion was a basic right necessary for women's economic and social well-being. Instead, the debate was squarely placed within a profoundly medicalized discourse. Much like abortion reform discourse in the UK, most of the CMA's arguments insisted that some form of legalized abortion was necessary in order to "tidy up" the abortion situation, so that the law and the common practice of abortion were once again aligned (Brodie, Gavigan, and Jenson 1992, 27). Mainstream arguments for abortion reform also revolved around the construction of women as mothers, albeit of varying forms. Some mothers needed abortion because they already had too many children, while other were not healthy enough, or were too young, to be mothers (29).

Largely employing this type of discourse, the CMA and CBA began discussing the possibility of reform in the early 1960s. The chief coroner of Ontario asked his coroners to call a public inquest into each death that resulted from illegal abortion – an act that created both increased visibility and data regarding the problems that existed under the existing legislation. By 1966, not only were these coroners' inquests calling for revisions to the law, but both the CMA and the CBA had also adopted official proposals calling for decriminalization.

These proposals were fairly reflective of mainstream public opinion. By 1965, polls found that almost 75 per cent of those surveyed supported therapeutic abortions in cases where the woman's health was in danger (Tatalovich 1997, 109). Given the combination of clear professional consensus and growing public support, all the movement needed was a political champion – and it found it in Justice Minister Pierre Trudeau. By the fall of 1967, under the guidance of Trudeau, the abortion debate had been brought "out of the backwaters of legal and medical journals and into the centre of Canada's political agenda," and on 3 October 1967, the House of Commons Standing Committee on Health and Welfare began hearings on abortion reform in Canada (Morton 1992, 20).

These hearings would take place over five months and would consist of twenty-five meetings, thirty-five briefs, and ninety-three witness testimonials. The submissions and testimonials came from a wide range of political and religious actors with an equally wide range of views, but with opposition to abortion reform unorganized and largely unmobilized, the majority of feedback favoured a change to the current law (Morton 1992, 21). Those voices that spoke against reform largely framed the issue around the traditional Christian argument that Canadian law must protect innocent life from the harm of abortion and that abortion was a threat to Canadian society as a whole (22). The most influential anti-reform submissions came from the Canadian Conference of Catholic Bishops and newly founded group the Emergency Organization for the Defence of Unborn Life, who testified that a more liberal abortion law would "foster an insouciance towards all vulnerable forms of human life and thereby plummet Canada into a 'second darkness'" (Cuneo 1989, 5–6). This early anti-abortion discourse relied on two interconnected arguments: first, a religiously grounded claim that the fetus is fully human and thus has a right to life and, second, a related assertion that in denying the essential humanity of the fetus, Canada was being taken down the path of moral decay.

The primary rationale in favour of abortion reform centred on the medically oriented argument that Canada must "put an end to the butchery of illegal abortions" (Morton 1992, 22). Religious groups that favoured some degree of decriminalization (such as United and Anglican churches) argued that abortion laws should be relaxed to include health exemptions for women, but they remained strictly opposed to abortion for social and economic reasons. Members of the CMA, conversely, conceded that self-interest was the primary motivator for their opposition to the current abortion law. The spokesperson for the CMA testified that the association's interest in abortion reform was "to end our life as lawbreakers" (quoted in deValk 1974, 43). One submission, however, foreshadowed the women's rights approach that would come to dominate the debate in the 1970s and 1980s (Morton 1992, 22). The testimony of Dr. Henry Morgentaler, a then relatively unknown doctor and the vice-president of the Humanist Fellowship of Montreal, advocated for the adoption of the British model of abortion on demand in the first three months of pregnancy. He framed this recommendation squarely within the language of women's rights, asserting that "it is a woman's inalienable right to have mastery of her own body" (quoted in deValk 1974, 48).

Ultimately, however, the proposed reforms of the late 1960s were primarily "framed and achieved within a discourse of medicalization" and not one of women's rights (Brodie, Gavigan, and Jenson 1992, 11). With the exception of Morgentaler's submission, the discourse downplayed the moral dimensions of abortion reform and defined reproductive decisions as medical, rather than political, in nature. In fact, the medical perspective was so influential that the new abortion law proposed to Parliament very closely resembled the CMA proposal of 1966 (Morton 1992, 19).

4.5 The Decriminalization of Abortion: Section 251

In spite of some opposition to abortion reform, on 21 December 1967, Justice Minister Pierre Trudeau introduced the Criminal Law Amendment Act, which had 104 new or revised clauses, including one that would decriminalize contraception and broaden the legal grounds for abortion in Canada. Although activists from both sides of the abortion debate contested it – some because it did not go far enough in its liberalization, others because it went too far – the omnibus bill ultimately passed in 1969, decriminalizing abortion and contraceptive use. While the bill did not fully legalize abortion, the new abortion law – section 251 of the Criminal Code of Canada – did authorized abortion when performed in an accredited hospital with permission from a therapeutic abortion committee (TAC). The role of TACs, which consisted of at least three doctors appointed by the hospital board, was to determine whether "the continuation of the pregnancy would or would be likely to endanger the life or health of the pregnant woman" (Brodie, Gavigan, and Jenson 1992, 11). Under the new law, the conditions for procuring a legal abortion were threefold. First, the abortion must be performed in an accredited or approved hospital. Second, the qualifying hospital must have a TAC, and the doctor performing the procedure must not be part of that committee. Third, the majority of the TAC must confirm in writing that the pregnancy would endanger the life or health of the pregnant woman (Muldoon 1991, 173).

With section 251, Parliament "replaced judicial control after the fact with medical control before the fact" (Canada 1998) in a way that attempted to "create a compromise solution to the abortion controversy" (Muldoon 1991, 173). For although section 251 undoubtedly liberalized access to abortion in Canada, it also defended fetal life by ensuring that TACs acted as "gatekeepers for abortions" (Muldoon 1991, 183), which meant that doctors were given control over women's reproductive decisions. As a consequence, women did not gain an individual or collective right to abortion in either theory or practice (Brodie, Gavigan, and Jenson 1992, 36). Rather, they gained the right to seek permission for an abortion from medical authorities. And women had no right to appeal the process in the case of rejection.

The implementation of the TAC system in Canadian hospitals turned out to be challenging and controversial. The central issue was the ambiguity that surrounded the terms "life" and "health" in section 251. The vagueness of these terms led to their being interpreted in differing ways by the TACs. And these TAC's were not immune to the larger political environment in Canada. Some employed relatively open interpretations of "life" and "health," which, in practice, liberalized access, but many others were staffed with anti-abortion doctors who denied the majority of applications. In some cases, TACs were even disbanded as a result of pressure from anti-abortionists (Arthur 1999).

A further complication was the fact that only a third of hospitals in Canada had accredited TACs in place. Because many women lived in communities far from any hospital, never mind one that had a TAC and abortion centre, real abortion access varied enormously across the country and created significant geographic disparities (Rauhala 1987; Arthur 1999). Moreover, as a result of a lack of resources, many accredited hospitals and abortion providers were forced to self-impose informal quotas on abortion care, further limiting access (Kellough 1996).

The medicalized orientation of section 251 had a profound influence on the way in which Canadian lawmakers would *talk* about abortion for the next two decades. By defining abortion as a medical decision, section 251 effectively dampened the political resonance of both pro-choice and pro-life attempts to frame the abortion debate in the language of rights (Brodie, Gavigan, and Jenson 1992, 11). In contrast to the US (where the language of rights had quickly become the dominant frame), Canadian discourse remained less politicized in one sense. Instead of being framed around women's relationship to her own reproductive health, the subsequent debate over abortion largely focused on the role that doctors played in providing abortion. As it was up to Canadian physicians to interpret section 251, the public debate largely remained focused on the actions of doctor, and not the demands or needs of women. But while this medicalized discourse largely made abortion reform possible (by drawing physicians into the debate), it also gave rise to feminist challenges that contested this discursive framing (as well as its practical effects) as far too constraining for women.

4.6 The Fallout over Section 251

Public concerns about the adequacy of section 251 quickly emerged as women's groups began to contest the medicalized framing of abortion almost immediately following the passage of the law. In 1970, the Vancouver Women's Caucus organized the Abortion Caravan. The caravan travelled over 4,800 kilometres from Vancouver to Ottawa, picking up abortion supporters along the way. By the time it reached Ottawa, the

Abortion Caravan comprised about 500 women. They held two days of demonstrations, culminating with thirty women chaining themselves to the parliamentary gallery in the House of Commons, closing Parliament for the first time in Canadian history.

With the success of the Abortion Caravan, women's groups across Canada started involving themselves more directly in the abortion debate, ultimately leading to the founding of the Canadian Association for the Repeal of the Abortion Law (CARAL) – the first national group promoting abortion rights in Canada – in 1974 (Brodie, Gavigan, and Jenson 1992). Adding to the momentum of the abortion rights movement was also the increasing popularity of Dr. Henry Morgentaler, a figure who would come to define abortion politics in Canada.

In spite of this early mobilization, however, turning abortion into a key plank of the women's movement would be a somewhat slow process in Canada. This was not because the early women's movement was unconcerned with the importance of abortion rights. The issue was that the "1969 reform had preceded the institutionalization and consolidation of the new women's movement" (Brodie, Gavigan, and Jenson 1992, 51). Thus, according to Jane Jenson, it "took time for the ineffective law to be felt" and its problems to be uncovered, especially because the majority of feminist activism was concentrated in urban areas where abortion services were more readily available and accessible (51).

As the limits of TAC-regulated abortion became increasingly clear and as anti-abortion groups began to emerge and mobilize against abortion access, existing feminist groups like the National Council of Women of Canada and the Fédération des Femme du Québec began to increasingly engage with the abortion issue, linking it to other women's issues like child care and pay equity. The issue would also be taken up by a broad-based coalition of reformers focused specifically on abortion – organized under the banner of CARAL (Brodie, Gavigan, and Jenson 1992, 46).

This increasing activism in favour of further abortion reform in the early 1970s highlighted the "gross inequalities [that] existed in the availability of therapeutic abortion to the women of Canada" and led to serious debates in policy circles about section 251 (Thomas 1977). In response, the federal government appointed the Badgley Committee to examine whether the TAC process functioned equitably across Canada. In 1977, the committee submitted its report, which was highly critical of the law.

The report's findings were fourfold. First, it found that TACs were not being implemented consistently across the country. Not only were they inconsistent in their interpretations the "life" and "health," but hospitals operationalized the process very differently. While some hospitals required women to meet face-to-face with the committee, others did not. The report concluded that women's access to abortion largely came down to the luck of the draw (Thomas 1977, 966). Second, the report determined that women were being forced to wait for up to eight weeks between the original consultation with a TAC and the abortion procedure, causing further complications in women's ability to access abortion services. Third, the report found that there was a financial deterrent that was affecting women's ability to afford abortion services, with hospitals subjecting approximately 20 per cent of abortion patients to extra billing. Finally, the report found that one in five Canadian women who had had an abortion had been forced to obtain the procedure outside Canada (between 1970 and 1975, over 50,000 Canadian women went to the US for their procedures). Given these figures, the report determined that abortion access in Canada was unsatisfactory.

Despite the increasing influence of the Canadian women's movement and its more rights-based discourse, the Badgley Committee continued to frame abortion in almost exclusively medicalized language. Indeed, because the committee had been constituted by the Minister of Health – and ordered to rule on the procedures of the various TAC – its report was largely restricted to medical arguments and language. So, while the Badgley Report espoused some "equality" arguments (i.e., that abortion services were *unequally* accessible for Canadian women), it ultimately produced a report that contributed to the medicalized discourse surrounding the abortion question.

4.7 The Emergence of the Canadian Anti-abortion Movement

Because abortion had been illegal in most of Canada from the mid-1800s to 1969, nothing that could be described as an anti-abortion movement existed prior to abortion reform in the late 1960s. However, by liberalizing many long-standing laws concerning not just abortion, but also contraception, homosexuality, and other "social" issues, Trudeau's omnibus bill provoked a significant reaction among some sectors of Canadian society. One consequence of this reaction was the creation of an explicit anti-abortion movement whose objective was to recriminalize abortion.

Immediately following the 1969 abortion reform, the Canadian Conference of Catholic Bishops became the most vocal critic of legal abortion. However, as the 1970s progressed, the group was slowly replaced by groups like the Knights of Columbus and the Catholic Women's League, resulting in the emergence of a more "grassroots" anti-abortion movement (Cuneo 1989, 7). Moreover, throughout the 1970s, both the Conference of Catholic Bishops and the larger Catholic Church would come to distance themselves from the abortion issue. While informal connections continued to exist between the anti-abortion movement and Canada's Catholic institutions throughout the 1970s (and the church provided activists organization with resources, such as meeting space, office supplies, refreshments, volunteer clerical work, and transportation), the church did not tend to publicly and explicitly fund or support the movement (Cuneo 1989, 7–8).

The first major grassroots anti-abortion group in Canada was the Toronto-based Alliance for Life. Founded in 1968, it provided the organizational muscle for the larger Canadian anti-abortion movement and aggressively argued against legal abortion for many years. These early years, however, were characterized by significant internal debate and disagreement over strategy and orientation (particularly over the appropriate role of religion in public discourse). Shortly after its founding, Alliance for Life's aggressive (and often very anti-woman) tactics were challenged by other activists. Louise Summerhill, who opened the first Birthright clinic in Toronto (also in 1968), for instance, was a vocal opponent of Alliance for Life, arguing that the group "distracted attention from the economic and emotional plight of many women facing unplanned pregnancies" (Cuneo 1989, 9).

Similar tensions continued to characterize the broader movement throughout the 1970s. In 1973, Alliance for Life, in conjunction with Toronto Right to Life, decided to found a sister organization that would concentrate exclusively on political advocacy. The result was Coalition for Life, whose responsibilities included canvassing, lobbying politicians, and developing election strategies (Cuneo 1989, 10; CLC, n.d.-a). While the executive of Coalition for Life was predominantly male academics – and, perhaps somewhat ironically, often NDP supporters – a strong and distinct grassroots presence emerged in the organization as well. The lower ranks of Coalition for Life were largely made up of conservative working-class and middle-class members "for whom abortion was a composite symbol of general cultural decadence as well as a threat to traditional family values" (Cuneo 1989, 11). As these militant and religious individuals became active in the movement, they increasingly took control of executive and other decision-making positions.

By the end of the 1970s, they had essentially sidelined the previous "progressive" and academic leadership. In 1978, a second, even more militant anti-abortion political action group – Campaign Life – was formed (CLC, n.d.a). These new grassroots anti-abortion groups and activists had a clear vision for the movement – one that, as we will see in chapter 5, would lead the movement towards a much more explicitly religious and confrontational strategy throughout the 1980s.

Despite rising internal politics, the anti-abortion movement of the 1970s was still relatively uniform. Largely Roman Catholic in its demographic composition, it was fairly limited in its political advocacy, and its main goal was understood as reminding the Canadian public of sustained opposition to legal abortion in Canada (Cuneo 1989, 40). Its activities included some political lobbying, the promotion of anti-abortion education, the occasional public rally, and smaller-scale protests outside of "abortion-intensive" hospitals (40).

In terms of discursive orientation, the relatively "progressive" pioneers of the anti-abortion movement intentionally framed their arguments in ways they believed would strike the widest public appeal. In Canada – a relatively secular country – this meant downplaying its religious underpinnings and motivations (Cuneo 1989, 41). According to historian Michael Cuneo, despite the Christian commitment of most activists, early "pro-life literature was notable for its avoidance of explicitly religious language or argumentation" (41). This meant that although mainstream anti-abortion discourse largely framed the issue in terms of fetal life, it did so primarily through medicalized and scientific rationales.

4.8 The Intensification of the Anti-abortion Movement in Canada

By the late 1970s and early 1980s, evangelical Canadians began to take a more active role in the anti-abortion movement in Canada – a phenomenon that would have a significant impact on the nature and discourse of the anti-abortion movement. In 1985, Choose Life Canada was founded by evangelical preacher Ken Campbell's Renaissance Canada Ministry. Its explicit purpose was to engage more evangelicals on the abortion issue (Cuneo 1989, 13). At first, the role and influence of evangelicals in the Canadian anti-abortion movement was not nearly as intense or widespread as was the case in the US, and the "fire and brimstone" discourse espoused by more militant strands of evangelical activists never really found widespread support across the anti-abortion movement or in Canadian society more generally. Thus, evangelical organizations and discursive patterns remained a "distinctly minority phenomenon with an underdeveloped tradition in the Canadian imagination" during the same period in which they were flourishing in the US (ibid., 13).

As the 1980s progressed, "the movement's simmering religious energy would have its cap unscrewed and anti-abortion protest would assume an unprecedented stridency" (ibid., 41–42). According to Cuneo, one important reason for this change was that, by the mid-1980s, many of the religious activists had decided that otherwise key doctrinal differences between Protestants (especially evangelicals) and Catholics were less important than their shared concerns about abortion (47). Moreover, social changes in Canada meant that these groups found a commonality in their "mutual feeling of estrangement from the secular character of modern Canadian society," and they bonded over the perception of a common (secular) foe (42). Increasingly then, members of the anti-abortion movement saw themselves less as Catholics or Protestants and more as Christians positioned against an unacceptably secular society and overly permissive social policies.

By the mid-1980s, anti-abortion discourse came to reflect this shift, taking on a more explicitly religious stance: "Scriptural passages appeared alongside civil rights slogans on pro-life placards and broadsheets, and public prayer, which was exceptional in the movement's early years, became a regular feature of pro-life rallies and demonstrations" (Cuneo 1989, 43). Anti-abortion activists increasingly believed that "facts alone will never sway people," opening up the possibility for more morally and religiously charged rhetoric (44). Increasingly, more moderate strands of the movement – which had advocated less explicitly religious forms of social and political protest – were pushed to the periphery and were replaced by more militant activists whose main perspective was profoundly anti-secular and anti-abortion (Cuneo 1989, 73; Herman 1994, 270). By the mid- to late 1980s, there had emerged a distinctly religious anti-abortion discourse, emanating largely from the newly formed Campaign Life Coalition, a new organization resulting from a merger between Coalition for Life and Campaign Life in 1986.

4.9 The Christian Right in Canada

As we saw in chapter 3, the rise of the Christian right in the US brought social conservatism into the mainstream of formal politics and allowed abortion to become one of the most controversial and central focuses of the intensely partisan struggles that have characterized US politics since at least the 1970s. As James Farney argues, the rise of the Christian right meant that "the United States generally accepted the social conservative concern with sexual morality and allowed that religious arguments had a place in the public square" (2012, 4). While religious arguments were not common in the judicial realm, the public and political debate over abortion in the US was saturated with fundamentalist religious language, which in turn gave rise to a number of more extremist anti-abortion groups (most notably Operation Rescue), and which reinforced the authority and utility of religious arguments in anti-abortion discourse.

In Canada, things were very different. Far from becoming a central issue in political battles, the debate over abortion after its decriminalization in 1969 primarily took place outside of Parliament and beyond the formal platforms and policies of political parties. Canada saw very little of the intense political polarization around abortion that characterized the US in the 1970s and 1980s. It was not a widespread, vote-determining issue in elections, and the anti-abortion movement was not able to exercise significant influence on party policy or election strategy. Neither the choice of party leaders nor the nominations of most candidates for the major parties were significantly influenced by the efforts of the anti-abortion movement.

In fact, unlike in the US, all three national parties largely treated the movement as a political liability (Cuneo 1989, 74). This was particularly true in regard to the most religiously oriented anti-abortion activists. Religious appeals were not major themes in the discursive justification of the anti-abortion position in Parliament. There were, of course, individual MPs, such as Jake Epp, the Health Minister under Prime Minister Mulroney and a devout Mennonite, who favoured a decidedly punitive approach to abortion law (proposing to ban abortions of malformed fetuses and enact criminal penalties for women who self-aborted). Epp publicly opposed abortion on explicitly religious grounds during the debates in the late 1980s and early 1990s. However, most scholars agree that, despite some individual examples, no Canadian equivalent of the American Christian right and its construction of the "Moral Majority" emerged in Canada (Farney 2012; Herman 1994). Didi Herman, for instance, argues that, during the 1970s and 1980s, not only did Canada not shift towards a Moral Majority–inspired conservatism, but it witnessed the reverse: the solidification of "a powerful 'liberal consensus' [that] largely dominated public debate and policy around such issues as abortion, education, public health and homosexuality" (Herman 1994, 268; see also Farney 2012). Jonathan Malloy, one of the few scholars to have directly studied the relationship between evangelicals and politics in Canada, also notes that even the most "social conservative" party in Canadian history, the Reform Party, "did not prioritize opposition to abortion and gay rights in its platform or official rhetoric," despite being founded by a leader who was both evangelical and "outspoken about his religious beliefs" (Malloy 2013, 186).

Contemporary Canadian conservatism has developed into something that is quite different than the peculiar amalgam of social and religious conservatism and radical free-market economics that has become the norm for conservative politics and thought in the US (Saurette and Gunster 2013). Most Canadian historians and political scientists suggest that, despite the existence of religiously inspired and oriented actors in Canadian politics (see McDonald 2010; Warner 2010; Martin 2010), and the fact that the re-emergence of a unified Conservative Party under Stephen Harper has been willing to promote certain social conservative issues that earlier conservative parties would not (Malloy 2013), the influence of religion and politicized religious groups is much more limited in Canada than it is in the US. To suggest otherwise, most scholars agree, would be to "over-emphasize the power of social conservatism in Canada and, by so doing, overplay the similarities between Canadian and American conservatism" (Farney 2012, 4).

4.10 The Discourse of the Early Canadian Anti-abortion Movement

If the Christian right was not the primary shaper of the anti-abortion movement and its discourse throughout the 1980s, what did the Canadian anti-abortion movement look like? According to Michael Cuneo's study of Canadian anti-abortion activism from 1965 to 1985, the movement was quite diverse. Despite being founded and organized by Catholics (often with indirect support from the church), religion was downplayed in the public discourse of the movement in the 1970s. By the 1980s, however, religious discourse became increasingly explicit. Cuneo (1989) argues that the Canadian anti-abortion movement of the 1970s and 1980s can be broken into three "emergent norms" – civil rights activists, family heritage activists, and revivalist Catholics – each of which employed their own version of public discourse.

The first group – made up of "civil rights" activists, who opposed abortion in every case except when the life of the pregnant woman was at risk – formed the nucleus of many of the earliest anti-abortion efforts. Their opposition to abortion was predominantly the result of an unwavering belief in the humanity of the fetus. While civil rights anti-abortion activists did not necessarily believe that abortion could be eliminated entirely, they did believe that by promoting education reform that focused on the humanity of the fetus and legislative reform that protected the fetus, the movement could change cultural attitudes and public opinion about abortion (Cuneo 1989, 85).

Civil rights anti-abortion activists founded their public discourse on fetal-right-to-life arguments. Their motto largely became "babies are being murdered and we've got to stop it" (quoted in ibid., 90). Their strategies were diverse, ranging from the operation of "crisis pregnancy centres" to promoting campaigns designed to educate the public about the humanity of the fetus. This faction promoted "patient dialogue" rather than confrontation and was openly critical of the emergence of aggressive protest tactics (89). These activists were not necessarily opposed to working with abortion advocates and feminists in reducing the number of unplanned and unwanted pregnancies, believing that "the shrill rhetoric on both sides of the issue stifles any chance of meaningful dialogue" (89). Moreover, their discourse typically avoided anti-woman tones and language. They also remained committed to working from within a liberal reformist conceptual framework. Civil rights activists believed that the case for fetal personhood should be made by exclusively engaging with both scientific evidence and basic principles of civil rights, and not grounded explicitly in religious discourse. In the words of one activist, "babies are being slaughtered daily and pious platitudes sure won't save them" (90).

While civil rights anti-abortion activists were influential in the beginning stages of the Canadian anti-abortion movement, they had been pushed to the periphery of the movement by the mid-1970s as more radical forms of anti-abortion activism began to flourish. These more radical activists were highly critical of the "liberal" approach taken up by civil rights anti-abortionists. According to one more militant activist, "abortion kills babies – pure and simple – and this is what has to be said time and again. They [civil right anti-abortion advocates] try so hard to make pro-life look nice and liberal. This isn't nice – this is about life and death. Who gives a damn about trying to make ourselves look good when babies' lives are at stake" (quoted in Cuneo 1989, 91).

Throughout the late 1970s and early 1980s, it was thus both "family heritage" and "revivalist Catholics" that increasingly saturated and defined the

Canadian anti-abortion movement. According to Cuneo, it was the family heritage activists that, as of the mid-1970s, provided the "basic imprint and impetus" for the anti-abortion movement (ibid., 96). Family heritage activists, who tended to be Protestants, were politically engaged and worked (however unsuccessfully) at building political alliances with MPs. They made financial donations, participated in rallies and marches, and ran local right-to-life groups across the country. At the core of their opposition to abortion was the belief that "liberalized abortion [was] the indisputable barometer of Canadian society's decline into moral viciousness ... [as] the 'slaughter of innocents' could be condoned only in a culture that is morally bankrupt and destined for possible extinction" (96). This was not the only theme, however, for these activists saw legal abortion as part of a larger attack on traditional conceptions of family and motherhood, which they believed underpinned Western civilization.

The public discourse espoused by family heritage advocates was aggressive and linked the struggle against abortion to the larger battle over traditional morality in Canadian society. The "legalized abortion holocaust," it was argued, "prov[ed] that our society has fallen into barbarism ... The abortion chambers are no different from Nazi crematories. They both have the same results and stem from the same nihilism" (quoted in Cuneo 1989 101). In this respect, family heritage discourse is very comparable to that of evangelical Christians and the larger Christian right in the US. The perceived enemy was not only abortion, but also secularism, feminism, and sexual permissiveness (98). In Canada, it would be the organization REAL (Realistic, Equal, Active, for Life) Women that largely came to represent the family heritage mentality and discourse. According to former president Grace Petrasek, what underpinned REAL Women's mission was the belief that Canadians must be made aware of the fact that the "feminist agenda" did not represent the grassroots of Canada. "We do not want our politicians capitulating to the anti-family, anti-life ideology of pro-abortionists," Petrasek argued, "They must know that there is a very strong pro-life voice that will not tolerate this pandering to a handful of extremist feminists" (100). Ultimately, the discourse taken up by family heritage activists drew on increasingly aggressive and radical religious arguments around fetal personhood and the decline of Canadian society.

Even more extreme was the final type of anti-abortion activism that emerged throughout the 1970s. Revivalist Catholic activists were even more fundamentalist than their family heritage counterparts and were considered the "most vigorous and indefatigable wing" of the

Canadian anti-abortion movement (ibid., 105). While sharing a number of similar beliefs and concerns with the family heritage wing (around the perceived threat of secularism), revivalist Catholics were a "distinct subculture" within Canadian Catholicism (105). Not only did the revivalist Catholic position often extend deeper than their opposition to abortion, these activists also often expressed anger towards the Catholic Church itself for what they believed was the relaxation of its sexual and gendered norms. They believed that the historically conservative ethical and theological positions of the church had been diluted under the influence of an increasingly secular Canadian society.

Revivalist Catholics considered it their duty to perform God's will "unstintingly and without compromise, leaving the final outcome to divine justice" (Cuneo 1989, 114). Their discourse was the most profoundly religious of all types. Using the organization Campaign Life as their platform, revivalist Catholic activists' mission was to "raise the pro-life movement from a political to a sacred place, where it would be guided more by nobility of purpose and religious valour than by concern for mere historical consequence" (114). Because they shared an ethical conviction of the humanity of the unborn with other wings of the anti-abortion movement, their discourse fused arguments about the humanity of the fetus with a radical religious discourse. According to one Revivalist Catholic, "abortion is the last line of defence. This is where we draw the line and say: These babies are created by God. They are sacred. Respect at least this. Have at least this much faith" (107).

Another feature that distinguished revivalist Catholic activists from earlier modes of anti-abortion activism was their commitment to confrontational protest. While the civil rights anti-abortion activists opposed such tactics, aggressive protest was considered by revivalist Catholics as a "signature of faith," something that set them apart from the "modernizing tendencies" of larger Canadian society (ibid., 106). Since Revivalist Catholics adopted a traditional world view in which women were regarded primarily as mothers, it was not surprising that their public discourse frequently employed anti-woman tones. Women who chose abortion were framed not only as "unnatural" but also often as immoral, sinful, and selfish.

4.11 Conclusion

This chapter has provided a historical overview of many of the key elements of the abortion debate in the UK and Canada from the beginning of the 1800s until the early 1980s. Canada's early laws largely followed the trend towards increasingly restrictive anti-abortion laws in the UK initiated by Lord Ellenborough's Act of 1803 and intensified throughout the nineteenth century. The limited public discourse that surrounded these shifts similarly paralleled tendencies in the UK. Largely driven by the professional self-interest of physicians and medical practitioners, laws criminalizing abortion were justified not only through a concern for fetal life, but also a relatively condescending attitude towards women, who were represented either as incapable of making moral decisions or as morally depraved. By the early twentieth century, certain legal loopholes opened for doctors, allowing them to perform therapeutic abortions in cases where the continuation of a pregnancy might compromise the psychological or physical health of the pregnant woman. Eventually, mounting pressure by the medical community and other groups convinced the UK government to legalize abortion in 1967.

Canada witnessed a similar liberalizing trend in the 1960s, as a coalition of the legal and medical establishments helped set the stage for new laws that decriminalized abortion in 1969 on the basis of a highly medicalized perspective. These new laws, however, had a variety of limitations and were far from universally accepted. They placed women's reproductive decisions in the hands of physicians and created a series of profound inequalities in abortion access across the country. The 1969 law did not settle the abortion question in Canada. Rather, it provoked strong opposition from both abortion rights activists, who wanted much greater and equitable access, and from the anti-abortion movement, which opposed the very idea of legal abortion. These two sides grew in strength throughout the 1970s and 1980s, and the nature of their discourse shifted as they responded to one another, changing social conditions, and the makeup of their own internal coalitions.

While the contest over public and political opinion intensified over the 1970s and 1980s, significant events in the political and legal spheres would largely define and frame the abortion debate from the late 1980s until today. In the next chapter, we turn back to the political and legal landscape of the mid-1970s to take up the story of abortion in Canada from a more institutional angle.

Chapter 5

The Abortion Debate in Canada: *Morgentaler* and Beyond

As we saw in chapter 4, for much of Canada's history, the debate over abortion was cast in highly medicalized terms and was dominated by political, medical, and legal elites. However, as both the women's rights and the anti-abortion movements emerged and intensified during the 1970s and early 1980s, this began to change. The result was the emergence of a debate characterized by "pro-choice" rights-based arguments on one side and religiously based fetal-centric discourse on the other.

In this chapter, we briefly return to the 1970s in order to examine some of the key political and legal events that came to play key roles in shaping the abortion debate in Canada. The chapter begins with an overview of Henry Morgentaler's legal fight against the abortion law and the political transformations that set the context for the Supreme Court's 1988 *Morgentaler* decision, which struck down section 251 of the Criminal Code as unconstitutional. It then traces the political and legal events that followed the *Morgentaler* decision. The chapter concludes by outlining certain trends that have characterized the Canadian anti-abortion movement and its discourse since the 1980s.

5.1 Abortion in the Courts, Round 1: *Morgentaler v. The Queen*, 1976

In the previous chapter we discussed some of the ways in which activists in the public sphere were organizing and advocating for and against legal abortion. Simultaneously, activists on both sides of the debate were also employing legal means to forward their positions. The most famous abortion rights advocate in this domain was Dr. Henry Morgentaler.

In 1968, Dr. Morgentaler closed his family medicine practice in Montreal and began performing illegal abortions in his own private clinic. Because the clinic was not an accredited hospital and did not have a therapeutic abortion committee (TAC), Morgentaler's actions directly violated section 251. In June 1970, for the first of many times, Montreal police raided Morgentaler's clinic and charged him with conspiracy to perform an abortion (and ten additional abortion-related charges). The Montreal raids marked the beginning of a twenty-year civil disobedience campaign by Morgentaler, who would go on to open abortion clinics across the country (Morton 1992, chap. 3).

Between 1970 and 1976, the Quebec government took Morgentaler to court three times. Each time, Morgentaler invoked the "medical necessity" defence. And each time he acquitted by a jury of his peers. In 1974, however, after he was acquitted by a jury of eleven men and one woman, the Crown appealed the decision. In a historically unprecedented move, the Quebec Court of Appeal overturned the jury's acquittal. Morgentaler appealed the decision to the Supreme Court of Canada, which began hearing the case (*Morgentaler v. The Queen*) in 1974. In his appeal, Morgentaler asked the court both to overturn the Court of Appeal ruling and to strike down section 251. His argument had two main parts. The first was that the health assumptions on which the original bill was based (that abortions were complicated and serious medical procedures that could safely take place only in a hospital) were no longer relevant and that therefore the bill could no longer be supported as being in the public interest. Second, he argued that the law violated the Bill of Rights, which had been passed by the Diefenbaker government in 1960.

Both were strong arguments. Partially as a result of Morgentaler's own research and innovation, the health risks associated with abortion had become much lower than the risks associated with continuing pregnancy (the death rate resulting from abortion under safe conditions is less than one-tenth the death rate resulting from childbirth). Moreover, the death rate associated with illegal abortions is several hundred times higher than that of legal abortions (Columbia University 2013). While one-third of the court supported some or all of Morgentaler's contentions, a majority of the justices rejected the idea that the rights contained in the Bill of Rights were a sufficient basis for overturning section 251. The court thus voted 6–3 to uphold section 251 and Morgentaler's conviction (Sharpe 2003, 6–13).

Morgentaler would pay a significant personal price for his actions. After Liberal Justice Minister Otto Lang (who publicly opposed a more liberal abortion law) refused to pardon him, Morgentaler started serving his eighteen-month sentence in March 1975. He was denied parole after he had served one-third of his sentence (despite the fact that parole was granted at this point in most cases); his medical license was suspended; he divorced; and he suffered a heart attack while in solitary confinement (Sharpe 2003, 14). Finally, after Morgentaler had served ten months of his sentence, Prime Minister Pierre Trudeau's government amended the Criminal Code and eliminated the power of appellate judges to strike down acquittals and order imprisonments – at which point the federal Justice Minister set aside Morgentaler's original conviction and ordered a retrial (Morton 1992, chap. 8).

In addition to these events, Morgentaler was charged for a fourth time in Quebec towards the end of 1976. However, the new Parti Québécois government, which replaced the Liberals in November 1976, announced that, in light of juries' consistent refusals to convict Morgentaler, the abortion law could not be enforced and Quebec would therefore no longer charge qualified medical personnel who performed abortions. The Quebec Minister of Justice also officially requested that the federal law be amended, although this request was refused by the federal government.

5.2 A Transforming Political and Legal Context

Over the course of the 1970s and 1980s, a number of important political and legal factors shifted in ways that profoundly influenced the abortion debate and future legal decisions regarding abortion. First, the movement in favour of legal abortion rights began to organize and mobilize intensely. A variety of new civil society groups such as the Canadian Association for the Repeal of the Abortion Law (CARAL – renamed the Canadian Abortion Rights Action League after the *Morgentaler* decision) were founded to help raise funds and support for Morgentaler's challenges to the law. Beginning in the early 1970s, feminist organizations began creating large networks to build and mobilize grassroots support in favour of a more liberal abortion law. Not only was Canadian abortion activism intensifying, it was beginning to reach a critical mass (Palmer 2012).

According to historian Beth Palmer, abortion rights activists started to recognize the strategic importance of presenting their cause to both the public and to Canadian legislators in "ways that highlighted the mass support for the issue" (ibid., 195). In fact, mobilizing and publicizing the "silent majority's" strong support[10] for abortion rights would become one of the primary goals of the Canadian abortion rights movement (199). The movement therefore invested heavily in building networks between the many individuals and organizations engaged in abortion reform. This was, for instance, an explicit goal of the Vancouver Women's Caucus (VWC), the organizers of the Abortion Caravan. In a 1970 memo titled "Abortion Strategy," the VWC argued, "it is our hope that we can utilize the abortion campaign not only to build toward better communication and more solidarity with women in [British Columbia] but across the country as well" (196).

Abortion rights advocates sought to create strong links to both the emerging women's liberation movement and the Canadian labour movement throughout the 1980s. Within the women's liberation movement, abortion offered a "concrete issue that could foster discussion on gender and class inequality" as well as a site for tangible political action (Palmer 2012, 202). Moreover, the emergence of the New Left in Canada – particularly in the Canadian labour movement – provided the growing abortion rights movement with an extremely important ally. Unions knew how to mobilize masses of people – something that would be increasingly important as the battle for abortion access intensified and increasingly moved from the boardrooms of elite policy discussion to public sites of mass political contestation. In this public context, unions began passing pro-choice motions at their congresses and demonstrated in support of abortion rights. The alliances between the labour and abortion rights movements came to play a key role in demonstrating the mass support that existed for abortion reform (ibid.).

The reality of the issue's mass appeal was also revealed in the degree to which it attracted "novice activists" – many of whom were participating in political events for the first time – who built a very strong grassroots movement (ibid., 216). These grassroots activists employed a wide range of tactics, "from in-the-street demonstrations to letter writing campaigns to compilations of personal narratives to lobbying government bodies" (195). Slogans and visuals – usually found on buttons, bumper stickers, and placards – were particularly effective strategies. Women also began publicizing their own personal stories of abortion.

---

10 According to a 1974 Gallup poll, 62 per cent of Canadian believed that "the decision to have an abortion should be made solely by a woman and her physician" (Palmer 2012, 199).

Such women often spoke of the barriers they faced in accessing abortion, underlining the problematic elements of Canada's abortion law through storytelling (200). Through personal narratives, women were able to highlight issues that were surprisingly absent from the legal and medical discussions of abortion. Interestingly, these stories differed greatly from past narratives of illegal abortion. Whereas these older narratives typically sought to highlight the most extreme examples of clandestine abortions, new abortion stories most often underscored how common the practice of abortion was – highlighting the issue as something that affected many Canadian women.

In the legal realm, the most important change came with the ratification of the Canadian Charter of Rights and Freedoms in 1982, for it offered new avenues of legal argumentation that were much more robust than those contained in its weaker antecedent, the Canadian Bill of Rights. Among the many important (and now constitutionally binding) rights contained in the Charter, one of the most influential and relevant to the abortion debate was section 7, which states, "Everyone has the right to life, liberty and security of the person and the right not to be deprived thereof in accordance with the principles of fundamental justice" (Canada 1982). This was especially important in the context of the debate over abortion, and the courts began to interpret the various Charter rights of individuals as disallowing a variety of governmental interventions that had previously been judged constitutional.

The Charter contained other sections that sought to balance these rights with other interests. Most relevant to the abortion debate was section 1, which states that "the Canadian Charter of Rights and Freedoms guarantees the rights and freedoms set out in it subject to such reasonable limits prescribed by law as can be demonstrably justified in a free and democratic society" (Canada 1982). This provision (one that makes it very different from the US Bill of Rights) means that the courts can rule that, even though a given policy or law violates specific constitutional rights, it can be judged constitutional overall if it can be sufficiently justified under section 1 (or another section).

Yet, successfully invoking section 1 is not easy. The burden of proof lies with the court/government – that is, it must prove that the limitation is justifiable. And the bar for what counts as acceptable proof and justification is high. Since 1986, the Supreme Court of Canada has employed what is referred to as the Oakes test (as it was first enunciated in *R. v Oakes*) to determine what counts as a "justifiable" reason. Briefly, the Oakes test identifies two main criteria that must be met.

First, the court/government must prove that the "objective to be served by the measures limiting a Charter right [are] sufficiently important to warrant overriding a constitutionally protected right or freedom" (*R v. Oakes* 1986, 105). Second, the limitation must pass a three-part proportionality test to ensure it is not overly broad.[11]

In many ways, the Charter opened up a new possibility for the legal contest over Canada's abortion laws. On one hand, as section 7 of the Charter identified a clear individual right to life, liberty, and security, abortion reformers had a new means by which they could ask the courts to strike down section 251. On the other hand, section 1 of the Charter meant that there were provisions that would enable anti-abortion groups to argue that, even if a woman's right to life, liberty, and security was found to be violated by section 251, the violation was justified.

5.3 Abortion in the Courts, Round 2: *R. v. Morgentaler*, 1988

In this dynamic and uncertain legal context, Henry Morgentaler decided to "force the abortion decision onto the courts" once again (Brodie, Gavigan, and Jenson 1992, 58). He began by challenging Canada's abortion law in other provinces – opening clinics in Winnipeg and Toronto in defiance of section 251. In 1983, Toronto police raided the Morgentaler clinic in that city, and, in 1984, Morgentaler along with two other doctors from his office were charged with providing women with illegal miscarriages. Once again, a jury acquitted Morgentaler of all charges. After the government appealed, the Ontario Court of Appeal rejected the acquittal and ordered a retrial. Morgentaler appealed this decision to the Supreme Court of Canada, which agreed to hear his case (*R. v. Morgentaler*).

Morgentaler's second case before the Supreme Court of Canada forwarded seven questions to the court regarding the constitutionality of section 251. The main two ones were as follows: (1) did section 251 infringe on a pregnant woman's constitutional right to "life,

---

11 In particular, the limitations must be proven to be "fair and not arbitrarily, carefully designed to achieve the objective in question and rationally connected to that objective." In addition, the "means should impair the right in question as little as possible."Finally, the larger the impairment of the rights ("the more severe the deleterious effects of a measure"), "the more important the objective interest must be" (*R. v. Oakes* 1986).

liberty and security" as guaranteed by section 7 of the Charter and, (2) if so, was this infringement justified under section 1?

In some respects, the court's decision was clear: its 5–2 decision unequivocally struck down section 251 as unconstitutional. At the same time, it was a highly complicated decision that had three separate justifications written for the majority position as well as one dissenting opinion for the minority position. Despite its complexity, the decision embodied a number of clear practical conclusions. First, and most importantly, the court ruled that section 251 did, in fact, infringe on a woman's right to life and security of the person in several ways. According to Chief Justice Dickson and Justice Lamer,

> Section 251 clearly interferes with a woman's physical and bodily integrity. Forcing a woman, by threat of criminal sanction, to carry a foetus to term unless she meets certain criteria unrelated to her own priorities and aspirations, is a profound interference with a woman's body and thus an infringement of security of the person. A second breach of the right to security of the person occurs independently as a result of the delay in obtaining therapeutic abortions caused by the mandatory procedures of s. 251 which results in a higher probability of complications and greater risk. (*R. v. Morgentaler* 1988, 32–33)

Second, although this was only explicitly identified by one justice (Justice Bertha Wilson), the court noted that section 251 violated section 7's guarantee of the individual's right to liberty, in addition to life and security. According to Justice Wilson,

> [T]he "right to liberty" contained in s. 7 guarantees to every individual a degree of personal autonomy over important decisions intimately affecting his or her private life. Liberty in a free and democratic society does not require the state to approve such decisions but it does require the state to respect them. A woman's decision to terminate her pregnancy falls within this class of protected decisions. It is one that will have profound psychological, economic and social consequences for her. It is a decision that deeply reflects the way the woman thinks about herself and her relationship to others and to society at large. It is not just a medical decision; it is a profound social and ethical one as well. Section 251 of the Criminal Code takes a personal and private decision away from the woman and gives it to a committee which bases its decision on "criteria entirely unrelated to [the pregnant woman's] own priorities and aspirations." (*R. v. Morgentaler* 1988, 36–37)

Third, the court determined that these violations of the basic Charter rights of individuals were "not in accordance with fundamental justice" and thus was not justified under section 1. Essentially, the majority held that section 251 passed neither the "importance of the objective interest" test nor the proportionality test as outlined in *Oakes*. In reaching this conclusion, the court noted the importance of the issue for individual rights of Canadian women; the huge disparities of access created by the requirements of having a TAC; the fact that systematic delays due to the TACs had the practical effect of increasing the health risks to pregnant women; and that the effects of the legislation far exceeded the minimum required to protect whatever societal interests might exist in regulating abortion. Thus, the court ruled that the violations created by section 251, to the life, liberty, and security of persons could not be justified under section 1 of the Charter. Section 251 was therefore struck down as unconstitutional.

Fourth, despite the fact that a majority of justices found that section 251 itself was not justifiable, some from the majority left open the possibility that legislation embodying much narrower limits on abortion access might be justifiable under section 1. Justice Wilson noted that "a woman's right to control her own person becomes more complex when she becomes pregnant" and the Canadian state might potentially have some justifiable interest (under section 1) in putting "reasonable limits" on the woman's right (*R. v. Morgentaler* 1988, 38). Justices Beetz and Estey also noted that, should much narrower legislation be passed, it might be able to pass the tests of the importance of objective interests and proportionality if the law's measures were linked precisely to the higher degree of danger to health in the late months of pregnancy (36).

Finally, the court was clear that it was not ruling on the question of whether the fetus had legal standing as a person and thus would have individual rights under section 7 of the Charter. This meant that the anti-abortion argument that the fetus has a constitutional right to life was neither accepted nor rejected by the Supreme Court in *Morgentaler*. As we will see later, the court would be forced to explicitly deal with the issue of fetal personhood in the coming years.

The *Morgentaler* decision was a major victory for Dr. Henry Morgentaler, feminists, and abortion rights activists across Canada. It also both reflected and broadened the discourse of the abortion debate that had previously characterized legal decisions. On one hand, it reinforced the medicalized perspective, as multiple justices (particularly Dickson, Lamer, Beetz, and Estey) largely agreed that section 251 was unconstitutional because the Charter's section 7 guarantee of security of the person "must include a right of access to medical treatment for a condition representing a danger to life or health without fear of criminal sanction" (Beetz, quoted in Tatalovich 1997, 76). On the other, it also marked a partial legal acceptance of the "women's rights" arguments of the Canadian abortion rights movement and "transplant[ed] the rhetoric of choice into the domain of law" (Brodie, Gavigan, and Jenson 1992, 59). As noted above, Justice Wilson's decision framed abortion as not simply as a medical issue of security or a necessary precondition to women's liberty. She also identified abortion as an integral part of women's constitutional right to freedom of *conscience* guaranteed by section 2(a) of the Charter and as such represented a choice that the state must respect, even if it does not approve.

While the court struck down section 251, it did not bar Canadian lawmakers from formulating a new abortion law. Rather it left open the door for Parliament to create a new law that reflected "a balance between the state's 'legitimate' interest in the foetus and the constitutional protection guaranteed to Canadian women under the Charter of Rights and Freedom" (Brodie, Gavigan, and Jenson 1992, 59). Despite claims that the decision was an example of an activist court used by like-minded legal elites to undemocratically create laws of their preference (see, e.g., Morton and Knopff 2000; Morton and Allen 2001), the court merely struck down the existing law and left it to Parliament to decide if and how it should regulate abortion. In fact, in comparison to the *Roe* decision in the US, the *Morgentaler* ruling was much less prescriptive. Whereas *Roe* outlined very clear guidelines about what constitutionally acceptable abortion legislation would look like (e.g., with its trimester framework), the *Morgentaler* decision refused to set any policy guidelines or restrictions for a new abortion law. Instead, it returned the issue to Parliament – which would struggle for three years about what to do.

5.4 Establishing a "Sense of the House": The Parliamentary Abortion Debate of 1988

On the political front, following the *Morgentaler* decision in January 1988, Prime Minister Brian Mulroney's Conservative government tabled a motion in Parliament regarding abortion. The motion – which proposed liberalizing abortion access throughout the first three months of pregnancy while criminalizing it in later stages – was meant to act as a guide in drafting a new abortion law. A free vote on the motion was held in Parliament on 20 May 1988, where it was defeated 147–76, with opposition coming from members of Parliament who advocated stricter regulation as well as those who advocated more liberal access to abortion. Reluctant to force a vote at such a dynamic and divisive moment, in July 1988 the government sought "a sense of the House" – an open debate on the issue, where MPs on both side of the debate were free to "air their views and to introduce their own amendments to the government's resolution" (Brodie, Gavigan, and Jenson 1992, 69). From 26 to 28 July, seventy-five MPs gave speeches – 57 per cent were clearly anti-abortion, 21 per cent were clearly pro-choice, and the remaining 21 per cent pressed for a middle ground (69).

Political scientist Janine Brodie argues that the pro-choice response in the House was defined by two complementary discourses: one focused on pragmatic health concerns and another centred on rights. Given the prominence that the pragmatic medicalized case for legal abortion had in North America (as necessary to address the dangers of "back-alley" abortions), it is not surprising that it was present in the 1988 Parliamentary debate. The House was reminded that "we cannot go back to making abortion illegal because ... it will simply force women to seek illegal abortion in unsafe, and completely unhealthy way" (quoted in Brodie, Gavigan, and Jenson 1992, 74). The speakers made reference to "used coat hangers" and "vacuum cleaners" to reinforce their point and continued to construct women primarily as mothers or potential mothers (74).

The rhetoric of rights and the feminist notion of bodily integrity and women's choices was a second major theme among pro-choice MPs. This approach argued that "only [women] can make [the choice] about the product of their womb" (quoted in ibid., 75). Within this discourse, women were increasingly framed by pro-choice MPs as independent moral agents capable of making their own reproductive decisions. As the Minister responsible for the Status of Women, Barbara McDougall, passionately declared, "Make no mistake, women make the right choice, a far better choice than you or I or all of the pageantry of institutions that have been invented ... from the beginning of time" (76).

On the other side, anti-abortion discourse sought to simultaneously "discredit the medical profession as arbitrators in moral disputes and, at the same time, embrace medical science as the irrefutable guarantor of the claim that life begins at conception" (Brodie, Gavigan, and Jenson 1992, 79). Ultimately, anti-abortion MPs depicted abortion as murder and vacillated between a negative discourse condemning women and a positive rhetorical campaign to "protect life" (79). These arguments were often reinforced with images of the fetus depicted as completely separate from the pregnant woman. On Brodie's analysis, "the pregnant woman, according to this discursive construction, represents shelter, nourishment, and time. She is a mechanical incubator ... The foetus, from conception, is autonomous and self-propelling" (81). Many of the anti-abortion speeches bear out this idea, with one MP telling the House that "the umbilical cords and the placenta belong to the baby. They are not part of the mother's body" (82).

This fetal-centric discourse was buttressed by additional themes. Some anti-abortion MPs opted to frame the abortion issue as "a concern for the entire human family" (quoted in Brodie, Gavigan, and Jenson 1992, 82). And women were frequently represented as morally bankrupt and in need of being controlled by legal deterrents. As one MP argued, "for those who have no moorings, no ethical guidance mechanism left, the only thing left is the law" (84).

After heated debate in the House, a free vote was held on five distinct possible abortion amendments. These ranged from the Bosley Amendment, which would have made abortion a decision strictly between a woman and her doctor, to the Mitges Amendment, which would have prohibited any abortion except when two doctors agreed that the continuation of the pregnancy would endanger the life of the mother. In the end, no clear consensus emerged. While the profoundly anti-abortion Mitges Amendment came the closest to passing, the government judged that it had gained no "sense of the House" to help it develop new legislation (Brodie, Gavigan, and Jenson 1992, 87).

The issue became less of a pressing political concern in Parliament when Mulroney called a federal election in November 1988. For despite the ambiguity surrounding the future of legal abortion in Canada, only 1.5 per cent of a national sample identified abortion as the most important issue of the election campaign (ibid., 88). The vast majority of Canadians were not overly concerned with the new status quo of abortion. This lack of interest did not deter the anti-abortion movement. Not only did the anti-abortion lobby publicize the positions of all of the candidates on abortion, it also targeted ridings where pro-choice candidates were seeking re-election by lending their organizational resources to anti-abortion candidates. Following the election, the Mulroney government waited almost a year before re-introducing a bill concerning abortion, as it was a divisive issue that had not been of central concern to most voters.

And during that year, several new rulings came down from the Supreme Court that would strengthen the constitutionality of abortion rights.

5.5 Abortion in the Courts, Round 3: Borowski's Attempt to Establish Fetal Rights

Despite the Supreme Court's attempt in *Morgentaler* to avoid several important questions, including the legal status of the fetus, and to explicitly return the abortion question to Parliament, it soon faced these questions again. In March 1989, a case brought by well-known anti-abortion activist Joe Borowski reached the court. Borowski was a former vice-president of the United Steel Workers of America and New Democratic Party (NDP) cabinet minister in the Manitoba legislature. He had long been known as a social conservative who left the NDP caucus to sit as an independent in order to try to prevent public funds from being spent on hospitals that provided out-of-province abortion referrals. After he lost his seat in the Manitoba legislature in 1977 (running as an independent on an anti-abortion platform), he devoted much of his life to anti-abortion activism. He spent time in prison for withholding income taxes for five years to protest against section 251. In 1977 he became coordinator of the organization Campaign Life in Manitoba, and in 1981, during the peak of his battle with the Canadian courts, he underwent an eighty-day hunger strike in honour of "the unborn children of Canada" (Morton 1992, 66).

Borowski's legal campaign began in September 1978, when he argued on behalf of fetal rights before the Saskatchewan Court of Queen's Bench. Issuing a "direct attempt to force the Canadian Supreme Court to grant legal protection to the unborn," he argued that section 251 contravened the right-to-life provision of the Canadian Bill of Rights, which was still in force at the time (Tatalovich 1997, 79). It would take Borowski five years of court battles before being granted legal standing to represent the unborn, during which time the Charter of Rights of Freedom was implemented. As a consequence, his final legal argument would use a strategy very similar to the one used by Henry Morgentaler, arguing that section 7 granted "everyone," including fetuses, the "right to life, liberty and security" (79).

In 1983, the Saskatchewan Court of Queen's Bench ruled against Borowski, maintaining that the fetus was not a legal person and thus was not protected by section 7 or section 15 of the Charter. Although Borowski appealed to the Supreme Court of Canada, by the time his case reached the court, in 1989 (*Borowski v. Canada*), section 251 had already been declared unconstitutional under *Morgentaler*. Accordingly, in its ruling on 9 March 1989, the court sidestepped the issue of whether the fetus has a right to life under the Charter by claiming that, since *R. v. Morgentaler* had already overturned Canada's abortion law, Borowski's appeal was moot. According to the Supreme Court, abortion was no longer considered a "live controversy" and it ruled unanimously that Borowski had effectively lost his court standing.

Borowski's discourse inside and outside the court reflected the angry and aggressive anti-abortion arguments of the period. Legally, Borowski's arguments were grounded in a fetal personhood discourse and emphasized the typical moral and scientific arguments supporting this contention. His extra-legal discourse, however, reproduced the other, more aggressive, tones of popular anti-abortion discourse. He would regularly depict women seeking abortions as "callous." He once arrived at the Supreme Court for a day of hearings carrying a bag with two large glass jars, both containing fetuses, claiming that if the judges had only been able to see them and "pass them hand to hand" it would have been "very convincing evidence" (Morton 1992, 271). When his appeal failed, he turned on the courts, declaring that if he had been in Ottawa for the announcement, he "probably would have gone into the court and punched the judges in the nose" (272) and that "if the court will not act to save babies then ... people ... will have to do it themselves" (quoted in Brodie, Gavigan, and Jenson 1992, 95). Given that many people saw Borowski as the spokesperson of the Canadian anti-abortion movement, this only further cemented impressions of the anti-abortion movement as an extremist movement.

5.6 Abortion in the Courts, the Final Round: *Tremblay v. Daigle*

Although *Borowski* was a blow to the Canadian anti-abortion movement, the next year would see an even more important ruling. Following the defeat of Borowski's constitutional challenge, a number of "fathers' rights" cases seeking to prohibit specific women from exercising their right to an abortion made their way through the judicial system. While these cases were not entirely unprecedented,[12] none

---

12 Alberta had rejected such a request and, in the ruling in *Medhurst*, the Ontario Supreme Court ruled that a man did not have the right to stop a woman from obtaining an abortion. Feminist scholar Janine Brodie argues that "the prevailing medicalized definition of abortion protected women from third party vetoes because medical treatment was seen to be the choice of women alone" (Brodie, Gavigan, and Jenson 1992, 91).

had been successful before July 1989. Then, within the span of several weeks, several injunctions were granted, beginning in Ontario with the *Dodd* case. The most famous was granted on 8 July 1989 when Jean-Guy Tremblay successfully obtained an injunction preventing his former girlfriend, Chantal Daigle, from terminating her pregnancy. In an unprecedented 3–2 decision, the Quebec Court of Appeal upheld the injunction, declaring the fetus a "distinct human entity," in accordance with the Quebec Charter, reasoning that "clearly echoed the central themes of pro-life discourse" (Brodie, Gavigan, and Jenson 1992, 93). The ruling was particularly shocking to many observers, as Daigle had testified that her relationship with Tremblay had been an abusive one and that he had intimidated her into discontinuing her use of birth control. Nonetheless, the court ruled that Daigle's pregnancy had been voluntary, further arguing that "the rule of nature is that pregnancy must lead to birth" and that "pregnancy is not an attack on a women's physical well-being"; thus abortion could never be justified as medically therapeutic (93).

Daigle immediately appealed the decision to the Supreme Court of Canada. While awaiting the decision, she disguised herself and procured an abortion in the United States, despite the Court of Appeal's ruling. Although the specific issue of Daigle's abortion was no longer relevant, the Supreme Court "decided not to skirt the issue" (Brodie, Gavigan, and Jenson 1992, 96). Indeed, it not only unanimously ruled against Tremblay's claim and the Appeal Court's decision, but it also unequivocally tackled the status of the "fetal rights" by deciding that "the substantive rights which are alleged to support [the injunction] – the rights accorded to a foetus or a potential father – do not exist" (*Tremblay v. Daigle* 1989, 572).

The ruling has several fascinating elements, but most important was the conclusive ruling that the fetus does not have the legal status and rights of personhood. According to the court, the issue of whether a fetus is a legal person cannot be settled by common usage (i.e., whether we usually use the term in that way in common discussion) or by medical usage (i.e., by the medical definition of the term fetus). Rather, the court clearly stated that the question of whether a fetus is a legal entity with the rights of persons must be decided by considering "substantive legal reasons that support a conclusion that the term 'human being' has a particular meaning" in a legal setting (*Tremblay v. Daigle* 1989, 532). In the court's unanimous view, it was patently clear that such reasons did not exist in Canada.

The judgment begins by noting that "a foetus is not included within the term 'human being' in the Quebec Charter" and that the Quebec Charter "does not display any clear intention on the part of its framers to consider the status of a foetus." This lack of explicit intention, the court stated, "is a strong reason in itself for not finding foetal rights under the Quebec Charter" (*Tremblay v. Daigle* 1989, 532). The ruling then determined that there was no evidence in the broader Quebec Civil Code to support the argument that a fetus is a legal person. Rather, the court concluded that the variety of provisions of the Civil Code regarding fetuses "do not accord the foetus any additional rights" beyond those already granted in the Code, which treat the fetus "as a person only where it is necessary to do so in order to protect its interests after it is born." The court therefore ruled that the Code cannot be understood to "generally accord a foetus legal personality" and further determined that, even in Anglo-Canadian law, "a foetus must be born alive to enjoy rights" (532).

With this finding, the court effectively extinguished the legal strategy of arguing for fetal rights in Canada based on the constitution and current laws. Fetal-centric arguments have remained highly visible and important in the public discourse of the anti-abortion movement and in the political realm. However, the Supreme Court's decision effectively nullified the possibility of using these arguments in a legal setting.

5.7 Drafting a New Abortion Law: Abortion in the Political Realm

As it became clear that the Supreme Court of Canada would not extend Charter rights to the fetus, Prime Minister Mulroney understood that his government "could no longer postpone introducing a new abortion law" (Brodie, Gavigan, and Jenson 1992, 97). On 3 November 1989, therefore, the Conservative government tabled Bill C-43, legislation that placed abortion back the Criminal Code. Bill C-43 prohibited all abortion unless a doctor ruled a woman's life or health would be threatened. Anyone found in violation of the law (whether the doctor who preformed the procedure or the woman who underwent it) could be sentenced to up to two years in prison. Framed largely within a discourse of medicalization, Bill C-43 went on to define the terms "health" in very general terms, as "physical, mental and psychological health," and "opinion" as "the generally accepted standards of the medical profession" (98).

The government regarded Bill C-43 as a much-needed compromise, with the prime minister delivering a passionate speech about the need for all sides to accept some concessions. Justice Minister Kim Campbell (who was presented as "a pro-choice woman of child-bearing years") stated that she was "very comfortable with the bill" as a necessary compromise (Brodie, Gavigan, and Jenson 1992, 99, 108). Bill C-43 continued to view abortion as an essentially medical issue – one to be decided by Canadian physicians – but it lowered the prerequisites that had been in place under section 251 by requiring that women needed the approval of only one doctor instead of three. However, it clearly recriminalized abortion and allowed it only under ambiguous terms, which seemed very likely to create the same inconsistency that was part of the reason why section 251 had been ruled unconstitutional.

Unsurprisingly, the new bill generated significant debate. Groups that represented the medical community, like the Canadian Medical Association, praised the government for continuing to define abortion as a medical procedure, but argued that the bill's poor design would ultimately "jeopardize the physician-patient relationship" (quoted in Brodie, Gavigan, and Jenson 1992, 103). Feminist abortion rights groups also criticized the ambiguity of the bill, arguing that if it was the government's intent "to allow abortion for environmental and socio-economic factors, it should have clearly specified this in the proposed legislation" instead of using the much more ambiguous statement that it would be permitted if the "health or life of the female person would be likely to be threatened" (102). They also criticized the degree of control that the bill gave to physicians, arguing that the bill failed to give women control over their own reproductive decisions.

On the other side, anti-abortion objections to the bill also revolved around the ambiguity of the term "health." Some predicted that the ambiguity would lead to "abortion on demand." Anti-abortion groups argued that the law failed to respect fetal life and, at a minimum, required gestational limits. The discourse espoused by anti-abortion MPs largely paralleled the arguments during the 1988 parliamentary debate: while they were predominantly concerned with the effect of Bill C-43 on fetal life, their discourse also included anti-woman tones and arguments.

On 29 May 1990, the House of Commons narrowly passed Bill C-43 (the vote was 140–131). Even though the bill would not be legally enforced until it received approval from the Senate, the Commons vote had immediate effects. Doctors, unsure of how Bill C-43 could affect them individually, withdrew abortion services, and hospitals across the country began turning away women seeking abortion services (Brodie, Gavigan, and Jenson 1992, 98).

Forceful public opposition to Bill C-43 emerged, with both sides using many of the same arguments that were represented in earlier parliamentary debates. In response, the Senate held two months of hearings before holding a free vote on the bill on 31 January 1991. Astoundingly, the result was a 43–43 tie, the first tie in the history of the Senate. Given the rules of the Senate, a tie constituted the defeat of the bill – the first defeat in thirty years of a government bill in the upper chamber. The government, perhaps sensing that Bill C-43's "defeat in a Senate dominated by Progressive Conservatives was due to lukewarm support [even] among their partisans" (Tatalovich 1997, 94), announced that it would not reintroduce new legislation on the issue. To this date, C-43 is the last abortion bill officially tabled by a government in the House of Commons.

5.8 Anti-abortion Violence

As the number of defeats grew for the anti-abortion movement, frustration intensified in certain sectors of the movement. In this context, some activists began to advocate and employ more extreme protest tactics, and a small minority of extremists resorted to violence. Drawing on tactics pioneered by groups like Operation Rescue in the United States, by the end of the 1980s some Canadian anti-abortion activists began a crusade of civil disobedience to "save the unborn" (Brodie, Gavigan, and Jenson 1992, 90). Popular targets of anti-abortion blockades were Vancouver's Everywoman's Health Clinics and Toronto's Morgentaler Clinic. Like their American counterparts, militant anti-abortion protestors announced that they were willing to go to jail in order to "save one baby" and to "serve the Lord" (90). However, these extremist discourses and tactics –taken up largely by Catholic revivalists – would prove less effective in Canada than they had been in the US. Court injunctions regulating where and in what ways protesters were allowed to demonstrate prohibited the most extreme attempts at clinic blockades. In Vancouver, protestors faced the threat of a five-month jail sentence for disobeying such an injunction. In Toronto, anti-abortion activists were prohibited from protesting within 500 feet of the Morgentaler Clinic (90).

As we saw in chapter 4, the use of these new confrontational strategies in the US was accompanied by the spread of violent anti-abortion attacks on clinics and doctors in the 1990s. Although somewhat less intensely, Canada also experienced this trend. Canadian abortion clinics were directly targeted and experienced both vandalism and arson attempts. In 1990, two men broke into a clinic in Vancouver and destroyed a variety of equipment. In 1991 and the early months of 1992, both the Edmonton and Toronto Morgentaler Clinics were damaged by arson attacks. On 18 May 1992, the Toronto Morgentaler clinic was completely destroyed by a firebomb. In November 1996, the Edmonton Morgentaler Clinic was the target of a butyric acid attack (Arthur 1999).

Anti-abortion terrorists also began targeting doctors who performed abortions. In 1994, British Columbian doctor Garson Romalis was shot at his Vancouver home. He survived only because his medical training allowed him to staunch the wound with a tourniquet (even so, he spent months in the hospital and never fully recovered). Shockingly, Dr. Romalis was attacked again in July 2000, when he was stabbed outside his medical clinic, making him the only Canadian abortion provider to be attacked twice. Despite the first attack, Romalis continued to work as both a general obstetrician and an abortion provider. After the second attack, he left his general medical clinic (so as not to endanger other medical providers) and concentrated exclusively on providing abortions and training other doctors in these procedures (Mickleburgh 2014). In Hamilton, Ontario, Dr. Hugh Short's career as a surgeon was ended in 1995 when a sniper shot him through the window of his home. Dr. Jack Fainman also had to end his medical career (one that included delivering over 5,000 babies as an obstetrician) after being shot in his house in Winnipeg in 1997 (Fainman and Penner 2011).

Anti-abortion violence in Canada never reached the same levels as it did in the US. Nonetheless, these acts of violence had far-reaching consequences that went well beyond the specific physical harm to the individuals, institutions, and organizations that were attacked. Clearly these acts had very significant and lasting effects on the medical practitioners and clinics that were attacked. Some clinics were unable to continue operating. All had to increase their attention to, and investment in, security. Others reduced their public visibility (even today, the annual National Abortion Federation conference locations are not publicly divulged). Medical practitioners and staff also had to increase their personal security measures, whether moving from their homes, keeping their windows permanently shuttered, hiring bodyguards, or wearing bulletproof vests when in public.

Equally importantly, these instances of violence had widespread impacts well beyond the individuals and clinics involved. As a pattern of increasingly aggressive protests accompanied by concrete cases of violent attacks and assassination attempts emerged, a major chill was sent throughout the abortion-provider community. This type of politically motivated anti-abortion violence displays all the hallmarks of the classic definition of terrorism. For the key characteristic of terrorism, as opposed to other types of violence, is that it uses violence or the threat of violence to achieve specific political aims and force behaviour change on a much broader group than those who were specifically targeted by that violence. Such anti-abortion violence was a classic case of terrorism, as the violence was clearly political in nature (i.e., a political and moral rejection of current abortion laws and practices) and was not simply aimed at stopping a particular clinic or doctor from performing abortions but also sought to terrorize other doctors, medical staff, and patients into refraining from similar procedures.

The strategy of violence was, ultimately, no more successful in Canada than it was in the US. It painted the movement as extremist and dangerous, alienating many Canadians from the cause. Today, virtually all anti-abortion organizations in Canada (including groups like the Canadian Centre for Bio-ethical Reform, which, as we shall see in chapter 7, employs the most confrontational street-level tactics in Canada) explicitly reject the use of violence. Moreover, since the early 2000s, explicit and overt anti-abortion violence has all but disappeared in Canada.

5.9 Recent Anti-abortion Legislative Efforts

If extremist violence was one political tactic that a very small minority of anti-abortion activists employed in response to the political and legal defeats of the 1980s, another more mainstream reaction was for anti-abortion MPs to introduce private members' bills into Parliament. Private members' bills or motions are introduced by individual MPs and do not require the official support of a party or government. Since 1988, forty-four separate private members' bills and motions that sought to limit abortion access in at least some respect have been tabled in Parliament. None have been passed by the House of Commons. Even so, these bills (and several other anti-abortion strategies) provide a glimpse into how Canadian anti-abortion politicians and lawmakers have framed their position between 1988 and the first decades of the twenty-first century. Although their specifics vary, most of these private members' bills have fallen into five categories: (1) general abortion bans, (2) fetal personhood bills, (3) "conscience clauses," (4) bills to defund abortion, and (5) bills that seek to protect women from abortion.

5.9.1 General Abortion Bans

Perhaps the most straightforward way in which Canadian lawmakers have attempted to limit abortion has been through efforts to fully prohibit abortion. Seven of the forty-four private members' interventions have simply asked Parliament to recriminalize abortion in Canada. Liberal MP Don Boudria led many of these efforts, tabling four bills between 1989 and 1994 that sought to prohibit abortion. Three of these attempted to ban all abortions "except to save the woman's life," and the fourth sought to criminalize "every person who directly or indirectly requires a physician, nurse, staff member or employee of a hospital or other health care facility to perform or participate directly or indirectly in an abortion procedure" and to impose a two-year prison sentence on anyone found guilty (ARCC 2012). All of these four bills would have re-regulated abortion under stricter conditions than it ever had been previously. Moreover, they all positioned women as following their own immoral self-interest in ways that harmed both the fetus and the moral and legal standing of the medical community. Recently, it seems that most anti-abortion advocates have realized that full criminalization is unlikely to be a winning strategy. Thus, the most recent bill of this type, Bill C-338, introduced by Liberal MP Paul Steckle in 2006/7, sought to criminalize abortion only after twenty weeks of gestation (which is largely the medical norm in Canada anyway, with only a handful of abortion clinics offering the procedure up to twenty-four weeks).

5.9.2 Fetal Personhood

While direct bans are the most obvious type of proposed anti-abortion legislation, it has not been the most popular. Instead, the most frequent tactic of anti-abortion MPs since 1988 has been to extend the legal definition of "human being" to include the fetus so that it would be covered by the legal protections afforded "human beings" under Canadian law. Given the long history of fetal-right-to-life arguments in Canada and the anti-abortion movement's failure to convince the courts that the fetus should be accorded all the rights guaranteed under the Charter, the anti-abortion movement has since sought to insert that protection explicitly into the law through acts of Parliament.

Since 1988, seventeen private members' bills and motions have adopted the fetal-personhood argument. The first, Bill S-16, introduced immediately after the 1988 *Morgentaler* decision by Liberal senator

Stanley Haidasz, asked Parliament "to amend the Criminal Code to give full [legal] protection to 'unborn children'" (ARCC 2012). This became a fairly standard template for a variety of similar bills over the next two decades. Other bills went further by attempting to define abortion as homicide. Liberal MP Tom Wappel's Bill C-275 (tabled in 1989, 1991, and 1996), for example, not only sought to "redefine human being to include an embryo and a fetus" but also proposed "extending the prohibition against killing a human being to include the killing of fetuses and embryos" (Interim, n.d.).

As with previous laws in Canada, most of these private members' bills sought to place constraints on physicians and medical professionals as the primary way to re-regulate abortion. However, some bills also sought to implicitly or explicitly criminalize women who sought an abortion. In March 1997, for instance, Reform MP Keith Martin (an outspoken opponent of legal abortion) tabled a bill that proposed to "charge pregnant women who abuse alcohol, drugs, etc. with criminal endangerment of the fetus" (ARCC 2012). Women found guilty of fetal endangerment would be sentenced to a treatment centre. His bill is exemplary of at least two other trends in anti-abortion legislative proposals. First, it employs an "anti-woman" tone that was common in several of the bills. Second, it embodies an oblique strategy. Rather than directly and explicitly targeting abortion laws, Martin attempted to indirectly make abortion illegal by extending the legal definition of human beings to the fetus in relation to another issue, knowing full well that if the fetus were granted legal protection from a pregnant women's decisions in one context, it would become the legal basis for prohibiting abortion.

Fetal personhood bills continue to be employed as a strategy of the movement. Conservative MP Stephen Woodworth's 2012 Motion 312, for example, asked Parliament to create a committee to review the part of the Criminal Code "which states that a child becomes a human being only at the moment of complete birth" and to examine the medical evidence and legal impact of this statement (ARCC 2012).

5.9.3 Conscience Clauses

At a general level, medical "conscience clauses" are legal clauses attached to laws that allow individual medical providers to abstain from providing certain medical services for reason of religion or conscience. Beginning in the 1990s, conscience clauses have increasingly been raised with respect to reproductive issues in North America, particularly in the US. In Canada, anti-abortion conscience clauses were most popular during the late 1990s and first decade of the new century, with eight conscience-related private members' bills tabled between 1997 and 2008 by Liberal senator Stan Haidasz (twice), Conservative MP Maurice Vellacott (five times), and Liberal senator Raymond Perrault (once).

All of these bills aimed at entrenching a conscience clause in Canadian law that would protect physicians from being forced to perform abortion procedures. Senator Haidasz's Bill S-7, for example, aimed at preventing "coercion in medical procedures that offend a person's religion or belief that human life is inviolable" and sought to protect physicians from potential employers that might refuse to hire physicians who would refuse to perform duties that offended a tenet of their religion (ARCC 2012). (Haidasz's bill also contained a fetal personhood aspect.)

In reality, had even one of these conscience clauses been passed, it would have had little direct impact on abortion access, as the only doctors who have the expertise to perform abortions must choose to train to gain these skills. In general, Canadian medical schools rarely devote more than one lecture to abortion and the actual training of future abortion providers takes place mostly when doctors choose to undertake voluntary, elective residencies at abortion clinics themselves (Groen 2015). There is no evidence that medical personnel in Canada are coerced into providing abortions against their beliefs. However, conscience clause bills would also ensure that family doctors, for example, would not have to provide birth control or abortion-related counselling or referrals if doing so was against their religion – something that would indirectly have an impact on access to abortion.

5.9.4 Defunding Abortion

Another indirect strategy used by anti-abortion lawmakers is to try to defund abortion, although this, too, has had very limited success. Although abortion is generally covered by Canadian health care, because funding decisions related to health care fall under provincial jurisdiction, there are many regional variations (for full breakdown of abortion access and funding in Canada, see, NAF, n.d.-a). In most provinces, public funding is linked to the gestational age of the fetus. Ontario (24 weeks) and Quebec (23 weeks) have the longest period, with Alberta and BC funding until 20 weeks. Manitoba (16), Nova Scotia (15), Newfoundland (15), and the Northwest Territories (14) are in the middle of the pack. Yukon, Nunavut, and Saskatchewan fund abortions only until week 12 of pregnancy (although Saskatchewan reimburses abortion providers in Alberta for Saskatchewan residents whose pregnancies are over 12 weeks).

Two notable exceptions lie outside the Canadian norm of full public funding of abortion offered by medically authorized providers. Prince Edward Island has no abortion facilities, making it the only Canadian province where abortion is not a provided medical service. While the province will fund abortions performed at hospitals off-island – *if* the woman can find a PEI physician to give her a referral – no legal abortions have taken place on the island since 1982 (Boesveld 2011). Furthermore, PEI women are required to cover all their own costs (including gas, hotel, meals, and bridge/ferry tolls) associated with travelling to a province that offers the procedure (usually Nova Scotia or New Brunswick).

Moreover, the PEI government has adopted and consistently maintained a clear anti-abortion stance. Less than a month after the 1988 *Morgentaler* decision, PEI passed Resolution 17, which declared not only that the PEI legislature "oppose[d] the performing of abortions" on the island, but also provided for the resolution to be forwarded to "all three Federal political parties requesting the passage of legislation consistent with the intent of this Resolution" (CBC News 2013b). In 2013, a group of doctors and the National Abortion Federation Canada (NAF) proposed the creation of an abortion centre at one of PEI's hospitals and provided a business case showing that such a decision would save the government $37,000 a year and PEI women seeking abortions between $23,000 and $46,000 in associated travel costs (CBC News 2014). This proposal was studied intensively by a working group convened by Health PEI, an organization that is "responsible for the operation and delivery of publicly funded health services" on the island (Health PEI 2014). It reportedly gained significant support from senior health officials, including the CEO of Health PEI, who apparently stated that, if the province "can offer a service that's reasonable, we're obligated" to do so (CBC News 2014).

When the proposal became public, anti-abortion groups in PEI staged large public demonstrations and engaged in an intensive lobbying effort, claiming that abortion was dangerous for women and that NAF was trying to bring abortion on demand to PEI. In late 2013, Premier Robert

Ghiz stated that the government's policy regarding abortion would not change. In January 2014, the CEO of PEI Health was called by Health Minister Doug Currie and informed that the project had to stop because "there's no point in putting more resources into a project … that's against government policy" (CBC News 2014).

The second province that currently lies outside the Canadian norms regarding the delivery of abortion services is New Brunswick. In fact, New Brunswick has been the most effective of all the Canadian provinces in defunding abortion. Even prior to the 1988 *Morgentaler* decision, New Brunswick amended its Medical Act to restrict abortion procedures to hospitals. Following *Morgentaler*, the McKenna government further amended the Medical Service Payment Act to defund elective abortions performed in clinics, effectively reclassifying it as an unentitled service in 1989. As it stands now, in contrast to all other Canadian provinces, New Brunswick funds only abortions performed in hospitals. Moreover, prior to November 2014, women had to receive official authorization from two doctors stipulating the procedure was medically necessary. Things may be slowly changing, however. The provincial Liberal government elected in September 2014 repealed the two-doctor authorization policy in late 2014, meaning that women do not need official authorization to have their hospital-provided abortion funded. However, at the time of writing, the government has not yet changed its funding policy. At this point, New Brunswick continues to refuse to pay for abortions performed in clinics – something that forced the Morgentaler clinic to close in 2014 and that continues to raise questions about the viability of the new clinic that opened in early 2015 on the site of the Morgentaler clinic in Fredericton. The New Brunswick funding policy, then, continues to have a significant impact on the accessibility of abortion for women across the Maritimes (Auld 2014).

While no other Canadian provinces have successfully defunded abortion, many attempts have been made to do so, both at the provincial and federal levels (by way of private members' bills and motions). Most notably, Alberta attempted to defund abortion in 1995. Facing intense pressure from the anti-abortion movement, Premier Ralph Klein put abortion funding to a free vote in the provincial legislature. The legislature voted in favour of defunding all abortions, except those that were deemed "medically necessary," and requested that the Alberta College of Physicians and Surgeons define what was a "medically necessary" abortion. In response, the College immediately condemned the actions of the legislature and defined all abortion as medically necessary.

The provincial government dropped the issue and continued to fund all abortions performed in hospitals. A year later, as required by the federal government, Alberta extended funding to private abortion clinics as well (Arthur 2011).

At the federal level, six bills and motions have been tabled in Parliament attempting to limit the use of provincial funds to pay for abortion services. Both Liberal MP Don Boudria and Reform MP Jim Pankiw tabled bills in the 1990s that sought to "amend the *Canada Health Act* to allow [the] federal government to penalize any province that paid for abortion deemed not necessary to preserve the life of the woman" (ARCC 2012).

Despite their relative lack of success up to this point, defunding initiatives remain popular avenues for the anti-abortion movement. Campaign Life Coalition (CLC), for example, has launched a national campaign targeting six provinces with the aim of increasing the barriers to accessible abortion by convincing these provinces to no longer fund abortion. Arguing that abortion is not a necessary medical procedure, but rather an expensive elective service, the campaign claims that it is "ludicrous to ask us to open up our wallets for these killings when the province is drowning in debt and genuine areas of health care are neglected." It argues that the funds used for abortions (in Ontario, for example) would be better used to "hire 200 family doctors, or 400 nurses, or purchase 20 MRI machines or provide therapy to 500 additional autistic kids" (CLC 2009a).

5.9.5 Bills and Motions Framed as "Protecting" Women from Abortion

Finally, as we will we elaborate on in Part II, there is an emerging anti-abortion discourse that claims to oppose abortion on the grounds that women need to be "protected" from abortion – language that has been mirrored in the justification for, and the character of, a variety of private members' bills over the past ten or fifteen years. Since 2002, six private members' bills and motions have positioned themselves as "protecting women." The first, M-523, tabled in 2002 by Alliance MP Garry Breitkreuz, asked that Parliament form a standing committee on health in order to "evaluate whether abortions are 'medically necessary,' and to compare health risks for women undergoing abortions to women carrying their babies to full term" (ARCC 2012). One year later, Breitkreuz introduced another related motion, this time asking Parliament to implement a Woman's Right to Know Act. This act, according to its proponents, sought to "guarantee women are fully informed of all the risk before deciding to abort their baby" (ARCC 2012). The motion also advocated the creation of penalties for physicians who performed an abortion without a woman's consent (regardless of the thorough regulation of consent by the medical community itself).

Since 2010, one bill and one motion have been tabled that oppose abortion on the grounds of protecting women. Bill C-510, tabled by Rod Bruinooge in 2010, sought to protect women from "abortion coercion," and MP Mark Warawa's Motion 408 asked Parliament to "condemn discrimination against females occurring through sex-selective pregnancy termination" (ARCC 2012). Bill C-510 and M-408 both depart substantially from their anti-abortion predecessors in that they are grounded in a seemingly progressive language of women's rights and health. While we will deal with both of these Parliamentary interventions in detail in the following chapters, what is important to understand here is that, while the majority of anti-abortion bills and motions tabled in the last two decades have focused primarily on argument of fetal personhood, there seems to be a new anti-abortion trend that increasingly attempts to frame anti-abortion legislation squarely within the feminist language of women's rights.

5.10 Conclusion

In this chapter, we have examined Canada's history of abortion politics since the 1970s and the ways in which the courts, Parliament, public opinion, and both the abortion rights movement and the anti-abortion movement engaged on this issue. These decades saw some important shifts in the discourse being used to define the issue and persuade Canadians to champion their position. While medicalized language that highlighted the dangers of illegal abortions remained an important resource for abortion rights advocates, these activists also increasingly appealed to women's right to choose and employed arguments that highlighted the equality dimension of abortion policy. Anti-abortion advocates, on the other hand, not only intensified their use of fetal-centric arguments, but they also increasingly framed their public discourse in religious and often "anti-woman" language. Following the 1988 *Morgentaler* decision, their protest tactics became more aggressive, and small pockets of anti-abortion extremists used terrorist tactics to try to force change violently. At the same time, anti-abortion politicians and lobby groups tried a variety of strategies to introduce new legal barriers (some direct, some indirect) in order to either prohibit abortion or decrease the real accessibility of abortion in Canada. None of these strategies have proved particularly effective or successful, however, and, between the mid-1990s and the end of the first decade of the twenty-first century, the abortion debate seemed largely closed and settled from a political, legal, and even civil society perspective.

Chapter 6

Intermezzo: The History of the Abortion Debate in North America

The preceding chapters covered a lot of historical ground in sketching the 200-year political, legal, and discursive history of the abortion debate in North America. Therefore, before we turn to the contemporary analysis of Part II, we want to distil some of the key implications our findings (up to this point) hold for two questions: (1) In what ways has the historical unfolding of the abortion debate in the US and Canada been similar, and in what ways has it been different; and (2) What does the historical record suggest about the accuracy of the traditional portrait?

6.1 Abortion Politics in the United States and Canada: Historical Similarities and Differences

One of the most obvious similarities in the history of the abortion debate in Canada and the United States is that, from the early 1800s to the mid-1960s, their respective arcs of abortion regulation followed broadly similar paths. Both countries, although in slightly different ways and at slightly different time periods, shifted away from a relatively permissive common law tradition that allowed pre-quickening abortion and was not especially punitive of post-quickening abortion. Although the United Kingdom and Canada moved to criminalize abortion from 1803 to the mid-1800s (when this transition was essentially complete), similar state level laws in the US did not begin to spread across the nation before 1850, and it was the first decade of the twentieth century before the process was complete. Nonetheless, all three countries ended up with broadly comparable laws that made abortion illegal. By the 1960s, the UK, Canada, and the US all saw the beginnings of what would become significant movement towards liberalization of abortion laws.

Moreover, the courts in both the US and Canada played central roles in shaping the course of abortion legalization since the 1970s.

However, there are also some important differences between the countries. Given the much more decentralized political system in the US (and the fact that abortion law is regulated at the state level whereas in the UK and Canada it is regulated by federal law) – both the criminalization and the liberalization of abortion policy at the legislative level looked quite different. In the US, for instance, efforts to criminalize abortion were state-by-state efforts, whereas in the UK (and in post-Confederation Canada), a single bill in Parliament covered the entire country. Moreover, since the 1970s, the nature of abortion legislation in the two countries has diverged dramatically. In the US, anti-abortion legislation has proliferated – to some degree at the federal level but most dramatically at the state level, with many different types of anti-abortion legislation (including laws that seem to contradict the dictates of *Roe*) having been passed in legislatures over the past forty years. The pace of anti-abortion legislation has increased dramatically over the past decade, with 2011 to 2013 being record years in terms of the number of anti-abortion bills being passed in the US. In contrast, since the 1969 reforms in Canada, there have been no successful legislative efforts to pass anti-abortion bills. Not only have none of the over forty private members' bills been passed, but even the federal government's attempt to introduce new laws in the late 1980s was defeated – and this in a context in which the Supreme Court of Canada had stuck down the only existing law regulating abortion.

If we compare the type of legislation that has been (often successfully) introduced in US legislatures with those bills that have been (unsuccessfully) introduced in Canada's Parliament over the past forty years, we can also see some important differences. There are, of course, some similarities: the anti-abortion movements in the US and Canada clearly share strategies, and lawmakers in both countries have attempted to pass various types of similar legislation, from conscience clauses to unborn victims acts. For the most part, however, even when the legislative efforts in the two countries appear similar on paper, there are nevertheless very important differences, not only in terms of the number of bills that are successfully adopted, but also in terms of the discursive justifications used to defend these bills.

In 2003, for example, under the guidance of President George W. Bush, the Unborn Victims of Violence Act was successfully passed by both the House of Representatives and the Senate and was eventually signed into federal law. The bill – colloquially known as Laci and Conner's Law after a pregnant California woman (Laci Peterson) who was murdered by her husband – was championed in part by the American anti-abortion organization the National Right to Life Committee (NRLC). The bill made it a separate crime to kill or harm an "unborn child" during an attack on a pregnant woman. Unsurprisingly, proponents of the bill framed it squarely in the language of fetal rights. Douglas Johnson, legislative director at the NRLC decried that "the criminals who commit these [acts of killing pregnant women] … are depriving these unborn children of the right to life" (Fox News 2004). Senator Rick Santorum supported this view, arguing that opposition to the bill from abortion rights supporters was "all about denying the humanity of the child" (ibid.). In the end, Congress was able to successfully pass the Unborn Victims Act into federal law by framing the bill almost entirely in the language of fetal personhood.

In 2007, Canadian MP Ken Epp introduced a very similar law in Parliament by way of a private member's bill. In some ways, Bill C-484 (named the Unborn Victims of Crime Act) paralleled the US law, both in its stated objective (to "protect fetuses from third-party attacks") and its fetal-personhood justification ("there are currently no criminal laws protecting children while they are still in the womb") (ARCC 2012). However, Epp's Canadian attempt differed in several crucial ways. Most obviously, it did not come close to being passed by Parliament. Similarly, as we will examine in more detail in Part II, fetal-centric arguments were not the only – or even the predominant – justification for Bill C-484. Rather, invoking traditionally feminist language, Epp argued that the bill was meant to respect and defend women's *choices*, suggesting that the act targeted situations "where the woman has made the choice to have the child, and that choice is taken away unilaterally, without her consent and usually with violence" (quoted in PWPL, 5 January 2008). In contrast, there was very little focus on women's choices and safety in the US debate – a difference, we would argue, that is illustrative of broader patterns of divergence between the two countries over the recent past.

There are also important similarities and differences regarding the question of real access to abortion (as opposed to the formal right to abortion). In the US, *Roe* unambiguously ruled that the formal right to abortion is constitutionally guaranteed during the first trimester. In the absence of a formal Supreme Court reversal of *Roe*, the anti-abortion movement has thus sought to create laws and policies that severely hamper the availability of real, practical access to abortion. Defunding bills such as the Hyde Amendment and state-level bills have, in practice, made it much harder to access abortion by ensuring that women have to pay for it themselves (something that does not make it impossible for women to get abortions, but certainly limits the real accessibility of abortion to low-income women and families). Similarly, targeted regulation of abortion providers (TRAP) legislation is designed to reduce (and has been very successful at reducing) the number of clinics and doctors who perform abortions by raising the costs and requirements of performing abortion to an unsustainable level.

Questions about real access to abortion exist in Canada as well. Real accessibility is strongly influenced by geography, since women in non-urban areas must travel much farther (and bear the associated costs) to access abortion. Indigenous women face many more obstacles in access-ing abortion care than other Canadian women, largely due to geograph-ical distance and the lack of confidentiality in their small communities (Smith 2010). Moreover, Prince Edward Island lacks even a single pro-vincial abortion provider, and legislation and policy in both PEI and New Brunswick hamper abortion access. That said, the defunding and TRAP bills so common in the US are essentially absent in Canada. In this respect, the experiences of American and Canadian women in access-ing abortion differ greatly. While barriers to abortion access continue to exist for some Canadian women, the main direct barriers are gen-erally limited to those living in remote indigenous communites, PEI, and New Brunswick. Moreover, in direct contrast to the US, provinces are not the main locus of anti-abortion politics, and no provinces, not even PEI and New Brunswick, have any piece of anti-abortion legisla-tion that is close to those of many American states. Instead, Canadian health care regulations ensure that the majority of abortion procedures throughout Canada are accessible and funded, at least in comparison to many American states.

The earlier chapters also reveal that the orientation of the main polit-ical parties to the abortion question – and the relationship between parties and the anti-abortion movement – is drastically different in the two countries. In the US, the anti-abortion movement has been enormously successful in influencing the Republican Party. A strong anti-abortion platform has been the official Republican policy since the 1980s. Not only are many of the most influential and vocal Repub-lican politicians strong anti-abortion advocates, but the movement has poured substantial resources into electoral politics and has had significant success electing anti-abortion members and translating that influence into legislation.

In Canada, the situation has been very different. Over the past forty years, the major political parties have treated abortion largely as a divisive issue to be avoided, rather than a mobilizing and polarizing wedge issue to be exploited. While vocal anti-abortion advocates have been elected as MPs for both the Liberal and Conservative parties (as well as the Reform Party, before it became part of the Conservative Party of Canada) and have publicly made their views known, these MPs and their bills have had no legislative success. Nor have they had much influence in shifting their parties' stance towards an anti-abortion position. Until 2014, the only major federal party to have an official policy on abortion has been the New Democratic Party, which has been officially in favour of abortion rights since the early 1970s. Traditionally, the Conservative Party of Canada and the Liberal Party have viewed the abortion issue as a question of conscience and have avoided imposing party discipline, instead allowing individual MPs to decide how they will vote on abortion-related issues. In May 2014, Liberal leader Justin Trudeau transformed this practice and announced that, under his leadership, all Liberal MPs would be expected to vote in favour of pro-choice positions (Saurette 2014). Moreover, even Conservative leader Stephen Harper explicitly ruled out reopening the debate throughout his tenure as prime minister. In direct opposition to the US, then, being outspokenly anti-abortion is generally viewed as a political liability rather than a career-advancing stance in Canada, even on the political right. In clear contrast to the US, the anti-abortion movement has essentially had no success co-opting or influencing the main political parties in Canada.

The role that the courts have played in influencing the nature of abortion policy is another interesting dimension of comparison between the two countries. On one hand, Supreme Court decisions in both countries have played defining roles in the abortion debate. Litigating and challenging laws has been a key strategy for both anti-abortion and abortion rights activists in both countries – and Supreme Court decisions have played key roles in decriminalizing abortion in both the US and Canada.

However, there are a variety of differences here too. *Roe* and *Doe*, for example, were decided fifteen years before the final *Morgentaler* case. Arguably, this meant that the Canadian public had much longer to acclimatize both to the idea of greater abortion access and to the idea that courts could justifiably strike down legislation such as section 251 of the Criminal Code. Furthermore, Canada had introduced the Charter of Rights and Freedoms only six years earlier. Thus the 1980s were a period of significant legal and constitutional re-interpretation – which may have influenced both the nature of the *Morgentaler* decision and the degree of intensity (or lack thereof) with which the broader public reacted to it.

The bases of the major US and Canadian decisions liberalizing abortion access were also quite distinct. In *Roe*, the primary principled argument centred on questions of privacy and choice – language that was quite close to the pro-choice discourse of the women's movement. In *Morgentaler*, only one judge, Justice Bertha Wilson, cited the right to liberty and choice in her reasoning. The majority decision instead focused primarily on the right to security (the right of women to access services crucial to their health) and equality of access (in light of the significant discrepancies in the ways in the which therapeutic abortion committees exercised their authority).

The precise content of the *Roe* and *Doe* decisions also differ from *Morgentaler* in important ways. In some ways, *Morgentaler* was much more sweeping than *Roe*, insofar as it struck down the abortion law of the land in its entirety. In other ways, it was quite deferential to Parliament. Not only did it leave open the possibility that the state might have an interest in regulating abortion, but it also refused to prescribe or even gesture towards what that regulation might look like, leaving all debate regarding the nature of a constitutional new law to Parliament. In contrast, *Roe* was much more prescriptive about future laws, establishing a clear framework that specified that there must be open access to abortion in the first trimester but that states could regulate abortion in the second trimester to protect women's health and safety and could regulate it even more strictly in the third trimester on the basis of fetal viability and women's health.

The post-*Roe* and post-*Morgentaler* legal history of the two countries is also very different. In Canada, subsequent decisions only solidified abortion rights, with the Supreme Court ruling against paternal rights on the issue of abortion and definitively stating that fetuses were not legally considered "human beings" under the Charter (and thus not protected by the Charter and its various rights). In contrast, post-*Roe* decisions in the US have incrementally eroded and watered down *Roe*, opening the door to a plethora of different types of anti-abortion legislation and policy at both the federal and state levels.

It is interesting to consider the similarities and differences regarding the question of religion in the abortion debate. As we have seen, none of the early efforts to criminalize abortion in the 1800s were driven primarily by religion in either country. Rather, both were motivated and spearheaded by physicians at a moment when they were seeking to establish their authority and control over the medical sphere. That said, institutionalized religion has operated as an important motivation and organizational network for the anti-abortion movement in both countries, particularly since the late 1960s. However, the influence of religious groups and discourse has been much more intense in the US. In particular, the religious fundamentalism and extremism that lies at the core of many parts of the American anti-abortion movement has been much less present in Canada – something that perhaps helps explain why Canada has not seen the same levels of anti-abortion violence and ultra-aggressive clinic blockading that characterized the US scene for several decades (although the legal injunctions and bubble zone laws that were quickly enacted in Canada are also an important explanatory factor).

Finally, there is the question of public opinion. Although it is difficult to measure public opinion across national borders (as regional differences, the phrasing of the questions, the timing, and the relationship to specific political events can all affect the results significantly), on the abortion question we can see some enduring and important differences. For the past forty years, Gallup has asked the following question in the US each year: "Do you think abortions should be legal under any circumstances, legal only under certain circumstances, or illegal in all circumstances?" The percentage of respondents who put themselves in each category has, perhaps surprisingly, changed very little since the early 1970s. In 1975, for example, 21% stated abortion should be legal under any circumstances, 54% under certain circumstances, and 22% illegal in all circumstances. Over the next 40 years, these numbers have varied somewhat, reaching a pro-choice high, for example, in 1994 (33% – 52% – 13%) and an anti-abortion high in 2009 (21% – 57% – 18%). Generally, the categories have remained relatively constant – within a few percentage points – over the past twenty years, as is confirmed by the poll in 2013 (26% – 52% – 20%) (Gallup, n.d.).

The situation is quite different in Canada. In its October 2012 poll, Forum Research asked the same question as Gallup uses. It found that 60% of Canadians believed that abortion should be legal in all circumstances, 30% thought it should be legal in some circumstances, and 8%

felt it should be illegal in all circumstances (Forum Research 2012). In other words, the percentage of Canadians who think abortion should be accessible in all circumstances is more than double that of Americans, and the percentage of Canadians who believe it should be illegal in all circumstances is less than half what it is in the US. Perhaps even more revealingly, the same poll showed that these numbers are not significantly different even among those who identify as conservative voters: a breakdown by partisan identification revealed that 47% of conservative voters believe that abortion should be legal in all circumstances, 37% in some circumstances, and 14% illegal in all circumstances.

In sum, while there are a number of obvious historical similarities between the two countries on the question of the political, legal, and social history of abortion, there are many key differences that should not be overlooked.

6.2 The Historical Abortion Debate and the Traditional Portrait

The historical overview in the past several chapters helps to contextualize what we have called the "traditional" portrait of the anti-abortion movement. In particular, it reveals that the image we have of the anti-abortion movement and its discourse is primarily a snapshot of the movement in a particular moment and place – primarily the US in the 1980s and 1990s – and that reading this image backward – or, for that matter, forward – risks misrepresenting the historical diversity of the debate around abortion in both the US and Canada.

One important characteristic of the traditional portrait is the notion that men have largely led the anti-abortion movement. Historically, this has been fairly true of both the US and Canada. Most of the major anti-abortion legislative efforts and organizations have been led by men – from Horatio Storer and the American Medical Association to Randall Terry and Operation Rescue. This was also largely the case in the UK and Canada (although it should be noted that, while the leadership of the movement was primarily male, much of the concrete organizing work in Canada in the 1970s was done by women).

Another element of the traditional portrait is its suggestion that the anti-abortion movement has always been motivated and structured by religion and religious institutions. In the early years of the movement, such a characterization is misleading, as the primary motivations and much of the organizational support for the move to criminalize abortion in the 1800s came from medical doctors who seem to have been primarily motivated by professional concerns about cementing their authority in the medical field. This changed dramatically in the 1970s and 1980s, as religious constituencies became politically mobilized around this issue. In the US, the rise of the religious right coincided and was intertwined with the emergence of the modern anti-abortion movement. In Canada, there was also a turn towards religious intensification in emergent anti-abortion organizations during the late 1970s and 1980s. While Canada and the US both saw the anti-abortion movement become populated and organized by religiously oriented activists throughout the late 1970s, 1980s, and beyond, this trend was much stronger in the US.

The traditional portrait also tends to represent the movement as focused almost exclusively on using legislation to ban and criminalize abortion. This captures an important dimension of the US movement, historically speaking. The first real mobilization of an anti-abortion movement in the US in the mid-1800s did focus largely on prohibiting abortion through legislation. Moreover, the post-*Roe* modern anti-abortion movement has also focused intensely on legislation and influencing electoral politics. That said, even in the US, most serious observers of the movement highlight that the anti-abortion movement has employed a wide range of activities (e.g., lobbying for legislation, counselling in crisis pregnancy centres, public protesting at abortion clinics, disseminating information to change public opinion) and used a wide variety of legislative tools beyond criminalization to work towards their goal. In Canada, long-term historical anti-abortion efforts focused primarily on criminalizing abortion through legislative changes and were much less involved in engaging in broader popular campaigns of persuasion until the 1980s. As we shall see in the next half of this book, however, the movement has significantly broadened its efforts since then.

The traditional portrait also tends to suggest that the strategies of persuasion and discourse used by the anti-abortion movement are marked by several characteristics. For example, the traditional portrait suggests that not only are anti-abortion activists motivated by religion, but also that anti-abortion discourse has always been suffused with explicitly religious language. Historically, this has certainly not been the case. Even in the US, before the 1970s, explicit religious appeals were not the primary discursive frames of those who argued for the criminalization of abortion. In fact, it was a largely medicalized language emanating from the American Medical Association (AMA) in the 1800s that was the primary discursive strategy for anti-abortion efforts. Even the early iterations of the modern US anti-abortion movement were relatively reluctant to use religious argumentation to forward their position. In the 1950s and 1960s, religious discourse was seen primarily as a rhetorical strategy associated with the progressive civil rights movement. At that time, religious language went hand in hand with Martin Luther King Jr., not with conservative attempts to limits civil rights. As the political relevance and influence of the Christian right grew, however, the anti-abortion movement began to internally debate how explicitly religious its discourse could be. Since the 1980s, the religious and fundamentalist nature of public anti-abortion discourse in the United States has been one of its defining characteristics.

For most of Canada's history, anti-abortion discourse also largely avoided religious frames. The early policy debates in Canada were primarily elite affairs, and while there was certainly moralized language, the debates tended to be framed through medicalized discourse, right up to the 1970s. By the end of the 1970s and in the early 1980s, however, important elements of the movement had embraced religious discourse much more publicly. Yet, given the fact that Canada did not witness the rise of anything comparable to the Christian right, its political discourse remained much less saturated by explicitly religious themes. Moreover, partly because the abortion reform legislation of 1969 was framed in markedly secular and medical terms, this more religiously oriented anti-abortion language gained little traction in the broader public and political realms.

Another key element of the traditional portrait is the notion that the anti-abortion movement has always used highly aggressive protest tactics, civil disobedience, and political violence to further its goals. Again, this has not been the case historically. In the US, aggressive street-level protests and blockades became widely used only in the 1980s as the movement became increasingly fundamentalist, politically radicalized, and frustrated with the perceived lack of progress taking place in the legal and legislative realms. Similarly, anti-abortion terrorism (bombings, arson, assassination of abortion providers) was certainly not present before emerging and dramatically escalating in the 1980s and 1990s. As discussed in chapter 3, the mainstream movement increasingly denounced anti-abortion terrorism as its counterproductive impact became clear, and anti-abortion violence has continued to fade since the late 1990s. Moreover, certain types of legislation (e.g., the Freedom of Access to Clinic Entrances Act) have limited some of the most aggressive types of protest (physically blocking the entrances to clinics, trespassing, threats of violence) since the mid-1990s (Wilson 2013).

In Canada, the anti-abortion movement had never adopted aggressive and violent tactics before the 1980s. In that decade, it did adopt some aggressive street-level protest tactics – including protesting outside clinics and attempting to block and harass staff and patients. However, bubble zone legislation and injunctions quickly limited the most intense types of protest around clinics. Thus, as we shall see in Part II, for the most part, anti-abortion street level protests have taken on quite different forms (with the notable exception of a few outliers such as protests by Linda Gibbons). As we saw in chapter 5, a small minority of extremist anti-abortion activists in Canada resorted to violence, including assassination attempts, bombings, arson, and acid attacks during the 1990s. However, by the next decade these intimidation tactics had fallen out of favour and have not made a significant comeback since that time.

Finally, the traditional portrait suggests that anti-abortion discourse has long been profoundly defined by anti-woman tones and has largely defended its position with reference to fetal-centric arguments. There is little doubt that, historically, there has long been a strong focus on fetal-centric arguments in the US. The focus on fetal personhood has been consistent from the beginning of the 1800s onwards. It seems more accurate to assert, however, that there have been several different tones regarding women and that these embodied varying degrees and types of negative representations of women.

The tone was perhaps less explicit and universal in the original push for anti-abortion legislation during the 1800s and early 1900s, focusing primarily on negatively portraying the "immigrant midwives" who were the primary providers of early abortion services. In fact, because these early discourses also were framed in medical terms, their tone towards the pregnant women seeking abortions was more infantilizing or patronizing than aggressively moralizing and judgmental. Although this historical discourse seems to have embodied a controlling attitude towards female reproductive health, it didn't primarily criminalize or explicitly vilify women. This dramatically changed in the 1970s and 1980s (especially with the rise of Operation Rescue), as the anti-abortion movement's discourse took on a highly charged, fundamentalist, and self-righteous "anti-woman" tone that characterized much of the religious right's discursive backlash against the changing gender norms and values of that period.

In Canada, the situation was fairly similar, as the early language justifying the criminalization of abortion was primarily a medicalized discourse stressing the importance of physician control and the medical dangers of abortion. However, during much of the early and mid-1800s, British and Canadian anti-abortion discourse and legislation took a much more punitive tone towards pregnant women themselves than in the US. Beginning in the 1970s, an even more explicit and aggressive anti-woman tone began to characterize anti-abortion discourse in Canada as activists such as Joe Borowski and Jean-Guy Tremblay demonstrated extreme misogyny at various points in their arguments.

In sum, our overview of the comparative political, legal, and discursive history of the abortion debate in Canada and the US demonstrates that the history of the anti-abortion movement is far more diverse and complicated than the traditional portrait suggests. While the traditional portrait helpfully highlights some characteristics of the American and Canadian anti-abortion movements and its discourse during the 1970s through the 1990s, many dimensions of this portrait cannot be extended back much beyond that time period. The question we are left with, however, is whether the traditional portrait remains helpful in understanding the discourse of the contemporary anti-abortion movement, particularly in Canada. This is the question we will now examine in Part II.

PART II

The Changing Voice of the Contemporary Anti-abortion Movement

Shifting Strategies: A Little Old, a Lot New, a Bit of Both

As outlined in the introduction to this book, many observers in North America interpret the abortion debate, and in particular the anti-abortion movement, according to what we have called the traditional portrait. With regard to the Canadian context, this portrait has encouraged many observers to make one of two related assumptions. First, to the extent that a contemporary anti-abortion movement exists in Canada, its character and its organizational and communication strategies are essentially the same as those used by earlier generations of Canadian and American anti-abortion activists. Second, because we don't see nearly the level or intensity of these traditional forms of anti-abortion advocacy in Canada, the movement has largely exhausted itself and is unlikely to be a particularly important player in abortion politics in the future.

How valid are these assumptions? As Part I has demonstrated, although there have been similarities between the abortion debates in these two countries, there have been important differences as well. We should not conflate the two, nor should we assume that the anti-abortion movements in these two countries are static or unchanging. This, in turn, suggests that we should periodically investigate, in a rigorous and empirical fashion, the nature of the organizational and communication strategies of the contemporary actors in the abortion debate in Canada. In Part II, we are particularly interested in examining the strategies of the contemporary anti-abortion movement in Canada. Do they conform to the main characteristics of the traditional portrait? Or has the movement and its public discourse departed from its historical predecessor and American counterparts?

As described in the introduction, the main way in which we have answered these questions has been by undertaking a systematic and empirically rigorous analysis of the public discourse of the contemporary Canadian anti-abortion movement. In chapters 8 through 11, we analyse what the movement is actually *doing* (discursively speaking) rather than what it *thinks* or *says* it is doing. We have chosen this as our primary method because profound changes of discursive strategy can sometimes take place across a movement, even if such a shift is not explicitly strategized and/or consciously intended by the actors within that movement.

That said, if there were to be indications that various actors within the Canadian anti-abortion movement have been consciously and explicitly debating their strategic vision, this would provide further evidence that the contemporary movement should be viewed as at least a partly distinct phenomenon with its own set of characteristics. Of course, the lack of this kind of strategic discussion doesn't rule out the possibility that a movement has changed its strategies of persuasion in practice. However, the presence of an explicit process of restrategizing would strengthen our contention of a significant shift and suggest that it is at least partially an intentional shift. This chapter's main objective, then, is to determine whether there are signs that some of the key actors in the contemporary anti-abortion movement in Canada have been engaging in a conscious and explicit reconsideration of their strategic approach.

Addressing this question is not without its challenges. When an established political or social movement fragments or consciously alters its strategy, it often experiences a sustained period of transition and reflection during which various actors discuss and debate the circumstances, the challenges and opportunities, the objectives, and the available means. Such processes often take place behind closed doors and usually can only be pieced together well after the fact through insider interviews and archival research. This is especially true in highly politicized and polarized environments since, in most cases, it is disadvantageous for advocacy groups to publicize their strategy for all, including their policy opponents, to see.

It seems possible that the contemporary Canadian anti-abortion movement might be experiencing such a moment today. On the one hand, because the movement has experienced very little success over the past twenty-five years, there is reason to suspect that key actors in the movement might be rethinking their strategy. Moreover, the movement itself is a diverse aggregation of different actors with shared goals but different motivations, reasoning, and strategic perspectives – conditions that generally lead to sustained debate across a variety of fora.

These conditions suggest that the movement might be ripe for an internal debate. On the other hand, given the highly polarized nature of the abortion debate (and, as we shall see, the generalized suspicion that many in the movement have towards the media, academia, and so on), any attempt to reconstruct the strategic debate is a fraught undertaking. For even if one were to interview the main actors, disentangling what is "accurate" information from what is self-interested "spin" might make the results highly unreliable.

One way to navigate these types of research challenges is to analyse what might be called "semi-public" sites of internal debate and discussion. While the medium and nature of these semi-public types of gatherings and conversations differ widely, what characterizes something as a semi-public site is that, although technically open to the public, it primarily functions to facilitate discussions between individuals and actors within the movement on issues that are most pressing to their political activism. What is so interesting about these types and sites of discussion is that the participants are often extraordinarily candid. It is almost as if, in a context where a large majority of the participants are known or assumed to be political allies and movement "insiders," participants forget that the event/space is still technically open. In this setting, it seems that many people can't resist, for the most part, acting and speaking as openly and honestly as they would in closed, confidential meetings. This seems to be true both of in-person events and of online discussion spaces.

Fortunately, the highly networked and increasingly online character of the contemporary anti-abortion movement lends itself to the creation of a rich set of semi-public spaces and debates that provide a window into the strategic thinking of the anti-abortion movement. These sources range from the annual March for Life youth conferences (during which strategic discussions and training are often key themes) to explicit Twitter and blogging posts by key actors to other members of the movement (again, often about anti-abortion strategy) and from the training materials produced by anti-abortion organizations (e.g., the National Campus Life Network, whose goal is to train new anti-abortion groups in effective strategy) to the detailed strategy documents posted publicly by some organizations (e.g., the Canadian Centre for Bio-ethical Reform). We do not mean to say that the conversations in these spaces are completely free from considerations of strategic communications and positioning. But, as the main purpose of these semi-public fora is to communicate and debate internally with other members of the movement, and many of such fora seem intentionally directed to other insiders, we believe that these sources provide a useful and reasonable data set, especially if it turns out that we find parallels between the explicit strategic discussions in these sites and the trends we analyse in chapters 8 through 11.

The central question that this chapter aims to answer is therefore the following: are there strong indications that key actors in the anti-abortion movement in Canada have been actively reconsidering their strategic approach? While the long answer is somewhat more complicated, the short answer is "yes."

7.1 Failing to Plan Is Planning to Fail: Results-Oriented Strategizing

One thing that is clear from a variety of the movement's semi-public discussions is that influential actors – ranging from those who most closely fit the traditional portrait to those who are the newest, youngest, and perhaps most active members – believe the movement must adopt new, results-oriented strategic perspectives. Consider a group that perhaps most closely fits the traditional portrait in Canada: the Association for Reformed Political Action (ARPA). ARPA is an explicitly religious organization, with an entirely male board of directors and leadership, whose goal is to "educate, equip and encourage Reformed Christians to political action and to bring a biblical perspective to our civil authorities" (ARPA Canada 2007). While it is a multi-issue advocacy organization, one of its most public efforts in the last several years has been the anti-abortion We Need a Law campaign.

This campaign acknowledges that the anti-abortion movement in Canada has, in one sense, failed entirely: "In the past 20 years, all attempts to pass a law protecting pre-born humans have failed" (We Need a Law, n.d.). Moreover, the campaign seems to implicitly admit that the movement has failed because it has been ineffective in its attempts at public persuasion, particularly in comparison with the abortion rights movement, which "has been very effective at convincing the Canadian people that there is no need for a law" (ibid.).

Yet this campaign suggests that, rather than feeling discouraged or resigned, anti-abortion activists should look to the future with optimism and recognize the many emerging strategic opportunities. In fact, ARPA believes that there is "hope that the fundamental right to life of all children will be protected by law in the very near future," given the fact that "a majority of Canadians think that children in the womb should be protected at some point during pregnancy"; that "scientific

and medical advances, combined with an increased awareness surrounding the abortion procedure, are affecting Canadians' view on
the status quo"; and the "startling reality that we are the only Western nation without protection for the pre-born child" (We Need a Law,
n.d.). We Need a Law thus envisions itself as a pro-active and innovative response both to the strategic failures of the anti-abortion movement in the political realm and to a changing Canadian context that it
perceives to be more supportive of fetal rights.

A variety of other groups in the movement have also been vocal
about the strategic opportunities that are emerging in Canada. Take
the Canadian Centre for Bio-ethical Reform (CCBR), for example. The
CCBR shares many characteristics of the traditional portrait. Like its
American counterpart (the Center for Bio-ethical Reform), the CCBR
has adopted an aggressive communications approach. This approach
includes an unreserved willingness to use of graphic visuals (pictures
of aborted fetuses) as well as unorthodox methods for sharing these
images (billboard trucks, giant banners, sidewalk demonstrations near
high schools, postcard campaigns targeting politicians). The CCBR's
argumentation is also reflective of traditional approaches and heavily
focused on the presentation of the fetus as fully human. In some ways,
then, one would not expect this group to be particularly vocal about the
movement's need to profoundly restrategize. And yet, it insists that this
is exactly what is necessary.

For the CCBR, it is crucial that actors in the anti-abortion movement
clarify their strategy. Its website therefore includes in-depth descriptions and justifications of its philosophy and approach, including
several detailed strategy documents explicitly outlining its vision,
objectives, strategies, and tactics. In their view, one of the key reasons
why the movement needs to revise its strategy is that many in the
movement seem to have forgotten its ultimate goal: "actually ending
abortion" (CCBR 2013b, 2). The CCBR, then, pushes other anti-abortion
actors to adopt a clear and unambiguous position: "End the Killing:
Make Abortion History" (CCBR 2011a, 2). The goal of the CCBR is not
to reduce the number of abortions or restrict their availability. Rather it
is to make "the killing of pre-born human beings unthinkable" (CCBR
2013h, 2).

Yet, pushing for the complete prohibition of abortion is not the
CCBR's only goal. It also believes that, if the contemporary movement
is going to capitalize on the potential opportunity it sees in Canada's
changing social and political environment, key actors need to develop

a far more focused tactical battle plan. The CCBR argues that activists must adopt a results-based perspective that focuses on methodically driving change by employing the most *effective* methods for the Canadian context. Members of the movement must "ask ourselves honestly: Do we really have a plan to accomplish this and are we evaluating our activities to test whether they help get us to this goal, or distract us from it?" (CCBR 2011a, 2).

The CCBR has therefore developed a detailed map of its advocacy tactics (some of which we will discuss later in this and following chapters), each with a clear analysis of its desired effect on different target audiences. The organization's strategic documents identify its target audience, including which regions to focus on, given the group's limited resources (Calgary and Toronto are the focus, reflecting the belief that Calgary leads the "new west" and the fact that "you cannot change the country with *only* Toronto, but you cannot change the country without Toronto"). In addition, these strategic documents identify the group's "pyramid strategy of communications," which outlines the purpose and impact of each of their various communication tactics (CCBR 2011a, 12–18). Moreover, cognizant of the criticism they face from both within and outside the movement (see, e.g., CCBR 2013a; CCBR 2007), the group's leaders explicitly claim to have "gone through the healthy process of questioning our approach, making sure we have good reasons and pure motives for it" and have outlined a strategic philosophy of their place and role within the anti-abortion movement that has "firmed our resolve that our work is right and effective" (CCBR 2011a, 5).

The CCBR appreciates the importance not just of *being* strategic and professional, but also of *appearing* highly professional, acknowledging the need for activists to "act seriously and convey a professional attitude," "reflect a high standard of professionalism," and be "respectful in all interactions with others" (CCBR 2013h, 40). As part of this professionalization, the CCBR advocates for clear and concrete timelines, arguing that, without this level of concrete granularity, it will not be able to actually drive change on the ground.

In order to mobilize concrete change, the CCBR has outlined an eighteen-year strategy of engagement, with the goal of ending abortion in Canada by 2030. Why eighteen years? Because that is the period between the first feminist abortion rights caravan in 1970 and the *Morgentaler* decision that struck down the federal laws criminalizing abortion in Canada (see CCBR 2013j). The CCBR thus sees itself as taking pages out of the women's movement mobilization strategy, forty years later. Moreover, like the 1970 Abortion Rights Caravan (see chapter 4), the CCBR's eighteen-year campaign is aimed not only at changing Canadian laws. Rather, it largely seeks to change public opinion, "because public policy is not likely to change unless public opinion does." As a result, the "CCBR's primary emphasis over the next two decades is an educational one" (CCBR 2011a, 3).

This focus on education highlights another one of the CCBR's new strategic goals: driving concrete culture change by training a new generation of young and vibrant anti-abortion activists. Believing its objective can be achieved only if public opinion shifts significantly – and aware that high school and university significantly liberalizes individuals' views on abortion[13] – the anti-abortion movement is currently investing in building a network of anti-abortion organizations in high schools and universities across the country. The National Campus Life Network (NCLN), for example, was founded in 1997 with the goal of "equip[ping] pro-life students across the country for campus life advocacy and network them with each other and the broader pro-life movement" (NCLN, n.d.). The NCLN's website and events aim to provide the tools and knowledge necessary to create effective anti-abortion university clubs. It holds an annual symposium for high school and university students and has also partnered with the Toronto Right to Life Association (TRL) to create a handbook for high school anti-abortion clubs (TRL 2012). What is clear from all of the NCLN's materials and events is that the next generation of activists is being taught to conceive of their advocacy in a strategic, communications-focused manner.

The TRL/NCLN high school manual, for example, stresses the importance of translating goals into specific, effective, and concrete actions. The entire package is designed to leverage the strategic vision of more established organizations to help build highly effective high school and campus groups. Such a purpose is evident in the way the manual describes the purpose of pro-life clubs ("a club that will save lives by using effective strategies"), how it encourages students to brainstorm about events ("choose and organize effective school events that will change hearts and minds and ultimately save lives"), and the inclusion of a sample calendar and materials that have already been

---

13 The National Campus Life Network (NCLN, n.d.), for instance, references a poll showing that support for full abortion rights increases from 33% in high school to 66% of university graduates.

field tested by the NCLN and TRL (TRL 2012, 4, 9, and 12). As one tweet from the 2013 NCLN Symposium put it, campus groups need to focus on "SMART goals: specific, measurable, achievable, relevant, time-oriented. Apply this to your #prolife activism. #NCLNSymposium" (Luluquisin 2013a).

Overall, it seems clear that a variety of important actors in the anti-abortion movement have acknowledged the need to re-evaluate the appropriateness of the strategies (or lack thereof) employed by earlier generations of activists. Anti-abortion actors are also trying to develop a more effective and results-oriented vision for the future. These are not the only signs of a movement working to redefine and reposition itself. There are also indications that a strong debate about *where* activists should target their efforts is emerging within the movement.

7.2 The Terrain of Contestation: Law and/or Culture

A key characteristic of the traditional portrait is the contention that the anti-abortion movement's main instrument for opposing abortion is legislation (passing laws that restrict, ban, and/or criminalize abortion; creating major barriers in real access; defunding abortion, and so on). As we saw in Part I, this representation is a largely accurate reflection of the earlier history of the movement – the criminalization of abortion in the 1800s, the reaction to abortion reform in 1969, and activism in the years leading up to and immediately following the *Morgentaler* decision. Moreover, it is certainly accurate in terms of both the historical and contemporary movement in the US.

Yet, it is far from clear that legislation is the main focus of the contemporary movement in Canada. This is not to say that the anti-abortion movement would not support anti-abortion legislation. It most certainly would: even groups and actors who sometimes caution against pursuing an anti-abortion legislative agenda usually lend vocal support to legislative efforts when they emerge. It is to say, however, that many parts of the Canadian movement are sceptical that wide-scale legislative success is likely to become a reality in the foreseeable future, leading a variety of actors to argue that it is more important to adopt strategies that do not focus primarily on political legislation.

On one hand, some actors in the anti-abortion movement are clearly committed to actively pushing for legislative change at the federal level. Groups such as the Association for Reformed Political Action (ARPA) and its We Need a Law campaign, for example, invest their time and energy in directly pushing for anti-abortion legislation. For ARPA, it is undeniable that "Canada needs federal abortion legislation," and thus its mission is to "build a groundswell of support among the Canadian public for federal abortion legislation" and "motivate and encourage our politicians to introduce legislation" (We Need a Law, n.d.). The We Need a Law campaign is clear that an incremental approach to creating abortion legislation is a legitimate and necessary strategy. Quoting Clark Forsythe (the president of Americans United for Life), campaign director Mike Schouten argues that "prudent political leaders must pursue a vision of complete justice – of complete legal protection for human life. But, in the democratic process, they must pursue the ideal in such a way that progress is made and with the willingness to accept something when all is not achievable due to social, legal, or political obstacles beyond their control" (CCBR 2013c).

As we discussed in chapter 5, there have been various contemporary attempts to pass anti-abortion legislation at the federal level. Between 2007 and 2013, three bills and two motions related to the anti-abortion cause have been introduced as private members' bills in the House of Commons. In 2012–13 alone, Stephen Woodworth's M-312 (calling on Parliament to revisit the definition of "human," with the purpose of extending this definition to include fetuses in such a way that would extend Criminal Code sanctions against murder to include abortion) and Mark Warawa's M-408 (calling on Parliament to pass a resolution condemning the practice of gender-specific abortions) gained surprising visibility and support. Although Woodworth's motion was defeated, 91 members of Parliament, including the Minister responsible for the Status of Women at the time, voted in favour of it (203 voted against). Perhaps even more interestingly, the committee ruling that deemed Mark Warawa's M-408 "non-votable" caused a mini-rebellion in the Conservative caucus and a significant amount of criticism even in the mainstream media. It is thus unsurprising that a clear theme of the 2012 March for Life was supporting the We Need a Law campaign and that, in 2013, the official theme of the march was supporting M-408 and the need to combat gender-specific abortion.

On the other hand, however, it is not clear that these legislation-oriented examples – often heavily covered by the media – represent the sole or even main strategic focus of the contemporary Canadian anti-abortion movement. Interestingly, in an interview with the CCBR, Mike Schouten noted that the Canadian anti-abortion movement has not been focused primarily on legislative change. When discussing the origins of We Need a Law, he stated that the campaign had grown out of the fact that, for the past several decades, the Canadian anti-abortion movement has spent very little effort actively advocating for abortion legislation. In his words, We Need a Law "was initiated as a result of a desperate need in the political arm in the pro-life movement for a group that was focused narrowly on pre-born human rights" (CCBR 2013c). Yet, even Schouten acknowledges that legislative change requires much more than simple political lobbying. He sees a deep connection between the political and educational arms of the movement, believing that public education is a prerequisite for legislative success. As he noted in the same interview, "it is never up to an individual or a group or an organization to introduce laws into the House of Commons, it is up to our members of Parliament ... and what we've been finding is that [MPs] are more and more willing to introduce something that is more in line with public opinion, and that's why we are strongly pushing the public opinion stance" (CCBR 2013c).

Moreover, even some organizations that are focused on "education" ultimately support and aim for legislative action. For example, Stephanie Gray, the co-founder and executive director of the CCBR until 2014, has argued that this group is "not going to lose sight of the fact that ... our ultimate goal is the total abolition of abortion" (CCBR 2013c). Jonathon Van Maren, who became executive director of the CCBR in 2014, echoes Gray's commitment: "We're in this to the end. We're in it to ban first trimester abortions. All abortions ... If people think we're going to be satisfied with a 24 week ban, I'm actually a little bit insulted" (CCBR 2013c).

If some anti-abortionist groups are actively pushing for legislative change, and some are engaging in public education in the hopes of supporting legislative change, others seem to have largely eschewed any focus on creating legal barriers to abortion. Instead, many within the movement seem to be increasingly focused on shifting what they call the "culture of abortion." The blog ProWomanProLife (PWPL) is an excellent example of this.

PWPL's main mission statement is "a Canada without abortion, by choice." This sentiment does not seem to be mere window dressing; rather, it is consistently reflected in its thousands of blog posts. For instance, the webpage devoted to explaining "the story" of PWPL explains that the blog is "calling on all women who believe the key to the cultural change is a grassroots movement of women, not legislation. Top-heavy legislation, that might criminalize abortion, for example, gets us nowhere with a culture of women who believe abortion to be anything from a necessary evil, to a compassionate act, to completely neutral ... We must be able to discuss the issue with complete and total freedom, and to highlight how uncompassionate abortion actually is, from a woman's perspective" (PWPL 2007). The bloggers on PWPL do not entirely disavow legislation – there are a variety of posts in support of Woodsworth's and Warawa's motions, for example. But, then again, neither of these motions technically called for legislation restricting abortion, even if they clearly seemed to be steps in that direction.

Much of the PWPL blogging argues that the movement should reorient its focus away from advocating legislative change and towards nurturing cultural change. In one illustrative PWPL blog entry, Andrea Mrozek (founder of PWPL) states that abortion "is not a criminal problem, like drunk driving, to be solved by ramping up penalties and fervent prosecution" but is instead "a moral, cultural and philosophical problem inextricably tied to our view about sexuality, motherhood and marriage" (PWPL, 27 March 2009). This blog is not an outlier. We identified forty-three PWPL blog posts between 2007 and 2011 that involved explicit discussions or comments about the strategy of the anti-abortion movement. In analysing whether they advocated cultural change, legislation, or both, a strong majority (58 per cent) explicitly champion driving change through non-legislative means. Only 25 per cent advocate legislative reform alone. Moreover, many of these legislation-focused entries did not advocate criminalizing abortion explicitly and instead argued for other types of state regulation. (As many of the posts were devoted to commenting on private members' bills C-484 and C-510, they often addressed the issue of criminalization somewhat obliquely.)

This orientation towards changing culture is not confined to bloggers. We also found evidence of it in a variety of organizational discourse. The anti-abortion organization Signal Hill, for instance, had run six advertising campaigns as of 2011. Not a single one of them focused on legislative change. Instead, they focused on changing "abortion culture." The group's website not only highlights women's negative experiences with abortion (by promoting the Silent No More campaign), it also has a Take Control campaign, which reflects the group's mission to provide "clear and supportive information, empowering women to make informed choices" (SH, n.d.). A similar tone defined the 2009 Ontario-wide campaign by Alliance for Life Ontario that sought to embrace women at the moment they were making their choice, rather than arguing for the criminalization of abortion through legislation.

It seems, then, that significant portions of the Canadian anti-abortion movement are increasingly acknowledging the advice Stephen Harper offered in a CBC interview several years ago: "What I say to people [is], 'If you want to diminish the number of abortions, you've got to change hearts and not laws'" (CBC News 2011a).

The point is not that the anti-abortion movement has given up on legislative change or that culture/values change is the only, or even the primary, dimension of the movement's strategy. Rather, the point we wish to make is that, although it often garners substantial media attention, pushing for legislative change is only one part of the work that the movement is undertaking. This is not only because even those activists who think legislative change is possible understand that a prior shift in public opinion is a prerequisite for legislative success but also because many activists think that a legislative strategy is unlikely to succeed and that changing culture and values is a more effective and realistic strategy. As the CCBR suggests, "since the vast majority of Canadians do not hold a pro-life view, the most basic job pro-lifers have is to educate the public on abortion. This task is the mandate of educational or 'prophetic' pro-life organizations. Only when the educational arm of the movement succeeds will the other arms of the movement succeed" (CCBR 2013f).

In an interview with the *National Post*, even Andre Schutten of the politically oriented organization ARPA noted this shift. "It used to be that the political arm of [the anti-abortion] movement was all or nothing. It was very idealistic. And in the last five years, there's been a huge shift ... Politics is the art of the possible and realizing that, we have a lot of things we need to change and culture is a huge one that needs to change first before we can change the laws in any meaningful ways" (Gerson 2015). Moreover, in Schutten's view, this reality also suggests that the movement might need to rethink its strategies of persuasion: "I think there is a reorientation about how to engage [within the anti-abortion movement] ... We have to find ways of making arguments and living within the pluralism of Canadian society" (quoted in ibid. 2015). Given this new approach, it is crucial to analyse how the movement is seeking not only to influence the formal political realm (something that the traditional portrait encourages us to focus on) but also to persuade Canadians beyond the political realm.

7.3 To the Web! The New Anti-abortion Network

According to many actors in the anti-abortion movement, one of the most important structural changes in the strategic landscape over the past decade has been the emergence and massive growth of the web as a communications and organizing tool. To understand the importance of this shift in relation to the anti-abortion movement, it is crucial to understand that many advocates believe that, from a communications perspective, the deck is heavily stacked against them. According to many within the movement, both the political realm and the mainstream media are highly inhospitable spheres that are strongly biased against the anti-abortion position. PWPL's Andrea Mrozek, for example, argues that "the only people happy with the status quo right now are very radical, very extreme pro-abortion types. But they have voice in the law schools, amongst judges, in the education system, and finally, in the media" (PWPL, 18 May 2010). Mrozek affirms the idea that "journalists are undeniably pro-choice, more so than the public at large" (PWPL, 11 April 2013). Anti-abortion publications and organizations regularly publish accounts claiming to show evidence of media bias in the treatment of the anti-abortion movement (see, e.g., Craine 2012). They have even created a variety of terms for this perceived condition, "abortion distortion" being one of the catchiest.

Anti-abortion advocates also claim that they are victims of vast censorship – both literal (in relation to Mark Warawa's M-408 in March 2013) and structural (having their stories suppressed by the mainstream media). Indeed, the movement often explicitly frames its communication strategies in response to this perceived censorship. The CCBR, for instance, argues that "since traditional media (e.g., television networks, newspapers, billboard advertisers) will generally not show the reality of abortion or allow for graphic pro-life advertising, the pro-life movement must create its own mass media projects to convince the public of what abortion is" (CCBR 2011a, 15).

Portraying the mainstream media as profoundly biased and systematically exclusionary is certainly not unique to the anti-abortion movement. It is a relatively common trope used by a variety of contemporary conservative (as well as many other political and social) movements and actors in North America. And as we shall see in the following chapters, it has a number of key rhetorical functions. These types of claims are made so frequently and intensely in the anti-abortion movement, however, that even some insiders have suggested that many anti-abortion activists "are given to exaggerated fears of media conspiracies of silence" that are not substantiated by the actual situation (PWPL, 11 April 2013). Regardless, this strategy continues to structure anti-abortion communication strategies in profound ways.

In this context, virtually the entire movement seems to agree that the advent of the Internet has transformed and invigorated the anti-abortion cause by creating a host of new types of outreach, advocacy, and networking that have generated new and very promising possibilities for the movement. The traditional portrait tends to portray the anti-abortion movement as a relic of the past, organized in church basements and coming into the public eye largely by protesting outside abortion clinics or organizing the odd annual political march. This is a far cry from the realities of the new digitally networked movement. In an interview in 2011, Joanne Byfield (then president of LifeCanada) offered a precise encapsulation of this new state. In her telling, the inhospitable political and media landscape has meant that anti-abortion advocates faced a situation analogous to that of the early Christian church (Newman 2011). Persecuted and driven underground, the early church had to develop unorthodox ways to organize and mobilize. The same, she believes, is true for the contemporary anti-abortion movement in Canada – but this time in a context where prolific networking has been facilitated by technological advances. According to Byfield, anti-abortion activists "have been pretty much shut out of mainstream media in just about every way. We've had to turn to the Internet – through blogs, Twitter and Facebook, to connect with each other, engage in discussions and get the info out" (Newman 2011).

One concrete example of this digital communication strategy is the online anti-abortion news outlet LifeSiteNews. At the 2013 March for Life Youth Conference in Ottawa, John Henry Westen, the founder of LifeSiteNews (one of the sponsors of the march and major information hub for the North American movement) spoke at length about the media conspiracy against the anti-abortion movement. Westen suggested that the media profoundly misleads the public with the information it does, and does not, provide. He argued that the only way to get out the truth to the members of the movement, and to the broader public, is to find ways to circumvent the mainstream media. This, he argued, was the purpose of LifeSiteNews (Prolife and the Media panel, March for Life Youth Conference, 10 May 2013, authors' observations).

The organizational and communication possibilities offered by the Internet have become central to a variety of other anti-abortion actors as well. Without the Internet, the aggressive and explicit visual campaigns of the CCBR, for example, would be significantly more costly to disseminate widely, making them much less effective. For as the group clearly notes, core to its overall strategy is to "develop commercials that would never be aired on TV due to graphic content, but will be widely viewed on the internet (and be free) via social media" (CCBR 2011a, 4).

Many in the movement underline the importance of the online realm to other efforts as well, such as effectively disseminating the anti-abortion message, organizing supporters, and creating a sense of community and shared purpose. Many of the speakers and participants at the 2013 March for Life Youth Conference spoke about the online realm as the lifeblood of the movement. According to the participants, social media and online resources were major organizing tools for many of the youth organizers and participants. While traditional institutions such as schools and religious groups remained important contributors – particularly in terms of providing financial and logistical support – participants felt that social media and online resources were key tools that allowed youth to feel connected the larger movement (March for Life Youth Conference 2013, authors' observations). It is no surprise, then, that social media was a major theme at the National Campus Life Network (NCLN) conference in September 2013. One tweet from the official NCLN account, for instance, read: "The importance of social media in the #prolife movement: primary form of communication. Get to people where they are #NCLNsymposium" (NCLN, 28 September 2013a). Another makes it clear that the online presence is as important as, if not more important than, the physical presence of student clubs: "Your club website is like your office, home base. Your social media profiles are like your info tables. #needboth #NCLNsymposium" (NCLN, 28 September 2013b). Clearly, the online realm is now of central importance in terms of networking within the movement and communicating to those outside it.

7.4 Communications, Communications, Communications

Given a context in which the mainstream media is viewed with suspicion and the online realm has opened up a variety of new communications possibilities, it is not surprising that there is significant evidence that many actors in the contemporary anti-abortion movement are investing considerable energy and resources in optimizing their communications efforts. Many actors believe that, in order to capitalize on political, social, and technological opportunities, the movement must develop innovative content and communication strategies that, unlike the strategies of the past twenty years, effectively respond to the "pro-abortion" culture they see around them. As Andrea Mrozek wrote in 2008 while musing about the implications of Barak Obama's victory, "we (pro-lifers) need to get creative. We need to look for new and different ways to stop abortion" (PWPL, 18 November 2008). Moreover, it seems that there is a fairly robust discussion in the anti-abortion movement about what exactly are the new and different methods that the movement should use.

Even a cursory examination of anti-abortion blogs, training sessions, and conferences provides ample evidence that important actors in the movement are actively and explicitly discussing what strategies are being used by the abortion rights movement and debating how the anti-abortion movement should effectively be countering them. As an example, consider the posts of Faye Sonier, who is legal counsel for the Evangelical Fellowship of Canada (EFC) and, according to her professional biography, advocates on a variety of social policy issues both in the political and legal realms (EFC 2013b). She is also a blogger and media commentator on the abortion issue, and one of the four young women portrayed in a *Faith Today* article about the growing generation of young female leaders of the movement (Newman 2011). In one post, Sonier ruminates about some of the "pro-choice" communication strategies, their consequences, and what the anti-abortion movement can learn from them. Perhaps the most interesting part of her blog is her opening comments about the conversations going on in the anti-abortion movement:

> As a member of the pro-life movement, I frequently engage in messaging meetings with other interested pro-life parties. I know that a movement cannot require that all members abide by certain communications standards. I also acknowledge the rights to freedom of speech and expression, even though I (we) sometimes wish certain individuals didn't attempt to advance the pro-life cause with questionable or nonsensical placards or banners. And of course, as in any movement, there is a small minority of extremists who definitely do not represent the whole. (PWPL, 4 July 2013)

Sonier is far from alone in considering these issues. Moreover, the sophistication of her reflections on the strategic challenges and opportunities is representative of a movement that is increasingly self-conscious about the importance, and potential pitfalls, of communicating in a context where members of the movement have very different views on what constitutes acceptable and effective tactics.

One of the touchstones for this debate has been the aggressive communications practices of the Canadian Centre for Bio-ethical Reform.

Over the last decade, the CCBR has developed a variety of controversial strategies. At the centre of its communications strategy is the belief that "the vast majority of Canadians don't know what abortion truly is about – and they don't care to know. In order for them to shift their views to the pro-life position, they need to understand the humanity of the pre-born and the inhumanity of abortion" (CCBR 2011a, 11). As we will discuss below, part of the CCBR's strategy is to engage directly with Canadians, and to train a broad array of grassroots volunteers to do the same, with the hope that such moments of interaction can change people's *minds* and make them understand "what abortion truly is about." However, the group also embraces a related, and more controversial, strategy, which might be called visual shock therapy – for it seeks to viscerally change people's *stomach* for abortion.

This visual shock therapy involves publicizing extremely graphic visual images of aborted fetuses. The CCBR has developed a variety of tactics to confront the Canadian public with these images, including driving "anti-abortion" caravan trucks with giant billboards showing these pictures, setting up static Genocide Awareness Project (GAP) billboards on Canadian university campuses, and undertaking mobile "choice-chain" on public sidewalks outside of high schools and on busy street corners. It has also used the same graphic imagery on postcard mail-out campaigns. The CCBR's Face the Children campaign has even used this strategy in an attempt to target and publicly shame high-profile conservative politicians, including Stephen Harper, in their own ridings.

The CCBR has spent significant energy explaining and defending this communications strategy in a wide variety of publications. The justification can take softer or harder edges, depending on the context. But all of such sources argue that there is a visceral effectiveness of extreme visual images. Defending its GAP (a campaign that many universities have sought to ban or limit on campus), the CCBR has argued that public exposure to graphic images is necessary because, "every day, babies are being dismembered, decapitated, and disemboweled. The enemy wants that hidden ... Words don't cut it like pictures do ... These pictures, then, are the undiluted argument that pro-lifers must exhibit uncensored if the validity of the pro-life perspective is to be understood by our culture" (CCBR n.d., 4–5).

In one of the CCBR podcasts, former director of communications and current executive director Jonathon Van Maren made this argument even more pointedly. Discussing how graphic imagery makes "visible" the "invisible" reality of abortion, Van Maren noted "it's like a punch in the gut, because that image really does pack that much kick, you know

I felt it myself, it's one of the reasons I joined the pro-life movement" (CCBR 2013c). For the CCBR, it's the kick, the punch in the stomach, that justifies these tactics.

The CCBR also has a sophisticated conceptualization of the collective impact these images can have on the broader debate and social/political context, for they believe that these visual tactics are the key to creating an anti-abortion cascade effect through society. In their view,

> Photos allow us to forge a consensus regarding the facts ... People who understand who the baby is and what abortion does to him/her are more likely to choose a crisis pregnancy centre than an abortion clinic in a crisis pregnancy ... They are more likely to boycott corporations which support the abortion industry. They are more likely to challenge their pastor's weak leadership in defense of life and vote for pro-life political candidates. Pro-aborts are more likely to be neutralized. Neutrals are more likely to be converted. Converts are more likely to be activated. Activists are more likely to donate time and money in defense of life. Pro-life volunteers are more likely to be pro-life professionals. (CCBR 2011a, 24)

Far from being a haphazard or unfocused expression of the moral beliefs of its members, the CCBR's use of images is a multilayered and clearly strategized communications plan.

It is a strategy, however, that the CCBR admits has "been fiercely debated, even inside the pro-life movement" (VanMaren, n.d., 1). In 2009, for example, Barbara Kay – a noted conservative columnist at the *National Post* – took public issue with the idea that graphic imagery and the GAP are appropriate and effective tactics. Seeking to give the anti-abortion movement some friendly advice, Kay admits that she "cannot think of anything more damaging amongst educated observers to the pro-life cause than the Genocide Awareness Project campaign, which draws a moral equivalence between abortion and the Holocaust." Although Kay goes on to clarify that her disagreement is not necessarily with the idea of showing graphic images of fetuses itself, she insists that the CCBR does not have the "ethical right to exploit for mere rhetorical advantage a human tragedy [i.e., the Holocaust] with no logical, moral or historical relevance to abortion." Hence Kay's advice to the anti-abortion movement: "Your cause deserves better than the GAP campaign. Because the result – and I think this is a very grave consequence for any movement – is that thoughtful, educated people do not take you seriously. They do not respect your strategies for persuasion.

You must consider whether the emotional impact of your message is so important to you that it is worth burning the narrow but sturdy bridge you could be using to reach people like me" (Kay 2009).

Even other anti-abortion advocates have publicly noted various degrees of discomfort with the strategies used by the CCBR. Andrea Mrozek at PWPL, for example, frequently refers to herself as a friend and supporter of Stephanie Gray and the CCBR. Yet she too has lodged various differences of opinion with the CCBR's tactics. She has argued that the sometimes over-the-top rhetoric is problematic. Reacting to a post in which Gray claims that every woman who has not been pregnant is a "mother-to-be" (the aim is to represent every woman who is actually pregnant as already a mother, as the fetus is a human baby), Mrozek argues that the neologism of a "mother-to-be" in this context is not only illogical and unsubstantiated but risks alienating a variety of women who might otherwise be allies. She writes, "the concept might also be considered terribly insensitive to women who are infertile – desperately wanting to be mothers but finding for one reason or another that they can't be. Who, in that circumstance, wants to be told they actually are 'mother-to-be'? Fan.Tas.Tic" (PWPL, 25 April 2013). These moments of friendly disagreement and divergence emerge over larger issues as well. For example, in reaction to the CCBR's campaign against politicians, Mrozek notes that "I have my issues with the campaign. I am not confident that the images without the voices of Stephanie and her team are a win. So while I don't have a problem with the use of graphic images, I do believe there should be a person there to discuss those images when people inevitably have a strong reaction" (PWPL, 25 May 2013).

Interestingly, while the CCBR recognizes it has been a flashpoint for criticism, it also believes it is important to remember that, at the end of the day, all anti-abortion activists are all working for a common cause. In this sense, the CCBR sees the various parts of the movement – even those that disapprove of one another's methods – as working together. Drawing on a concrete scenario, the CCBR outlines how this cooperation might work:

> A GAP display is set up at a university campus. In the days and weeks preceding and following it, the local pregnancy care centre and post-abortion ministries advertise their services. During GAP-days, these same groups have a visible presence on campus by setting up an information table/exhibit either near the display or in another high-pedestrian traffic location. Post-abortion ministries like Silent No More Awareness can share the testimonies of women who regret their abortions.

Thanks to GAP, a new climate of debate is created and other pro-life groups can organize presentations and debates that draw a larger crowd ... With this kind of coordination expanding from a campus into the general public, a greater impact will occur and political initiatives, such as campaigns to defund abortion, will be positively impacted. (CCBR 2013h, 29)

Ultimately, the strategy debates within the movement remain cordial, and most anti-abortion actors have adopted the idea that the movement is like a diverse extended family or team comprising different approaches and roles but all pulling more or less in the same direction. As the CCBR states, "[our] comments are not made to be gratuitously critical of ... fellow pro-life workers. CCBR's views are not made to deprive people of hope, to drive them into despair. They are made so that the pro-life movement will become as effective as possible in reaching its goal of ending abortion" (CCBR 2013f).

What seems clear is that various actors in the movement are actively and self-consciously debating which innovative communication strategies are best suited to the contemporary situation and are seeking to develop new ones that are not necessarily beholden to historical practices.

7.5 Persuasion in the Streets: Reason, Rhetoric, and Respect

While the anti-abortion movement is taking communications seriously and increasingly mobilizing online, this does not mean that it has forgotten about being in the streets. For important actors in the anti-abortion movement are investing heavily in developing a much more effective and robust street-level outreach program by training a new generation of grassroots "persuaders" (whose goal, as we will see, is to engage Canadians face-to-face). However, the ways in which they are doing this – and to what end – are quite different than those highlighted by the traditional portrait. Rather than seeking to intimidate pregnant women by protesting outside abortion clinics, the contemporary movement is focusing its face-to-face efforts on engaging impressionable citizens in an attempt to change public opinion.

This is not to say that the old-style protests outside abortion clinics have completely disappeared: studies show that some anti-abortion actors continue to protest outside clinics (Wu and Arthur 2010). Moreover, certain protest tactics developed in the US have been introduced in Canada. The 40 Days for Life Campaign, a large US-based and overtly religious campaign whose mission is to "access God's power through prayer, fasting, and peaceful vigil to end abortion," has recently been imported into Canada (40 Days for Life, n.d.). Central to the campaign's strategy (in addition to individual prayer) is the holding of vigils outside of abortion clinics over the forty days of Lent. According to the Campaign Life Coalition website, the Canadian version of 40 Days for Life targeted seventeen clinics across Canada in 2013 (CLC 2013b). Other sources confirm increased levels of anti-abortion protest during these campaigns (Wu and Arthur 2010).

Moreover, the anti-abortion movement still frequently celebrates Linda Gibbons – an anti-abortion activist who has spent significant time in jail for violating legal injunctions that protect abortion clinics from having protesters directly block access and harass patients. (Most of these laws establish a small buffer zone in front of clinics or doctors' offices – from ten to fifty metres – in which individuals are not allowed to protest.) MP Maurice Vellacott nominated Gibbons for a Diamond Jubilee Award (which she received). Thus, the anti-abortion movement continues, to some extent, to employ, and support, these types of street-level strategies.

Tactics such as Gibbons's, however, are hardly the predominant form of contemporary anti-abortion street-level engagement. While many activists celebrate Gibbons's civil disobedience, very few actually advocate using her strategies. A newspaper article published after one of Gibbons's arrests reported that Jim Hughes, the president of Campaign Life Coalition (CLC), "admires Ms. Gibbons for her willingness to go to jail for the cause but does not see the injunction as a major issue for his group" (Lewis 2011).

An examination of several of the main street-level activist models used by the anti-abortion movement in Canada further highlights the degree to which Gibbons's more "traditional" approach has been revised by most contemporary groups. It seems that, faced with various legal barriers and a shifting strategic view, the movement has both broadened and (to some degree) shifted the targets and the tone of its street-level presence, adopting techniques that are quite different than those highlighted by the traditional image. Take, for example, the 40 Days for Life Campaign. In contrast to the portrait of an angry mob-like group of mostly male protesters shouting and physically blocking abortion clinics in an attempt to harass and dissuade staff and patients from entering those clinics (Faludi 1991), even the US version of the 40 Days for Life Campaign strategy is premised on taking a much more strategic, "professional," and "compassionate" approach.

Founded in Texas in 2004, the 40 Days campaign grew into a national effort across the US in 2007 and was extended to Canada and a variety of other countries in 2009. It is notable that, despite the fact that the campaign is explicitly religious and thus seemingly quite traditional, the tactics of even this organization are somewhat different than those suggested by the traditional portrait. The original American campaign literature, for example, makes it very clear that protests in front of clinics should be peaceful, calm vigils – not loud, aggressive protests. The "visible, public centerpiece of 40 Days for Life is a focused, 40-day non-stop, round-the-clock prayer vigil" outside of abortion clinics (40 Days for Life, n.d.). This is intended to be a "peaceful and educational presence," and is not a direct action aimed at physically or verbally intimidating staff and patients. The campaign believes that the stereotypical mode of aggressive confrontation is not the only, or even most effective, model of persuasion. Rather, its strategy reflects the belief that even a relatively silent, testimonializing presence can have important effects.

Moreover, the overall campaign is designed to be a sophisticated and integrated effort that extends beyond the vigil itself. Far from viewing the protest itself as the main goal, organizers often focus on the positive impacts the campaign can have on building a stronger anti-abortion community. The campaign's literature clearly articulates the important effects it has had on recruiting and mobilizing new supporters, developing "dynamic new leaders to increase the future impact of pro-life efforts," and increasing "local financial support for pro-life efforts" (40 Days for Life 2014). It also highlights the value of generating "enormous buzz by getting pro-life news coverage – even from biased media outlets" (40 Days for Life 2014).

In this sense, the campaign is organized like a professional political campaign. The central organization invests heavily in creating basic campaign material and has adopted a business model that allows it to send out some material to local campaigns (for a registration fee of approximately $200) and provide additional training and messaging materials that local campaigns can easily leverage. It encourages local campaigns to be highly organized as well, with a campaign director, outreach coordinators, communication coordinators, and church and vigil coordinators all being recommended roles (40 Days for Life 2014). Far from being primarily an angry protest limited to abortion clinics, the strategy and organizational structure make it clear that these campaigns are well organized and designed primarily to engage the broader community through media and community outreach efforts that far outstrip (both in effort and, likely, in impact) the vigil itself.

Many of these elements also seem to characterize Canadian versions. A scan of the 2013 Facebook and blog postings of the Calgary chapter of

40 Days for Life (one of the more active campaigns in Canada) reveals many pictures of young women, often holding much more pro-woman-sounding signs than one would expect – "Abortion Hurts Women," "I Regret My Abortion," "You Are Loved," "I Was Scared Too," "A Pregnant Woman Needs Support Not Abortion" (Calgary 40 Days for Life, n.d.). The pictures also show that the size of the protests on the sidewalks outside the bubble zones are quite small and often made up of the same few people. One photo showing four women with signs was titled "Full Sidewalk!!" (Calgary 40 Days for Life 2013). While the limited size of the protests might be explained partly by specifics of the bubble zone bylaws, the size and diversity of the protests seems minimal all the same.

The fact that even the 40 Days vigils are relatively small in Canada is consistent with other analyses that have suggested that, compared to the US context, clinic blockades and protests in Canada are much smaller and less intense and effective. For example, survey data suggest that, while protests in front of abortion clinics are sometimes aggressive (sixteen Canadian clinics reported that protests negatively affected patients or staff), often they seem to have little effect (eight clinics reported that such protests did not affect them at all). Some clinics even suggested that some of the protests were not particularly noticeable (Wu and Arthur 2010, 9). It seems, therefore, that the traditional image of large groups of aggressive, male protesters physically blocking and verbally harassing staff and patients is not a type of protest that is common or growing in Canada.[14]

Perhaps equally telling is the fact that even some of the anti-abortion organizations that are the most active, influential, and assertive proponents of street-level engagement are also employing practices and strategies that are different – in subtle, but very important ways – than those outlined in the traditional portrait. Take, for example, the Canadian Centre for Bio-ethical Reform, one of the most aggressive anti-abortion organizations in Canada (it focuses on fetal rights, explicitly seeks to ban all abortion, uses graphic imagery, and so on). We might expect this group to retain street-protest tactics very similar to those of the previous generation and focus its energy on highly confrontational battles in

---

14 This is not to say that the 40 Days of Life protest doesn't have negative effects. It is merely to say that it is a slightly different mode of protest than that in the traditional portrait and that it doesn't seem to be a central and growing strategy.

front of institutions that provide abortions. If the group is willing to confront and alienate powerful politicians such as Stephen Harper for being complicit in what it sees as the unquestionable evil of abortion, it would seem likely that it would be especially aggressive in targeting abortion providers and clinics.

Yet, the CCBR's strategy champions face-to-face engagement with the public on the streets rather than the targeting of abortion clinics. Key to its perspective is the widely shared anti-abortion belief that, "too often," gatekeepers such as "media, teachers, principals, clergy and parents censor the injustice of abortion" (CCBR 2011a, 4). In response, the CCBR contends that its projects "[must] involve mass education that bypasses gatekeepers": "because others persist in facilitating the cover up, the projects for EndtheKilling [CCBR's organizing strategic plan] will deliver uncensored messages online and on community streets ... We will engage passersby on public sidewalks where we don't need the permission of institutions to get the pro-life message to them ... We will continue to give presentations in institutions where such are welcomed" (4). One of the two "fundamental truths" that underpins the strategy of CCBR is the contention that "Canadians will not understand abortion until pro-lifers understand that the frontlines of the abortion debate are in their communities, neighbourhoods and even homes ... Pro-lifers must learn to take individual responsibility to educate the public even if it requires personal sacrifice" (11).

Given the CCBR's commitment to graphic visual imagery, it is not surprising that the group's approach to public engagement accepts and defends the necessity of some degree of controversy and confrontation. However, the way it defends this necessary confrontation is interesting. For most frequently, it is justified in terms of its effectiveness. For example, the CCBR is becoming well known in the media precisely because it has chosen to set up large graphic images of aborted fetuses on public property beside high schools, arguing that these graphic sidewalk displays are key tools to spur conversation and reflection. In its view, the controversy and resulting media coverage are not unfortunate by-products: they are part of the purpose of these events, and the CCBR believes that they help spread its message even further (CCBR 2013g).

In fact, the CCBR argues that it is critical to clearly, and rationally, evaluate the type of anger and reaction that its tactics generate: "It all depends on *why* people are angry. If they are angry because pro-lifers are mean, then that is grounds for pro-lifers to change their behaviour.

But if they are angry because they don't like a particular truth message, then that is grounds for pro-lifers to persist" (CCBR 2013h, 26). Moreover, it justifies its tactics and the public response with reference to a long historical lineage of social justice movements: "The history of successful social reform movements reveals societies getting angry at peaceful but persistent activists who communicated what was right, albeit unpopular ... These people and their causes show the irony of social change: *effective reformers are rarely popular and popular reformers are rarely effective*" (ibid., 26–27; emphasis in original). The important point here is that even the CCBR's confrontational tactics are very clearly and rationally strategized – employed not as an expression of outrage or blind assertion of the deep beliefs of its adherents but rather as a historically tested tool to drive social change. Thus, it is not surprising that the CCBR unequivocally also rejects the use of violence against abortion providers and "condemn[s] all forms of abortion-related violence and will not collaborate with groups or individuals who fail to condemn such violence" (55).

In this sense, the CCBR self-consciously sees itself as something of a hybrid model. There are continuities between it and older forms of anti-abortion street-level protest. For example, both the CCBR and protesters who picket abortion clinics generate extreme (and often negative) emotion in people who encounter them. In this respect, the CCBR sees a relationship between its public demonstrations and the protest tactics used by a previous generation of anti-abortionists. However, while it recognizes some similarities, it also explicitly and self-consciously understands that it is doing things quite differently. Having undertaken a critical strategic analysis of the conventional tactics of the anti-abortion movement, its conclusion is that "educational pro-life groups should continue doing public demonstrations but simply *improve* them" (CCBR 2013h, 15).

How are CCBR protests different from previous iterations of anti-abortion protest? Three characteristics are particularly important. First, the CCBR has attempted to improve the effectiveness of street-level demonstrations by making sure that they target the right audience. In light of statistics that show that students become increasingly in favour of abortion rights as they proceed through high school and university, the CCBR has made students a prime target audience for its events. Moreover, a significant portion of its public engagement is devoted to giving talks to persuade certain audiences (especially high school students) or training sessions to develop the skills and strategy of anti-abortion activists (especially in high schools and universities).

A second key difference is that the CCBR insists that the anti-abortion movement must be very rational and cost effective in its attempt to build the human capital such a project needs. Not surprisingly, the CCBR focuses intently on increasing the "manpower" of the movement. Its literature is fond of quoting the claim of Gregg Cunningham (the founder of the US Center for Bio-ethical Reform, which is the parent of the Canadian group) that "there are more people working full-time to kill babies than there are working full-time to save them." The CCBR "bore that in mind and built an organizational structure to have a large team of full-time pro-life staffers" and stated that it will "continue to expand our base of full-time staffers so that we can achieve the goals of EndtheKilling" (CCBR 2011a, 7). What is particularly clear about the CCBR is that it seeks to leverage its own full-time staff to train a much larger segment of anti-abortion activists so that its message can be delivered to Canadians by a wider group of activists. The heart of its mission, therefore, is to "equip activists to become effective pro-life ambassadors, pro-actively taking our message to the very people who need to change their minds on abortion" (ibid., 11). Given this commitment, it is not surprising that a significant part of the organization's website is devoted to providing educational material, communication training, and communication materials for anti-abortion activists.

The third and most important difference concerns both the *content* of the arguments that are conveyed by these demonstrations and the *tone* and *attitude* that the demonstrators embody. For, what is clear is that the anti-abortion movement is pro-actively and self-consciously working to create grassroots activists whose arguments and demeanour actively dismantle the popular image of anti-abortion activists as angry, older, male, and confrontational and replace it with modes of debate that are potentially much more open and "pro-woman," despite the graphic visual and discursive content of many of its campaigns.

Consider Stephanie Gray's speech to the 2011 Pro-Life World Congress. In it, she outlines the CCBR's thoughts on how the anti-abortion movement must communicate more effectively. For Gray, one of the most important elements that activists must remember is that they are not simply machines spouting information. Rather, Gray emphasizes that "when we debate, we become representatives – *ambassadors* – for the pro-life perspective ... [and] that it is vital to our success that we be *good* ambassadors" (Gray 2011, 3).

What does it mean to be a good anti-abortion ambassador? To be sure, it requires that the advocate communicate the right "knowledge" – arguments and facts – and present them clearly and persuasively.

In Gray's words, "we mustn't merely state *that* abortion is wrong; but rather give *evidence* to back up our claims" (Gray 2011, 3). Thus, a significant amount of the training offered by the CCBR focuses on the content of the arguments to be used. Interestingly, none of the arguments provided by the CCBR focus on religious grounds. Rather, focusing on how best to convince non-believers, Gray advises the use of several different argumentative gambits. One tactic she discusses is how anti-abortion advocates might use science to make their case. Another technique she supports is offering philosophical counter-arguments to the idea that fetuses are alive but not persons deserving equal protection. A third set of suggestions concerns how to respond to abortion rights arguments that use structural or individual circumstances (e.g., poverty, rape, health) to justify abortion. All of these strategies – especially the appeal to science – highlight the interesting and often innovative ways in which the anti-abortion movement is making its arguments (something we will discuss in more detail in the following chapters).

If Gray offers substantive advice about the types of arguments anti-abortion advocates should use in debates, what is even more interesting are her thoughts on the *style* of debate that anti-abortion advocates should adopt. For Gray, mastering the non-verbal and emotional aspects of debating are central aspects of being a good anti-abortion ambassador. According to her, the success of a debating stance is often only partially due to the information, reasoning, and argumentation that is presented. It is also often highly dependent on two other aspects. Gray terms the first additional element the "wisdom" of the debating position. Wisdom, in her view, "guides *how* we share our knowledge. It is one thing to be able to explain why abortion is wrong, but it's another to do so in a winsome manner, to help people think through things on their own, retain what you're sharing, and be persuaded" (Gray 2011, 3). Wisdom, in other words, is essentially the ability to choose the best rhetorical strategies (analogies, questioning, finding common ground), and mastering it is crucial to becoming an effective anti-abortion advocate.

Gray also argues that the tone and other more affective elements (e.g., body language, intent, and good will) of an ambassador's "character" are equally crucial. Thus, in addition to being given information and training in rhetorical "apologetics," activists are also taught to think about how they can use their "character" to persuade others. According to Gray, the tone and attitude "must not distract from what we're saying but reinforce it. If we speak about respect for humans, we need to show respect to the human we're talking with. The pro-life message is about compassion, empathy, love and kindness for the other, so we must show that in our character" (3). For the CCBR, "*how* we say and do things is just as important as *what* we do ... Therefore it is essential that pro-lifers remain hopeful, kind and courteous to those they interact with" (CCBR 2013h, 19).

The challenge, according to Gray, is the tendency in the anti-abortion movement "to compartmentalize pro-life approaches" and behave as if "the counselling arm is about compassion [but] the educational arm is about truth." In Gray's mind, "both arms need truth *and* compassion" (Gray 2011, 12). From her perspective, once activists understand the importance of character in wining a debate, ensuring that they come across as compassionate and capable of listening are just as important as, if not more important than, being able to explain and justify their own position. Gray even quotes Martin Luther King Jr. and his claim that "whom you would change, you must first love, and they must know that you love them" as a way of explaining why cultivating and embodying a persona marked by patience, generosity, wisdom, and "character" is as important as the content of the argument (3).

In many ways, then, the CCBR is an excellent example of a hybrid approach. Its willingness to employ shocking visuals, confront students on the street, and elicit highly negative emotions from the public seems quite similar to the images of anti-abortion protesters in the traditional portrait. However, it is important to recognize that, despite these similarities, the CCBR's tactics are also very different from these traditional forms. Not only is the CCBR much more strategic and self-conscious about its use of provocative techniques, but the debating ethos that it wants to ingrain in activists is the exact opposite of the old stereotype of anti-abortionists as aggressive, angry protesters who scream at or accost women in front of clinics.

The CCBR is certainly not alone in focusing on some of these dimensions. While some actors in the anti-abortion movement may have issues with the aggressive imagery used by the CCBR, its goal of cultivating a new mass of anti-abortion activists is one dimension that seems almost unanimously supported. The NCLN, for example, is very clear that a key element of anti-abortion campus and high school clubs is building the human capital for the movement. Given the turnover intrinsic to such clubs, the need to constantly grow the next generation of high school and campus anti-abortion leadership is a key theme for the NCLN. One of the organization's key points in one session at its 2013 symposium was that clubs need to "continually build new leaders to transition in after you graduate from #university. Make room for your members to succeed" (NCLN, 29 September 2013a and 2013e). Its high school manual spends several pages discussing the importance, and the logistics, of turning a potential member into a member, then into a future leader (TRL 2012, 14–16).

The process of growing the organization and cultivating leadership is multidimensional. Assigning tasks appropriately and encouraging members to stretch is key: "Teach your members how to run the club. Lead by letting your members lead" (NCLN, 29 September 2013a). But the TRL/NCLN manual also stresses that "softer" human relationship techniques, such as ensuring that the club recognizes the contributions of all members and potential members, or organizing "socials" like apple picking, tobogganing, a salsa evening, or a local concert, are also indispensable (TRL 2012, 15).

It is thus unsurprising that the messaging frequently reinforces the idea that this campaign is a long one – one that participants will be involved with well beyond their time at school. As a tweet from one attendee at the NCLN Symposium put it, "the long path #outofthe-shadow: endurance. #marathon" (Luluquism 2013a). Such tweets highlight that a key purpose of these clubs is to build the future leadership of the anti-abortion movement well beyond high schools and universities.

If the broader movement seems to agree with the CCBR's focus on cultivating the next generation of activists, it is also clear that CCBR's objective of teaching activists how to engage in effective and respectful tactics of street-level persuasion is indicative of a wider trend in the movement. Alex Newman approvingly writes of the fact that the CCBR approach tries to get a conversation going by using a solicitous and engaging style and presentation. When describing the CCBR's ideal interaction, Newman suggests that "instead of debating right or wrong, she [the facilitator] asks students why they believe what they do about abortion and listens to their stories to see how they came to these views. The Socratic method of debate – asking questions – is most effective if pro-life activists first listen" (Newman 2013, 20). The importance of employing active and respectful listening as well as a calm demeanor is frequently reinforced when activists talk about online engagement. One tweet from the 2013 NCLN conference suggested that activists "treat your online confrontations like your personal confrontations. If being attacked personally, respond kindly. #NCLNsymposium" (NCLN, 28 September 2013c). Another suggested that the online realm actually allowed for this type of character to be demonstrated to an even greater degree than did street-level discussions: "There's a need for sensitivity. Take the time to make a good response, an advantage you don't have in in-person convos. @NCLNsymposium" (NCLN, 28 September 2013d).

7.6 Conclusion

In sum, there are significant indications that many influential actors are seeking to re-invigorate the anti-abortion movement in Canada by actively pushing the movement to self-consciously reconsider its overall vision and strategies of persuasion. Key individuals and organizations seem to be pushing the movement to intensify its strategic focus and to create innovative and effective communication strategies. They have understood that changing cultural values and public opinion is a task that is, at this historical juncture, at least as important as directly attempting to recriminalize abortion through legislation. They have begun to exploit in sophisticated ways opportunities offered by the online environment, with the aim of networking their movement and reaching far more Canadians than was possible previously. They are investing significant resources to cultivate a new generation of street-level activists and to train them to engage with the Canadian public in ways that are quite different (despite some continuities) from those used by previous waves of anti-abortion protesters. Important actors in the movement have also raised a series of foundational questions about the strategic direction of the anti-abortion movement and are encouraging the movement to hone its existing strategies and create new and hybrid approaches in order to more effectively convince the Canadian public of the rightness of its position.

So how, precisely, does the contemporary discourse of the Canadian anti-abortion movement achieve this? The next four chapters are devoted to identifying the most important rhetorical strategies employed by the movement's contemporary public discourse, explaining how these strategies function to persuade Canadians, and outlining the ways in which these strategies embody and/or differ from those tactics highlighted in the traditional portrait. In the next chapter, we examine the explicit arguments of contemporary anti-abortion discourse before moving on to some other, more subtle, techniques of persuasion in chapters 9 through 11.

Chapter 8

Women Up Front, God Out Back: The Changing Anti-abortion Arguments

If you were to ask people to identify the most obvious way we try to persuade one another, most would likely name explicit argumentation – i.e., stating a position and then giving reasons, principles, and evidence in favour of it. This is far from the only technique of persuasion, and not necessarily the most effective, but it is the most commonly conceptualized form of persuasion in Western thought. Given the fact that our educational, political, and legal worlds are largely conceptualized in adversarial terms that highlight these persuasive practices (whether in a high school debate, parliamentary question period, or a courtroom), explicit argumentation is one of the key modes of persuasion in contemporary politics. Therefore, if we want to analyse how the contemporary anti-abortion movement in Canada is currently seeking to persuade Canadians (and the degree to which this reflects or departs from the traditional portrait), one of the first places to start is with an analysis of the movement's explicit arguments.

The traditional portrait tends to describe the explicit arguments of the anti-abortion movement as centred on the contention that the fetus has a right to life and as largely grounded in general philosophical/moral appeals to religion (often with a punitive, anti-woman tone). This is certainly the dominant image of American anti-abortion discourse, and one that can find support in many high-profile examples over the past few years.

Former Republican vice-presidential candidate Sarah Palin – who has publicly stated that she would not support abortion for her own daughter even if she had been raped – is perhaps most representative of this view. Not only is Palin strictly opposed to abortion unless a doctor has determined that a pregnant women's life would end due to continued pregnancy, she also grounds her position in religious and moral reasoning. In 2010, for instance, she advised pregnant women who might be considering abortion to reconsider, stating "God will never give [you] something [you] cannot handle" (Montopoli 2010). Palin is far from alone in her anti-abortion beliefs and justifications. Senator Rick Santorum – who ran for the 2012 Republican presidential nomination and is one of the most vocal anti-abortion lawmakers in the country – recently offered the following advice to victims of sexual assault: "In lots of different aspects of our life we have horrible things happen ... We have to make the best out of a bad situation and I would make the argument that [not choosing abortion] is making the best" (Huffington Post 2012). By casually paralleling the experience of rape to "other horrible things," Santorum's comments, to many people's ears, not only exemplify a dismissive attitude towards women's experiences of sexual assault, but they also mirror the traditional tendency to position the rights of the fetus above the rights, health, and experiences of women through the use of highly moralistic and often religiously tinged language.

It is certainly the case that the traditional portrait continues to accurately capture many characteristics of the American anti-abortion activism. However, the question this chapter asks is, to what degree does the anti-abortion movement in *Canada* continue to reflect this traditional portrait? To test whether the traditional portrait remains accurate in Canada, we analysed and coded each of the 401 cases in our data set (see the methodological discussion in the introduction) to identify whether they included (implicit or explicit) religious appeals and which explicit arguments (if an explicit argument existed) were being used to defend the anti-abortion position. We also listened carefully for these elements during our naturalistic observations of a variety of anti-abortion events. In particular, we paid attention to *who* was making what arguments and the possible ways in which their subject position reinforced the power of the argument (something we call visual signalling).

Section 8.1 describes what we found in regard to religious justifications in the Canadian movement. Sections 8.2, 8.3, and 8.5 are devoted to examining the key explicit arguments used by contemporary anti-abortion discourse. In between, in section 8.4, we briefly look at who is making these arguments and how practices of visual signalling are amplifying the force of some of the most important explicit arguments that are being used.

8.1 God and the Public Sphere

While analysing the semi-public fora of internal debate discussed in chapter 7, we noticed some interesting trends regarding the role of religion in the Canadian anti-abortion movement. On one hand, some actors in the anti-abortion movement continue to clearly and explicitly state their religious perspective and use it to philosophically ground their position. The Association for Reformed Political Action (ARPA), the Evangelical Fellowship of Canada (EFC), and Campaign Life Coalition (CLC) are particularly explicit about the fact that their anti-abortion position is grounded in religious faith. Others are also relatively clear about their faith-based perspective, even if they are explicitly religious. Life-Canada, for example, states that its goal is "to advocate for the preborn, the disabled, the infirm and the elderly who are all uniquely created by God" (LC 2010a).

However, it also seems that many in the movement are actively debating the role that explicit appeals to religion should play in public debate. There are influential and vocal anti-abortion actors who (regardless of what their own personal religious beliefs might be) advocate that the movement should temper the role of religious rhetoric, arguing that it is not the most effective type of argumentation in the political and social context of Canada today.

Many of the bloggers at ProWomanProLife (PWPL), for example, explicitly contrast the religiosity of the previous generation of anti-abortion activists with the character of the contemporary movement. Rebecca Walberg, responding to a column in the Ottawa *Citizen* about the PWPL blog, suggests that "there is a distinctly patronizing flavour to the column, which is built on some rather, shall we say, outdated perceptions. The pro-life movement is mostly led by Christian fundamentalist men? (And, abortion advocates are all women?) ... Pro-life women are 'church ladies'? I don't know if that was even true in the 1970s, but it's certainly not the case now" (PWPL, 27 March 2009). The mission statement of PWPL makes explicit the belief that abortion is not merely (or even primarily) a religious issue. Rather, it states that "ProWomanProLife believes abortion is a human, social issue, not a religious or faith matter, whereby women and men of any faith or no faith at all can stand up in support of women's rights and life, at the same time" (PWPL 2007).

Some of the PWPL bloggers go as far as to renounce using religion in public argument. In response to an article posted on LifeSiteNews, blogger Brigitte Pellerin (who was at one point a reporter with the parliamentary bureau of Sun Media) responded, "My short answer to 'Why aren't there more non-Christians in the pro-life movement?' is this: Because some Christians can be real off-putting. Especially the ones who won't shut up about religion even when surrounded by ostensibly non-religious people ... One of the reasons I agreed to join PWPL was Andrea's [founder Andrea Mrozek] insistence that it be non-religious" (PWPL, 17 July 2008). Pellerin reinforces this in another post, where she states that "when we write the biography of ProWomanProLife (and why shouldn't we?), my part will read something like: I wasn't wild about abortion, but I'd never really felt like joining the usual pro-life groups. I found them either too religious or too preachy or too shrill or all of the above. But when Andrea asked me to join a group devoted to trying to change the culture – trying to end abortion by influencing the culture in a way that would make demand for abortion dwindle without resorting to legal threats and harsh punishment – now that was different" (PWPL, 13 June 2009). While few in the anti-abortion movement would express it as sharply as Pellerin, it is clear that at least some influential actors in the movement are openly questioning the effectiveness and value of public religious appeals in ways that are at odds with the traditional portrait.

But how representative is this current in contemporary anti-abortion discourse? Are these the views of only a few outliers in the movement? To what degree do religious appeals remain central to the public discourse of the contemporary anti-abortion movement in Canada? To answer these questions, we coded our data set for any reference to religion, ranging from explicit appeals to religious authority to more "implicit," metaphorical allusions to religious tropes (sometimes called "dogwhistling").

What did we find? Unsurprisingly, we found that religious appeals do still exist in contemporary anti-abortion discourse. Although PWPL founder Andrea Mrozek claims she usually "doesn't tend to post things overtly Christian," she does occasionally speak of her own religious choices, as well as the role they play in her anti-abortion activism (PWPL, 16 August 2013). For instance, in one blog defending the anti-abortion position from claims that it is not "cool," Mrozek writes, "I hope for every Christian – for those who claim that label – that we are truly following the call of God on our unique lives ... and not choosing to do instead what looks cool or what we are comfortable with. (And by the way, I don't rule out that God might call people to do things that look cool, too)" (PWPL, 16 August 2013). This implicit presentation of anti-abortion activism as "the call of God" seems very representative of the traditional portrait.

To some extent, religion also continues to characterize the public positioning of some parts of anti-abortion activism as well. As mentioned earlier, a variety of anti-abortion organizations including ARPA, the EFC, LifeCanada, and the CLC publicly acknowledge their religious foundations. The CLC, for example, devotes a section of its website to marrying political (largely anti-abortion) activism with religion. This section, aptly titled "Pastor's Corner," links to a two-page "election guide for serious Christians" as well as to a series of anti-abortion sermons for both Catholics and Evangelical leaders. The CLC argues that, because "many pastors do not have time to do all the research related to abortion ... CLC makes it easy for you, whether Protestant or Catholic, to preach a powerful pro-life sermon in tune with the scripture readings for your Sunday service (or Mass)" (CLC 2009b).

The continued relevance of religion in the anti-abortion movement is also evident at many anti-abortion events. For example, a number of speeches at the 2012 and 2013 Marches for Life made religious references, as did a number of speakers and panels at the two Youth Conferences that followed them. Both Youth Conferences, for example, opened with a church service, and, in the lobby of the conference centre, at least ten different religious organizations had booths set up, some handing out information for private Christian colleges, while other sold rosaries and other religious mementos and apparel. Moreover, the majority of the youth attending the conference were involved with anti-abortion groups at their largely Christian high schools (2012 and 2013 March for Life Youth Conference, authors' observations). Clearly, religion still plays an important role in the motivation, mobilization, and organization of anti-abortion activists.

Given this context, we expected that our data set would contain a significant level of explicit and implicit religiously oriented discourse. What we found, however, completely surprised us.

In contrast to our assumptions, our analysis shows that contemporary Canadian anti-abortion discourse almost entirely eschews religiosity as a mode of publicly grounding its explicit argumentation (see figure 8.1). In fact, despite our active search for both explicit and implicit religious references in our data set, religious appeals and themes occurred in less than 2 per cent of the 401 cases. Most notably, and in distinct contrast to the US, there was not a single explicit reference to religion among any of the four anti-abortion MPs' speeches, press releases, or websites.

What does this finding tell us? First, let us be clear about what it does *not* tell us. It does not tell us about the personal motivations or beliefs

Figure 8.1 Religious References in Canadian Anti-abortion Discourse (% of cases in data set)

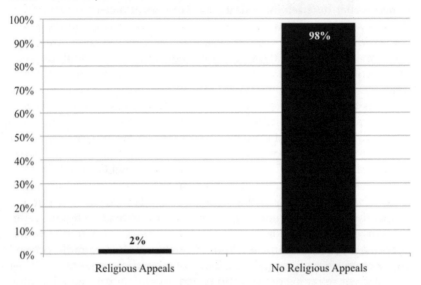

of the anti-abortion activists whose discourse we have studied. People are often motivated by many reasons that they never publicly note. Our findings therefore should not be taken to say that anti-abortion activists are not motivated by religious beliefs. Many clearly are. Moreover, we are *not* saying that religious institutions and networks are unimportant actors in the anti-abortion movement in Canada. They clearly remain central actors in the anti-abortion movement. Religious institutions are key funders and organizers for the annual anti-abortion marches in Canada. Religious organizations fund many high school anti-abortion clubs and help pay for – and organize – the many buses carrying high school students that converge on Ottawa for the annual March for Life on Parliament Hill. Various Catholic school boards in Ontario give their students time off for the trip and provide teachers as chaperones (Stone 2013b). Moreover, there are regular reports of religious schools inviting groups like the Canadian Centre for Bio-ethical Reform (CCBR) to speak at school assemblies and encouraging students to sign anti-abortion petitions (Hasham 2012). And a brief examination of the CCBR's "past events" page reveals that the groups frequently present to religious gatherings and high schools (CCBR 2013i).

Furthermore, some anti-abortion figures and organizations speak publicly from a clearly religious perspective on this issue. Organizations such as the ARPA, the EFC, and the CLC and individuals such as Charles McVety (a politically mobilized evangelical leader) and a handful of MPs all speak from a religious stance on this issue. And the institutional resources of established religious groups seem to be crucial, from a logistical and funding point of view, to the success of many of the movement's most visible rallies and events.

However, based on the result of our discourse analysis and on the basis of our naturalistic observation, what also seems to be true is that, despite the continuing importance of religion as a motivational factor for activists and an organizational aid for events, many major actors in the movement have concluded that appealing to religious grounds *is not a winning strategy with most Canadians and that the movement should therefore focus on other argumentative strategies in the public realm.*

Consider the case of ARPA, one of the most explicitly religious anti-abortion groups. In 2012 and 2013, its legal counsel and Ontario director, Andre Schutten – whose role in the anti-abortion movement has been described as "something of a political translator" (Van Dyken, n.d.) – gave a presentation to packed (approximately 400 people) non-denominational Protestant church before the annual March for Life rallies. Both years, the format was similar. A traditional church service, with a sermon, hymns, and prayers, opened the proceedings. Then, a significant portion of the service was given over to several presentations aimed at increasing the argumentative skills of the audience. Schutten's presentation, entitled "Pro-Life 101," essentially aimed at giving participants debate training by providing them with what ARPA describes as "the very easy and step-by-step logical defense against the so-called 'right to choose.'" The aim of the training was to give anti-abortion activists "pro-life arguments [that] can be employed during the March and in the coming year" (ARPA Canada 2013).

Given the setting (an explicitly religious service) and the source (an explicitly religious political organization), one might expect that the training would focus on biblical argumentation against abortion. But Schutten's advice was just the opposite. Although he maintained that, "as Christians, we know that the answer is in the Bible. The Bible tells us the unborn is precious in God's eyes," he also noted that this argument has limited utility in the public realm. "That [argument] is ok for us," he said, "But if you're arguing with someone who doesn't believe in the Bible, does that mean you're lost?" (authors' notes on Schutten's

"Pro-Life 101" presentation, 10 May 2012). According to Schutten, not at all – as long as pro-lifers are willing to use different arguments in the public realm. His advice is that, in these circumstances, believers must leave biblical verse in the background (as it won't resonate with non-believers), and instead "go to science" (authors' observation). In his 2013 presentation to a new audience at the same church, he explained that believers should, in all good faith, engage non-believers from a scientific perspective because it is "consistent with our religious beliefs, since God made the laws of nature" and, equally important, it "jibes with what people out there think" (authors' notes on Schutten presentation, 9 May 2013). The rest of the presentation, therefore, saw Schutten walk the audience through a series of empirical biological "facts" and consequential "logical" arguments that sought to make the case against abortion based on scientific arguments rather than appeals to biblical authority.

This approach is not an outlier, either. The same pattern also characterized the 2012 and 2013 Marches for Life. Yes, there were religious references in some of the speeches. However, given the level of religious organizational support underpinning the march, religious discourse was surprisingly limited in the speeches at the march itself and on the large majority of the placards.

The absence of religion at events such as the March for Life is also reflected in a variety of organizations that seem to minimize their appeal to religious sources in their broadly public discourse. Take the CCBR, for example. As we discussed in chapter 7, the CCBR often uses hybrid strategies that resemble the traditional portrait in certain ways – especially given its fetal-centric perspective (and its use of graphic imagery) and the frequency with which it presents to religious schools and institutions. In this sense, it would be completely unsurprising if its material were characterized by religious appeals. However, religious appeals are almost entirely absent from the CCBR's public materials. For example, none of the fifteen main web pages devoted to providing training in "pro-life apologetics" in school classrooms (all of which have very pointed arguments against abortion) have any religious references. And this is not atypical of CCBR. Regardless of the personal religious views of its members, its material and arguments assiduously avoid religious appeals and instead focus on scientific, visual, and historical rhetorical resources.

As such, although religion seems to continue to operate as a motivator, a financial and logistical resource, and a source of rhetoric that can be used to mobilize anti-abortion activists (primarily in "in-group" settings), it is clear that explicit religious appeals have become far less prevalent in the movement's public strategy of persuasion. To use a distinction that Tom Flanagan, one of the major architects of the contemporary Canadian conservative movement, likes to employ – the anti-abortion movement in Canada has undertaken a process of "sanitizing" its public discourse. According to Flanagan (2012), most social and political movements have at least two types of discourse. Unsanitized discourse is how activists talk among friends. In this space, activists can express their own deep commitments, as the aim of the discourse is not to convince opponents nor will it be subject to external evaluation. Sanitized discourse, on the other hand, is the public discourse that is crafted to appeal to and convince target audiences – audiences whose own principles and views might be very different than those of the activists themselves and thus who might require different arguments to be persuaded.

On Flanagan's read, the irony of politics is that often "in doing what it takes to win you have to give up what makes you strikingly different" (Flanagan 2012). In these cases, successful political persuasion usually requires "sanitizing the political playbook" in order to build political coalitions with groups that may not historically align with a particular party's or movement's politics, which often means that activists must carefully control and regulate what they say in public and resist the urge to speak the same way and use the same arguments with outsiders that they would with insiders.

The anti-abortion movement would certainly not be the only political movement – nor even the only "conservative" political movement – to have concluded that it needed to sanitize its religious appeals. For over a decade, Preston Manning has been writing and speaking about how conservatives of a religious persuasion should behave in order to most effectively "navigate the faith/political interface" (see, e.g., Manning 2009). The Manning Centre, in fact, has offered what it calls the Faith-Politics Interface program since 2006, and it claims to have trained 600 people in small-group settings and shared its message to more than 5,000 in larger venues (Dobbs 2010). There is no question that Manning argues for a larger place for religion in public discourse – and offers advice on how this might be achieved in the longer term. However, he advises religious conservatives to be "wise as a serpent but as gracious as a dove in the public arena" and suggests that activists can learn lessons from earlier successful religious campaigners such as William

Wilberforce and his efforts to abolish slavery. Manning argues that Wilberforce demonstrates not only the importance of religious activists' adopting an open and generous tone when making their case, but also that it can be much more effective to firmly, but calmly, "publicize the human *suffering*" caused by a certain practice rather than foregrounding one's religious principles and "moralizing self-righteously or legalistically against the evil to be remedied" (Manning 2009).

When it comes to religious appeals, the majority of the contemporary anti-abortion movement in Canada certainly seems to have adopted this approach. It seems to have decided that overt religious appeals are too limiting and that scientific and analogical reasoning in reference to historical injustices (something we will discuss more in chapter 9) is more likely to resonate with a wider audience. In this sense, God certainly isn't dead in the contemporary Canadian anti-abortion movement. But it does seem that the marketers of the movement have decided that leaving him quietly in the guest suite might make their house more inviting to Canadians. And while this change might seem like little more than window dressing, it would be wrong to underestimate its consequences. For an anti-abortion discourse that does not publicly ground its arguments in overtly religious foundations might resonate in very different ways with the broader Canadian public than a highly religious one would.

8.2 Think about the Women: The "Abortion-Harms-Women" Argument

There are, of course, many ways to make the anti-abortion argument. Religious appeals have been one traditional mode. Another has focused primarily on fetal-centric, highly moralized arguments (which can be, but are not necessarily, linked to religious foundations). There are indications, however, that over the past decade, at least some actors in the anti-abortion movement believe that new types of argumentation are necessary to replace old fetal-centric arguments as well.

In 2009, *National Post* columnist Barbara Kay offered some advice to the Canadian movement, suggesting that the effectiveness of appealing to the rights of the fetus is questionable. Are such appeals, she asked, "the best use of your advocacy time? I would advise moving away from the rights of the fetus, which arouses defensiveness and hostility." Instead, she suggests moving "towards the rights of women, an area staked out as the moral high ground of the pro-choicers" (Kay 2009).

Why the rights of women? According to Kay, because the abortion rights movement's claim to defend women's "choice" is "compromised by their ignorance: There are physical and psychological risks to abortion that pro-choicers and abortion clinics wilfully suppress, such as the irrefutable link between induced abortion and a risk of pre-term delivery in future pregnancies. An uninformed choice is not a real choice." Her suggestion is that anti-abortion activists "should end the so-called pro-choicers' monopoly on women's 'rights'" with "A Woman's Right to Informed Consent" and "A Woman's Right to Optimal Reproductive Health" campaign. The advantages of such a rhetorical move, according to Kay, would be significant, for she believes that arguments based in "women's rights" and "women's health" hold political capital. By "focusing the debate on women's health, you would occupy the moral high ground feminists claim as their particular precinct. What campus union could in conscience refuse an information session on women's health?" (Kay 2009).

As surprising as it may be, given that Kay's suggested positioning runs counter to the image presented by the traditional portrait, this perspective is not completely alien to contemporary anti-abortion discourse in Canada. Rebecca Wahlberg, one of the bloggers at PWPL, has made very similar points about anti-abortion strategy. In 2008, for instance, she blogged, "I have my own beliefs about the sanctity and rights of an unborn baby, but I don't think we'll change many minds by arguing about that ... We need more discussion, then, of abortion as a women's issue. Abortion damages women. It does them physical and psychological harm, which is multiplied by the fact that very few women seeking abortions give their informed consent" (PWPL, 4 February 2008).

Other activists in the movement have also supported this new line of argumentation. Gail Reid, the managing editor of *Faith Today*, published an editorial in the May/June 2011 issue that applauded this approach as unexpected and "refreshing": "This movement manifests a concern for unborn children – but also, very importantly, a concern for women – that is confident, sincere, and focused on a positive approach by changing minds and hearts. Against the background of bitter past protests, it offers a refreshing understanding of the issues and a clear intention to intervene in positive ways" (Reid 2011, 6). Moreover, she also highlighted the fact that these contemporary anti-abortion arguments are being developed and popularized by women: "Many of these young women have been encouraged by the stories of older women, who have turned their regrets about abortion into action. They are well aware of strong evidence today that shows abortion has negatively affected women's lives in a very profound way – physically and mentally" (6).

These types of "pro-woman" argumentation are increasingly characterizing even the most traditional strains of anti-abortion activism in Canada. Even the president of Prince Edward Island Right to Life recently argued against loosening provincial restrictions on abortion by stating that "the science is pretty straightforward. Women are being harmed by abortions. It is the best-kept secret in North America. Women suffer in silence following an abortion from a number of different consequences, whether it's a short term risk of infection or a punctured womb from surgery itself, to the later implications psychologically" (Hudes 2014).

The question for us is, where does Canada's anti-abortion movement stand overall on this idea of "pro-women" argumentation? Have important actors taken up this new mode of argumentation, focused on women's health and rights? Or are they the musings of observers and activists who are profoundly out of touch with the larger (and more traditional) movement?

To determine the nature and weight of this and other explicit argumentation in the anti-abortion movement's public discourse, we analysed and coded each case in our data set to identify which explicit arguments (if an explicit argument existed) were being used to defend the anti-abortion position. Based on our pilot analyses, we coded for six different anti-abortion arguments: fetal-personhood arguments, abortion-harms-society arguments, wrong side of history arguments, abortion-harms-men arguments, abortion-harms-women arguments, and one category for other miscellaneous anti-abortion arguments.[15]

When we began this study, we believed that, given the pervasiveness of the traditional portrait, it would be noteworthy if we found evidence that the abortion-harms-women argument was present in 10–15 per cent of cases (as this would indicate it was a strongly emergent new argument). As with the question of religious references, however, what we found left us very surprised.

---

15 These categories were developed after extensive preliminary qualitative sampling and analysis of a smaller sub-set of anti-abortion discourse. The coding of the arguments was not mutually exclusive (i.e., if two arguments existed in a single case, we coded both as present). This method both gave an overall picture of the frequency of each argument and avoided the need to make judgments about which was the "primary" argument when two or more arguments co-existed.

Figure 8.2 Explicit Anti-abortion Arguments (% of cases in data set)

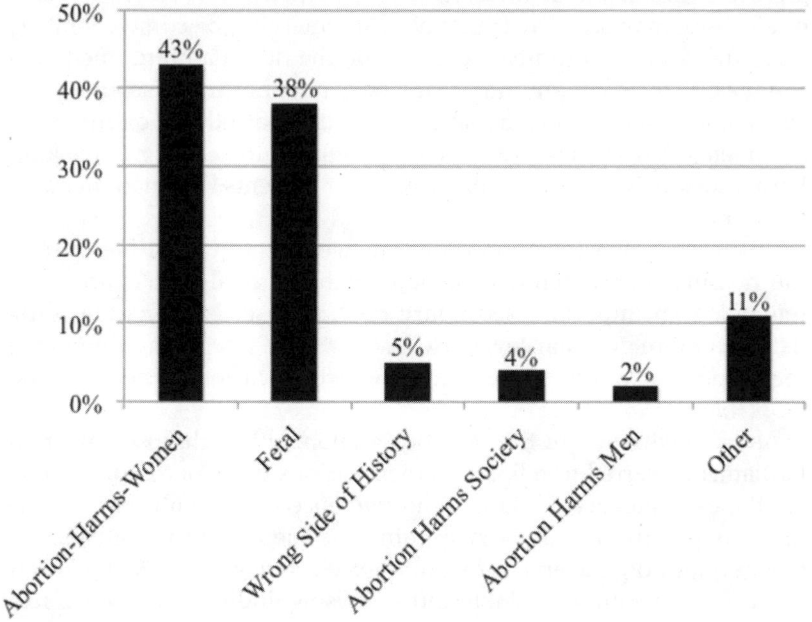

Note: Percentages are not mutually exclusive – if a case had two distinct arguments in it, it was coded twice (once for each code).

Figure 8.2 shows the percentage of cases in our data set that make reference to each of the six types of arguments.

The results of our analysis suggest some significant continuity in the types of explicit argumentation used in anti-abortion discourse. We found, for example, that fetal personhood remains an important argument, used in 37.7% of all cases. However, beneath this apparent continuity lies significant change. On the one hand, as we will explore in a later section, our qualitative analysis of contemporary fetal-centric arguments shows that the nature of the contemporary version of this argument is quite different from older versions. More important, however, is the fact that, although our analysis shows the continued importance of fetal-centric arguments, it also clearly demonstrates that they have been overtaken by a new type of argument, which we call the A-H-W (abortion-harms-women) argument.

On aggregate we found that, while the fetal personhood arguments are present in 37.7% of cases, A-H-W arguments are present in 42.9% of all cases analysed. Far from being an emerging discursive strategy, then, the A-H-W argument seems to be the dominant argumentative framework for contemporary Canadian anti-abortion discourse. Less surprising, but still very notable, is the fact that other, "culture war" arguments that seem to remain very popular in the US (e.g., "abortion-harms-society" arguments) are very minor currents in Canadian public discourse.

If it is clear that the abortion-harms-women argument has become the dominant argument in Canada (with the fetal-centric argument remaining an important secondary one), a closer examination of the data at a more granular level also reveals some interesting differences regarding which arguments are preferred by various types of actors (see table 8.1).

As we mentioned in the previous section, although no members of Parliament referred to religion in their various types of discourse, they are the one category of actors who referenced fetal-centric arguments more frequently than A-H-W arguments. The other two categories – bloggers and organizations – significantly privileged the A-H-W argument. These are highly notable and surprising findings. For even if fetal personhood remains an important argument, our analysis demonstrates that a sea change has taken place in anti-abortion discourse over the past twenty years.

If we analyse the data set with an even more precise mode of measurement, however, we can see that the A-H-W argument is even more dominant than the above metrics suggest. Allow us to explain. Sometimes, analysing the mere presence/non-presence of an argument in

Table 8.1 Explicit Anti-abortion Arguments (Number and Percentage of Cases Where Category Present)

Type of Argument	Blogs	Organizations	MPs	Total
Fetal Personhood	101 / 34.5%	34 / 46.6%	16 / 45.7%	151 / 37.7%
Abortion Harms Society	8 / 2.7%	3 / 4.1%	4 / 11.4%	15 / 3.7%
Wrong Side of History	18 / 6.1%	2 / 2.7%	1 / 2.9%	21 / 5.2%
Abortion Harms Men	6 / 2.0%	2 / 2.7%	1 / 2.9%	9 / 2.2%
Abortion Harms Women	117 / 39.9%	44 / 60.3%	11 / 31.4%	172 / 42.9%
Other	24 / 8.2%	17 / 23.3%	5 / 14.3%	46 / 11.5%

Note: Codings are not mutually exclusive – if a case had two distinct arguments in it, it was coded twice (once for each code).

a case can be imprecise. For example, what about the case of a text in which two arguments are referenced, but one argument is discussed in much more detail? In such cases, one methodological practice is to supplement the presence/absence coding with an analysis of the total number of words devoted to one argument or the other. The idea, of course, is that if a text spends more time and energy (i.e., words) on a given argument, in most cases it is reasonable to suggest that the longer argument carries a heavier weight in terms of its impact on the audience, and thus should be measured as such.

This is not merely a theoretical possibility. Take, for example, the page entitled "What to Expect" on the Signal Hill website. In this case, both the fetal personhood and the A-H-W argument were coded as present, which would mean that, on that metric, it would look like abortion-harms-women and fetal-centric arguments were equally present, and thus should be interpreted as equally important. However, when one analyses this case more closely in terms of the relative time spent on each argument, we find that only 37 words (or 6 per cent of the words of the web page devoted to explicit argumentation) were devoted to outlining a fetal-personhood argument while 567 words (or 94 per cent of words of the web page devoted to explicit argumentation) were used to outline an explicit A-H-W argument.

We therefore analysed all of the data set cases according to this second metric so that we would have a more precise measurement of their importance in the overall discourse. What we found was even more convincing evidence that the discourse of the contemporary movement is changing.

Whereas the original frequency-of-argument analysis in table 8.1 suggests that the abortion-harms-women argument is slightly more prevalent than the fetal-centric argument (approximately 43 per cent compared to 38 per cent), the more precise word count metric demonstrates that the A-H-W argument carries a much greater weight in terms of total words: 21.4 per cent of the words used in all the cases analysed were devoted to arguing that abortion harms women whereas only 8.2 per cent of the total words argued from a fetal-personhood perspective (see figure 8.3). This means that the relative weight of the abortion-harms-women argument is more than two and a half times that of fetal-centric arguments.

Breaking down the word count results by actor reveals that even the discourse of the one category of actors (MPs) who appeared to use fetal-centric arguments more than A-H-W arguments (on the case count analysis) actually spent much more time outlining A-H-W arguments

Figure 8.3 Explicit Anti-abortion Arguments (% of words)

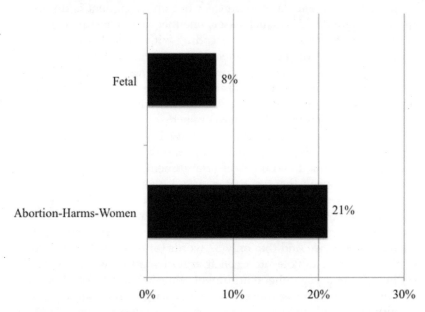

Note: Percentages are not mutually exclusive – if a case had two distinct arguments in it, it was coded twice (once for each code).

than they did fetal-personhood arguments. For although 46% of all MP cases contained fetal-centric arguments (compared to only 31% with A-H-W arguments), only 8.7% of the total words written by MPs were devoted to fetal-centric arguments. In contrast, 19.2% of their total words were devoted to A-H-W arguments – more than twice as much as fetal-centric arguments.

Other qualitative methods of analysing the discursive primacy of arguments further reinforce our quantitative finding that the A-H-W argument has become the dominant strain in Canada. One such oft-used qualitative method is to hone in on a limited number of central texts or sites (those that are seen to be the most important in the over-all structure of an organization's advocacy and self-promotion efforts, or those that are likely to be the most visited web pages or parts of the texts) and analyse those sources carefully to determine the logical primacy of the information contained within them. This method also returned results that strongly corroborated our quantitative findings.

Consider, for example, the layout of the PWPL's homepage, entitled "The Story," which describes the mission, mandate, and beliefs that govern the PWPL's approach to blogging and lists ten "core beliefs" that characterize the blog. What becomes immediately clear is the predominance of the A-H-W argument. For example, of the ten core beliefs, six can be described as advancing some kind of A-H-W messaging. Similarly – and once again mirroring our larger findings – only two of the ten beliefs advanced fetal-personhood arguments (one of which contains an A-H-W element).

It is not just the frequency and word count of these arguments that matter, however. The prioritization and placement of arguments can also substantially determine the overall impact (and thus importance) of a given argument. One way to think about this is to consider the force of what is often called the "inverted pyramid structure" – a familiar concept in media analysis and journalism (Gitlin 1980). According to media scholars Pan and Kosicki, by placing the most important (or salient) arguments first, "certain elements of the issue get a greater allocation of an individual's cognitive resources. An important consequence of this is that the selected elements become important in influencing individuals' judgments or inference making" (1993, 57). Simply put, because more people are inclined to read the beginning of an article or blog post, as opposed to the end – and because the frame that is first encountered by the reader often stays with them the most powerfully – the content that is put first usually has the most impact (hence the reason it is also a journalistic teaching tool used to guide how reporters write articles).

As the order of arguments and persuasive techniques is itself a "meta-technique" used to enhance specific arguments by subtly emphasizing and de-emphasizing certain frames or arguments, analysing the sequence of arguments provides clues about how important various arguments are in a given discursive universe. Once again, we found that using this type of qualitative analysis corroborates and reinforces our quantitative findings. Applying this technique to the PWPL web page mentioned above ("The Story," see PWPL 2007) we can see very clearly that its pyramid structure focuses our attention on the A-H-W argument. In fact, all of the first five core beliefs advance A-H-W arguments. It is not until the sixth point that the PWPL web page mentions the fetus, or fetal personhood.

The PWPL blog is not an outlier in this respect. The majority of the anti-abortion organizations that we analysed structured their websites in similar ways. For instance, of the thirteen CLC web pages that deal solely with abortion, only three sections use exclusively A-H-W arguments. However, on the homepage, among the thirteen sections, the three A-H-W ones are listed second, third, and sixth. In comparison, only one of the sections on the homepage (a section entitled "prenatal development") deals primarily with fetal personhood, and, perhaps most surprisingly, it is listed last. Similarly, on the Alliance for Life Ontario (AFLO) site, of the twelve web pages that deal exclusively with abortion, four advance exclusive A-H-W arguments, and these pages are listed second, third, fourth, and fifth. Moreover, in the case of AFLO, while fetal personhood no doubt underpins many of these web pages, not one of them deals exclusively (or even primarily) with fetal personhood. What is very clear, then, is that the A-H-W argument is not only predominant in its frequency and word count, but is also being highlighted by anti-abortion bloggers and websites in the basic structure of their arguments.

Overall, our findings demonstrate that the A-H-W argument is not merely an emerging argument. Nor is it merely one that has narrowly overtaken the traditional fetal-centric argument. Our results show that the A-H-W perspective has become the dominant (but certainly not exclusive) explicit argument in contemporary Canadian anti-abortion discourse – something that is nothing less than a discursive tectonic shift.

If these quantitative findings tell us that this transformation has occurred, they don't reveal what the precise nature of the A-H-W argument is. In the next section we analyse the new anti-abortion discourse to determine what type of harm it asserts abortion visits upon women and how the discourse attempts to convince women that abortions are harmful for them.

8.3 Framing Harm: Discursive Medicalization, Progressive Cooptation, Repetition

To address these issues, we analysed every case where the A-H-W argument was present to further identify what type of specific harm was being asserted. Based on the findings of our pilot analysis, we coded for five different types: physical/medical harm; psychological harm; harm to personal life; general unspecified harm; and other types of harm.

As with the question of religion discussed above, one of the most interesting findings is again what was not present. As mentioned previously, there is very little if any reference to the spiritual, moral, or religious harm that a "culture of abortion" might be seen as doing (although this discourse is clearly present in the American culture wars surrounding the abortion debate). In fact, what stood out very strongly was the degree to which contemporary Canadian anti-abortion discourse differs strongly from this trend. So what did we find?

As shown in figure 8.4, the most prevalent type of harm asserted was psychological harm – the idea that women are being psychologically harmed and emotionally devastated by abortion.[16] Of all the cases where the A-H-W argument was present, 36.6 per cent argue that abortion causes women to experience long-term and severe psychological harm. Moreover, when we consider this category in conjunction with the other category we used to track a specific type of primarily psychological harm ("personal harm" – which was present in 12.2 per cent of cases), it is clear that claims about psychological forms of harm form the central core of the abortion-harms-women argument. It is also clear that claims about physical harm are an important part of this argument, with more than 30 per cent of cases referring to this form of harm.

Interestingly, however, we can also see some distinct tendencies in the discourse of different actors, which are shown in table 8.2. For example, only 29 per cent of blogging cases referred to psychological harm, whereas both organizations and politicians focused on this area at least 50% of the time. Bloggers were much more likely to simply assert that abortion caused general unspecified harm, something that MPs did very rarely.

Besides their relative quantitative weight, several other dimensions are particularly noteworthy about the sub-categories of the A-H-W argument and the ways they are used by various actors. For example, across the board there is a very strong rhetorical attempt to frame the anti-abortion position as based in definitive scientific and medical studies and statistics. A typical example is an article posted on MP Maurice Vellacott's website, which has the appearance of scientific validity but

---

16 Again, the purpose of this book is not to evaluate the soundness of these arguments. We map the claims of the anti-abortion movement rather than evaluate their logical, philosophical, medical, and scientific validity. Nonetheless, we should note that the medical research community strongly challenges the existence and significance of the abortion-harms-women claims, with the vast majority of studies (and meta-studies reviewing the aggregate findings of all the relevant individual scientific studies) showing no significant long-term differences, for example, in mental health outcomes as a result of elective pregnancy terminations. See, for example, Charles, Polis, Sridhara, and Blum 2008 and Major et al. 2009.

Figure 8.4 Types of Abortion-Harms-Women Arguments (% of cases in data set)

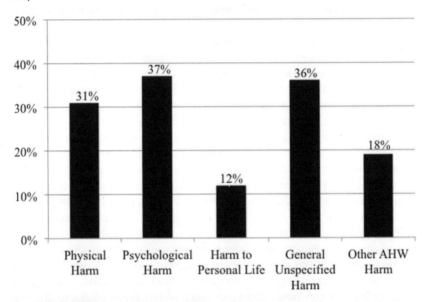

Note Percentages are not mutually exclusive – if a case had two distinct arguments in it, it was coded twice (once for each code).

tends to conflate random correlation with causality: "Since the 1970s, there has been a marked increase in North America in the number of abortions and repeat abortions, which may explain the significant

Table 8.2 Types of A-H-W Arguments (Number and Percentage of Cases Where Category Present)

Type of Abortion Harms Women Argument	Blogs	Organizations	MPs	Total
Physical Harm	28 / 24.5%	19 / 47.5%	6 / 50%	53 / 30.8%
Psychological Harm	33 / 28.9%	23 / 57.5%	6 / 50%	62 / 36.6%
Harm to Personal Life	13 / 11.4%	7 / 17.5%	1 / 1.8%	21 / 12.2%
General Unspecified Harm	51 / 44.7%	9 / 22.5%	2 / 3.6%	62 / 36.0%
Other Abortion-Harms-Women Argument	20 / 17.1%	7 / 15.9%	4 / 36.4%	31 / 18.6%

Note: Codings are not mutually exclusive – if a case had two distinct arguments in it, it was coded twice (once for each code).

increases in pelvic inflammatory disease (PID), uterine haemorrhage, sepsis, pain due to endometritis, retained fetal or placental tissue, and the increasing evidence of an abortion-breast cancer link" (deVeber Institute for Bioethics and Social Research 2004). Interestingly, despite the fact that this study is not peer reviewed, it is regularly cited as an authority on the issue. Similar examples can be found throughout the blog entries and on virtually all the organizational websites. The Toronto Right to Life website, for example, argues that, during the three month period after their abortions, "women had a more than four times higher rate of hospitalization for infections, a five times higher rate of 'surgical events' and a nearly five times higher rate of hospitalization for psychiatric problems than the matching group of women who had not had abortions" (TRL 2010a). A large majority of the top responses to a Google search of the "medical effects of abortion" are anti-abortion counselling sites that reproduce similar claims. There is little objectively generated evidence to support these types of claims, but as James Hoggan has shown in other subject areas, this does not necessarily impede their usage or force in the contemporary public sphere (Hoggan 2009).

The medicalization strategy is also employed when discussing psychological harm. Perhaps the most notable expression of this strategy is the coining, and attempt to popularize the concept, of "post-abortion syndrome" (PAS). A term that was first introduced in the early 1980s by American anti-abortion activist David Reardon (see chapter 12 for full discussion), it is not recognized by the American Psychological Association or the American Psychiatric Association (or any Canadian equivalent), nor can it be found in the Diagnostic and Statistical Manual of Mental Disorders or the International Statistical Classification of Diseases. Despite the fact that there is no credible medical or scientific proof of this condition, it is used widely in contemporary Canadian anti-abortion discourse. According to information posted on the Alliance for Life Ontario website, for example, PAS is said to emerge out of the "trauma of an abortion [and] can follow a woman for the rest of her life" (AFLO, 2010c). According to its proponents, PAS is experienced by almost all women as a result of the feelings of sorrow, grief, and regret following their abortions, and these feelings often lead to mental illness, suicidal thoughts, nervous disorders, depression, and/or substance abuse (AFLO, 2010a).

One of the reasons the reference to PAS is a powerful rhetorical strategy is that it subtly calls to mind other medically recognized syndromes and, in doing so, activates a medically credible "network of associations" (Westen 2007, 457) in ways that encourage the audience to accept PAS as a medically and scientifically validated condition (despite the fact that it is nothing of the sort). In this case, the term PAS seeks to evoke a parallel with post-traumatic stress disorder (PTSD). As with PTSD, PAS portrays "victims of abortion" as experiencing "recurrent and intrusive thoughts about the abortion or aborted child, flashbacks in which the woman momentarily re-experiences an aspect of the abortion experience, nightmares about the abortion or child, or anniversary reactions of intense grief or depression on the due date of the aborted pregnancy or the anniversary date of the abortion" (TRL 2010b).

Proponents also use this rhetorical strategy to make a link between abortion and sexual assault. Contemporary anti-abortion discourse often implicitly (if unsubtly) encourages us to make this association by suggesting that abortion is emotionally or metaphorically similar to sexual assault, such as when the Toronto Right to Life website states that some women "report that the pain of abortion, inflicted upon them by a masked stranger invading their body, feels identical to rape." Other times the link is made explicitly. For example the Toronto Right to Life website asserts that "many [women] are forced into an unwanted abortion by husbands, boyfriends, parents, or others" and, consequently, "abortion may be perceived as the ultimate violation in a life characterized by abuse" (TRL 2010b). Extending this to a broader public policy level, blogger Tanya Zaleski suggests that "a link was also found between domestic violence and women seeking repeat abortions. 30% of women having a second abortion reported relationship violence and women having a third or subsequent abortion were over 2.5 times as likely to report a history of physical or sexual abuse by a male partner" (PWPL, 5 August 2009). In using this rhetorical device, contemporary anti-abortion discourse manages to frame the anti-abortion position as being just the opposite of a reactionary, conservative, anti-woman stance. Instead, it appears as nothing less than a logical extension of the anti-violence concerns of progressive feminism.

Finally, it is interesting to note that in 36% of A-H-W cases (only 0.6% less than the psychological harm sub-code), the anti-abortion materials simply assert that abortion harms women, without specifying how. Interestingly, this strategy was most prevalent in the blogger's discourse (45% of A-H-W cases) and much less so in the case of organizational websites (23%) and politicians (16%). Through these non-specific statements, anti-abortion advocates repeatedly assert that abortion is damaging to women. Why is this tactic of "content-free assertion" rhetorically interesting? Because far from being discursive flotsam with little to no impact, repetition is a very potent rhetorical technique. As Drew Westen (1985; 2007) discusses, the process of repetition is an effective way of transforming "value paradigms" into "psychological values." In other words, the more frequently a speaker repeats a statement, the more likely that statement is to be internalized by its receiver. As the neuroplasticity literature likes to say, neurons that fire together, wire together. Ultimately, Westen is arguing that "the more the repetition, the greater the probability of communicating the message" (Westen 1985, 301). Repetition – even the repetition of completely false claims – creates feelings of familiarity in an audience. And feelings of familiarity often function for many people as a gut-level indication of a statement's truthfulness. It is thus literally the case that the more a lie is repeated, the more it starts to feel like the truth to us. This is why the discursive strategy of simply repeating a non-specific claim of harm is, far from being irrelevant, a key rhetorical strategy.

8.4 Visual Signalling: The Changing Face of the Movement

As we saw in chapter 7, the strength of an argument is only partially grounded in its content. *Who* is doing the saying can be equally important as *what* is being said. If the tone, the style of speech, or the visual impact of the speaker is at odds with the content, it can have a powerful negative impact – encouraging the audience to question the authenticity of the debater or judge the argument as a cynical attempt to "sell" the idea. And this can be fatal to even the most convincing of arguments. It is not surprising, then, that the key point of Preston Manning's advice to any religious political activist is to "find and train the 'right' spokesperson(s) to advance your cause (it might not be you) by asking the question 'Out of whose mouth would this message be most credible'" (Manning 2009).

The relevance of this advice for the anti-abortion movement is clear. An anti-abortion movement that visually (and otherwise) reinforced the stereotype of the movement as male-controlled, conservative, and anti-woman would face a significant challenge. For even if the arguments were about "women's health," the visuals would likely seem to contradict the messaging, which would risk making the entire position appear to many Canadians as a hypocritical and/or cynical marketing effort.

In this context, it is notable that the anti-abortion movement in Canada seems to be actively working to cultivate an increasing number of young women to play highly prominent and much public roles. This visual shift is rife with important implications for the way the anti-abortion message will be received in Canada. Here, Barbara Kay's critical reflection on the anti-abortion movement is again helpful to set the stage. One of her key insights was that the anti-abortion movement must break down the traditional visual portrait of who the anti-abortion movement is: "Don't let the media and student unions pigeonhole the pro-life movement as Christian evangelists and stay-at-home moms with 10 children (not that there's anything wrong with that). There are many secular career women who sympathize with or actively support your cause" (Kay 2009).

As we will see throughout the remainder of Part II, there is little question that the communications strategies of the movement's public discourse are increasingly aligned with Kay's advice. Not only have the anti-abortion *arguments* and *rhetoric* shifted; the "who" making these arguments has also changed. And the fact that young women are increasingly the public face of the movement means that the visuals of the movement now also seem to actively embody the pro-woman argument of the contemporary discourse.[17] We might call this a strategy of visual signalling or performative embodiment, for the foregrounding of young women as the spokespersons and leaders of the movement visually reinforces the credibility of the "pro-woman" message by performing it, literally, in the embodied gender of the spokeswomen.

It seems that a variety of influential anti-abortion actors explicitly recognize the performative value of having women, especially young women, speak out publicly on this issue. Since the mid-2000s, Andrea Mrozek has been one of the most eloquent champions of this view. In a 2009 interview, she argued that "the unconvinced in our country are

---

17 We are not saying, of course, that the anti-abortion movement is now made up only of women. Men continue to be active and visible members and leaders of the movement. This is particularly true in the formal political realm, where women are substantially under-represented in the ranks of MPs. Our point is that women – and especially young women – seem to be more heavily highlighted in the public communications and strategies of the movement than they were in the previous wave of anti-abortion activism. It may also be that the relative percentage of anti-abortion activists that are women has increased, but we do not have reliable data on this. What is clear is that the number of young women running anti-abortion organizations and acting as primary spokespeople for the movement is much higher than what the traditional portrait suggests.

willing and able to listen to a young woman's voice more than a man, no matter what his age" (quoted in Newman 2011, 18). Why does she believe this? In Mrozek's words:

> The beauty of being a woman who is pro-life is that it is fairly easy to annoy my opponents simply by showing up. I don't need to say all that much, when combating the anachronistic notion that "abortion is a woman's right." I simply need to stand there (with shoes on, outside the kitchen!) and ask – hey, why is that self-evident? Because I don't get it. And I don't believe it. And by the way – that's your opinion, not a fact. (PWPL, 29 April 2009)

In Mrozek's view, foregrounding women who advocate an anti-abortion position is a powerful communications technique not simply because it defuses the old stereotype of the movement being male led and anti-woman. Its force also stems from the fact that it challenges feminist assertions that abortion rights are *necessarily* in the interests of women. Having *women* question this assumption makes the critique appear more authentic (as these women, in a very different way than men, would have to directly live the consequences of such a policy). The visibility of women making such arguments is, according to Mrozek, a crucial rhetorical advantage.

Moreover, the movement seems to be marketing itself using visual images that increasingly represent the movement as much more women led and focused. As we will discuss in the following chapters, this idea has become central to its external communications strategies with respect to the broader Canadian public over the past few years. But it is notable that this image rebranding has also increasingly characterized the ways in which the movement represents itself to its internal members. The May/June 2011 issue of *Faith Today* – the magazine of the EFC – is symptomatic of this shift. The cover story of the issue is titled "The New Face of the Pro-Life Movement: How Young Women Are Having an Influence" (Newman 2011) and the cover features four of the most prominent young spokeswomen of the movement – Andrea Mrozek, Stephanie Gray, Faye Sonier, and Ruth Lobo.

The article focuses on two main themes. One is the idea that the anti-abortion movement is increasingly embracing a "women's rights" perspective in its messaging. As the author approvingly writes, "as surprising as it might sound, it's women's rights that actually inform much of the pro-life message these days" (Newman 2011, 18). The other is the fact that it is increasingly young women who are the most visible faces of the movement: "Articulate, educated young women who embrace the gains of the women's liberation movement – this is the face of today's pro-life movement." (18). Two years later, the same visuals were emphasized in the magazine's article "Why Is It So Hard to Talk about Abortion in Canada" (Newman 2013): five of the six photos that accompany the article show only female faces. Such an approach is not unique to *Faith Today*. The Toronto Right to Life/National Campus Life Network high school student club manual (see chapter 7) also shows picture after picture of young women, with almost no young men. In fact, seventy out of the eighty-five people shown in the pictures of that manual were female, and almost all appeared to be under the age of twenty-five (TRL 2012).

Although the movement obviously has a clear interest in promoting this image makeover, this does not seem to be simply marketing. Consider the following. The most popular anti-abortion blog in Canada, ProWomanProLife, is made up entirely of women bloggers. Several of them are also highly visible in the public debate outside their blogs. As mentioned, Andrea Mrozek is the executive director of the Institute of Family and Marriage Canada (IMFC) and a frequent contributor of opeds to, and one of the go-to anti-abortion commentators and interviewees for, the national media. Faye Sonier is the legal counsel for the EFC and a frequent commentator in the media. Brigitte Pellerin has also been a frequent contributor to print media in Canada and was a Parliamentary Bureau reporter for Sun Media and the Sun News Network. Moreover, one of the explicit goals of the PWPL blog is to cultivate more vocal women to engage in the public debate against abortion: "ProWomanProLife aims to develop a nationwide network of mentors, 'big sisters,' who can speak confidently to their views on why abortion is not a woman's right, and help other women to understand the same" (PWPL 2008).

Women also seem to occupy prominent leadership positions in many other anti-abortion groups. For example, our analysis of the leadership structures of prominent anti-abortion groups in Canada in 2013/14 revealed that many of them were headed and staffed by women. The executive directors of the two major anti-abortion organizations (the CCBR and NCLN) were both young women (the CCBR was headed by Stephanie Gray, the NCLN by Rebecca Richmond). Moreover, all five of the staff members at NCLN were young women, while the CCBR listed ten women and seven men on its staff. In terms of the other anti-abortion organizations we examined, the executive director of Alliance for Life Ontario was a woman, Jakki Jeffs, with seven of the eleven other executive and board members being female. The President of LifeCanada, Monica Roddis, was also female, as were eight of the nine members of the executive. Signal Hill's executive director was male, but the seven staff members were women. The national director of the CLC is James Hughes, but women led six of the eight provincial offices on which the group provides information. Moreover, the primary lead on their youth-outreach efforts was Alissa Golob – a highly visible spokesperson in the movement. Unsurprisingly, the 2013 National Pro-Life Conference speaker list also reflected this trend. Of the fourteen speakers that were slated to present at the October conference, ten were women, including many of the ones discussed above. Furthermore, even a brief glance at the pictures from the national March for Life rallies in 2012–15 highlights the fact that there were many, many young female faces in the crowd. This is no doubt partially due to the fact that the March for Life, other anti-abortion groups and a variety of Catholic school divisions, anti-abortion clubs, and so on, invest heavily in bussing school-age youth to the rally from all over Ontario. But regardless of the reason, they are there, for each other and the cameras to see.

This is not to say that there has been a complete, 180 degree transformation and that women are now the sole face of the movement. Up to this point, none of the anti-abortion private members' bills introduced since 1988 have been tabled by a female MP. At the 2013 March for Life event in Ottawa, only two of the twenty or so MPs and senators who were officially announced were women. And, currently, the most outspoken anti-abortion MPs are all men. Moreover, there are several largely male-dominated organizations that, while not primarily focused on the abortion issue, publicly intervene from an anti-abortion perspective. For example, when we examined their organization in 2013/14, ten of the eleven board members of the EFC appeared to be male, as was the president and six of ten members of its leadership team. All eight members of the board of ARPA also appeared to be male, as well as the individuals occupying the three senior leadership positions.

The point, then, is not that there are no men left in the movement. Rather, it is that, in contrast to the traditional image, which portrays the movement as almost exclusively male led, a brief analysis of the organizational structure of anti-abortion organizations in Canada reveals that there is a much larger and influential cohort of female leadership in the movement than has been traditionally suggested, and that these women are increasingly dominant and visible, especially in the communications realm.

8.5 Fetal Personhood Renewed

The rise of the A-H-W argument, combined with the increased visibility of women within the movement, paints a significantly different picture of contemporary Canadian anti-abortion activism and its explicit communications strategies than does the traditional portrait. However, it is crucial to note that despite this, the A-H-W argument is not the only important contemporary argument used by the movement today. For despite its demonstrated prominence, some important actors in the Canadian movement strongly disagree with the idea that an A-H-W argument should be at the core of the anti-abortion movement's messaging. The CCBR, for example, explicitly disagrees with the strategy of focusing on this argument. On the one hand, it is dismissed as being "reactive": "the idea that pro-lifers need to change what they're doing *simply* because people respond badly is not only flawed, it is entirely reactive – which is what the other side wants" (CCBR 2013a, 2). The CCBR also sees a significant weakness in the A-H-W argument itself, and the group insists that relying primarily on this argument substantially weakens the anti-abortion position:

> When pro-lifers put too much emphasis on the risks women face from abortion, they lose ground. As an abortion advocate could point out, there are risks inherent to many medical procedures ... But more to the point, if pro-lifers claim that abortion is wrong because it hurts women, what happens if it doesn't hurt women? ... Would this mean that abortion becomes morally acceptable. (CCBR 2013h, 33)

Perhaps most importantly, the CCBR argues that the A-H-W argument must be rejected because it ignores the fundamental problem of abortion and, in doing so, plays into and intensifies a individualistic conception of society and obligation:

> If pro-lifers allow themselves to be distracted by arguments focusing on why abortion is not in a *woman's* self interest, then we are implicitly reinforcing the pro-abortion position and not our own. We are legitimizing the pro-abortion principle that the women's interests take precedence over the child's life ... [But] abortion is *not* wrong because it hurts women. Abortion is wrong because it intentionally kills an innocent human being. *That* is why it hurts women. Because abortion involves killing one's children, it hurts women psychologically ... [and] physically. (CCBR 2013h, 33)

Although the CCBR understands the value of the A-H-W argument, it thinks it should be at best an add-on strategy. For the CCBR, "testimonies and personal appeals are powerful – and important – but they shouldn't replace the foundational message about what abortion does to the unborn" (CCBR 2013a, 3). Thus, to the question "should we *primarily* appeal to a women's interests or concerns" when arguing against abortion, the CCBR would answer "no."

Unsurprisingly, then, the CCBR is by far the most vocal supporter retaining a focus on fetal-centric arguments. Although it is no longer the uncontested dominant argument in the anti-abortion movement, fetal personhood remains a profoundly important one. That said, the contemporary version is not necessarily identical to older variants of the fetal-centric argument. As we have seen, even those actors who employ fetal-centric arguments now do so almost exclusively on the basis of scientific and visual arguments, rather than the religious ones highlighted by the traditional portrait. In one of the most recent private members' interventions, for instance, Stephen Woodworth's M-312 called on Parliament to establish a committee to examine if the Criminal Code's definition of "human beings" should include fetuses. Using the language of modern science, Woodworth's speech in the first hour of parliamentary debate on M-312 declared that any law "defining a human being must absolutely be an honest law based on cogent evidence and sound principle." He further argued, "perhaps that ancient definition [the one that does not define the fetus as a human being] made sense when leeches and bloodletting were standard medical practices but does it make sense in the twenty-first century?" (Woodworth 2012a). By presenting his own argument as scientific, medically relevant, and modern, Woodworth's fetal-centric approach represents both some continuity with certain characteristics of traditional fetal-centric arguments but also differs significantly from the religiously grounded appeals to the sanctity of life that dominate the traditional portrait of anti-abortion discourse.

It is also important to note that many contemporary fetal-centric arguments avoid contrasting the rights of women with the rights of the fetus. Instead, advocates fuse the interests of the fetus and the woman in order to argue that abortion harms women and the fetus simultaneously – a much softer and more palatable version than previous iterations. In fact, contemporary fetal personhood arguments often go to great lengths to represent the interests of the fetus and woman as necessarily and inextricably intertwined and symbiotic. As one blogger puts it, "you can't protect a foetus without protecting the woman. You can't hurt a woman without hurting the foetus. When a foetus is aborted, you have to hurt the woman to hurt the foetus. This is why we are pro-life because we are prowoman" (PWPL, 14 May 2008).

The movement has also created a variety of visuals that underline this fused viewpoint. Consider the image that Alissa Golob, youth coordinator for the CLC, shared on Twitter in March 2013 (Golob, 29 March 2013) in support of Mark Warawa's M-408 motion against sex-selective abortion (see figure 8.5).

Many elements of this graphic are notable: the black-and-white colouring, the exaggerated eye liner, the dark features of the young women, her fear-widened eyes, the male hands of her assaulter, and the explicit text all function to analogically define abortion as a "violence against women" issue. What is particularly interesting about this graphic, however, is that it also explicitly fuses the interests and bodily security of actual women with those of a fetus. Whereas previous fetal-personhood rhetoric represented abortion as exclusively violating the right to life of the fetus, now abortion is depicted as equally harmful and dangerous for women as well.

This strategy of discursively merging the interests of the fetus and the pregnant woman has also characterized some of the more recent anti-abortion attempts at federal legislation. Consider Conservative MP Ken Epp's 2007 private members' Bill C-484 – colloquially titled The Unborn Victims of Crime Act. The goal of the bill was to "protect fetuses from third-party attacks" (ARCC 2012). However, when many of the bill's critics argued that it sought to introduce some form of fetal personhood into the Criminal Code, anti-abortion activists countered that the bill was in fact designed to buttress women's rights and safety. Epp himself argued that the bill went "very narrowly at one issue – where the woman has made the choice to have the child, and that choice is taken away unilaterally, without her consent and usually with violence" (quoted in PWPL, 5 January 2008). By framing themselves not simply as protectors of fetal life, but also as defenders of women's choice and safety, these anti-abortion arguments attempt to avoid the common feminist charge that the anti-abortion movement discounts women's health and choices in the name of the unborn fetus.

Virtually all fetal-centric arguments are now positioned with a tone and framing that actively work against the old stereotypes of the traditional portrait, seeking to present the fetal-argument as profoundly "pro-woman." We will examine these in detail in the following three chapters (particularly in the context of Mark Warawa's M-408 against

Figure 8.5

Source: Personhood USA. Images: Dunca Daniel Mihai/Alamy (top); Eric Fahrner/Shutterstock (bottom)

sex-selective abortions). What is important to understand here in relation to explicit argumentation is that the anti-abortion movement has
found subtle ways of combining the A-H-W argument and the fetal-
centric argument, while expressing them using overtly pro-woman,
pro-girl language and symbolism. Moreover, as we will show in the
following chapters, even the most vocal defender of the fetal-centric
approach – the CCBR – is simultaneously deeply committed to communicating its arguments in a "compassionate" tone and to reframing
the fetal-centric argument in ways that link it to a variety of identities
and values that are far more "pro-woman"-sounding than older versions have traditionally been. All of which is to say that, while fetal
personhood arguments remain important in contemporary Canadian
anti-abortion discourse, even these are quite different than the image
offered in the traditional portrait.

8.6 Conclusion

In the previous chapter, we provided evidence suggesting that many
actors in the contemporary Canadian anti-abortion movement have
been advocating for a strategic reorientation, including the development of new and innovative communication strategies that would drive
a change in cultural values among the wider Canadian public. In this
chapter, we began to examine new modes of persuasion in the contemporary anti-abortion movement and the degree to which its discourse and
communications strategies actually reflect these calls. Beginning with an
examination of the most explicit modes of persuasion – the practice of
justifying a political position by reference to philosophical reasoning and
specific argumentation – we found strong evidence that approaches have
shifted considerably from the assumptions of the traditional portrait.
Our analysis revealed that, rather than appealing to religious sources
for its philosophical grounding, contemporary anti-abortion discourse
largely avoids referencing religious themes. We also demonstrated that,
rather than relying solely on fetal-centric arguments, contemporary anti-
abortion discourse employs a variety of other arguments, the most dominant of which is the "abortion-harms-woman" argument. We showed
that this explicit "pro-woman" argument is reinforced by the fact that
many of the movement's most visible spokespersons are now women,
especially young women – something that lends additional credibility to
its pro-woman positioning. And finally, we highlighted that the contemporary content of even the seemingly traditional fetal-centric arguments

has changed significantly from previous eras and has been crafted into a much more "pro-woman" package.

Explicit philosophical justification and argumentation are only the most obvious techniques of persuasion employed by anti-abortion discourse, however. Many other, less explicit, techniques also play key roles. Thus, in the next chapter we turn to a discussion of "framing" techniques and examine the ways in which identity/brand framing has been used by the anti-abortion movement to reinforce the "pro-woman" orientation communicated by its explicit argumentation.

Chapter 9

We're All Progressives Now: Rebranding the Movement

The common-sense understanding of language is that it is a system in which words primarily represent and express clear and explicit meanings. In this view, while the explicit meaning conveyed by language might be political, language itself is transparent and neutral, allowing debaters to clearly communicate the similarities and differences between their positions. This view of language is one reason why explicit argumentation is usually the first rhetorical technique people imagine when thinking about how social and political movements seek to persuade constituents. However, explicit argumentation is only one way in which political discourses can convince audiences to agree with a given political position. There are many techniques of persuasion that, although more subtle and less obvious, are actually far more influential than explicit argumentation. And they are more influential precisely because they are less obvious. One concept that captures several of these techniques is that of "framing." In this and the following chapter, we will explain how and why framing can be an effective technique of persuasion, identify several different types of framing, and analyse the ways in which the contemporary Canadian anti-abortion discourse uses a variety of framing techniques.

9.1 Essentially Contested Concepts, Networks of Association, and Framing

Although the common-sense view of language sees it is as a clear and neutral medium, most people know from everyday experience that interpretations of the meaning of the same words, even in the same context, can vary widely. Representational (or common-sense) theories of language tend to try to explain away many of these contests over meaning as if they were exceptions and errors. But not all disagreements around meaning can be understood in this way. In many cases, the parameters of what counts as a reasonable and defensible interpretation are wide enough to include substantially differing understandings.

In fact, many scholars suggest that struggles over the meaning and implications of certain words are not exceptional but are instead the norm, particularly in politics. William Connolly, for example, suggests that the battle over words arises from the fact that politics "is the ambiguous and relatively open-ended interaction of persons and groups who share a range of concepts, but share them imperfectly and incompletely" (Connolly 1993, 6). What does it mean that we share a range of concepts imperfectly and incompletely? And why does it matter?

It is useful to think about this in two ways. First, Connolly reminds us that, although it may appear that everyone involved in a given discussion agrees on the terms of debate, individuals and groups may differ profoundly about what these terms mean, what and to whom they apply, and what consequences they imply. He argues, moreover, that this is particularly true for certain types of political concepts that express commonly accepted and deeply valued normative commitments. We may all agree that "liberty" is the most relevant value when evaluating a certain policy question, but there are a variety of understandings of what "liberty" means, and each may lead to a different policy conclusion.

Isaiah Berlin's classic distinction between negative and positive liberty is an excellent example of these different understandings (Berlin 1969). A "negative" interpretation of liberty assumes that liberty is freedom from other people restricting you from acting. You are unfree if, for example, someone physically stops you from playing the piano. "Positive" interpretations of liberty assert that liberty is the freedom to do certain things. Thus, if you want to play piano but cannot afford to buy or rent time on a piano, you are unfree – even if it is the abstract functioning of the market that creates these barriers, rather than a specific individual stopping you. People who hold negative and positive interpretations of liberty might both support policies they see as reducing "piano unfreedom." However, the one who holds the negative liberty perspective would support only those policies that ensured that individuals were not literally stopping others from playing piano, whereas the person with a positive liberty perspective would not only support those laws but would also champion a policy of using state funds to provide improved access to musical instruments to underprivileged populations. Or that person might support a political movement devoted to replacing a capitalist market economy with one that is more socialist. Both perspectives could sincerely claim to be acting in the name of freedom, but they would be arguing for very different policies.

One reason that concepts like freedom are interpreted so differently in the political realm is because these terms have both a descriptive element (they seek to describe whether something is or is not free) and a valued normative element (in contemporary Western society, liberty is usually viewed as something good, all things being equal). According to Connolly, the dual descriptive-normative nature of these terms means that they are key resources in political debate. If advocates of one position are able to ensure that a highly valued concept is, in the dominant discourse, defined in the way they prefer, it tilts the broader political debate in their favour. Connolly suggests that there are a variety of terms that are (a) so flexible in terms of their meaning, and (b) so powerful in regard to the rhetorical force they provide, that we should think of them as "essentially contested concepts." An essentially contested concept, in other words, is a term that is constantly subject to interpretive battle and is thus continually being defined, contested, renegotiated, and redefined. Once we recognize the existence and importance of these types of terms, we can then see that public political discourse is often characterized by a series of interactions in which different sides struggle over the meaning of the same concept by attempting to "adjust, extend, accommodate and transcend" the very meaning of words (Connolly 1993, 6).

Beyond the struggle over the meaning of specific terms, there is a second, politically relevant, way in which we share concepts incompletely and imperfectly. As many thinkers have demonstrated, the most important moment in a debate is often the moment when the questions, and the relevant evaluation criteria, are defined. For if you can gain a relative advantage in a debate by defining a given concept or value in your favour, you can gain an even greater advantage by predetermining how the question is posed and which of the many potential concepts are viewed as most relevant for evaluating a given issue. A classic example often used to illustrate this idea is the frequent battle over whether "equality" or "liberty" should be the pre-eminent value employed to evaluate a specific policy. If you can ensure that an audience believes that income equality is good (or at least that high levels of income inequality are bad) and can also ensure that the value of equality is foremost when they think about policies regarding higher taxation and income redistribution, you are much more likely to garner support for those types of policies than if your audience holds a negative liberty perspective and is thinking about the idea that "free" competition drives more innovation and overall wealth creation.

In contemporary theory, the contest to define these core values and determine which of them audiences use to evaluate an issue is often called the battle over "framing" an issue. The idea of a "frame" and "framing" is useful because it captures so many different aspects of the struggle to shape political meanings. Consider the following common meanings of framing:

- a physical skeleton or structure. The frame of a building gives it shape. It both enables and limits the other features that can be added and helps determine where everything else (windows, doors, roof, hallways) may appear;
- a structure that borders and bounds a picture or piece of art. Frames of this type highlight certain aspects of the picture, draw the eyes to select areas, de-emphasize others, and, with photographs, often literally exclude much of what the original photograph captured. In this way, frames profoundly influence the reception and interpretive message of the piece within the frame;
- a single, stop-action photograph that is only one part of a sequence of dynamic cinematic shots;
- a linguistic structure or pattern (framework) that is widely used generically and establishes a general expectation about the type of meaning of a formulation, even if the specific content varies;
- a verb meaning to pin the blame on someone else – that is, to manipulate perceptions by drawing attention to certain things in a way that is not necessarily "accurate."

What all these common meanings of "frame" have in common is the idea that pre-structuring the overall context/design of an object, event, or discourse can have a significant impact on its final shape and reception.

The concept of framing has become important to a variety of disciplines. In particular, the concept of discursive framing has become an increasingly popular theoretical tool for analysing political movements and their strategies of persuasion. One of the pioneering theorists of the idea of framing, Erving Goffman (1974, 21), suggests that to frame is to identify a "schema of interpretation" that enables individuals "to locate, perceive, identify, and label" everyday life experiences. Following Goffman,

Snow and his colleagues explain that frames have two related roles. On one hand "frames function to organize experience" – that is, how we understand the world and the way it works. But frames also work to "guide action, whether individual or collective," partially as a function of shaping our explicit understanding of the world, partially through other mechanisms (Snow, Rochford, Worden, and Benford 1986, 464). Moreover, many insist that we are collectively involved (although often in different ways) in the processes of producing, reinforcing, transforming, and contesting a wide variety of frames in our societies (e.g., Goffman 1974; Snow et al. 1986; Snow and Benford 1992; 2000). Our engagement with these frames (which most often takes the form of our unconsciously accepting and employing them) has a crucial impact on how we make sense of our experience. Moreover, the more these frames become accepted and solidified as common sense, the more they encourage us to accept certain ideas with less and less critical evaluation.

It is important to recognize that the playing field of framing is not an equal opportunity arena. Some groups and individuals have more power to reinforce or contest certain frames, given their position in, and access to, the discursive means of dissemination in the public sphere (i.e., what type of resources they have to make their frame seem credible and widely available). And, regardless of their resources, certain groups and perspectives will have an easier time establishing their frame as the dominant one. This is because the effectiveness and popularity of a frame can often be highly influenced by the degree to which it builds on, and responds to, historical frames and other ideological formulations. In particular, frames that mimic or piggy back on other preexisting, widely shared/recognizable frames are often adopted more easily – for our brains tend to be less critical of, and accept more readily, frames (and other phenomenon) that already have a common-sensical or normal "feeling" (Kahneman 2011, chap. 5). This is one reason why Hollywood blockbusters do so well, despite the fact that we can all predict what will happen well before we see the movie: we experience a certain pleasurable feeling from the cognitive ease with which we can easily identify the stereotypical characters and guess which of the archetypical plots we have seen many times over the movie will follow.

The fact that our brains are predisposed towards interpreting cognitive ease as something positive (and indeed "truthful") also explains why a key strategy in political persuasion is what Snow and his colleagues call "frame extension." Frame extension is the attempt to "encompass auxiliary interests not obviously associated with the movement in hopes of enlarging its adherent base" (Snow et al. 1986, 472). In other words, it is a strategy to incorporate familiar frames that are usually not associated with a certain position into that position so as to attract new supporters. Moreover, frame extension can take a wide variety of forms. Through frame extension, "new values may ... be planted and nurtured, old meaning or understandings, and erroneous beliefs or 'misframing' reframed in order to garner support and secure participants" (473).

The impact of successful "framing" and frame extension can be quite profound. It can allow a group to pre-position an issue in relation to a very specific set of values and considerations and rule out others. And it can establish the dominant questions, arguments, and criteria of evaluation defining a debate. One characteristic that makes framing so powerful as a rhetorical technique is the fact that it also operates below the level of explicit reasoning. The work of Drew Westen – a political psychologist – is helpful to understanding why this is the case. According to Westen, the strength of a given frame's resonance (i.e., the degree to which a particular framing is accepted by and structures the issue for a given audience) is very much influenced by degree to which it activates non-explicit "networks of association" (Westen 2007, especially 80–93).

For Westen, the term *networks of association* describes the phenomenon in which certain images, words, thoughts, and actions can call forth a wide variety of other ideas, assumptions, and emotions in an audience. The origin of this phenomenon lies in the fact that our brains often jump ahead of our senses to predict the meaning of a word or event, and often does this on the basis of familiarity (i.e., assuming it will replicate previous experiences) and context (i.e., assuming that it follows the logic of the rest of the context). We do this all the time when we read – studies consistently show that we constantly fill the in the blanks and are much more likely to read words and interpret meanings that fit with conventional scripts (Westen 2007, 90–93). We also do this much more widely, and, in these cases, certain explicit frames can heavily influence our cognition. For example, studies have demonstrated that, in tests, individuals who see the phrase "angry insect" just before the phrase "bad mug" are much more likely to read the second phrase as "mad bug" (ibid., 85). This is because the meaning of the first phrase primed the subjects to expect and interpret the second set of words in the context of insects. Another experiment has shown that, when asked to name a type of laundry detergent, participants who had previously been shown word pairs that included the pair ocean-moon were much more likely than others to say "Tide" (84).

Network associations not only influence how we think, they can also profoundly influence how we behave. The academic studies reported on in Malcom Gladwell's book *Blink: The Power of Thinking without Thinking* offer a variety of important insights on this subject. Like Westen and Kahneman, Gladwell's work highlights the fact that we make judgments far more quickly and unconsciously than most of us want to believe. To buttress his thesis, he outlines the results of a wide-ranging set of experiments in many fields of study. One set, undertaken by a Columbia University psychologist John Bargh and his colleagues, showed that when subjects were subtly primed with network associations related to being "old" (through wordplay tasks), they actually walked out of the office and down the hall more slowly than those who were not primed with words associated with oldness (Gladwell 2007, 52–53). Even more notable is another test that Bargh and his colleagues performed. In it, they primed subjects with network associations by having them undertake wordplay tasks with subtle themes linked either to "rudeness" or "politeness." Then, they were asked to return to the experiment supervisor's office to get their next assignment. The wrinkle was that the supervisor was going to be purposefully busy and the real experiment was how long it would take the subjects to interrupt. The people who had been primed for rudeness waited on average five minutes before interrupting. What was particularly stunning was that 82 per cent of those subjects primed with politeness associations never interrupted at all before the ten-minute time limit expired on the experiment (55).

Other studies show that a variety of stereotypes, if subtly activated by network associations, can have significant impacts on how we think, feel, and act. Gladwell discusses the fact that stereotypes about gender and race can powerfully influence people, even people whose explicitly stated conscious values reject those stereotypes. The Implicit Association Test (IAT) highlights this fact. Gladwell reports that he was shocked (especially as his own mother is Jamaican) when the results of his personal test revealed that he had a "moderate automatic preference for whites" as measured by the way and the time it took him to associate certain words with race (Gladwell 2007, 84). He is far from alone in this. Eighty per cent of those who have taken the IAT race test ended up having subtle or not so subtle pro-white associations. This is not to say that 80 per cent of people who took the test are consciously racist. The more shocking reality is that even many of those who are self-consciously anti-racist still harbour unconscious network associations that influence their subconscious decisions and evaluations when it comes to race.

These tendencies are not hiccups or exceptions in how we reason. It has now been solidly established – including by the work of Nobel Prize–winning economist Daniel Kahneman (a pioneer of behavioural economics) – that our brain profoundly relies on what he called "System 1" reasoning to process the vast majority of the information we receive and the decisions we make during each day. According to Kahneman (2011, chap. 1), System 1 thinking is much faster, much more prevalent, and often much more emotionally powerful than the step-by-step, logical, and critical thinking that characterizes our "System 2" thinking. Importantly, System 1 thinking is also much more automatic – and thus much less self-conscious and explicit. Westen and others suggest that the different characteristics of each system are explained by reference to the fact that the two systems largely operate in different parts of the brain that have very different physiological characteristics. System 1 is processed largely through the more primal and much faster amygdala, which quickly processes basic threat information to inform flight or fight responses. System 2, in contrast, is largely processed through the, evolutionarily speaking, newer frontal cortex, which operates more consciously and slowly (Westen 2007, chap. 3). These physiological differences also mean that conceptual and verbal stimuli are processed quite differently. For example, one reason why System 1 thinking is so much quicker is because it relies heavily on the unquestioned use of stereotypes and other unconscious assumptions and judgments that allow it to "leap" to conclusions based on previously learned patterns and network associations (Kahneman 2011; Westen 2007).

It is the ways in which these subconscious network associations and stereotypes can be primed in the amygdala and then used to convince an audience to support one candidate, party, policy, or ideology that are particularly relevant to the political realm. What Westen (2007, 93) terms "stealth attacks" are perhaps the most obvious version of the way network associations can be used for political advantage. According to Westen, the famous Willie Horton ads used by George Bush Sr. against Michael Dukakis are an excellent example of this (the ads essentially accused Dukakis as being soft on crime by focusing on Willie Horton – an African-American man who raped and assaulted several people while out on weekend furlough from jail). As Westen's analysis highlights, the Horton ads – one of the key turning points in the campaign – were exquisitely designed to activate a subconscious but highly intense fear reaction by using a series of visual, musical, and verbal cues to frame the ballot question around powerful network associations – and the attitudes and feelings they give rise to – about race, crime, and threats (63–68).

These findings hold profound implications for how we understand political persuasion and framing. They suggest that the political framing of an issue can have demonstrable effects on the ways the audience will interpret it. They also indicate that framing does not have to be explicit – nor does the audience have to be aware of it – for it to be effective. In fact, they suggest that framing is often most effective when it is not explicitly recognized by the audience. For if it is made explicit, this increases the possibility that the audience might engage its System 2 thinking and critically evaluate and question the frame, rather than simply allows its System 1 thinking to unconsciously accept and follow the frame without evaluation. Moreover, these studies suggest that, through various types of framing and frame extensions, political movements can tap into the "bundles of thought, feelings, images, and ideas that have become connected over time" by various patterns of network associations and can use these emotions, passions, and habits of thought to mobilize political support among their audience (Westen 2007, 3). They also suggest that often subtle, and even ridiculous-seeming, shifts of framing or frame extensions can have significant effects if they resonate with other well-established cultural frames.

We believe this discussion is highly relevant for the discursive struggle over abortion policy in Canada. For what we have found is that contemporary anti-abortion discourse has extended several of its frames to include significant elements that have traditionally been associated with feminist and progressive politics. Seeking both to shed the old, anti-woman stereotypes and to increase its appeal among a broader swathe of the Canadian population, contemporary anti-abortion discourse seems to be increasingly framing itself as a sort of twenty-first-century, next-stage feminism, presumably in the hopes that this frame extension will activate progressive networks of association in the Canadian public and win new supporters.

In this and the following chapter, we examine four types of frame extensions that are key to this attempt to win supporters. The first is the extension of the identity/brand frame of the anti-abortion movement. In the remainder of this chapter, we will outline this concept and demonstrate the ways in which the movement has increasingly sought to present itself as a righteous heir to a long litany of historical progressive causes. Then, in chapter 10, we will look at the ways in which the anti-abortion movement has also extended other types of frames (regarding values, issues, and epistemological dimensions) – all in ways that seek to piggy-back on pre-existing frames that have been traditionally associated with progressive, and particularly feminist, perspectives.

9.2 Identity/Brand Frame Extension: Progressives against Abortion

As anyone who watches commercials for cars, alcohol, or fashion can attest, one of the key principles behind marketing is the idea that it is often more effective to sell a product by framing it as a reflection of a particular identity, rather than by framing it as a collection of technical features. Marketers know that today, in a context of conspicuous consumption, people often buy products based not only on whether the products meet their specific concrete needs but often on what those products will communicate to others. A Toyota and a Lexus may be made by the same company and be nearly technically equivalent, but they don't say the same thing about who you are. Which is also why one company owns Old Navy, the Gap, and Banana Republic: each brand reflects and communicates very different identities and attracts very different consumers.

Moreover, marketing firms have long understood that one of the best ways to reshape your brand/identity is to piggyback off the cultural capital of other symbolic markers. In this sense, a rebranding effort often does not materially improve anything about the products themselves. Rather it seeks to make the products seem more attractive by creating an appealing identity by association. Why do watch companies pay exorbitant amounts of money to tennis players even though they never wear their watches on the court? Celebrity endorsements makes sense only if one believes that, at some level, our perceptions of a product and brand can be influenced by association with another, valued object, person, or position.

Political parties and movements – which increasingly focus on the need to communicate, protect, and strengthen their brands (see Delacourt 2013) – also intimately understand the importance of the identity that they project. As Drew Westen has shown, many voters do not make political decisions based primarily on which policies they prefer. A much stronger predictor of political behaviour is political identity (Westen 2007, chap. 5). Voters' emotional commitments to a given political identity not only profoundly influence their willingness to support certain policies and candidates, but they also make voters much less willing to critically evaluate their own assumptions and those of their preferred candidate. In fact, strong commitments to political identities tend to make individuals more likely to ignore evidence that disadvantages their preferred candidate or movement, while at the same time making them much more likely to creatively construct ad hoc explanations to justify away apparent contradictions (Westen 2007, xi–xiv and chap. 5).

In politics as in business, who and what your brand is associated with matters a lot. For your audience will often use those associations as shorthand to pre-judge your identity and to determine whether you, your cause, and your reasoning should be taken seriously or dismissed out of hand. A movements' brand identity – and its use of framing – functions like a super-magnet. Get it right and you attract supporters. But get it wrong (i.e., fail to align yourself with your audiences' values) and you can reverse polarities and drive them away, regardless of the strength of your arguments and data. It is therefore fairly predictable that political movements will sometimes seek to rebrand their identity by framing their ideas in association with other, already established, frames that would expand the movements' appeal beyond their base. This process is especially likely to happen in cases where the movement has large ambitions regarding policy change but has a small base and a traditional brand/identity that does not resonate well with the broader population.

One of the most brazen recent attempts to reframe a political liability in Canada has been the effort to rebrand Canada's bitumen oil reserves (originally popularly known as the tar sands until the industry shifted the lable to oil sands) as "ethical oil." The energy industry in Canada is, of course, worried that public opinion may eventually lead to increased regulations that might limit its ability to develop and profit from energy extraction. The industry has therefore engaged in a substantial and multi-pronged public relations effort designed to convince Canadians to support extensive oil sands extraction, low royalties, and other policies that benefit industry. It is a story no doubt worthy of its own book, but, for our purposes here, what is crucial about this campaign is that it is an excellent example of rebranding a contentious position (strong support for unimpeded development of the oil sands over environmental concerns) as something that should be supported by Canadians (and others) with progressives values.

The crux of this attempt is to move our gaze away from the nature of the bitumen itself and the environmental costs of extracting, shipping,

Figure 9.1

Source: Ethical Oil (www.ethicaloil.org)

and refining it and instead focus attention on the fact that the oil is from a country in which progressive human rights are respected much more so than in many other oil-producing countries. Consider the example in figure 9.1 (one of a half dozen similar postcards).

The use of a pro-woman progressive framing could not be more obvious, as this campaign attempts to bind the women's rights that exist in Canada to the process of oil extraction in Canada. The campaign then uses this link to override progressive environmental concerns by forcing the audience to ask whether they'd prefer oil that was environmentally problematic or oil that supported regimes where women's rights are not respected. And if you doubt that such a crude strategy could be successful, try it out as a topic for discussion at a dinner party with people whose opinions you respect.

Our findings suggest that the Canadian anti-abortion movement has been employing similar techniques in an attempt to redefine its own identity as a modern movement that is both reflective, and protective, of women's concerns and interests. As we have seen in previous chapters, important voices of the movement explicitly understand that certain elements of the perceived identity/brand of the anti-abortion movement (old, male, religious, anti-woman) represent significant marketing problems in a twenty-first-century Canadian political context. What we will now show is that one way the movement has responded to the anti-woman critique has been to analogically link itself to a variety of other progressive movements in hope that, by creating positive network-associations between these movements and the anti-abortion movement, more Canadians might be open to considering the anti-abortion position.

9.3 Historical Progressivism

One identity-frame extension strategy that is frequently used by the contemporary anti-abortion movement to broaden its brand appeal is to imply through analogy that the fetus is like other marginalized groups (e.g., slaves, women) that have been historically denied personhood and oppressed on this basis. This framing encourages new audiences to accept anti-abortion ideas and policies as responses that are necessary to alleviate a great injustice and boosts the appeal of the brand identity of the anti-abortion movement itself – that is, as the twenty-first-century heir to the progressive, compassionate social justice movements that fought against other historic injustices.

Blogger Veronique Bergeron's post entitled "The Ultimate Goal" exemplifies this trend by comparing the end goal of the anti-abortion movement to the abolition of slavery:

> Let's parallel this human rights issue (abortion) with another one from another era, when William Wilburforce [sic] first introduced a bill to criminalize the slave trade. He was ridiculed and success seemed far off. He was always up-front with his ultimate goal. Through creative and gradual measures, by more means than simply introducing his annual bill, his goal was eventually realized ... I would hope that every person who speaks out for the right for the unborn would have as an ultimate goal that these tiny humans' rights be held up as equal to our own ... Our dismal historic track record in deciding who – or what – is human suggests that we should stop

the circus act and recognize that determining humanity based on human-
made criteria has embarrassed more than one civilization. Will our treatment of the unborn shame us in a few generations? I have no doubt about
it, particularly in light the demographic decline of Western civilizations.
(PWPL, 23 February 2008b)

By explicitly suggesting that the status of fetuses and slaves are identical, insofar as both were deprived of their intrinsic right as persons on
illegitimate grounds, this rhetorical strategy aligns itself with the progressive, humanitarian cause of abolitionist William Wilberforce.

This technique is one of the strongest trends in the brand-identify
framing of a wide variety of anti-abortion activists and organizations.
It is particularly crucial to the Canadian Centre for Bio-ethical Reform's
(CCBR) communication strategy. On one hand, The CCBR clearly links
its project with many historical social justice movements. Quoting
Gregg Cunningham, the founder of the American parent organization (the Center for Bio-ethical Reform [CBR]), the CCBR argues that,
like earlier anti-slavery reformers, it "must prove the humanity of the
oppressed because many victims are popularly perceived to be subhuman." Cunningham, however, believes that the problem is even
greater than this. Thus, "proving their humanity is necessary, but it
is seldom sufficient. It is also important to expose the inhumanity of
the relevant injustices, because the magnitude of their evil is often
inexpressible and, therefore, underestimated" (CCBR 2011a, 19). The
difficulty of achieving the social justice goal of proving the humanity
of the oppressed and revealing the magnitude of their evil becomes
the justification for the strategy of using graphic images. This strategy, Cunningham argues, is "based on principles derived from our
analysis of successful strategies for social reform throughout history.
A common theme which unifies those strategies is the use of visual
imagery to establish the humanity of targeted victims, and the inhumanity of the injustices by which they have been victimized ... [for]
words alone can't change hearts and minds when the injustices sought
to be described are indescribable. Words only serve to trivialize evils
of that magnitude – particularly when listeners have a bias which pre-
disposes them to reject terrible truth" (19). Not only does this historical analogy seek to justify the CCBR's tactics by showing that earlier
progressive campaigners used them, but it also seeks to subtly imply
that the very fact that the CCBR uses these tactics proves it an heir to
progressive movements.

This strategy of progressive brand-identify frame extension also helps define the content of many of the groups' posters and public displays. As discussed in chapter 7, the CCBR's strategy has been to combine the use of very graphic imagery and public outreach and discussion, especially in the areas around high schools and universities. One of its main techniques is the Genocide Awareness Project (GAP), "a visual display composed of 4x8-foot (or 6x13-foot) billboards which graphically compare the victims of abortion to victims of other atrocities, such as Jews in the holocaust or African Americans during the civil rights struggle in the US. It is typically exhibited at universities or colleges by campus pro-life clubs. Participants engage passers-by in discussions about abortion as well as hand out pro-life literature." The belief is that "past genocides occurred because widespread killing of human beings was rationalized on the basis that the victims were subhuman, inferior and non-persons," and the hope is that just as "pictures challenged that thinking about past genocides ... they do so now for the debate on abortion" (CCBR 2013e).

The use of shocking visual representations has two effects. Its most obvious one is to create a metaphorical link between pictures of the victims of modern genocides such as slavery and the Holocaust and those of aborted fetuses. The idea is that because visual information is processed by a part of the brain that is much less subject to conscious critical questioning (Westen 2007; Kahneman 2011), this strategy is a particularly effective way of fusing intense emotional force to the arguments and, in doing so, bypassing any critical consideration of whether the analogy between dead adults and aborted fetuses is accurate or not. From a perspective of framing, however, it also has the valuable effect of visually placing the anti-abortion movement alongside other progressive social justice movements, thus painting a picture of the anti-abortion movement as a contemporary version of these historic battles against injustice.

This framing is also widely employed in the political realm. In a speech to anti-abortion supporters, Preston Manning (the former leader of the federal Reform Party) spent time drawing "a direct parallel between the struggle to end abortion and the fight to end slavery in the British Empire" (PWPL, 21 May 2009). This framing also characterized one of the most recent anti-abortion private members' motions in Parliament – Stephen Woodworth's Motion 312, which sought to have Parliament revisit the definition of "human" under the Criminal Code so as to give the fetus legal personhood. In his speech to Parliament, Woodworth explicitly framed his bid as analogous to other progressive social justice movements. The reason why it is important that fetuses be defined and protected as full human beings, Woodworth stated, "is that powerful people can strip vulnerable people of all rights by decreeing they are not human beings. The only way to protect the inalienable rights of all is to protect the inalienable rights of each. As the wise and courageous Dr. Martin Luther King Jr. said 'Injustice anywhere is a threat to justice everywhere!' If basic rights can be denied to even one vulnerable person, they can be denied to anyone!" (Woodworth 2012a). Both the language of human rights and the appropriation of Dr. King clearly seek to frame the anti-abortion movement as the heir of the historic civil rights movements.

9.4 Contemporary Progressivism

Contemporary anti-abortion discourse also seeks to present the movement as progressive and humanitarian by situating its fight alongside other contemporary signifiers linked to progressive social movements. Despite the Conservative Party of Canada's relative disdain for the United Nations (UN) (Berthiaume 2013), anti-abortion Conservative politicians nonetheless link their cause to the perceived progressive project of the UN. MP Maurice Vellacott, for example, argues that "whether the target is black babies, or female babies, or babies with some other characteristic we might screen for, when we single out certain categories of children for destruction, we undermine our commitment to the ideals expressed in the UN Declaration – the dignity and equality of all Canada's children" (Vellacott 2008).

Two elements are notable in this example. First, Vellacott analogically frames the abortion issue as a question of discrimination – whether on the basis of race, gender, or other elements – something that is generally considered a progressive issue. Second, by explicitly appealing to the authority of the UN, Vellacott links the anti-abortion movement to a major symbol of progressive international human rights. This brand-identity frame extension also appeared in Woodworth's speech in defence of his Motion 312. In it, he explicitly appealed to the UN's authority: "Here's the way the UN Declaration of Human Rights puts it: 'Recognition of the inherent dignity and of the equal and inalienable rights of all members of the human family is the foundation of freedom, justice and peace in the world.' That's why we should never accept any law that decrees some human beings are not human beings! No policy justifies it! No ideology justifies it!" (Woodworth 2012a).

Even more notable than extending the anti-abortion brand-identity by drawing parallels with the UN is the length some bloggers are willing to go to link the movement with human rights movements that are far less palatable to the traditional anti-abortion movement. One PWPL blogger, for example, framed the anti-abortion position as the logical outcome of a gay rights perspective:

A number of gay rights activists (in the US more than here) oppose abortion, full stop, because they think that when the genetic basis for gay identity (sorry for the question begging) is discovered, people might abort gay fetuses. The thing is, they have the intellectual integrity to work backwards and realize that if they don't want babies being aborted for being gay (or likely to become gay), they also have to speak up against babies being aborted for being the wrong sex, or having other medical problems. (PWPL, 13 May 2009)

Other activists have used visual graphics to make the point even more dramatically. Alissa Golob, the youth coordinator of Campaign Life Coalition (CLC) Canada at the time, tweeted "if she suspcts baby she's carryng is gay & wnts 2 abort him, will u rspect her 'freedm of choice'? #cdnpoli #ProChoice," accompanying the tweet with the graphic shown in figure 9.2 (Golob, 19 August 2013).

The poster is highly explicit in its use of progressive language and visual symbols to make its case. Linking abortion to "bigotry," the poster's text explicitly identifies the anti-abortion position as part of the progressive tradition of supporting and expanding human rights claims and challenging various forms of racism, sexism, homophobia, and many other types of intolerance and discrimination. The visual seeks to further persuade its audience of the progressive nature of the anti-abortion position by framing its identity as progressive in a variety of ways. The pink colour palette might be taken as a technique to visually persuade the audience that her message is "pro-woman." It also signals a "gay friendly" orientation (referencing the pink triangle campaign), a message that is reinforced by the use of the traditional LGBT rainbow symbol twice, including to highlight the fetus.

Seeking not only to challenge and upend traditional progressive assumptions, these types of frame extensions also function to promote the anti-abortion movement as an heir of historical social justice movements and as a sibling of contemporary progressive social justice movements. These strategies represent the anti-abortion movement not as a

Figure 9.2

Source: American Life League (www.all.org)

conservative, repressive movement, but as a heroic driver of progress and a fighter for persecuted victims.

These representations of the movement as a progressive hero are both reinforced by, and reinforce, another politically important discursive strategy – representing the movement not merely as a hero but also as a persecuted victim. The anti-abortion movement presents itself as paying a great price for standing on the right side of history against common but barbaric practices. As one blogger writes, "if fighting abortion does not constitute social justice, then I don't know what does. The victims have no voice. The perpetrators have entrenched interests, deny other information and make money by it. This culture will be embarrassed in not too long for offering the barbarity of abortion. We will wonder how we excused it, ignored it, concealed it, sanitized it, normalized it" (PWPL, 6 May 2008). Once again, this identity extension solidifies the anti-abortion identity as heroic and progressive. Anti-abortion activists are fighting for real, progressive social justice. They are the righteous Davids going up against powerful Goliaths, the "perpetrators" with "entrenched interests."

Finally, we are seeing signs that the next element of this brand-identity extension strategy may well be to link the anti-abortion movement to groups that fight for disability rights. At the March for Life in May 2013, several of the speakers explicitly framed the movement as defending the value of all life, and they condemned decisions to have abortions when fetuses are discovered to have significant genetic abnormalities. One senator even brought his daughter who has Down syndrome to the stage and asked her to thank the crowd for working to save the lives of other people like her. This strategy is apparently increasingly visible in the United States as well (Soloman 2013). And it is not hard to see why. It encourages the audience to make parallels between progressive movements that seek to protect the rights of (and ensure adequate resources for) disabled people and the anti-abortion movement and once again frames its identity as a progressive defender of the vulnerable.

9.5 Seekers of Truth, Defenders of Free Speech

Finally, the anti-abortion movement has increasingly sought to extend its progressive hero-victim brand-identity in one other culturally powerful area – that of the underdog persecuted for speaking truth to power and defending free speech. According to blogger Tanya Zaleski, the anti-abortion movement is fundamentally about naming the elephant in the room that society doesn't want to acknowledge: "It's evident that more than one important factor is still being ignored: the act of abortion itself, and the serious mental and physical repercussions to the woman. Talk about a herd of pink elephants!" (PWPL, 26 May 2008). Andrea Mrozek also frequently reinforces this identity framing. Referring to a defeated Quebec bill (Bill 34) that would have placed additional medical standards on abortion clinics, Mrozek references the commonly cited anti-abortion belief that the mainstream media and society actively engage in "abortion distortion" – hiding the truth about the reality and harmful consequences of abortion – and suggests that anti-abortion advocates are up against an ideological double standard sanctifying abortion that they must overcome and overturn. "Behind the hysteria lies the phenomenon known to pro-lifers everywhere as 'the abortion distortion'... The abortion distortion dictates that where abortion is mentioned, or even just implied as in this case, a double standard comes into play. Even where women's health is at stake" (PWPL, 10 October 2008).

Elsewhere, Mrozek hones this line of argument when she claims to summarize the common views of "pro-abortion" society: "Summarizing, then, the freedom of speech issue – when you support abortion, you are a catalyst for an important debate. When you are against abortion you are a pesk, some spending time in jail, others sidelined from their working spheres be it politics, law, medicine, or journalism. Again, euphemisms are the hallmark of the 'abortion rights' world. It's almost exclusively through concealing what they stand for that they win" (PWPL, 11 October 2008).

This framing of anti-abortion rhetoric as revealing the "truth" has increasingly become one of the major elements of the movement's public identity. The CCBR, for example, justifies its use of graphic imagery and direct, public engagement strategies on this basis. The group's extreme methods are justified because "many people refuse to go out of their way to learn about abortion, let alone learn about it from a pro-life perspective." The CCBR, then, has no choice but to "stimulate a debate on abortion that has long been silenced" and ensure that "Canadians who do not want to think about the issue are compelled to deal with its gravity" (CCBR 2013b).

This fearless, progressive, truth-to-power brand-identity extension is mobilized in the political realm as well. It was, in fact, at the core of the debate over Stephen Woodworth's Motion 312. Because this motion requested a committee to study the definition of "human" but did not formally propose an answer or seek to regulate abortion directly, Woodworth argued that any opposition to his motion was actually an explicit affront to free speech. Citing Émile Zola, a liberal author known for fighting censorship and inequality in France throughout the nineteenth century, Woodworth claimed:

> Those who believe that the moment of complete birth does somehow transform a child from a non-human into a human being should have enough confidence in their own belief to expose it to an examination of

the evidence!! What have they to fear from the full flood of light? Why oppose a mere study?

Zola's words apply again and I paraphrase them: The reason they oppose a mere study is "because they dread your good sense – they dare not run the risk of letting us tell all and of letting you judge the whole matter."

Again using Zola's words, I have had to "fight step by step against an extraordinarily obstinate desire for darkness." "A battle is necessary to obtain every atom of truth" … "It is on your behalf alone that [I] have fought," "that this proof might be put before you in its entirety, so that you might give your opinion on your consciences without remorse." (Woodworth 2012a)

The advantage of this framing is that it takes the traditional progressive defence of free speech (including echoes of civil libertarian arguments, a perspective that is often viewed as antithetical to social conservatism) and uses it to further the anti-abortion cause (a position that is traditionally very difficult for free speech advocates to support, given their championing of principles of individual privacy and choice).

The political value of this brand-identity extension became even more apparent with MP Mark Warawa's Motion 408. Following the defeat of Woodworth's motion in September 2012, Warawa introduced his own motion, which asked "that the House condemn discrimination against females occurring through sex-selective pregnancy termination" (quoted in Huffington Post Canada 2012). In March 2013, a Conservative-controlled Parliamentary committee ruled (without giving reasons for doing so) that the motion was "non-votable," which meant that it would not come to Parliament for a vote. This decision ignited a firestorm of controversy. Social conservatives were furious and responded aggressively with, among other strategies, a campaign to target Prime Minister Harper and four other Conservative politicians with a postcard and billboard attack in their own ridings. Moreover, for the first time, a significant minority of backbenchers in the Harper caucus were willing to openly criticize the prime minister. At the 2013 March for Life, some of these MPs explicitly called on the social conservative base to become much more involved in riding nomination processes during the next election.

Anti-abortion publications also took up the free speech banner in response to the quashing of the motion. The front page of *Faith Today*, for example, framed it as an issue of gendered suppression of free speech. With the main title asking "Why is it so hard to talk about abortion in Canada," the cover also featured an arresting image of a young woman's face with her mouth either taped over or ripped off – suggesting that young women's voices were being tyrannically and violently stolen from them (Newman 2013).

What was perhaps most notable was the degree to which many in the mainstream media also framed the issue as a question of free speech. Columnist after columnist argued that the government's decision to rule the motion non-unvotable was a travesty of parliamentary tradition and censorship of the first degree. In this process, it was free speech, rather than abortion, that became the major issue (Saurette 2013). Although it lost Motion 408, the anti-abortion movement arguably achieved something much more important through this debate: it managed to burnish the image of the anti-abortion movement as censored underdogs, victims of a pro-abortion society. The irony was that, this time, the group that the anti-abortion movement traditionally portrays as bullying censors (the so-called liberal media) was in fact championing the anti-abortion movement's claims to victimhood at the hands of the movement's erstwhile allies – the Conservative government.

This episode was one more event helping to move the perceived identity of the anti-abortion movement away from the traditional view of a social conservative attempt to control the behaviour of others towards a much more progressive one of defenders of free speech and open debate. By doing so, it helped shift the movement's identity into one far more Canadians would be sympathetic to.

9.6 Conclusion

In chapter 7 we demonstrated that the contemporary Canadian anti-abortion movement has been engaged in very real strategic reflection regarding its organizational and communication strategies. In chapter 8, we demonstrated that the movement has developed and increasingly deployed explicit arguments and other rhetorical techniques (such as visual signaling) that depart significantly from the traditional portrait insofar as they focus on representing abortion as harmful to women and thus the anti-abortion position as pro-woman. In chapter 9, we have shown how contemporary Canadian anti-abortion discourse employs a variety of other subtle techniques of framing, which further represent the anti-abortion movement as far more progressive than the traditional portrait suggests. Whether framed as an heir to historical civil rights and social justice movements, the logical extension of contemporary rights battles, or an oppressed minority voice fighting for truth and justice (against feminists, pro-abortion society, and even a watered-down Conservative Party), contemporary anti-abortion discourse is increasingly framing the identity of the movement by associating itself with a variety of progressive identities. And this reframing matters. As Westen and others have shown, perceptions about brands and political identities can be as important as – if not more important than – policy decisions when it comes to attracting supporters. Thus, rebranding the identity of the anti-abortion movement as progressive might allow the movement to resonate more strongly (and/or more easily) with broad swathes of the Canadian public who do not currently hold anti-abortion views.

Brand-identity framing, however, is not the only framing technique that the anti-abortion movement is using to make its position more amenable to the mainstream. Three other framing techniques – regarding values, issues, and epistemology – are examined in the next chapter.

Chapter 10

Anti-abortionism as the New Feminism: Reframing the Position

As discussed in the previous chapter, framing is a wide-ranging communications strategy that seeks to orient a given issue or movement in relation to characteristics that will positively resonate with a target audience. In particular, we suggested that frame extension is a strategy aimed at attracting new supporters by piggybacking on previously established frames that enjoy significant cultural and intellectual influence with potential new supporters. We argued that contemporary anti-abortion discourse seems to be attempting to increase the credibility of its explicit "pro-woman" arguments by extending its identity/brand frame into traditionally "progressive" territory. In this chapter, we discuss three other key areas – values, issues, and epistemology – in which the anti-abortion movement has sought to extend its frames, and we show that, through framing, the anti-abortion movement is seeking to persuade Canadians of its position by presenting it as more pro-woman than feminism itself.

10.1 Values Framing: Equality and Choice

As we discussed in chapter 8, appealing explicitly to religious authority is one way in which anti-abortion discourse has sought to philosophically ground its position. However, philosophical or moral values can also be used to frame an argument in other ways. The most obvious is to identify a given value and explicitly build an argument around it. Values can also play other roles. One way of using values is to exploit the "moral capital" of a secondary value (one that is not the central value of a discourse) to lend additional credibility to a position. Good lawyers, for example, never rely solely on their primary arguments. They also often build in secondary appeals to a variety of values, norms, and precedents in the hope that if a jury member isn't persuaded by the main argument, one of the appeals to secondary values might resonate and sway that jury member. In a similar way, contemporary anti-abortion discourse has become well versed at employing certain secondary values in ways that seek to frame the anti-abortion position as more progressive than people would normally assume.

10.1.1 Substantive Equality

Values are some of the most frequently and intensely contested concepts. Of these, few are contested more vigorously and actively than the concept of equality. Some interpretations of equality limit it to the establishment of formal equality – that is, equal access to the law and market. Others suggest that it should be understood as a more robust equality of opportunity. Still others suggest that it means equality of condition. Moreover, there is significant debate about whether equality should be analysed on an individual basis or whether collective, structural patterns of equality and inequality should also be considered.

While feminism comprises a diverse set of perspectives and many different views on the question of equality, it is fair to say that most feminist theories defend a "thick" conception of substantive equality between genders, which, at minimum, is seen as a very robust equality of opportunity that understands and takes into account informal structural patterns of inequality and power. Thus, for much of the twentieth century, equality has been a primary value frame used by feminists to advocate for equal rights, equal pay, and equal treatment. Moreover, as we saw in Part I, since the mid-twentieth century, the feminist conception of equality has been linked to the belief that women must be able to control their reproduction and thus be afforded access to abortion care. As a result, feminists and abortion rights advocates often effectively frame their arguments for abortion access around equality.

For a variety of reasons – including the success of the women's movement and the civil right movements in the 1960s and 1970s – the progressive equality frame has achieved a high level of social, political, and moral capital around certain issues in North America. Unsurprisingly, it has also been subject to a forceful backlash from perspectives that do not agree with it. Perhaps less widely understood, however, is the fact that the equality frame also has a long history of being redefined and redeployed by conservative movements. In this sense, it is a perfect exemplar of the "essentially contested concepts" we discussed in the previous chapter (Connolly 1993). Rather than cede this value to the other side, political movements constantly struggle to redefine "equality" in ways that help their positions. Thus, many types of conservative ideology accept equality as a value, but they define it as formal equality before the law.

Our analysis found that the contemporary anti-abortion movement in North America has participated, and continues to participate, in the contest over the definition of "equality" as a way to support their position. As we saw in Part I, the movement has traditionally appealed to equality through its demand for equal respect for the fetus under the law. However, this fetal-centric equality frame is no longer the only appeal to equality we are seeing on the part of anti-abortion activists. Anti-abortion discourse is increasingly extending the value frame of equality in a way that includes women's equality – something that traditionally has been the exclusive purview of progressive and feminist political movements. The ProWomanProLife (PWPL) blog, for example, forwards the notion that the anti-abortion movement is, and always has been, devoted to women's equality. One blogger argues that it is one of the strongest frames for the anti-abortion position:

> It is a million gazillion times easier to defend life in the public square – precisely because the arguments – and the sound bites – are rights based. They are equality based. Equality and dignity for both mom and child. There's this shaky notion pro-abortion types put forward that abortion serves women's rights because they are "in control of their own bodies" but it's a superficial argument, and one that is fairly easily overcome by unpacking the euphemism and looking at what really happens. (PWPL, 14 May 2009)

Attempting to break the discursive link between abortion access and women's equality, the anti-abortion message seeks to integrate the ideas of "equality and dignity" into its argument in order to paint the anti-abortion position as arising from and reflecting progressive values. "Equality for women," adherents argue, "is not contingent on access to abortion." Instead, the anti-abortion movement claims to represent the many "women across Canada who are against abortion, precisely because we are in favour of women's rights" (PWPL, 1 June 2008). Challenging the abortion rights movement's ownership of "equality" is thus an important concern of contemporary anti-abortion bloggers and politicians.

Figure 10.1

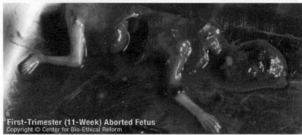

HOW CAN ONE PROTECT AND HELP WOMEN
BY KILLING THEM AS BABIES? –Suffragette Alice Paul
She fought for women's equality without threatening the lives of children. Can't We?

First-Trimester (11-Week) Aborted Fetus
Copyright © Center for Bio-Ethical Reform

Alice Paul fought for women's right to vote. **WILL YOU FIGHT FOR PRE-BORN CHILDREN'S RIGHT TO LIVE?**

Learn more here:
END THE KILLING.ca

If you've had an abortion and want healing, there's help: www.healingandhelp.ca
Copyright © Canadian Centre for Bio-Ethical Reform

Source: Canadian Centre for Bio-ethical Reform

The contemporary anti-abortion appropriation of the feminist frame of equality goes well beyond pro-woman bloggers and a thin interpretation of equality. Consider a postcard campaign (reproduced in figures 10.1 and 10.2) from the Canadian Centre for Bio-ethical Reform (CCBR) and its appeal to a thick conception of substantive equality.

The postcards visually and verbally suggest that Alice Paul – an American suffragist and women's rights advocate – would be fighting against abortion today. It acknowledges and valorizes equality before the law, such as the right to vote, and argues that it is unjust to violate this type of equality. But it then goes much further and asserts that denying women equal pay for equal work – a structural problem of substantive equality – is also unjust. Finally, it concludes its message by deploying the language of substantive, thick equality by stating that the audience should be like Alice Paul and fight for "True Equality for All." This message is also customized for a Canadian audience in a CCBR

Figure 10.2

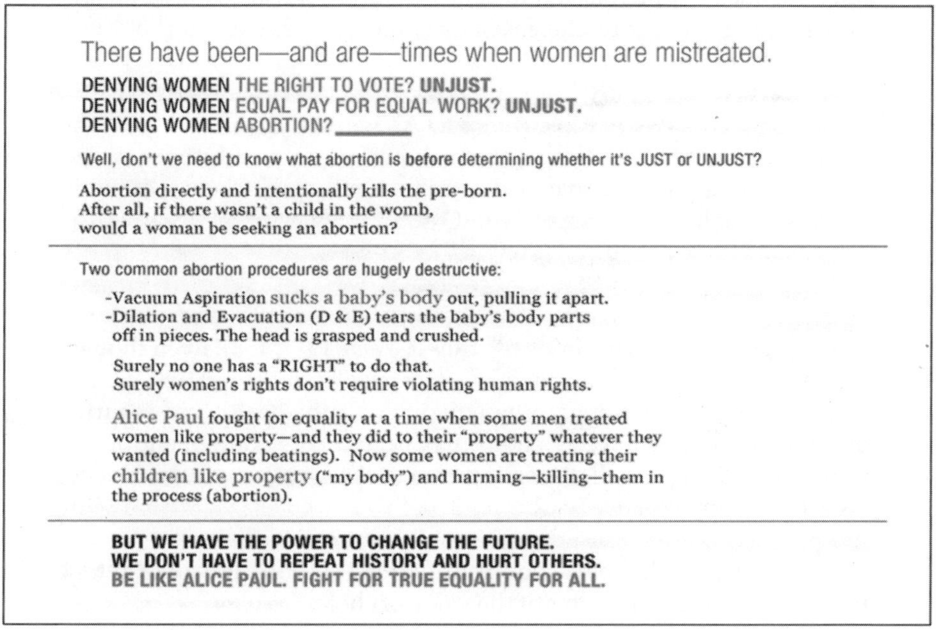

There have been—and are—times when women are mistreated.
DENYING WOMEN THE RIGHT TO VOTE? **UNJUST.**
DENYING WOMEN EQUAL PAY FOR EQUAL WORK? **UNJUST.**
DENYING WOMEN ABORTION? _____

Well, don't we need to know what abortion is before determining whether it's JUST or UNJUST?

Abortion directly and intentionally kills the pre-born.
After all, if there wasn't a child in the womb,
would a woman be seeking an abortion?

Two common abortion procedures are hugely destructive:

-Vacuum Aspiration sucks a baby's body out, pulling it apart.
-Dilation and Evacuation (D & E) tears the baby's body parts
off in pieces. The head is grasped and crushed.

Surely no one has a "RIGHT" to do that.
Surely women's rights don't require violating human rights.

Alice Paul fought for equality at a time when some men treated
women like property—and they did to their "property" whatever they
wanted (including beatings). Now some women are treating their
children like property ("my body") and harming—killing—them in
the process (abortion).

BUT WE HAVE THE POWER TO CHANGE THE FUTURE.
WE DON'T HAVE TO REPEAT HISTORY AND HURT OTHERS.
BE LIKE ALICE PAUL. FIGHT FOR TRUE EQUALITY FOR ALL.

Source: Canadian Centre for Bio-ethical Reform

video devoted to examining "how the pro-life movement can learn from the history of Canada's Famous Five – five women who fought for the right to be considered 'persons' under the law" (CCBR 2011b). The anti-abortion movement is thus not just contesting and attempting to use a conservative definition of equality to frame its position. It is also employing a thick feminist definition of equality to frame itself as the true feminist position.

10.1.2 Choosing Anti-abortionism

Perhaps even more surprising than the anti-abortion movement's adoption of the substantive-equality-for-women value frame is its incorporation of the pre-eminent feminist value around abortion: choice. The value of "choice" has a long history of being tied to feminist activism, literature, and ideology and has long been an anchor point for feminist discourse. Recognized feminist thinkers, from de Beauvoir to Butler, have advanced numerous feminist articulations, constructions, and critiques of the concept of choice. Choice, then, has become a rhetorical foundation of feminist discourse.

Choice has also clearly been at the very heart of much North American discourse around abortion rights. As we will discuss in the conclusion, there is an emerging debate about its continued utility (some advocates of a reproductive justice frame argue that "choice" alone is a highly problematic perspective). Overall, however, the language of "choice" has almost entirely defined the arguments of abortion rights activists in the United States since the US Supreme Court ruled that "the government may not place obstacles in the path of a woman's exercise of her freedom of choice" (*Roe v. Wade* 1973, 153). Even though the majority of justices in Canada's *Morgentaler* decision (1988) relied primarily on concerns regarding equality and the health and security of women, the language of choice has been a core component of the Canadian debate as well. When it comes to the issue of abortion policy, then, the value of choice has been virtually exclusively associated with progressive feminism and the support for abortion access.

In contrast, traditional, fetal-centric anti-abortion discourse rarely framed the question in terms of the value of choice (at most, it countered the dominant feminist definition of choice by advocating that the fetus also should have a "choice to live"), instead actively challenging the appropriateness of choice as a defining value. Challenging choice continues to be an important strategy for some actors in the Canadian anti-abortion movement. Stephanie Gray, for example, has noted that one of the explicit strategies of the CCBR is to critically examine the limits of "choice" in other areas of life and then reason analogically about the need to limit the scope of choice regarding abortion (CBC Radio 2013). It engages high school students in a conversation that starts by focusing on the fact most people agree that, while you should be free to *choose* to swing your arms around in public, you shouldn't be able to *choose* to swing them around and hit someone else in the face. It then extends this logic to the question of abortion to argue that you shouldn't be able to *choose* a medical procedure that harms another person. Choice, it seeks to highlight, is not an unlimited right; it can and should legitimately be restricted when it comes to the question of abortion.

Others within the contemporary anti-abortion discourse are seeking to break the tight link between choice and the defence of abortion rights by redefining the value of choice and employing it to support the anti-abortion position. Perhaps the best example is the slogan of the PWPL blog – "A Canada without abortion. By choice" – a theme that is paralleled in many posts and statements regarding its aim of celebrating "women's legitimate choices, freedoms and rights" (PWPL 2007). But contemporary anti-abortion discourse does not merely superficially mouth the word "choice." Instead, at the heart of the refashioned choice argument is a repurposed structural analysis of the "real life" limits to choice that sounds very much like analyses forwarded by many feminist perspectives on different issues. The core of this anti-abortion choice frame is the charge that, even if women have a "formal" choice, they are not presented with enough legitimate and informed choices to have a "real" choice.

This argument is not entirely new, as the anti-abortion movement in the US has attacked the idea of "informed consent" for decades. However, the Canadian version of this argument is notable due to the extraordinary degree to which it employs highly feminist-sounding language to make its point. PWPL founder Andrea Mrozek argues that the problem is not merely that women don't have proper information, but that "women don't really get choices" (PWPL, 15 May 2008). In a blog titled "This Pro-abortion Culture Is Brought to You By ..." Mrozek recounts three stories of marginalized women, all of whom were single and without support, who faced unplanned pregnancies. In all three stories, the pregnant women reached out to health care professionals and were offered information about abortion. Mrozek, outraged by the presentation of abortion as a pregnancy choice, writes:

> Is this what passes for compassion, for help? What kind of choice is this? Have these health care workers lost any semblance of compassion or empathy? Do they not care? Do they think providing an abortion constitutes care? Such a response is incredible. How can they so completely fail to register the real issues at hand – to send women packing with nothing more than the words "I can get you an abortion" ringing in their ears? (PWPL, 15 May 2008)

Mrozek's response frames abortion as an uncompassionate and non-empathetic false choice that is foisted upon women by abortion supporters who "love the slavery of abortion: slavery to a false freedom, a choice that isn't freeing at all" (PWPL, 28 December 2008).

As we will highlight in the following chapter, the stories narrated by contemporary anti-abortion discourse reinforce this framing by portraying real choice as compromised because women are victims who are trapped, coerced, and deceived into abortions by a variety of villains. We can see the same message portrayed in the values framing of a variety of other anti-abortion organizations as well. The LifeCanada website, for instance, contends that "it is often easier for a woman to obtain an abortion than pregnancy support or crisis pregnancy counselling. As a result, many a woman finds the only choice available to solve her problems is a dead baby" (LC 2003).

Contemporary anti-abortion discourse also combines this "no-choice" framing with the slightly more traditional "uninformed choice" framing, arguing that women are being "tricked" into abortion because they are not offered the "facts." In an article titled "15 Years of Choice?" LifeCanada argues that

> An informed abortion choice must start with the clear understanding, easily available through ultrasound, that a child is really there, beating heart and all. Next, why are women not being told about studies reporting a strong correlation between abortion, especially of a first pregnancy, and breast cancer risk? They should also be warned of the risk of post-abortion emotional trauma and harmful premature delivery of future children. Withholding basic information shows disrespect for women and is both dishonest and patronizing, since it implies that women are "intimidated" by the truth. Ignoring or suppressing what we now know about the dangers of abortion serves a coercive agenda, which fails to care about women's most important needs. (LC 2003)

Framing itself as the non-patriarchal defender of women's health and real choice, LifeCanada presents abortion, and those advocating abortion, as "dishonest and patronizing." The very title of the article questions the feminist formulation of the concept of choice. LifeCanada's argument is that women are being lied to by pro-abortion forces about the ramifications of abortion. The suppression of "what we know about the dangers of abortion" serves as a means of coercing women into abortion. Central to this claim is the notion that women's choices are eliminated by the mere existence of abortion, which implies that it is anti-abortion activists who are the ones actually standing up for women. LifeCanada (and other anti-abortion advocates) thus argue that it is the anti-abortion movement that ultimately "care[s] about women's most important needs."

Politicians often use this frame as well. A common theme in MP Maurice Vellacott's discourse is that women need better support so that "they don't feel trapped into killing their unborn child" and so that they have a "real choice" and are able to "choose life" (Jalsevac 2009). Even bills aimed at introducing fetal personhood rights into law are often characterized by this type of value extension. In October 2007, when Conservative MP Ken Epp introduced private member's Bill C-484, under which harming a fetus would constitute a crime, his primary justification centred almost entirely on choice. Epp described the bill as focusing "very narrowly at one issue – where the woman has made the choice to have the child and that choice is taken away unilaterally without her consent and usually with violence" (PWPL, 5 January 2008) and argued that "if the woman has chosen to have a child and she ... has done everything possible to protect her unborn child, why should she have to stand alone?" (Canada, House of Commons 2008b, line 1155).

10.2 Issue Framing: Anti-abortionism as a Women's Issue

As we have seen, a frame extension strategy can be applied to a political movement's brand-identity and the values it employs. A third way to subtly persuade an audience to accept a position is to frame it as analogous to other "issues" the audience strongly cares about. For example, "progressives," broadly speaking, are more likely to consider the position of individuals or groups who can show that their proposal is similar to other "progressive" issues and concerns. This can be achieved explicitly (by outlining similar logic) or it can be achieved more subtly (often below the level of conscious thought) by making a position look as if it is analogous to other specific issues. Contemporary anti-abortion discourse attempts to achieve exactly this result by framing the anti-abortion cause as if it is an extension of classic feminist concerns about a diverse set of women's issues ranging from women's rights to gender-based domestic and sexual violence.

10.2.1 Anti-abortionists as True Advocates for Women's Rights and Interests

In North America, the idea that women have a right to abortion was popularized by second-wave feminists who no longer considered abortion merely as "a matter of medical intervention allowed by state-defined 'health' indications but, instead, a fundamental right of all women" (Brodie, Gavigan, and Jenson 1992, 72). Much like the value frame of substantive equality and choice, the issue frame of "women's rights" has become a major component of arguments in favour of abortion access. In response to this assertion of women's rights and security, the traditional anti-abortion rebuttal has largely been to deny that abortion is a woman's right while simultaneously maintaining the right to life of the fetus.

This perspective continues to characterize contemporary anti-abortion discourse to some degree. A variety of actors repeat the traditional anti-abortion argument that "it's not a woman's right to have an abortion" and that "there's no such thing as a right to an abortion, not for women, not for men. It doesn't contribute to women's rights and freedoms at all, because having an abortion is, put simply, not a right" (PWPL 2007). However, as we found in the case of feminist value frames, contemporary Canadian anti-abortion discourse also frames itself in relation to "women's rights" in a variety of new ways. The main difference is that contemporary discourse does not simply critique and challenge the traditional portrait. Much of it tries to actively incorporate feminist ideas and language around women's rights in order to frame the anti-abortion movement as a champion of women's rights, freedoms, equality, and health. It does so partly by framing the anti-abortion position as more genuinely "pro-woman" than the pro-choice position. According to Mrozek, the belief that abortion is a right – and a good thing – is simply the result of consistent brainwashing by "pro-abortion" culture:

> I was taught that abortion was a right through years of schooling. It takes years of reading to discover that offering or withholding an abortion has nothing to do with women's rights and freedoms at all, and that the mantra "my body, my choice," isn't true. It is my goal to educate on this: Abortion is not a right and it does not enhance women's lives. Once we disconnect abortion from "rights talk" and other assorted euphemisms about "reproductive choice," we'll be able to truly and compassionately assist women who feel trapped in an unwanted pregnancy. (PWPL, 11 December 2008)

The last part of the quote is key. For here, Mrozek flips the narrative and essentially accuses feminism of being the outdated and almost male perspective – mechanically applying abstract "rights talk" and "euphemisms" that stop feminists from "truly and compassionately" assisting women. By breaking the assumed *a priori* connection between abortion and women's rights, contemporary anti-abortion discourse frames the anti-abortion position as pro-woman while similarly reinforcing the identity/brand of anti-abortion adherents as better advocates for the interests of women than are feminists.

10.2.2 Anti-abortion and the Issue of Informed Consent

The struggle to protect informed consent for women in a variety of contexts has long been a major theme in feminist perspectives – whether in regard to ensuring that women have control and informed choice about the medical procedures they choose or in regard to safeguarding sexual choice. And the doctrine of informed consent has been argued from a feminist perspective in order to defend abortion rights. Feminist legal scholar Susan Bordo (1993) argues that informed consent supports the fundamental "right to one's person" by honouring personal bodily integrity so broadly that judges have consistently refused to force individuals to submit to medical procedures without consent, even if the life of another human being is threatened by the refusal. Since the right to one's person privileges one's own bodily integrity over anybody else's, the pro-choice rhetorical framing of informed consent has been used to strongly defend women's legal right to abortion.

For the past several decades, anti-abortion discourse has sought to frame its position by arguing that women's rights are being systematically violated by coercive and unethical abortion practices. The anti-abortion group Signal Hill, for example, outlines the concept of informed consent and how its enforcement is being neglected in the case of abortion in Canada. Its website argues that "the concept of informed consent is fundamental in Canadian medical practice … However, this standard is not being met within the community of doctors and health care professionals who are working in women's reproductive health. Women are not being informed about the numerous studies showing a statistically significant link between abortion and breast cancer, information that may have serious bearings on their decision to carry through with an abortion. This is a violation of a woman's right to know" (SH 2010a).

10.2.3 Motherhood as the New Feminist Issue

Classic feminist arguments about pregnancy, motherhood, and the roles available to women in society are also being reformulated and incorporated into larger anti-abortion discourse. Veronique Bergeron, a PWPL blogger, writes about the professional and personal sacrifices that she has made throughout her life because of her choice to become a mother:

> I have completed some of my studies but my career is unmistakably mommy-tracked. I had dreams of traveling the world and I now find myself the least traveled person of my acquaintance. I have carried my pregnancies to term and I do harbour regrets about all the things I might have been able to do, especially when I look at my peers who are paying off their mortgages at 35 while I wonder how the heck I will pay back the $60 000 line of credit I incurred to buy a Master's degree and with it, the possibility of developing a career. (PWPL, 19 July 2008)

Not only does Bergeron use explicitly feminist concepts (e.g., "mommy-tracked"), she further acknowledges the merits of a life without children. She admits that she "harbours regrets" and insecurities about her own choices. In some important ways, her personal narrative parallels feminist Betty Friedan's articulation of the unspoken "yearning that women suffered in the middle of the 20th century in the United States ... As she made the beds, shopped for groceries ... she was afraid to ask even of herself the silent question – 'Is this all?'" (Friedan 1963, 19).

In one sense, both Bergeron's and Friedan's stories are framed in the same way. They both argue that there is a structural oppression created by gendered norms around motherhood and identify the insecurity, self-questioning, and personal and professional sacrifices that these norms impose on mothers. Both perspectives suggest that motherhood is undervalued, given its importance to the functioning of society. However Bergeron's frame departs from the traditional feminist perspective when she presents her theory about what causes this devaluing. Whereas feminists point to patriarchy and gender inequality, Bergeron blames feminism in general, and abortion in particular. For her, abortion has led to the societal devaluation of mothers because it transforms motherhood into just another choice that "reinforces prejudices against mothers":

> When we flaunt abortion as the panacea for our inability to recognize motherhood as an important contribution to society and to acknowledge that mothers may have ambitions in life other than motherhood – ambitions that are not per se incompatible with motherhood but that are made so by a myopic outlook on motherhood and ambition – we effectively reinforce prejudices against mothers, children and families. This is the heart of

my position against abortion. I am not "anti-choice." I only firmly believe that choice in matters of pregnancy has effectively reduced the range of options available to women in society. And this occurred principally when we made childbearing a personal choice for which women alone are held accountable. (PWPL, 19 July 2008)

As did many of the original feminist analyses, Bergeron personalizes her theory by discussing her own experience and suggests that she, like the mothers of the 1950s, has been discriminated against as a consequence of her choice to be a mother. As she says, "if I aborted my babies, I would have plenty of [work] experience by now. Employers demand this experience, why? Because they can. And certainly since pregnancy is a choice, they don't need to accommodate women who don't choose experience over life" (PWPL, 19 July 2008). Starting from what appears to be a feminist issue-frame, she subtly shifts the analysis to argue that abortion is incompatible with feminist ideals of equality and the proper valuation of motherhood. In the end, Bergeron's discourse combines a rewritten "feminist" analytic frame with a repurposed "feminist" testimonial format to argue that a challenge for modern women – how to balance a career and a family – is made far more difficult by a misguidedly and blindly pro-abortion, pro-feminist society.

10.2.4 Pro-Choice = Pro-Patriarchy

Contemporary anti-abortion discourse also seems to generalize the types of critiques discussed above to a more abstract level by extending its issue frame into traditional feminist tropes. Most notably, it explicitly seeks to reverse the common feminist interpretation of abortion as freeing women from a variety of patriarchal pressures and reframe it as both reflecting and reinforcing patriarchy. As Andrea Mrozek succinctly puts it, "show me an abortionist and I'll show you a misogynist" (PWPL, 3 July 2008).

How does contemporary anti-abortion discourse accomplish this reframing? First, abortion rights advocates are accused of encouraging "young girl[s] to believe [they are] not equipped, not strong, not able to carry a pregnancy to term" (PWPL, 17 April 2009). In contrast, anti-abortion activists are presented as inspirational, self-reliant icons for young, pregnant women by demonstrating that women "are strong enough, and smart enough and equipped enough to deal with [an unplanned pregnancy]" (PWPL, 13 November 2008).

Second, contemporary anti-abortion discourse reproduces one of the most fundamental tropes of second-wave feminist analysis by suggesting that support for abortion serves to further the particular patriarchal privilege of "a male standard of sexual behaviour." According to blogger Veronique Bergeron, society

> institutionalize[s] equality according to a male standard of sexual behaviour. That is, to be equal, we have to be able to have sex without having the kids. To achieve this great ideal, women have to stuff themselves with synthetic hormones, contraceptive devices and, failing that, undergo invasive surgery in the form of abortion. Then, having convinced women that they are really like guys, we will bombard them at a very young age with suggestions of proper sexual behaviour: "51 tricks that will make him jump for joy," "Release your inner vixen" and "How Hally [sic] got her bikini body back only 3 months post-partum." (PWPL, 13 November 2008)

Were it not framed as an argument against sexual and reproductive freedom, this blog could easily be mistaken for a feminist analysis, as just one more example of the ways that society reproduces patriarchal privilege. But in this case, the practice of abortion is added to the causes that traditional feminist modes of analysis highlight as being responsible for patriarchy. The analytic frame is the same. Its normative purpose is very different.

10.2.5 Abortion as Sexual Assault

Perhaps the most powerful attempt to extend the anti-abortion position through issue framing, however, is the effort to link it to the issue of sexual assault and intimate partner violence – issues that continue to be foundational for the feminist movement. Susan Brownmiller's (1975) famous analysis of the politics of rape as a technique perpetuating male dominance by ensuring all women remain in a state of fear expressed one of the central beliefs of second-wave feminist thought. With contemporary debates over "rape culture," her analysis remains as important to feminism today as it was forty years ago.

While most people would imagine that the feminist analysis of sexual violence fits naturally with, and supports, the feminist defence of abortion rights, anti-abortion activists have increasingly sought to link their position with a critique of male sexual privilege in general and sexual violence against women in particular in several distinct ways.

On one hand, anti-abortion discourse frames abortion as representing a similar level of violence against women as sexual assault. The first part of this strategy is to extend the feminist sexual oppression frame to include the anti-abortion position by suggesting that "pro-life feminists have also come to see abortion as part of a male agenda to have women more sexually available" (Vellacott 2009).

The second part of the strategy then seeks to concretize this analysis beyond mere generalizations about male sexual privilege by claiming that the abortion procedure itself is literally sexual assault. Anti-abortion activists therefore suggest that anyone against sexual assault should also fight against abortion access. The Toronto Right to Life (TRL) website, for example, informs its readers that "women report that the pain of abortion, inflicted upon them by a masked stranger invading their body, feels identical to rape" (TRL 2010b). The Alliance for Life Ontario (AFLO) website affirms the comparison between rape and abortion, asserting that abortion is a form of "medical rape":

> Many women report that their abortions felt like a degrading and brutal form of medical rape. This association between abortion and rape is not hard to understand. Abortion involves a painful examination of a woman's sexual organs by a masked stranger who is invading her body. Once she is on the operating table, she loses control over her body. If she protests and asks for the abortionist to stop, she will likely be ignored or told: "It's too late to change your mind. This is what you wanted. We have to finish now." And while she lies there tense and helpless, the life hidden within her is literally sucked out of her womb. (AFLO 2010c)

Here, the feminist argument that rape is a form of violence inflicted on women by men is clearly stitched into a vivid anti-abortion narrative. In this version, the abortion provider is the violator and the victim is the pregnant woman. The medical provider is a "masked stranger" (TRL 2010b) who does not care about the wishes or safety of the woman. He ignores the woman's pleas and "invades her body." The abortion provider is by metaphor a rapist who gives his victim no choice.

Many images circulated by Canadian anti-abortion activists reinforce this framing even more dramatically. Alissa Golob, the youth coordinator for Campaign Life Coalition (CLC), tweeted the image reproduced in figure 10.3 with the caption "#Abortion is the ultimate exploitation of women – American suffragette/women's rights activist #prolife #prochoice" (Golob, 13 June 2013).

Figure 10.3

Source: Campaign Life Coalition Youth. Image: NinaMalyna/Thinkstock

This is quite an arresting image. Given the wide-eyed look of horror on the woman's face and the aggressive posture of a man's large hands around her neck and mouth, the visual clearly suggests that an act of violence – and most likely sexual violence – is about to take place. Moreover, the colour, coarseness, and dirtiness of the man's hands activate a series of long-standing, and still highly operative, racialized and classist stereotypes about lower-class and racialized men violating young white women. Having visually primed the viewer into a heightened emotive state in which thoughts and fears about violence towards women are foregrounded, the image quotes the American suffragist Alice Paul to directly equate abortion with the horror of sexual violence and use the emotive force of the visual image to pull the viewer towards an anti-abortion position.

Creating visceral and intellectual links between abortion and sexual assault is a theme that is frequently reinforced across much anti-abortion discourse, particularly through the use of frames that imply that the after effects of abortion are "identical" to the emotions women experience after being sexually assaulted. A common assertion is to claim that "research shows that after any abortion, it is common for women to experience guilt, depression, feelings of being 'dirty,' resentment of men, and lowered self-esteem" (TRL 2010b). What is most significant is that these feelings are portrayed as identical to what women typically feel after rape. In "a sexual rape, a woman is robbed of her purity," whereas "in this medical rape [abortion] she is robbed of her maternity" (AFLO 2010c). Both sexual assault and abortion, it is argued, harm women – albeit with slightly different effects. This framing also applies to abortion performed in cases of rape. In such cases, it is claimed, the abortion only adds to and accentuates the traumatic feelings associated with sexual assault. Rather than easing the psychological burdens of the sexual assault victim, abortion exacerbates them. By focusing on the detrimental effect abortion has on women, anti-abortion discourse can simultaneously argue the wrongness of abortion in any and all circumstances (including sexual assault) while claiming sympathy for sexual assault survivors.

10.2.6 Abortion as Gendercide

Recent attempts to extend the anti-abortion frame into traditionally progressive and feminist territory are perfectly illustrated by MP Mark Warawa's 2012 Motion 408, which asked "that the House condemn discrimination against females occurring through sex-selective pregnancy termination" (Warawa 2012). What was so notable about this motion is that it became the centrepiece of a significant campaign that framed opposition to abortion as stemming entirely from concern about gender inequalities, women's rights, and the plight of girls.

For if the wording of the motion reflected the "more-feminist-than-feminism" framing strategy of contemporary anti-abortion discourse, the marketing efforts surrounding this motion revealed even more clearly the degree to which the movement is seeking to employ pro-woman/girl frames to reposition anti-abortion policy. As the motion progressed through Parliament, Warawa's website became increasingly saturated with language and links that sought to suggest that his life-long political mission has been to address all types of women's issues.

The language used to describe the problem of sex selection is a good example: "Sex selection is part of a global problem ... [of] discrimination against women and girls" (Warawa 2013). The website goes on to explain that "sex selection is the act of terminating a pregnancy based on the gender of the child. In Canada and around the world, women and girls are missing because females are valued less than males." Such language frames the issue almost entirely as one of gender inequality and discrimination – two of the central tenets of modern feminism. It also links it to the violence frames discussed above, as well as some of the more traditional identity framing discussed in the previous chapter. According to Warawa's website, sex selection is "an act of discrimination [that] contributes to the global problem of gendercide." Gendercide, according to the website, is "the systematic killing of a people group because of their gender ... Today the United Nations states that there are 200 million missing women and girls. Gendercide is a growing problem all over the world, and Canada needs to be part of the solution" (Warawa 2013).

The effect of this overt issue frame extension is fairly clear. Rather than debate the issue of abortion, the gendercide frame focuses the audience's attention on one issue (inequality and discrimination against women) and then pushes the audience to accept the additional assertion of condemning abortion as well. The use of the term "gendercide" to accomplish this is particularly telling, as the concept was originally developed by Mary Anne Warren (1985) – a philosopher and feminist who staunchly opposed gendercide and femicide *and* argued that abortion was ethically justified, as, according to her, fetuses do not have all of the prerequisite qualities of full personhood.

The wider marketing efforts of the anti-abortion movement on this issue highlight the degree to which simulated "feminist" frames regarding concern for gender equity have now become mainstream in the movement. Consider, for example, the main visual image employed by supporters of Motion 408 (used on the websites, petitions, banners, postcards, and so on) in figure 10.4.

The multiple ways in which this marketing reinforces the feminist framing are ingenious. The motto itself – "Protect Girls. Stop Gendercide. Support M-408. The anti-discrimination motion against sex selection" – reads as if it were a clearly and explicitly women's rights motion, and it is strongly reinforced with visuals. From the colour theme (pink and black), to the multicultural collage of adorable little girls, to the heart and traditional women's symbol in the middle of the "0" of M-408,

Figure 10.4

Source: Mark Warawa (www.markwarawa.com, defendgirls.ca)

everything reinforces the women's rights frame. Who wouldn't support efforts to stop gendercide, especially if one didn't know that the effort was an anti-abortion motion? And it is entirely possible to view the visual and not be aware of the link, as abortion and fetuses aren't mentioned anywhere in the promotional material. Rather than images of aborted fetuses, you have "missing" girls. This subtly, but crucially, shifts the "ballot question" away from fetuses (who have no legal rights) towards little girls (who have full legal rights). Rather than making it clear that the motion is against sex-selective *abortion*, the material suggests only that it is a principled motion against discrimination and sex selection in general.

Given the extraordinary advantages that this frame extension offers, it is perhaps unsurprising that even the largest and most "traditionalist" public anti-abortion gathering in Canada – the Ottawa March for Life – has increasingly used this frame. Given that the march is heavily supported and logistically aided by religious institutions, it is usually a place where religious discourse and traditional communication tropes are more present than elsewhere in the movement. Yet in 2013, the main theme of the march was framed around Warawa's motion and the issue of gendercide. "End Female Gendercide! 'It's a Girl' should not be a death sentence" was the official motto, which was prominently displayed on many of the official banners and placards, as well as the exclusive focus of the minute-long promotional video distributed to promote the march (CLC 2013b). Given its broad adoption, it seems likely that framing the anti-abortion position as a women's issue is a strategy that will continue to grow in the movement in the years to come.

10.3 Epistemological Framing: Standpoint Anti-abortionism

Finally, contemporary anti-abortion discourse has sought to extend its frame by broadening its epistemological frame. Epistemology is the study of knowledge – or, more precisely, the study of what counts as knowledge. What is the nature of knowledge? How does one acquire knowledge? What markers, signifiers, or methods guarantee the validity of certain types of knowledge claims? These are some of its key questions. As many theorists have shown, most disciplines and discursive contexts follow, implicitly or explicitly, certain epistemological norms that are recognized as being largely authoritative.

Two characteristics regarding the ways that epistemological norms function are particularly relevant for our study. First, seemingly "formal" epistemological norms (i.e., beliefs about what steps one must follow to create valid knowledge) can have a significant impact on determining what type of substantive knowledge claims are viewed as worthy of serious consideration in a given context. If a given debate largely accepts scientific norms of large, double-blind comparative studies, then qualitative and anecdotal feedback from individuals might be ignored (something that often creates a strong possibility that minority accounts/experiences are not taken into consideration as seriously as the average results). The second key characteristic is that the formal and informal rules about what counts as legitimate knowledge, and the means to arrive at such knowledge, can be slippery. Epistemological norms vary from discipline to discipline within academia. As Thomas Kuhn (1962) has demonstrated, even *within* disciplines, norms can sometimes change very quickly and in dramatic ways. Moreover, even in periods of relative epistemological calm in a given discipline, there are often contending alternative norms that seek to challenge dominant ones, even if these are only minor voices. This is especially the case in the public sphere beyond academia, where there are often active, politically motivated actors who consciously and unconsciously seek to promote epistemological norms that will allow them to present their political views in the most hospitable epistemological context.

10.3.1 Feminist Standpoint Epistemology

One of the major goals of standpoint feminism has been to make the voices of women heard in authentic ways, even in policy environments that are not epistemologically hospitable to their lived experience and preferred modes of communication. Activists and writers from Mary Wollstonecraft and J.S. Mill to Betty Friedan and Andrea Dworkin have made arguments about the degree to which women's specific experiences have been ignored in the public sphere (including, crucially, in politics and policymaking) and the importance of taking these experiences into account. In the 1970s and 1980s, this debate became particularly intense as scholars such as Sandra Harding (1986), Nancy Hartsock (1998), and Donna Haraway (1998) highlighted the political and gendered effects of certain accepted epistemological norms of scientific disciplines and the public sphere, which they believed largely privileged patriarchal political positions and policies, and argued for epistemological approaches that allowed women-specific experiences to be privileged.

One way feminists responded to these concerns was to forward a "standpoint" theory, which posited that an individual's standpoint (meaning the location from which people view the world) affects how that individual experiences political reality. Reality is seen as socially constructed and relational. Standpoint feminism championed the practice of creating more space for individual women (and other marginalized identities) to speak to their own personal experiences and argued that policymakers should take these experiences as valid data points and design policy that responded to them.

A good second-wave feminist example of this position is that of Catharine MacKinnon, who argues that women's voices have been largely absent from public and legal debate. For MacKinnon, "the candid description Justice Stewart once offered of his obscenity standard, 'I know it when I see it,' becomes more revealing than it is usually understood to be, if taken as a statement that connects epistemology with power. If I ask, from the point of view of women's experience, does he know what I know when I see what I see, I find that I doubt it, given what's on the newsstands" (MacKinnon 1996, 38). To counterbalance the dominance of patriarchal standpoints, many feminist projects have attempted to "uncover and claim as valid the experience of women" (MacKinnon 1989, 116).[18]

This standpoint perspective has long been central to feminist activism and discourse around abortion (Palmer 2012). The famous 1972 American feminist "We Had Abortions" petition, for example, was a highly visible campaign to de-stigmatize abortion (the "A-word") by allowing women's voices, experiences, and preferences regarding abortion to be forcefully heard in the public sphere. Such strategies remain important today. In the US, for example, Planned Parenthood has been using a campaign called Not in Her Shoes, which is based on the idea that "abortion is a deeply personal and often complex decision for a woman to make" and that nobody should "make that decision for someone else. Nobody knows a woman's specific situation – we're not in her shoes" (Planned Parenthood 2013). Through this campaign, the organization is emphasizing the individual lived realities of women facing unplanned pregnancies.

10.3.2 Anti-abortion Standpoint Epistemology

Given the other ways in which the anti-abortion movement has learned from and sought to extend its frames in relation to progressive and feminist identities, values, and issues (and given the reality that women's experiences, preferences, and political perspectives are not homogeneous), it is perhaps unsurprising that contemporary anti-abortion communication strategies have begun to extend their own epistemological

---

18 The question of what constitutes a feminist standpoint epistemology and whether it is even possible to have a single "women's" standpoint has, of course, been strongly debated within feminism. Authors such as Audre Lorde (2003), bell hooks (1981), Chandra Mohanty (2003), and others argued that many second-wave feminist standpoints represented that of white, middle-class women. They suggested that feminism itself needed to diversify further and create more space for a wider diversity of voices and experiences, especially in regard to sexuality and race. Here, however, we are more concerned with the early model of standpoint epistemology, as it is closer to the one the anti-abortion movement is now redeploying.

frame by adopting a standpoint approach that highlights the perspectives of women in their movement. Andrea Mrozek stresses the
importance of foregrounding women's perspectives in the abortion
discussion, arguing that "we need to talk about why women choose
abortion, how that choice affects them and those close to them in the
short- and long-term, and what we can do to help women, after they've
had an abortion and especially before they make that choice" (PWPL, 18
January 2009). Instead of adopting the stereotypical anti-abortion perspective that focuses entirely on the experience of the fetus, Mrozek's
approach claims to listen to and represent women's standpoint. She
suggests that women's voices need to be included in the anti-abortion
discussion because "how that choice affects them" is a crucial aspect of
being able to "help women" especially before they "make that [abor-
tion] choice." Implicit in this statement is the assumption that, once
women's voices are introduced into abortion discourse, these voices
will convince others that abortion is not a viable choice.

Whereas, previously, feminist abortion rights advocates were able to
frame themselves as the true representative of women's experiences by
using standpoint testimonials (among other strategies), anti-abortion
standpoint epistemology now allows anti-abortion activists to also
claim to be the recorder and defender of women's "real" lived realities.
In ways reminiscent of pro-choice feminists, moreover, anti-abortion
activists argue that individual women's experience in society (and with
abortion) is a reliable and important site of analysis. They also highlight
some of the same experiences women have with abortion that feminists
highlight, but they derive very different conclusions from their analysis. Both abortion rights feminists and this new anti-abortion standpoint acknowledge that women are often forced to experience abortion
in solitude and silence with little chance to discuss it openly and seek
support publicly. In a press release posted on the Toronto Right to Life
website, anti-abortion activist Natalie Hudson argues that "society
tends to shut down discussion about the after-math of abortion" (TRL
2006). However, rather than arguing that this is a result of social processes of shaming and stigmatization and concluding that the solution
is to demoralize the issue and discuss it openly as a medical procedure
(that, like many procedures, requires various types of pre- and post-
procedure supports), Hudson suggests that we need to talk more about
the ills of abortions so that women will stop having them. Referring to
the standpoint testimonials of women who regret their abortion, Hudson notes, "You cannot argue with the lived experience of these women.

For them, abortion is a physically painful, humiliating experience that has denied them motherhood and left them coping with long-term grief reactions" (TRL 2006).

While the epistemological frame is the same (empowered women expressing their lived realities) and thus resonates in important ways with more progressive-minded audiences, the contrast with the historic "We Had Abortions" abortion rights campaign is clear. Where that campaign was designed to promote the need to destigmatize and legalize abortion, the anti-abortion campaign serves as a personal standpoint framing rejoinder to the "medicalization" strategies of explicit argumentation we discussed in chapter 8. If the aim of the anti-abortion epistemological framing could be summed up in one phrase, then, it would be the hope that Canadians would reject abortion because they believed that every woman would "regret the day [she] decided to have an abortion and wish that [she] could take it back" (PWPL, 2 June 2008).

One tactic the anti-abortion movement has used to try to generalize this standpoint frame is to publicize the experience of particularly symbolic women, especially those whose backstory makes them unlikely converts to the anti-abortion movement. Like the "We Had Abortions" campaign, the idea is that the individual experiences and voices of certain women with certain characteristics and experiences will be given higher visibility and granted more epistemological authenticity and authority in the public debate. The US movement likes to highlight the fact that Norma McCorvey (the women who used the pseudonym Jane Roe to launch the famous *Roe v. Wade* case) later expressed remorse for her decision to have an abortion, rejected her pro-choice views, and actually worked for the anti-abortion movement. This strategy is also widely used in Canada. Signal Hill's website tells the story of Josephine Woodgate who, when she was twenty-five, "had one of the UK's earliest legal abortions. Today, 40 years after women were given the legal right to abortion, she remains haunted by the choice she made." Woodgate's personal testimonial, which is posted on the website, reads in part, "over the years, the regret I felt has never waned. Even now, I still catch myself wondering about the child I might have had, if only I had been given more information at the time" (SH 2010b). "Catching oneself wondering," in Signal Hill's framing, is represented as almost akin to psychological and emotional torture.

This epistemological framing strategy is the foundation of one of the most innovative international anti-abortion campaigns. The Silent No More campaign (of which the Canadian variant is a particularly strong exemplar) is as clear an embodiment of standpoint epistemology as possible. It began in 2002, when co-founders Janet Morana and Georgette Forney decided that "women suffering from abortion needed to be given the message that they are not alone and that help is available" (TRL 2006). The campaign runs a series of outdoor and radio advertisements but, more importantly, also administers a website that offers its visitors putative facts, statistics, and resources about the different ways in which abortion harms women. The core of this campaign is the collecting and publicizing of individual women's narratives. In doing so, the campaign seeks to show that, for women, abortion "is not freeing ... is not liberating," but instead "is the most humiliating experience of [their] li[ves]" (TRL 2006). The most important element of the website is the webpage titled "Testimonials," in which women (and some men) write about the ways in which abortion harmed them. This page is primarily a confessional for those dealing with the after effects of abortion, providing a consistent message that abortion leads to "physical, emotional and spiritual pain" (Silent No More 2010b).

The Silent No More campaign self-consciously employs these entries to "dispute" the abortion-rights activists' politically motivated portrayal of abortion with women's "own stories of post-abortion trauma." Activists like to argue that these anecdotes not only "show the pro-woman face of the pro-life movement" but also reveal the falseness of feminist standpoints on abortion (PWPL, 16 February 2009). Silent No More is portrayed as a more authentic standpoint that is "painfully resonant for many women today, whose regret[s] over past abortions have led them to buck feminist orthodoxy on the issue ... and dispute that storyline with their own stories of post-abortion emotional trauma" (TRL 2006).

This frame is also particularly popular with bloggers. One link posted to the PWPL blog suggests that anti-abortion standpoint epistemology is far more reflective than feminist perspectives of the experience and views of young women today: "The feminist establishment has tended to dismiss such stories as evidence of patriarchal brainwashing. That explanation may comfort pro-choice feminists who see their ranks dwindling. Yet today's young women are questioning abortion not because they know too little, but because they know too much. They have paid the price for the modern feminist embrace of counterfeit liberation. Now they are standing up to demand the real thing – whether or not their elders approve" (PWPL, 20 February 2008). This passage seeks both to refute the feminist, pro-choice position on abortion and frame the anti-abortion position as a refusal to kowtow to any ortho-doxy. As such, it is presented as a brave stance on behalf of women's real experiences and needs. In contrast, feminist abortion policies are depicted as outdated, anti-woman, and based in myth.

As with the gendercide issue framing, this epistemological strategy is increasingly highlighted and employed in many of the most traditional anti-abortion events in Canada. The Silent No More women and visuals played a prominent role in the 2013 and 2014 March for Life. In 2013, the opening forty-five minutes of speeches were carefully framed to highlight these women by ensuring that the cameras would catch what-ever speaker was at the podium in front of a backdrop of about fifteen women of different ages and ethnicities, all holding posters that read "I Regret My Abortion" and by heavily promoting the fact that, as part of this campaign, twenty-five women (representing the twenty-five years since the *Morgentaler* decision) walked from Montreal to Ottawa to pro-test against abortion.

10.4 Conclusion

In this chapter we have built on the discussion in chapters 8 and 9, fur-ther demonstrating the ways in which contemporary anti-abortion dis-course has sought to present itself as more pro-woman than feminism by framing the anti-abortion position in relation to traditionally femi-nist values, issues, and epistemological modes. Taken together, these three chapters have captured many of the key rhetorical strategies of contemporary anti-abortion discourse in Canada. Before concluding our contemporary Canadian analysis, however, we will examine two final and crucial strategies of persuasion in the following chapter – the ways that the overarching tone and the key narratives of anti-abortion discourse support its pro-woman positioning.

Chapter 11

From Jezebel to Snow White: Moralizing through Narrativizing

So far, Part II has examined the rhetorical strategies of persuasion used by the anti-abortion movement in a descending fashion, starting from the most explicit and obvious techniques (explicit argumentation and philosophical appeals) and moving to those that are more subtle and implicit (visual signalling and four aspects of frame extension – brand identity, values, issue, and epistemological). Our analysis has demonstrated that, on all of these dimensions, the contemporary Canadian anti-abortion movement has developed a sophisticated and multilayered discourse that seeks to persuade Canadians by making it appear far more modern, progressive, and "pro-woman" than the traditional portrait suggests. In this last chapter on the Canadian context, we want to examine two final techniques of persuasion to show how deeply this new orientation characterizes contemporary anti-abortion discourse. In this chapter, we examine the overall "tone" of anti-abortion discourse and the highly normative narrative structures embedded in it.

11.1 Metaphorical Tone: Strict Father or Nurturant Parent?

We are being asked to be accomplices in this medieval act of barbarism, forcing our doctors and nurses to commit murder ... so a handful of cheap, third-rate tramps ... can escape the consequences of their actions.

Joe Borowski, 1977

What does it say about the college coed Susan Fluke who goes before a congressional committee and essentially says that she must be paid to have sex, what does that make her? It makes her a slut, right? It makes her a prostitute. She wants to be paid to have sex ... So Miss Fluke, and the rest of you Feminazis, here's the deal. If we are going to pay for your contraceptives, and thus pay for you to have sex, we want something for it. We want you to post the videos online so we can all watch.

Rush Limbaugh, 2012

George Lakoff is a cognitive scientist whose work over the past decade and a half has focused on unpacking the dominant – but often implicit – metaphors that structure much of our everyday political discourse (Lakoff 2009 and 1996; Lakoff and Johnson 2003). According to his theory, our political "world views" are shaped largely by a set of metaphors that determine how we understand and evaluate political options. At the heart of Lakoff's theory is the contention that there are two ideal-type ur-metaphors – the "strict father" and the "nurturant parent" – whose respective characteristics help explain the coherence of, and differences between, conservative and liberal political mindsets.

The core of the conservative strict father metaphorical mindset is its championing of a punitive sensibility. According to Lakoff, this mindset views the world as a place where individuals need strict rules, rewards, and punishments to cultivate the self-discipline, self-reliance, and deep respect for legitimate authority that is required for a well-functioning society to survive (Lakoff 1996, 66). For the strict father, the idea of "character" and "moral strength" are given extremely high value, and individuals who fail to make choices in line with this value framework are seen to be entirely responsible for their actions and their consequences. Strong authority and consistent and often harsh punishment are seen as morally sanctioned and instrumentally necessary. Lakoff further suggests that the strict father perspective tends to highly value "traditional" gender roles, as the "father knows best" attitude mirrors the larger belief in the importance of authority.

Lakoff argues that the strict father mentality is the backbone of the contemporary US conservative viewpoint, and that it almost always leads to a very strong stand against abortion (viewing it both as murder and as unnatural and undermining traditional gender roles). Perhaps most important for our project, Lakoff suggests that the strict father world view tends to "blame" women for abortion, portraying women according to two main stereotypes. One is the irresponsible and promiscuous stereotype, in which the woman is viewed as having taken actions that demonstrate "a moral weakness, a lack of self-discipline, a form of immoral behavior" and thus "deserves punishment" because "she has to be responsible for the consequences of her actions" (Lakoff 1996, 267). The second stereotype is that of the selfish career woman who decides that her interest in a career is more important than her "child" and who needs to be coerced by legislation to make the morally sanctioned and traditional choice (268).

In contrast to the strict father, Lakoff suggests that the nurturant parent mentality assumes that individuals develop best by positively interacting with their community and being nurtured. "Support and protection are part of nurturance," and parents require "strength, courage and patience to create the open, two-way and mutually respectful communication" that is the environment that allows for healthy self-exploration and self-growth (ibid., 108–9). Crucially, the nurturant parent model assumes that some individuals will, through no real fault of their own, find themselves in challenging situations or make poor choices and that in these circumstances society should not seek to punish but should respond with "maximal empathy" and seek to help those individuals (112). Lakoff argues that the nurturant parent model almost always leads to support for abortion. In the nurturant parent view, women are mature individuals with a right to make choices on the basis of their own moral and political views. The view also recognizes that sometimes the consequences of people's choices are not what they wanted, and punishing those people or making them "pay" a price for their actions doesn't make things better for anyone.

Lakoff's rendition of the strict father world view captures the traditional tone of anti-abortion discourse in the US and Canada (at least in the 1970s through the early 1990s). In many ways, it mirrors the portraits of the anti-abortion movement sketched by feminists such as Susan Faludi (1991) and Andrea Dworkin (1983), who highlight the male-dominated, controlling, and explicitly "anti-woman" character of the anti-abortion movement and discourse. That said, Lakoff's perspective embodies a number of limitations in regard to our project,[19] the

---

19 We are not convinced, for example, by some of Lakoff's more ambitious claims about how accurate his findings are across different cultural and temporal contexts, nor do we subscribe to his beliefs that some of these metaphors are hard wired into the brain. Moreover, we find the gendered component of his analysis to be lacking – despite the obviously gendered nature of strict "father" versus nurturant "parent" dichotomy, where the nurturant parent clearly plays on the stereotypical mother role, he spends little energy exploring the implications of this and in fact de-genders it by describing that position as the nurturant "parent." Finally, in the context of our study, we will not

most important of which are his description of the strict father / nurturant parent aggregates as ur-metaphors; his tendency to claim that this model, developed in reference to the US, can be unproblematically generalized; and his assumption that a strict father perspective necessarily underpins all anti-abortion positions (and vice versa).

We therefore slightly revised Lakoff's approach to make it more useful to our study. First, rather than treating the "strict father/nurturant parent" binary as ur-metaphors, we have chosen to consider them more as part of a spectrum of "metaphorical tone." By metaphorical tone, we mean the overall "tone" or "sensibility" of a given political discourse as evidenced and communicated by the metaphors, analogies, and the emotive language it employs. This, we believe, gives us a rigorous and systematic method of investigating the overall tone of contemporary anti-abortion discourse. Second, as our previously discussed findings have already demonstrated that, on many dimensions, contemporary Canadian anti-abortion discourse is quite different from that suggested by the traditional portrait, rather than *assume* that the strict father tone defines that discourse, we sought to *test* whether it does. We contend that, if a "strict father" tone is the dominant metaphorical tone, this will show that contemporary Canadian anti-abortion discourse continues to employ at least one important implicit rhetorical strategy similar to the traditional model. In contrast, if that tone is not strongly present, it will further underline the degree to which contemporary Canadian anti-abortion discourse departs from the traditional portrait. In our study, we analysed and coded each of our data set cases to determine whether a metaphorical tone existed and, if it did, whether it fell into the strict father or nurturant rarent realm.

Unsurprisingly, we did find evidence of a continuing strict father tone in contemporary Canadian anti-abortion discourse. A good example of this is found in an article posted by LifeSiteNews, which argues that one of the many problems with abortion is that it makes "pre-marital sex feasible by apparently taking the possibility of consequences out of sex and taking responsibility with it" (Hudson 2004). Echoing the same sentiment, blogger Tanya Zaleski writes, "Don't want lung cancer? Quit smoking. Don't want to be obese? Eat sensibly and exercise. Don't want

---

use the "strict father/nurturant parent" tones as a tool to distinguish "conservatives" from "liberals," but will use it rather to investigate the tone of the new anti-abortion discourse.

to be pregnant? ... Refrain from having sex outside a committed relationship!" (PWPL, 20 May 2008). Veronique Bergeron reiterates her colleague's sentiments when discussing the case of Julie, a "pro-choice" blogger who, when faced with a pessimistic pre-natal diagnosis, decided to end their pregnancy. In response to Julie's admission that it was a difficult decision Bergeron blogs, "No Kidding ... That feeling of distress, could it possibly be your conscience telling you that terminating a disabled life was likely a selfish decision based on your needs rather than compassion for the child?" (PWPL, 23 February 2008a).

These examples embody the strict father demand that individuals "take responsibility" for their actions, and they employ the two stereotypes Lakoff identifies with respect to abortion – promiscuous girl and selfish career woman. But how prevalent is this trend? According to Lakoff and the traditional portrait, the vast majority of anti-abortion discourse should employ a strict father tone, and it should be particularly targeted at pregnant women considering abortions. Moreover, as Lakoff believes that the strict father tone is an expression of the most basic value perspective of the anti-abortion mindset, there should be virtually no evidence of a nurturant parent tone. What we found, however, was markedly different.

In strong contrast to the traditional portrait and the hypotheses generated by Lakoff, however, we found that a mere 17.2 per cent of Canadian cases reflect a strict father tone (see figure 11.1). Although the tone still clearly exists in contemporary Canadian anti-abortion discourse to some degree, it is far from being the dominant tone. For if 17.2 per cent of cases embodied this tone, this means that almost 83 per cent of cases did not.

Moreover, even the 17.2 per cent figure is misleading insofar as it strongly exaggerates the continuity of the traditional strict father tone. For the "target" of most of this tone in contemporary discourse is very different from that in the previous era. In the traditional portrait, the strict father tone concentrated largely on vilifying and shaming pregnant women who were considering an abortion. Our analysis reveals, however, that only 6.5 per cent of contemporary cases used a strict father tone against pregnant women. In the other 10.7 per cent of cases, the tone was aimed at other actors – for example, partners who were seen to be coercive, abortion providers, and a pro-abortion society. This suggests that nearly 94 per cent of cases did not target the pregnant women with a strict father tone. The fact that not a single case of the discourse employed by members of Parliament reflected a strict father tone, moreover, is a remarkable change.

Figure 11.1 Strict Father versus Nurturant Parent Tone (% of cases in data set)*

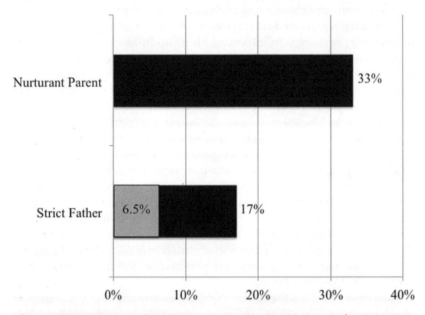

* Percentages are not mutually exclusive – if a case had two distinct tones in it, it was coded twice (once for each code). The lighter shading shows the subset of cases in which the strict father tone was directed at pregnant women.

The scarcity of the strict father tone is perhaps less surprising, however, than our other key finding: the much greater prevalence of a nurturant parent tone. Despite Lakoff's contention that a nurturant parent mindset necessarily reflects and leads to a "pro-choice" position, our findings suggest that contemporary Canadian anti-abortion discourse has strongly adopted this tone, with almost a third of cases employing a nurturant tone towards pregnant women considering an abortion. In other words, contemporary Canadian anti-abortion discourse uses a nurturant parent tone towards pregnant women five times more frequently than it employs a strict father tone.

This trend is entirely consistent with our other findings regarding the public discourse of the Canadian anti-abortion movement. The movement's discourse no longer resembles the traditional, religiously grounded, fetal-centric, anti-woman model in its explicit argumentation, ad hominem presentation, or its frames around identity brand, values, issues, and epistemology. In all of those dimensions, a significant portion of contemporary discourse clearly employs sophisticated, modern, and "pro-woman" tropes to make the anti-abortion case. From this perspective, it makes sense that the contemporary movement in Canada has not only downplayed the strict father tone but also has increasingly emphasized a nurturant parent one.

11.2 From Jezebel to Snow White: Narratives in Action

> Abortion providers are the wicked witches in a fairy tale, holding a bright, shiny apple ... In short, [abortion] is a malicious lie, pushed at the cost of babies' lives and women's health – but it's attractive nonetheless, all in an anxious moment.
>
> PWPL, 20 April 2009

The use of metaphorical tone is not the only technique that lends an implicit "pro-woman" patina to contemporary discourse. The stories told by the anti-abortion movement – and the narratives structures and implicit normative conclusions embodied in them – also play a key role in cementing this affective foundation.

There are many different ways to understand narratives and their importance. At a general level, we follow Fiske's suggestion that studying narratives allows us to "understand how people make sense of the world" (Fiske 1982, 115). For narratives are one of the primary ways that we, as humans, process our experiences and preferences. In fact, they are often much more influential on our judgments than are conscious debate or evaluation. There are, of course, many different methods and angles from which to investigate narratives. As we are interested in tracing dominant narratives and the ways in which "most people" would tend to interpret and interiorize these narratives (rather than, for example, exploring the multiple and often conflicting interpretive possibilities that every text embodies), we sought to develop a straightforward approach designed to identify the ways in which anti-abortion discourses reproduce and resonate with the typical (indeed, often stereotypical and archetypal) plots and character representations of the deeply historically and culturally embedded narratives that define our social and political context.

Here the work of Drew Westen is once again helpful. A political psychologist who has spent his career examining the psychological effects of various communication practices, Westen argues that political discourse is often framed by a "narrative" or "story," and that this narrative frame almost always encourages the audience to accept a certain world view, replete with a series of principles, preferences, and beliefs. In Westen's view, a politically relevant narrative is "a coherent story [that] has ... a protagonist, a problem that sets up what will be the central plot or story line, obstacles that stand in the way, often a clash between the protagonists trying to solve the problem and those who stand in their way or fail to help, and a denouement, in which the problem is ultimately resolved" (Westen 2007, 146). For Westen, narratives are so politically relevant because they almost always include implicit lessons we can sense, even if we don't realize it, because they are so familiar to us. In Westen's words, "most stories – and all that try to teach a lesson, as political stories do – have a moral. Many stories are complex with subplots and submorals. But in general, they follow a similar and recognizable structure that gives them their rhetorical power" (146).

This last point is crucial. As Westen (and many literary theorists before him) notes, the power of many narratives comes from the fact that they reproduce predictable plots and often rely on recognizable stock characters that communicate the basic moral lesson to the audience almost instantaneously. It is thus unsurprising that most political narratives are structurally similar to typical Hollywood blockbusters or childhood fairytales. These stories generally revolve around three main characters: the victim who needs to be rescued, the hero who rescues the victim, and the villain who harms the victim and stands in the way of the hero. Given its prevalence, this structure is intuitively recognizable to almost anyone raised in Western culture: the villain represents what the discourse cannot accept; the victim represents the honourable principles that must be protected/rescued from an injustice; and the hero is the device that gives nobility, honour, emotional resonance or motivation, and moral worth to the political quest.

A political narrative need not have an explicit moral outlined at the end. Rather, it is often simply through the presentation of the characters and the accompanying plot that the discourse's implicit argument is made. Because we have seen these structures and stock characters so many times, we can anticipate and recognize the implicit lesson, even if we hear or see only a fragment of the story. In fact, we can usually intuit the moral arc from even just a brief view of one or two of the main characters. For the very "role" they are assigned triggers our expectations about the plot to come and thus leads us to the moral conclusion even if the plot itself is never outlined.

We sought to analyse the narrative structures of contemporary Canadian anti-abortion discourse by systematically examining the existence (or lack of) and substantive nature of key character roles and the moral lessons they contain. Concretely, this meant that we analysed and coded our cases for a variety of categories designed to track the existing narrative structure and character roles, including how often narrative-like structures were employed, how women were represented in general, what type of actors were "attacked" as the enemy, and what type of actors were accorded the role of villain, victim, and hero.

Overall, we found that a very high percentage of anti-abortion discourse employed narrative techniques, with more than 88 per cent of cases mobilizing at least one stereotypical character role that pointed to a moral lesson. This supports our contention that narrativization is an important rhetorical strategy for political discourse. But it also raises the question of what specifically are the roles and the moral lessons conveyed by these narratives.

11.2.1 Villains

In the traditional portrait of anti-abortion discourse, the primary villain in the abortion drama is the pregnant woman seeking an abortion. As Faludi (1991) and Lakoff (1996) highlight, in this narrative, women tended to be depicted as either irresponsible sexually promiscuous Jezebels or as selfish, uncaring careerists. Our study found that Canadian anti-abortion discourse does continue to occasionally employ this strategy. Even the founder of ProWomanProLife, Andrea Mrozek, reproduces this narrative at times. Mrozek's response, for example, to another ("pro-choice") blogger who defended her abortion decision argues:

> I was raised by tough and courageous parents, who moved across the ocean to escape an immoral regime. Maybe that's why I find I'm often short on the sympathy file. If you claim to want to do the right thing, then just do it. Don't write long meandering tracts on how you wanted to but couldn't possibly be brave ... You know what I'm sorry about? (Because I'm not feeling sympathy for her right now, to be sure.) I'm sorry a person can be so spineless as to kill her child in favour of a Masters degree. And then claim "it was the right thing to do" to the nodding affirmation of New York Times types. (PWPL, 19 June 2009)

In line with the strict father world view, an impatient Mrozek presents abortion as a spineless option and the woman as a villain whose selfishness and self-pity stops her from seeing who the real victim is. Moreover, by contrasting a woman facing an unplanned pregnancy to her parents, who "moved across the ocean to escape an immoral regime," Mrozek draws on another popular narrative (hard-working immigrants sacrificing everything to live up to their political principles and give their children a better life) to suggest that hard choices can be made, which in turn justifies the self-righteous tone and punitive orientation.

However, our analysis shows that these types of narratives turn out to be surprisingly rare in contemporary Canadian anti-abortion discourse. In fact, pregnant women were identified as the villain in less than 7 per cent of the cases we analysed (see figure 11.2). Notably, none of the members of Parliament's statements targeted pregnant women. In this respect, then, Mrozek's narrative is not representative of the main narrative currents of anti-abortion discourse.

However, her post is instructive and broadly representative for another reason. For Mrozek's narrative not only targets the pregnant woman, it also blames the "New York Times types." Although the decision to abort a pregnancy is represented as a selfish individual decision, Mrozek implies that its origins are societal. Fellow blogger Veronique Bergeron makes explicit this shift in responsibility, arguing that, as a society, we are "not really pro-choice, we are pro-Me. Me support your choice to whatever as long as it doesn't affect Me. That's why Me supports abortion" (PWPL, 13 November 2008). These examples are indicative, moreover, of a significant transformation in contemporary anti-abortion discourse.

As we can see in figure 11.2, contemporary discourse identifies a pervasive, abstract, yet very real pro-abortion societal mentality as the villain in 26.7 per cent of all cases – a rate that is almost four times the frequency of those that blame the pregnant woman. Although this might seem like a subtle and unimportant difference, the implications are significant. For shifting the object of blame and villainy alters the overall tone and moral lesson of the story dramatically. In this version, pregnant women are portrayed less as the Jezebel who should be punished and more as a Snow White seduced by the shiny apples presented to them by a pro-abortion society. This representation allows anti-abortion discourse to present abortion as a selfish choice while simultaneously avoiding a punitive tone towards women. And this, in

Figure 11.2 Villains in Anti-abortion Narratives (% of cases in data set)

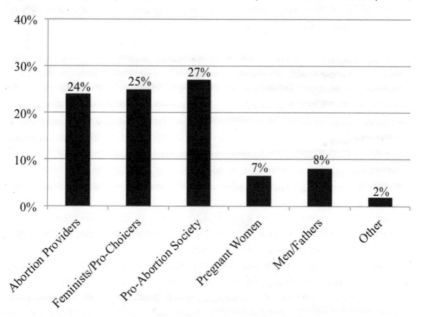

Note: Percentages are not mutually exclusive – if a case had two distinct villains in it, it was coded twice (once for each code).

turn, allows anti-abortion discourse to create the appearance of embodying sympathy and compassion towards women considering abortion.

As figure 11.2 demonstrates, our analysis also found that contemporary Canadian anti-abortion discourse is committed to finding a rich new cast of villainous characters to flesh out the somewhat impersonal bogeyman of the pro-abortion society. Men, feminists, and abortion providers have become increasingly prevalent stock villains.

Let's begin with men. In contrast to traditional anti-abortion narratives, where men are largely discursively constructed as opponents of abortion, our analysis shows that, in recent narratives, men are increasingly blamed for the pro-abortion culture that is plaguing Canada. Notably, the most common representation of the male subject is that he coerces women into unwanted abortions. Anti-abortion activists claim that "women often state that it was their male partner who decided on the abortion" (LC 2010) and that "many women who have an abortion feel coerced or pressured to do so by their boyfriends" (AFLO 2010c). As shown in figure 11.2, in 8.2 per cent of the cases, coercive men were portrayed as the villains.

While this percentage may not seem particularly high, two factors suggest that it is nonetheless a significant strategy. First, given that the casting of men as villains often happens in conjunction with claims that abortion is analogous to sexual and intimate partner violence, this discourse mimics other feminist tropes, reinforcing the notion that anti-abortion activists are crusaders against patriarchy and champions of women's rights (see the discussion in chapters 9 and 10). Second, if we examine the results of our analysis at a more granular level, we can also see that, while men as villains is not the most dominant narrative overall, it is dominant in one of the most visible and influential sites of discourse: the political realm. In fact, more than one third (37.1 per cent) of the narratives employed by MPs identified men or fathers as the villain (in contrast, this narrative was found in only 4 per cent of the blogs and 10 per cent of organizational cases).

This narrative has, for example, been a major framing device for both of the anti-abortion private members' bills introduced in Parliament in the past few years. Male coercers were identified as the primary villains and targets of MP Rod Bruinooge's Bill C-510. His 2010 private member's bill, commonly referred to as "Roxanne's Law" after a woman who was killed by her abusive boyfriend, allegedly for refusing an abortion, sought to criminalize any person who "coerces a female to procure or attempt to procure an abortion for herself" (Bruinooge 2010a). Bill C-484, the "Unborn Victims of Crime Act," is another example of influential representations of the villainous man within anti-abortion discourse. When defending the proposed law, MP Ken Epp argued that, "the man should not have power over her [the woman's] body. Usually, not always, the attacker is a man. The man is saying to the victim, 'You want to have your baby? I am sorry, I'm going to prevent that.' ... Women are not getting justice" (Canada, House of Commons 2008b). Although neither bill passed, the tendency to highlight male violence to justify the anti-abortion position has become a popular image and seems likely to grow stronger in the coming years, especially as it resonates with and borrows from feminist positions against domestic violence. And since debates in Parliament are often covered by the mainstream media more closely than some of the other arenas in which the anti-abortion movement is active, the men-as-villains narrative might seem far more visible than the aggregate number of 8 per cent might suggest.

Another popular villain that has taken the place of pregnant women in contemporary anti-abortion discourse is feminism, feminists, and pro-choicers. In fact, 24.7 per cent of the cases analysed characterized feminists as the villain – a rate that is well over triple the frequency of portrayals of the women seeking abortions as the villain. The feminist/pro-choice villain often shares the stage with the abortion provider. In 24.1 per cent of cases (again, more than three times the number of cases where women were portrayed as the villain), abortion providers were characterized as the villain (see figure 11.2).

Targeting feminists and abortion providers as the villain is not particularly new, of course. What is new is the main reason given for *why* they are villainous. Feminists and abortion providers are no longer primarily cast as villains because they are godless or anti-fetus. Rather, building on the larger strategy of representing the anti-abortion position as more pro-woman than feminism, contemporary discourse intensifies the claim and vilifies feminism for being actively *anti-woman*. In what might be thought of as a reverse "j'accuse" (in which those who claim to be defending women's rights are actually revealed as gender traitors who put their own elite interests above those of actual women), this narrative charges feminists and abortion providers with being uncaring patriarchs – biased, uncompassionate, and knowingly harming women by forcing them into unwanted abortions to further the feminists' and abortion providers' own ideology. A representative blog post entitled "When You Work in an Abortion Clinic" epitomizes this by arguing that medical professionals at abortion clinics are "are encouraging women to be completely distant from their own child, from their own bodies in which the child is living so that they can experience a short-term relief" (PWPL, 9 March 2009).

With this final turn, the transformation is complete. The villain in this story is no longer the pregnant woman. Indeed, the new villains – whether in the form of a nebulous pro-abortion society, men, feminists, or abortion providers – are now defined precisely by their well-camouflaged, but ultimately nefarious, intentions towards women. These new villains are those who "meet women in their personal deserts and offer a refreshing drink of cyanide. Only [they] call it Sprite and add ice and one of those fun umbrellas" (PWPL, 16 September 2008). By freeing pregnant women from the role of villain, contemporary anti-abortion discourse avoids reproducing one of the key negative dimensions of traditional anti-abortion narratives (i.e., the appearance of treating women as villains and thus being perceived as anti-woman). It also creates space for a more welcoming characterization of women that reinforces their pro-woman position. For as pregnant women who consider abortion are represented less and less as the conniving and blameworthy Jezebels of the past, they can increasingly be cast in the more "pro-woman" role of the pure Snow White, who must be protected from dark interests, poisoned apples, and spiked Sprite.

11.2.2 The Victims of Abortion

Traditionally, anti-abortion narratives have tended to represent the fetus as the primary victim. Throughout anti-abortion storytelling, the fetus is referred to as the "unborn," "the baby," or the "preborn," in order to stress its personhood. At the heart of the traditional anti-abortion discourse is the fetus, cast in the role of an innocent and powerless victim so as to ground the moral lesson that "the fetus is deserving of our protection" (PWPL 2007). To what extent is this narrative found in contemporary anti-abortion discourse?

We did find that the characterization of fetus as victim remains an important trend in contemporary Canadian anti-abortion discourse, with 24.2 per cent of all cases portraying the fetus as a victim (see figure 11.3). This narrative remains especially visible in the public realm, as one of the most controversial and aggressive organizations, the Canadian Centre for Bio-ethical Reform (CCBR), makes this a centerpiece of its communications strategy. Moreover, the portrayal of the fetus as a victim is particularly frequent in the political realm, with almost a third of all political cases using this frame.

However, if there is some continuity with traditional narratives around the representation of fetuses as victims, in other respects the differences between the traditional portrait and contemporary discourse are profound. The traditional portrait of the anti-abortion movement as classic religious culture warriors would suggest that contemporary anti-abortion discourse should spend a significant amount of energy portraying society and morality/spirituality as a significant victim of a pro-abortion culture, there is relatively little focus on that in Canada. In fact, only 6.5 per cent of cases made any narrative references to this thematic at all.

More importantly, several new actors have replaced the fetus as the main victim. As is clear from figure 11.3, the most obvious is the almost wholesale inclusion of pregnant women in the victim role. This is accomplished largely through the representation of pregnant women

Figure 11.3   Victims in Anti-abortion Narratives (% of cases in data set)

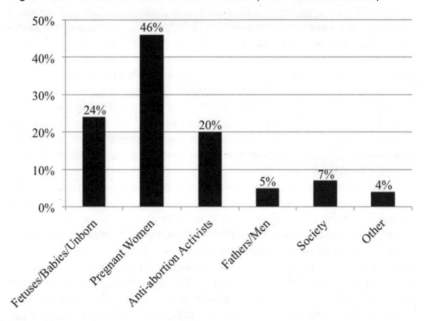

Note: Percentages are not mutually exclusive – if a case had two distinct victims in it, it was coded twice (once for each code).

as victims of overt coercion and/or implicit peer/social pressure. Consider the coercion plotline implied by the cast of villainous characters. Here, women are implicitly and explicitly represented as coerced, traumatized, and forever affected victims of abortion. They are no longer autonomous agents making selfish choices. They are victims whose decisions are not their own.

To effect this representation, anti-abortion discourse has expanded (as have many feminist theories, although to different ends) what counts as coercion-like influence. According to one blog entry, "coercion can be subtle. If a woman is scared her mate will leave her unless she has an abortion, she's being coerced. If a woman is made to feel guilty, as though she's choosing an unborn baby over the man she's currently with, she's being coerced" (PWPL, 3 December 2008). Organizational websites and bloggers suggest that between 51 and 64 per cent of women "do not feel free in making their [abortion] decision but felt pressured by others" (AFLO 2010a; PWPL, 17 July 2009). The website for Toronto Right to Life (TRL) reinforces this narrative and increases its intensity by comparing this coercion to domestic abuse, suggesting that many women "are forced into an unwanted abortion by husbands, boyfriends, parents, or others. If the woman has repeatedly been a victim of domineering abuse, such an unwanted abortion may be perceived as the ultimate violation in a life characterized by abuse" (TRL 2010b). In today's anti-abortion discourse, then, the logic used by activists such as Joe Borowski has been flipped on its head. No longer is it "third rate tramps" forcing "doctors and nurses" to commit "medieval acts of barbarism." It is now the doctors, nurses, and partners who are villains coercing vulnerable women to become victims of their own so-called choices.

This portrayal of women as victims is not a minor pattern. In our study we found that the dominant representation of women in contemporary Canadian anti-abortion discourse is as the coerced/pressured victims of abortion. In a stunning 45.9 per cent of all cases, women having abortions were portrayed as victims. This is almost twice the percentage of cases that represent the fetus as a victim and over seven times more frequent than the 6.5 per cent of cases that portrayed women as selfish/self-interested villains. It is also worth noting that the representation of women as victims is particularly strong in the formal political realm, with 68.6 per cent of politicians' discourse forwarding this portrayal. This perspective also increasingly defines the framing of anti-abortion themes in new laws. The proponents of Bill C-510, for example, described the bill as giving "vulnerable women ... the legal recourse to press charges when they feel they are being coerced into an unwanted abortion, potentially averting escalation into violence and even murder" (Bruinooge 2010a).

Interestingly, other new actors are also being portrayed as victims. The anti-abortion movement itself and its activists are often portrayed as victims. However, this is almost entirely limited to the blogosphere, with only 3 per cent of anti-abortion organizations and politicians portraying the movement as a victim. Most surprising perhaps, is the fact that men are beginning to be represented as victims of abortion. It is still a nascent pattern – only 4.7 per cent of cases suggest that men are harmed or victimized by abortion – but we suspect it will become more important in the coming years. In this narrative, a man whose partner had an abortion is also a victim, "suffer[ing] in silence because [he] is confused about [his] feelings, trying to put up a strong front, and ignored by society" (AFLO 2010b). Both the Alliance for Life Ontario (AFLO) and

Signal Hill websites have entire web pages dedicated to counselling and comforting men. This discourse also often uses the male victim narrative to once again vilify feminism. According to one organization, "many feminists, both male and female, see abortion solely as a woman's issue. It's her body, therefore, it's her choice. Unfortunately, this cut-and-dry approach fails to take into consideration that all people have emotions, both sexes" (AFLO 2010b). Bloggers have also taken up this characterization, accusing feminists of removing "men from the equation" and arguing that "we don't talk enough ... about what it's like to be a man whose child is aborted without his consent, or sometimes even his knowledge until after the fact" (PWPL, 18 March 2008).

The loss of traditional masculinity is also often highlighted as an element of men's victimization by abortion. MP Maurice Vellacott's website quotes material stating that "men are negatively affected and sense a loss of control and pride, especially when their partner has had an abortion without their being consulted," and that this leads to a variety of symptoms, including "depression, guilt, anger, and feelings of powerlessness" (deVeber Institute for Bioethics and Social Research 2004). The AFLO highlights abortion as a loss of traditional masculinity even more explicitly:

> Abortion rewrites the rules of masculinity. Whether or not the male was involved in the abortion decision, his inability to function in a socially prescribed manner leaves him wounded and confused. As a man, you naturally begin to take on the responsibility of protecting the child. It's how you are wired. But, because of the abortion, you are no longer able to fulfill this role. You may develop anger, resentment and guilt. You may not even realize where these feelings are coming from. They often come out in destructive behaviours – excessive drinking, drug use, depression, suicidal feelings, risk taking or maybe running from relationship to relationship unable to make commitments. (AFLO 2010b)

The moral of these gendered stories is clear. Men who advocate for abortion rights are coercers and criminals. And women who advocate for abortion rights and perform them are gender-traitors – anti-woman peddlers of outdated and self-interested ideology. In contrast, men and women deciding whether to choose abortion or not are worthy of discursive sympathy. They are victims of an abstractly pro-abortion society and elitist "pro-abort" activists (as many anti-abortion activists like to term them) and should not be vilified for their choices, but instead treated with compassion and kindness, even as the anti-abortion movement seeks to persuade them to make different choices. These distinctions, for all their potential logical inconsistencies and gaps, nonetheless allow anti-abortion narratives to subtly but powerfully reinforce the positioning of the anti-abortion position as modern, compassionate, and pro-woman.

11.2.3 Anti-abortion Heroes

If narrative characterizations of villains and victims convey important moral lessons about abortion, no political narrative is truly complete without its heroes. In the anti-abortion discourse of the past, men have traditionally been portrayed as standing at the forefront, and it was men who have until recently represented the heroes and martyrs of the anti-abortion movement. In Susan Faludi's defining sketch, men inhabited all the leadership and "warrior" positions of the anti-abortion movement with "the wives and daughters of the 'warriors' lined up in neat rows ... their palms raised towards the heavens. 'We're not allowed to speak,' one of the women says when approached for an interview" (Faludi 1991, 411).

So who are the heroes of the contemporary anti-abortion discourse in Canada? Figure 11.4 outlines what we found.

Unsurprisingly, men who have taken a clear public stand against abortion make up one category of heroes. In 8.7 per cent of all cases, men were identified as the hero of the narrative (see figure 11.4). A good example of this is PWPL blogger Rebecca Walberg's entry in which she offers extensive praise for the anti-abortion efforts of MP Rod Bruinooge:

> Bruinooge could curry favour ... and set himself up for a smooth climb through the party. He's also got a young family ... and therefore no end of claims on his time. But instead of playing it safe and keeping his mouth shut, as the CPC [Conservative Party of Canada] would prefer, he's speaking his conscience, leading the most-unsecret-ever secret pro-life caucus, and setting an example more of us should follow ... We need more MPs like him. (PWPL, 3 January 2009)

This is a traditional anti-abortion hero narrative. Despite it being an unpopular stance, despite the fact that it will harm his political career in the party, and despite the fact that it takes time away from his young

Figure 11.4 Heroes in Anti-abortion Narratives (% of cases in data set)

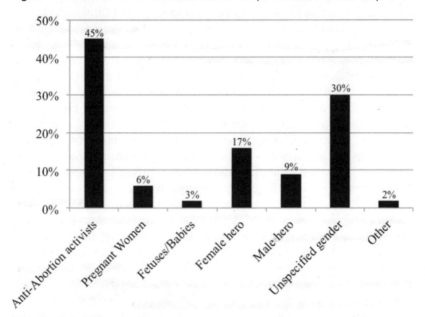

Note: Percentages are not mutually exclusive – if a case had two distinct heroes in it, it was coded twice (once for each code).

family, Bruinooge chooses to sacrifice his own personal interests in order to speak truth to power.

However, as is the case with the other character roles discussed above, contemporary anti-abortion narratives have also widened the cast of characters who are portrayed as heroes. Most obvious in light of our previous findings is the very strong move to tell the stories of heroic anti-abortion women. In fact, the emergence of women as heroes of the anti-abortion movement has become a key rhetoric tactic through-out the movement's discourse. PWPL founder Andrea Mrozek writes, "I started ProWomanProLife.org in order to provide a voice for those women who are pro-life because they are pro-woman. I believe ours is a unique approach to the abortion debate" (PWPL 2008). Current anti-abortion discourse repeatedly asserts that the movement is designed *for* women, *by* women. PWPL blogger Rebecca Walberg argues that "there is an excerpt containing the old chestnut that most anti-abortion activists are men, that it's about controlling women, that if men got pregnant this wouldn't be an issue. It's to put this to rest that I think PWPL is so timely and necessary" (PWPL, 4 February 2008). Again and again, contemporary Canadian anti-abortion discourse tells stories of the strong anti-abortion women who represent the cause. As Mrozek writes, "I'm glad to hear about women like [Michelle] Bachman, [Sarah] Palin, Laura Ingraham ... Strong pro-life women are a very scary thing to the pro-abortion side. Not to belabour the point, but they should be worried. We're not just coming. We're already here" (PWPL, 21 October 2008).

Celebrating women as anti-abortion heroes is a consistent and notable strategy. In our analysis, we identified women anti-abortion activists as the hero of the tale in almost 17 per cent of all cases – double the rate for men as the hero. Interestingly, however, there were some notable differences on this issue between the different sites. While bloggers and organizations strongly emphasize the role of women in the anti-abortion movement (for example, bloggers represented women as heroes more often than men – 17.2 per cent to 6.8 per cent – and organizations highlighted women even more strongly), this trend is reversed in the realm of formal politics, where men are represented as heroes in 25.7 per cent of cases and women in 20 per cent. Given that the electoral realm in Canada generally continues to be characterized by significantly unequal gender representation (particularly in conservative politics, where the anti-abortion position is more popular) and that only 28 per cent of Canada's MPs are female, it is perhaps not surprising that men continue to be – and continue to represent themselves as – key leaders in the formal political realm.

Interestingly, however, in almost 30 per cent of the cases, the hero was not gendered at all, and in 45 per cent of cases, the anti-abortion movement itself was held up as a hero, sacrificing its own self-interests for the good of the broader community, coerced women, and defenceless fetuses. Nowhere is this more dramatically exhibited than in one PWPL blog entry in which Andrea Mrozek explicitly channels Martin Luther King's "I have a dream" speech:

I have a dream! Women, loved and supported, loving and supporting their kids and families. Women, strong women, doing what they choose – aware that sex is also an action to be responsible for, and it is quite often, though not always, linked to having kids. Women, aware that some things simply aren't a choice, and that we don't kill to solve our problems. Women accepting life as it comes, with all the ups and downs. I have this idea that women want to love their kids, even the unplanned ones. And that the minority who don't still don't need to kill those kids. (PWPL, 8 March 2009)

Drawing on tropes that clearly attempt to link the movement with the women's rights movement and the civil rights movement before it, the contemporary anti-abortion movement seeks to portray itself as a selfless, courageous, and compassionate battle against profound social injustice.

11.3 Conclusion

In this chapter, we explored the degree to which contemporary anti-abortion discourse in Canada has embedded a modernized, pro-woman ethos in some of its deepest and most implicit rhetorical layers, including its overarching metaphorical tone and its narrative structure. We have found that, although there are some traces of traditional traits in the tone and narrative structure, to a large extent these dimensions profoundly reinforce the modernized "pro-woman" argumentation and framing that we discussed in previous chapters.

Our analyses have demonstrated how complex and multilayered political discourse can be and how some of the least evident rhetorical techniques can nonetheless be some of the most powerfully persuasive dimensions of a given discourse. Our findings make it very clear how much more complicated contemporary anti-abortion discourse is than the traditional portrait would imply.

What do our findings mean? And why do they matter? How does contemporary Canadian anti-abortion discourse compare to that of the contemporary American context? And what are the general implications of our findings – for academics, for citizens, and for activists? These are the questions we will address in the next chapter and in Part III.

Chapter 12

"Pro-woman" Discourse in the United States

Given the related but distinct histories of the United States and Canada – and the fact that the abortion debate is more contested in the US than in almost any other country – our analysis of the Canadian anti-abortion movement obviously raises questions about the nature of the American movement and its strategies of persuasion. Although a full and systematic comparison with the United States will have to wait for future research, the preliminary analyses contained in this chapter offer some very interesting findings and highlight the importance of examining this question in a more systematic and robust way.

12.1 The Enduring Relevance of the Traditional Portrait in the United States

It would be easy to assume that the traditional portrait remains a relatively accurate description of the contemporary movement in the US, and there is significant evidence to back up that assumption, especially with respect to certain key dimensions of the movement. As we saw in chapter 3, the US movement remains highly focused on contesting and limiting legal abortion in the legislative realm, making record-breaking gains in terms of new legislation over the past decade. Republican lawmakers continue to table a cascade of anti-abortion bills at the state level, the majority of which appeal to traditional conceptions of fetal personhood. And abortion remains a go-to issue through which Republican politicians regularly establish their conservative credentials. In the words of 2008 Republican vice-presidential candidate and conservative movement icon Sarah Palin, abortion continues to be a crucial way to "identify and unify" the Republican Party (Vander-burgh Right to Life 2009).

Most high-profile political candidates also continue to use traditional religious and fetal-centric discourse to defend their position. Minnesota Congresswoman and 2008 Republican presidential contender Michelle Bachmann is typical, declaring herself "100 percent pro-life" and defending her position by arguing that "our Declaration of Independence said it's a creator who endowed us with inalienable rights given to us from God, not from government. And the first of those rights is life. And I stand for that right. I stand for the right to life" (OnTheIssue 2013a). Moreover, as we discussed in the preface, there have been several high-profile cases in the past several years in which anti-abortion politicians such as Todd Akin have combined religious and fetal-centric discourse with extraordinarily anti-woman tones and arguments.

The picture is similar at the organizational level as well. The largest and oldest anti-abortion organization in the US, National Right to Life Committee (NRLC) (with 50 current state affiliates and over 3,000 local chapters), continues to highlight a number of traditional characteristics. Its mission statement explicitly cites "our Creator" as the philosophical foundation for the equal "rights to life" of the unborn. Moreover, it asserts that its main tasks include "sponsoring legislation which will advance the protection of human life" and its "supporting the election of public officials who will defend life" (National Right to Life Committee n.d.-b). The most robust part of the group's website is devoted to these legislative efforts and what individuals can do to support the campaigns. Even more recent major organizations, such as the Susan B. Anthony List (SBA List) (founded in 1993), operate more as political action committees (PACs) that are primarily devoted to raising and spending funds for and endorsing anti-abortion legislation and candidates. (The SBA List has endorsed and supported many candidates with quite extreme views, such as Rick Santorum and Todd Akin.)

Religious and fetal-centric arguments also seem to accurately characterize several women-founded organizations that are active in the American anti-abortion movement. Concerned Women for America (CWA), for example, proudly announces its religious roots, claiming that "the CWA is built on prayer and education," and defines itself as an organization devoted to "protect[ing] and promot[ing] Biblical values among all citizens" while also helping "our members across the country bring Biblical principles into all levels of public policy" (Concerned Women for America, n.d.). The CWA website has a long, explicit, and quite literalist statement of faith as the foundation of its self-description. Unsurprisingly, its abortion-specific discourse falls squarely within the traditional portrait, focusing almost entirely on influencing electoral politics, passing anti-abortion legislation, and using fetal-centric arguments to justify its cause. Nowhere in CWA's discourse (or that of similar organizations, such as Phyllis Schlafly's Eagle Forum) can we see the abortion-harms-women (A-H-W) argumentation or pro-woman framing that are now so characteristic of the Canadian movement.

The differences between the Canadian and American branches of organizations that have arms in both countries are also revealing. Consider the American Center for Bio-ethical Reform (CBR) and the Canadian Centre for Bio-ethical Reform (CCBR), for example. While the CCBR might use visuals and techniques that are very graphic by Canadian standards, they are notably less graphic than those used by the US parent. Moreover, the composition of the US leadership team fits the traditional image quite well. In 2013/14, seven of their directors were men, while only three were women; almost all appear to be white and middle aged or older. The majority of the biographies on the CBR website also mention the religious backgrounds of the directors in some detail (Centre for Bio-ethical Reform n.d.-a).[20] The CCBR is quite different. As previously discussed, in 2013/14 its masthead picture showed its entire staff, most of whom appear to be in their mid- to late-twenties or early thirties, and their staff information page confirmed that a strong majority of their staff were women. Equally interestingly, while pro-woman language and the A-H-W argument suffuse many of the CCBR's web pages, these themes were much less dominant on the CBR's website.

Also, although the projects and content of the two organizations are similar in many ways (they both, for example, use "choice chains" and Genocide Awareness Project (GAP) materials), there seem to be some important differences. For example, in line with the much greater and more explicit role of religion in the US anti-abortion movement, the CBR has an "church outreach" project titled Matthew 28:20. The CBR describes this as an "offshoot of the Genocide Awareness Project," but one that is "directed at the spiritual community, using biblical arguments" rather than

---

20 It should be noted here that Stephanie Gray was both a director of the CBR and the head of the CCBR.

the "civil-rights arguments" the GAP uses to address the "secular community" (Center for Bio-ethical Reform, n.d.-b). The CBR uses the Matthew 28:20 materials to engage the congregations of "big churches that are failing to discharge their biblical mandate to be a witness against evil. Being exposed to the horrible reality of abortion, Sunday after Sunday, these churches will no longer be able to trivialize or ignore baby-killing" (ibid.). Tellingly, the American CBR has two separate sections in its online store, one for secular-themed materials and the other for religious materials. In contrast, the Canadian version almost never mentions religion in its public discourse. Its list of presentations clearly shows that it frequently liaisons with and presents to religious institutions, schools, clubs, and events. Even so, it does not highlight religion as a relevant philosophical foundation in its public discourse. Moreover, only one of the fifteen staff bios makes any reference to religion – and, in that case, it was simply an indirect reference, as the name of one of the organizations the staff member worked for clearly indicated its religious basis. In sum, significant evidence suggests that there are important differences between the dominant anti-abortion discourse in Canada and the US and that many organizations in the US continue to use the strategies that are central to the traditional portrait.

Anti-abortion lawmaking in the US also tends to reinforce the traditional portrait. For instance, when Congress passed the Partial Birth Abortion (PBA) Ban in 2003 and 2007, its fetal-centric discursive rationale was that the ban "expresses respect for the dignity of human life" (quoted in Gee 2007, 984) – something that was mirrored in the majority decision penned by Justice Kennedy in the US Supreme Court ruling in *Gonzales v. Carhart* (see chapter 3). Personhood laws, which seek to change states' definition of the word "person" to include a fertilized egg, embryo, or fetus, with the intent of outlawing abortion, have also become increasingly popular across the US. In 2013 alone, nine state legislatures introduced "personhood measures." In November 2014, both North Dakota and Colorado put the issue to a referendum (voters in both states rejected the proposals) (NARAL 2015).

Many anti-abortion advocates also argue for similar laws at the federal level. Paul Ryan, the Republican nominee for vice-president in 2012 and current Speaker of the House of Representatives, has been a highly vocal proponent of a federal personhood amendment, as have other Republican hopefuls. Iowa Republican Senator Joni Ernst, who voted for a personhood amendment in the state legislature in 2013, has stated that she would support a federal bill that gives legal personhood rights to fetuses at the moment of fertilization. Her justification for supporting such a ban (that she "has been shaped by [her] religious beliefs through the years") also replicates many of the traditional characteristics of anti-abortion discourse (Basset 2014). And finally, in the thirty years between 1973 and 2003, a Human Life Amendment (which would embed "respect" for fetal life in the constitution) was proposed over 330 times by the National Committee for a Human Life Amendment, with seven of these actually having been introduced into Congress (only one reached a formal vote and failed by eighteen votes).

12.2 The Emergence of Woman-Protective Anti-abortion Arguments

Despite the continuing applicability of the traditional portrait to the US context, however, there are indications that it may not provide the full picture. For, as the American anti-abortion movement has grown over the past forty years, it has also diversified and fragmented. And there is evidence that some of the arguments and rhetorical tactics that we have found in Canada are also slowly becoming more visible in the US.

12.2.1 Rethinking the Strategy: Absolutists versus Incrementalists

While many view the American anti-abortion movement as monolithic and homogeneous, we saw in chapters 2 and 3 that this is not historically accurate, as different arms of the movement have adopted different legal and political strategies at various points. Historically, for example, strategic diversity could be seen in responses to *Roe v. Wade*. However, while there was some internal debate over which strategies to adopt immediately following *Roe*, the dominant belief was that the movement should work to directly challenge its constitutionality. Moreover, as the 1980s progressed, there was an increasing sense that "*Roe* was ripe for overturning" (Gee 2007, 981). However, disappointment over the fact that *Planned Parenthood v. Casey* (1992) did not overturn legal abortion (see chapter 3) led many activists to question the wisdom of gambling on an absolutist legal strategy.

In this context, a new, and perhaps intensified, strategic debate has grown within the contemporary American movement. On one side are the "absolutists," largely believing that the movement must direct all its efforts towards opposing *Roe* and overturning legal abortion completely, as one should "approac[h] evil categorically and without compromise" (Siegel 2008a, 1706). However, another perspective has come to argue that the most effective way to curb abortion is to challenge its legal and moral legitimacy "incrementally, in a manner that allows for the reeducation of the public" (1706). This incrementalist approach believes that to capitalize on *Casey*'s legal openings, the movement should invest more anti-abortion resources in enacting practical and often indirect barriers to real abortion access, mostly through the introduction of seemingly innocuous state-level legislation. Thus, where the traditional portrait would lead most people to believe that the primary legislative strategy of the anti-abortion movement is to enact absolute bans on abortion, we can see that there is more diversity regarding legislative strategy than that portrait might suggest.

In fact, the fracture between absolutists and incrementalists has led to sharp disagreements within the movement. For example, absolutists derided the PBA Ban (which was largely considered an incrementalist effort), with some local chapters of the NRLC criticizing the ban as a "waste of effort" and accused its supporters of having "adopted moral relativism and legal positivism, obsessing on process and overlooking fundamental justice" (Siegel 2008a, 1711). It seems that the influence of the incrementalist faction of the movement has grown – especially because, in its elaboration of the "undue burden" doctrine, *Casey* opened up many new avenues for this approach. Indeed, political critics and observers argue that the "undue burden standard" (as elaborated in *Casey*) has become the anti-choice movement's "most potent weapon," effectively limiting abortion access to urban areas and along the east and west coasts (Pieklo 2014). While certain characteristics of the incrementalist strategy fit within the traditional portrait, others do not. It seems that the traditional image on its own is likely too simple to capture contemporary anti-abortion strategy in the US, even when it comes to anti-abortion legislation.

12.2.2 Rethinking the Language: The Problems of an Anti-woman Tone

If the US anti-abortion movement has, since the late 1980s, experienced a strategic debate regarding legislative and legal tactics, it has also engaged in another internal debate regarding its strategies of persuasion, as many incrementalists worried that the absolutist discourse was alienating the broader American public (Siegel 2008a, 1706). As we saw in chapter 3, by the late 1980s, hard-line and at times violent protest tactics pioneered by groups like Operation Rescue were becoming the mainstream representation of the American anti-abortion movement. Increasingly, the movement was being (at least somewhat accurately) publicly characterized as extremist, violent, uncompromising, and anti-woman.

This public representation became a problem for the movement, as the increasing popularity of aggressive "rescue" tactics, the rise of anti-abortion violence, and the assassination of a number of abortion providers effectively "estranged the American electorate" (Siegel 2008a, 1714). Public support for the movement was falling. Polls throughout the late 1980s and early 1990s consistently suggested that, while many might be sympathetic to the argument that the fetus is a human being, the majority of Americans continued to support (at least some level of) legal abortion access for women (Gee 2007, 981).

Since the 1970s, the main rhetorical techniques of the anti-abortion movement were heavily fetal-centric, religious, and fundamentalist in content and angry and retributive in tone. This discourse was often supported by particularly graphic imagery, aggressive protest action, and sometimes even overt violence (see Siegel 2008a, 1713; Faludi 1991, 421). Eventually, this discourse and strategy encouraged many Americans to view the anti-abortion movement as profoundly anti-woman. Capitalizing on this shift in public opinion, abortion rights advocates accused anti-abortion activists of treating women as maternal incubators, of privileging the lives of embryos over the lives of adult women, of opposing abortion even in extreme cases of rape and incest, and of lacking basic compassion. And these criticisms often stuck. In the words of legal scholar Graham Gee, Americans continued to be "unsettled by the anti-abortion movement's neglect of a woman's experience in the face of an unplanned pregnancy" (2007, 981).

This anti-woman critique, combined with the growing popular perceptions of the movement as zealous and violent, ultimately "prompted deep concerns inside the anti-abortion movement about the confrontational frames that dominated 1980s advocacy" (Siegel 2008b, 1665). By the mid-1990s, the failure to make significant progress on public opinion ensured that even some of the most militant anti-abortion activists began openly questioning the fetal-centric and uncompromising strategy that had dominated the post-*Roe* era. In the words of one activist, the public "felt that pro-life people were not compassionate to women and that we were only 'fetus lovers' who abandoned the mother after the birth. They felt that we were violent, that we burned down clinics and shot abortionists. We were viewed as religious zealots who were not too well educated" (quoted in Siegel 2008a, 1716–17). This public relations challenge would ultimately lead some activists to employ a secondary anti-abortion discourse, one that focused on the fetus *and* women.

12.2.3 The Origins of Woman-Protective Anti-abortion Arguments in the United States

While the dominant anti-abortion argument throughout the 1980s was a fetal-centric one, it was never the only line of anti-abortion argumentation (Siegel 2008a; Siegel 2008b; Gee 2007; Rose 2011). As we saw in chapter 2, historically there have been a variety of arguments including, in the nineteenth century, the idea that women needed protection from dangerous midwives and abortionists. But even in the past forty years, there have been a small number of voices within the American anti-abortion movement that have positioned their opposition to abortion in ways that are similar to what we have seen in contemporary Canadian anti-abortion discourse.

Legal scholar Reva Siegel has spent much of the past decade tracking the emergence of what she calls "women-protective anti-abortion arguments" (WPAAs) and their growing influence on the American anti-abortion movement. Siegel traces the origins of WPAAs to the proliferation of "crisis pregnancy centres" in the 1980s. In order to dissuade pregnant women from choosing abortion, crisis centre staff stressed the alleged physical and psychological harms abortion inflicted on women. According to Siegel, before WPAAs emerged as a unified political discourse they existed as a "therapeutic, mobilizing discourse" deployed primarily "among women volunteers and clients in the 'crisis pregnancy' network during a period when the anti-abortion movement generally argued the moral and political case against abortion in fetal-focused terms" (Siegel 2008b, 1657).

By the mid-1980s, this therapeutic discourse gained steam after it was further developed by psychotherapist and anti-abortion advocate Vincent Rue. Drawing on the emergence of post-traumatic stress disorder (PTSD) – a new concept being used to explain the trauma experienced by Vietnam veterans – Rue argued that women who had had abortions were, like Vietnam vets, suffering in silence. According to Rue, the vast majority of women who had an abortion suffered from what he called post abortion syndrome (PAS). While PAS has never been listed in the official Diagnostic and Statistical Manual of Mental Disorders, the idea was nonetheless widely disseminated by the Christian Broadcast Network throughout the 1980s (Siegel 2008b, 1662). PAS was also embraced by some women within the movement, many of whom would go on to organize new groups and campaigns such as Women Exploited by Abortion (WEBA) and Silent No More. However, it was not until activist David Reardon, an engineer from the University of Illinois, picked up the idea of PAS that it would gain the attention of the mainstream anti-abortion movement.

For the past three decades, Reardon – who has been described as the "Moses" of the anti-abortion movement – has been arguing that the movement should offer an anti-abortion vision that focuses as much on women and their interests as it does the fetus (Bazelon 2007). Reardon has suggested that "it won't be the moral arguments that topple the abortion industry; it will be women's rights" (quoted in Rose 2011, 12). With this vision as a backdrop, he founded the Elliot Institute in 2005 and has written a series of books and published a variety of studies that support his position. Through his work and research with the institute, Reardon has advocated the deployment of new public anti-abortion arguments that largely depart from those popularized by the movement in the 1980s. He argues that "while committed pro-lifers may be more comfortable with traditional 'defend the baby' arguments, we must recognize that many in our society are too morally immature to understand this argument … The best way to lead them to it is by first helping them see that abortion does not help women, but only makes their lives worse" (quoted in Siegel 2008a, 1718). Reardon's first book, published in 1987 by Loyola University Press (a press that describes itself as "a Jesuit Ministry"), was titled *Aborted Women, Silent No More*. In many ways, it has become one of the foundational works for WPAAs in the US.

Reardon's research relies largely on "scientific" arguments about the medical and psychological harms abortion causes women. It is worth noting that none of his research is peer reviewed and that his PhD in biomedical ethics comes from an unaccredited and online university with no physical campus (Rose 2011). Reardon has developed a detailed discourse that "seeks to persuade voters who ambivalently support abortion rights that they can help women by imposing legal restrictions on women's access to abortion" (Siegel 2008b, 1669). His public rationales for opposing abortion fuse arguments about fetal personhood with those about women's rights and health. By invoking medicalized arguments about informed consent, he argues that victimized women are being lied to about the various harms abortion inflicts on them. In formulating and publicizing these arguments, Reardon has been credited as the pioneer of WPAAs and has succeeded in transforming them into a significant and salient political discourse, effectively setting out the main tenets of a new anti-abortion discursive strategy (Siegel 2008a; Siegel 2008b; Gee 2007; Rose 2011).

12.3 The Prevalence of Woman-Protective Anti-abortion Arguments in American Anti-abortion Discourse

Siegel's research suggests that there is at least some A-H-W argumentation and overall "pro-woman" rhetorical positioning in the American anti-abortion movement as well. Moreover, the emergence and development of concepts and arguments, such as PAS and WPAAs, suggest that these "pro-woman" arguments might be growing in importance for the American anti-abortion movement. The fact that a number of American observers have begun to comment on this trend lends credence to this possibility. While the emergence of this new discourse has been "unacknowledged by most in the press and punditry" (Rose 2011, 2) and "barely noticed in the mainstream press or by scholars outside the public health field" (Siegel 2008b, 1649), a number of journalists have begun to notice the rise of the PAS studies and have sought to examine and evaluate the scientific validity of the arguments (see, e.g., Bazelon 2007; Chamberlin 2006; Mooney 2004). More recently, several commentators have also started to note that WPAAs, and even some other less explicit "pro-woman" themes, are beginning to appear more frequently in some of the mainstream discourse of the anti-abortion movement (see, e.g., Sanneh 2014; Reitman 2014). Several academic observers have also examined this "pro-woman pro-life theme" in the US. Perhaps most notable is Reva Siegel's work in the legal realm, which argues that WPAAs are infiltrating key court decisions. Political scientist Melody Rose has also made a related argument about US anti-abortion discourse, suggesting that some segments of the movement are now increasingly employing pro-woman tones.

While there is perhaps a growing awareness of the relevance of WPAAs in the US, however, what remains unclear is just how prevalent these arguments and other "pro-woman" framings are. We have demonstrated that contemporary Canadian anti-abortion discourse is now clearly dominated by a set of arguments and rhetorical techniques predicated on defending the anti-abortion position from a "pro-woman" perspective. In contrast, the situation seems much more complicated in the US. As we saw at the beginning of this chapter, there is ample evidence to suggest that the traditional portrait continues to accurately represent the dominant nature of contemporary American anti-abortion discourse. Yet, it is also clear that there are an increasing number of voices that speak in terms that are much closer to the dominant "pro-woman" perspective in Canada. Fully addressing this issue would require a systematic study along similar lines to the one we have undertaken in regard to Canada. We can say, however, that our preliminary analysis suggests that a "pro-woman" anti-abortion discourse is becoming increasingly visible in the US, although it seems fairly clear that, in comparison to Canada, it remains a contested and secondary voice in the American anti-abortion movement.

Throughout the 1980s, for example, early versions of WPAAs were strongly opposed by key stakeholders, who argued that anti-abortion discourse that focused on women would distract from the "real moral stakes of the abortion debate" (quoted in Siegel 2008b, 1662). Francis Beckwith, for example, argued that the movement should not "stress the alleged harm abortion does to women" but instead should be "calling on society to fulfill its moral obligation to protect pre-natal persons" (Beckwith 2001, 155). During Ronald Reagan's presidency, prominent conservative activist Dinesh D'Souza urged Surgeon General Koop (a vocal and passionate opponent of legal abortion) to find that abortion harmed women. Much to the surprise of many within the anti-abortion movement, however, Koop refused, arguing not only that the scientific evidence was lacking but also that "the moral emphasis [was] wrong" (Siegel 2008a, 1713).

By the mid-1990s, some activists were slowly beginning to recognize the potential of this new discourse. Facing an increasingly unreceptive American public, anti-abortion leaders were looking for new ways of communicating their position to the "mushy middle." Siegel argues that, in this context, "the movement's leadership began to experiment with using talk of post-abortion harms, not simply to deter pregnant women from choosing abortion or to recruit them to the movement's ranks, but also to persuade Americans *outside* the ranks of the anti-abortion movement that government should impose legal restriction on women seeking abortion" (Siegel 2008a, 1715). In order to hone new arguments capable of convincing Americans undecided on the abortion question, the anti-abortion movement performed extensive market research, focus groups, polling, and testing of new ideas (1716). What it found was that anti-abortion discourse that focused on the alleged harm abortion inflicts on women had the potential for gaining support from demographics that had previously eluded the movement.

The fact that even John Willke began to supplement his fetal-centric arguments with woman-protective justifications is perhaps representative of the beginning of a new era in American anti-abortion strategy and discourse (Siegel 2008a). Willke, in most ways, can be characterized as a classic traditionalist/absolutist activist. He was the president of the National Right to Life Committee (NRLC), is well known for justifying his absolutist opposition to abortion (even in cases of rape) by using a discredited theory that "legitimate" rape rarely results in pregnancy, and is considered one of the pioneers of the fetal-centric advocacy model (1716). By the mid-1990s, however, even Willke was questioning his strategy. In 2001, he wrote that the "facts" of fetal-centric arguments were increasingly falling "on deaf ears, for this did not address the new argument of women's rights." In response, the movement "did the market research and came up with some surprising findings ... We found out that the answer to their 'choice' argument was a relatively simple and straightforward one. We had to convince the public that we were compassionate to women" (1716–17).

Today we can now find traces of this pro-woman discourse much more frequently in political debate, although it often co-exists alongside more extreme and traditional "anti-woman" tones. Take the position and tone of 2012 Republican presidential candidate Mitt Romney in response to statements by Congressman Todd Akin that women who had experienced "legitimate rape" rarely became pregnant as a result (Jaco 2012). Despite the fact that Romney had previously underscored his anti-abortion position, not only did he immediately urge Akin to step down from the Senate race in Missouri, he also told National Review Online that "Congressman's Akin comments on rape are insulting, inexcusable, and, frankly, wrong ... Like millions of other Americans, we found them to be offensive" (Johnson 2012). This "pro-woman" discourse is not simply found in moderate Republicans like Romney. For example, two of the most extreme anti-abortion lawmakers in the country – Senator Rick Santorum and Governor Rick Perry (both Republicans, representing Pennsylvania and Texas, respectively) – showcased their support for a Texas proposition that effectively banned any abortion after twenty weeks by arguing that the bill protected women. With the passage of the Texas bill into state law in July 2013, Perry stated that it was an important day for "those who support the health of Texas women" (Basset 2013c). Using even more empathetic sounding language, Santorum echoed Perry's view, arguing that the passage of the Texas anti-abortion bill was "an important moment for everyone to recognize where the abortion debate really is in America. The face of the pro-life movement [is] people out there every day embracing women, whether they decide to have an abortion or not. They love them ... It is the movement of love. That's what this movement is about" (Bendery 2013).

This trend is, to some extent, reflected at the organizational level as well. The organization Feminists for Life – of which Sarah Palin is a member – largely frames its position using arguments about the advancement of women's rights and health. In one recent advertising campaign, Feminists for Life called on American women to "Question Abortion." Its rationale? "Abortion rights activists promised us a world of equality and reduced poverty. A world where every child would be wanted. Instead, child abuse has escalated, and rather than shared responsibility for children, even more of the burden has shifted to women. Question abortion. No law can make the wrong choice right. Refuse to Choose. Women Deserve Better" (Feminists for Life of America 2013). This ad, as well as numerous others that can be found on the Feminists for Life website, highlights the way in which some American anti-abortion activists are repositioning themselves as defenders of women's rights and safety. By appealing to the feminist conception of the gendered burden faced by American women, Feminists for Life provides an example of the way in which "pro-woman" themes exist in American anti-abortion organizations.

Another relevant example of this trend is the Susan B. Anthony List (SBA List). In one sense, its very existence is a result of the insights and strategies of feminist organizations, as SBA List's election-focused strategy was directly inspired by the pro-choice organization EMILY's List. Beyond this, SBA List's strategies reveal a number of other similarities with those that have become dominant in Canada. For example, in using advanced grassroots tactics around fundraising, networking, and electioneering, it understands the importance of women-centric messaging and optics. According to journalist Kelefa Sanneh, SBA List president Marjorie Dannefelser "understands that [SBA List]'s messages are significantly more effective when delivered by women which is why [she] wants to elect more of them" (Sanneh 2014). According to Dannefelser, she learned this lesson while watching the dramatic 1993 abortion debate between Henry Hyde and Patricia Schroeder over Hyde's defunding bill. Although Hyde won the debate, Dannefelser noted that he was vulnerable to charges of sexism: "He could speak to the fundamentals of the issue but he couldn't speak with authority as a woman" (ibid.).

Dannefelser believes that a shift towards a women-centric focus should influence the content and the tone of SBA List's messaging, the messaging of her political allies, and even the bills they introduce into legislatures. Dannefelser herself apparently holds views that are highly religious and fairly intense: she is a Catholic who believes in the full implications of the Catholic conception of a "culture of life," arguing that life begins at conception and opposing practices as diverse as contraception and the death penalty as being contrary to a culture of life (ibid.). However, she does not believe that the messaging and the bills promoted by SBA List should necessarily reflect these views. Doing so would be a "bad idea driven by good intentions" because it would not serve to build a stronger, broader anti-abortion coalition. She may believe that life begins at conception, but she also believes that SBA List should advise candidates and allies to focus on issues and use language "on which there is, or might be, a broad consensus" (ibid.).

Dannefelser argues that the aim should not be to speak less about abortion, as some within the Republican community have argued. According to Dannefelser, the strategy should be to speak differently and better. In her view, this means tailoring and delivering specific messages to specific audiences in ways that do not necessarily focus on the key beliefs of the speaker but rather on those messages that will resonate most powerfully with the audience. Avoiding anti-woman tones and communicating compassion for pregnant women considering abortion is a key element of this approach. Dannefelser "counsels politicians to talk about pregnant women in ways that sound helpful not punitive" (ibid.). This strategy extends into the content of the legislation that SBA List champions. For example, despite Dannefelser's personal beliefs, SBA List does not promote or encourage legislators to support absolutist "personhood laws" that specify that life begins at conception and seek to ban all abortions as a consequence. Because those laws are potentially highly polarizing, Dannefelser thinks that they are not the most effective strategy for the movement (ibid.). In this respect, she marries an incrementalist legal strategy with a pro-woman discursive shift – something that is becoming increasingly common throughout the movement.

In some legislative and legal arenas, Dannefelser's vision of a more "effective" anti-abortion movement is coming to fruition. Current anti-abortion legislation is increasingly reflecting the incrementalist strategy of limiting the conditions under which abortions are available (as opposed to the absolutist approach of banning abortion). And such legislation and lobbying seem to be employing "pro-woman" language and arguments more frequently. Let us look at the policy guide released by Americans United for Life (AUL) in 2011. Titled "Women's Ultrasound Right to Know Act: Model Legislation and Policy Guide," the document is meant to empower state-level anti-abortion lawmakers to "chang[e] laws to protect human life, state by state" (Americans United for Life 2011, 1). Despite this explicit mission (which relies on a fetal-focused discursive framing), the document opens with the following passage about *women*:

> With each passing year, more and more women emerge from the silence after abortion. They are wounded and speak out in anguish on the physical, emotional, spiritual, and psychological harm they have suffered and still suffer as a direct result of their abortions ... Women's experiences reflect the fact that abortion clinics often fail to provide adequate and accurate medical information to women considering abortion. In the abortion industry, paternalistic attitudes toward women still prevail and, as a result, women continue to be uninformed of the risks and consequences of abortion. States have the constitutional power to take prophylactic measures to prevent this harm by passing comprehensive and carefully-drafted informed consent laws. (Americans United for Life 2011, 2)

AUL staff counsel Dorinda Bordlee rationalized this approach by explaining that, "what we have realized is that the woman and the child have a sacred bond that should not be divided. What's good for the child is good for the mother. So now we're advocating legislation that is good for the women" (Yeoman 2001). And this approach seems to be working. Many states used this policy guide to successfully enact new legislation in 2011. As of March 2012, twenty states had successfully passed legislation that mandated ultrasound viewing, many going even further by forcing women to listen to the fetal heartbeat.

Clearly, incremental and more pro-woman-sounding anti-abortion lawmaking – like "informed consent" laws – has become an increasingly popular strategy throughout the US, pointing to the growing presence and success of WPAAs. As we discussed in chapter 3, bills "targeted at regulating abortion providers" (TRAP bills) are becoming an increasingly common and effective way of curbing abortion access. Pioneered in the mid-1990s by lawmakers in South Carolina and Mississippi, TRAP laws can include "building regulations that specify ceiling heights, hallway and door widths, counseling-room dimensions, air-circulation rates, outdoor weed-control practices, and separate changing room for men" (Yeoman 2001). Critics argue that TRAP bills "go well beyond what other health providers must follow while doing little or nothing to improve the outcome of an already safe procedure," but such bills have nonetheless become a very effective method of shutting down abortion clinics (ibid.).

There are reasons to believe that TRAP bills are going to become an even more popular anti-abortion tactic. On the day of the 2014 midterm elections, for instance, Congressman Rick Womick proposed a federal bill that would mandate that women view their ultrasound (and listen to the fetal heartbeat) no less than twenty-four hours and no more than seventy-two hours prior to procuring an abortion. In the words of Reva Siegel, "advocates of incremental and absolute abortion restrictions have increasingly come to justify such regulation in the frames of their opponents, and now often portray abortion restrictions as promoting women's informed consent, women's health, women's welfare, and women's freedom" (2008a, 1706).

Perhaps the biggest indication of the rise of WPAAs in the US are their inclusion in the US Supreme Court decision *Gonzales v. Carhart*, which upheld Congress's PBA Ban in 2007 and criminalized a specific type of abortion procedure known as dilation and extraction. In many ways, *Gonzales v. Carhart* can be interpreted as one of the most punitive abortion-related Supreme Court decisions, most notably for its denial of a woman's life or health exemption (see chapter 3). Moreover, most aspects of the decision seem to be aimed at protecting the unborn and not women. By banning the procedure (a procedure that Congress regarded as "brutal and inhumane"), the court claimed that it was expressing "respect for the dignity of human life" (Gee 2007, 984). However, the court bolstered its fetal-centric arguments about "human dignity" with an additional "woman-protective justification for the ban that congressional findings never mentioned" (Siegel 2008a, 1697). The court's decision (penned by Justice Kennedy) reads in part, "while we find no reliable data to measure this phenomenon, it seems unexceptionable to conclude some women come to regret their choice to abort the infant life they once created and sustained ... It is self-evident that a mother who comes to regret her choice to terminate the pregnancy must struggle with grief more anguished and sorrow more profound when she learns, only after the event, what she once did not know: that she allowed a doctor to pierce the skull and vacuum the fast-developing brain of her unborn child, a child assuming the human form" (*Gonzales v. Carhart* 2007, 1634). To support this claim, the court cited the testimony of 1,000 women – gathered by an anti-abortion group by the name of Operation Outcry – virtually all of whom claimed that their abortions were uninformed or coerced or both (Siegel 2008a, 1732). Siegel argues that the incorporation of this language was no accident and largely "reflects the spread of abortion restrictions that are woman-protective, as well as fetal-protective, in form and justification" (Siegel 2008a, 1699).

12.4 Conclusion: Comparing the United States and Canada

It seems clear, then, that WPAAs and pro-woman framing are no longer an entirely peripheral discourse in the US but, instead, are beginning to permeate many important and influential realms of American abortion politics. This trend raises a host of fascinating comparative questions about the anti-abortion movements and their discourse in Canada and the US. How does the American context and discourse compare to that of Canada? How are they similar? How are they different? How dynamic are these patterns? How were pro-woman ideas popularized in Canada? Were they simply imported from the US into Canada? Or was there a more complicated genealogy? And why have they flourished in Canada so quickly while they have taken much longer to spread in the US? Once again, a fully authoritative comparison would require further study. We can, however, offer some tentative thoughts based on our preliminary analysis.

12.4.1 Similarities

The emergence of WPAAs in many political arenas throughout the US points to an increasing presence of "pro-woman" anti-abortion framing. Perhaps most relevant to our discussion is the fact that those developing this discourse (e.g., David Reardon and the Elliot Institute) are often cited to support the A-H-W argument in Canada. Moreover, the strategies being deployed by the Canadian anti-abortion movement clearly mirror many of the tenets set out by Reardon (largely seen as the pioneer of this discourse in the US) in important and noteworthy ways.

This discursive convergence is perhaps the most evident when comparing WPAAs with the explicit A-H-W arguments being deployed by the Canadian anti-abortion movement. The fusing of fetal and women's rights argument – something strongly advocated by activists such as Reardon, Willke, and others – is one of the key components of the shift in Canadian anti-abortion argumentation, as discussed in chapter 8. The increasingly common American anti-abortion assertion that "one cannot help a child without helping the mother [and] one cannot hurt a child without hurting the mother" is reproduced (sometimes even word for word) by the "pro-woman" approach taken up by Canadian activists such as Andrea Mrozek and her colleagues at the ProWomanProLife (PWPL) blog.

Parts of the US movement also seems to understand the strategic benefits of WPAAs in many of the same ways as their Canadian counterparts. As Reva Siegel notes, this new anti-abortion vision has "offered a framework for arguing with those *outside* the ranks of the anti-abortion movement – the 'conflicted middle' – who might not share the movement's animating conviction about matter of faith or family" (Siegel 2008b, 1672; emphasis in original). This observation corresponds closely with our own understanding of the sanitized/ unsanitized differences in anti-abortion forms of argumentation in Canada (see chapters 8 and 13). Like its Canadian counterpart, the American movement seems to be increasingly strategic not just about *what* arguments it deploys but also about *where and in what context* different arguments are most effective. In this context, important parts of the American movement have developed extensive training programs to school politicians and lobbyists on how to debate the abortion issue from a "pro-woman perspective" (Siegel 2008a, 1722).

It also seems that some activists in the US are, although in a more tentative way than in Canada, re-imagining the movement's public relationship with religion. While WPAA proponents such as David Reardon do not completely eschew religion in the formulation of their public arguments, they do argue that by publicly deploying WPAAs as important elements of anti-abortion discourse "we [anti-abortion activists] bear witness to the protective good of God's law in a way which even unbelievers must respect" (quoted in Siegel 2008a, 1721).

The movement towards WPAAs is also consistent with many other shifts in rhetorical strategy that we have discovered in Canada. Siegel argues that American anti-abortion discourse increasingly combines "the public health, trauma, and survivors idioms of PAS with language of the late-twentieth-century feminist and abortion-rights movement" through its appropriation of progressive and feminist values and language (Siegel 2008a, 1715). David Reardon, for instance, goes as far as to argue that anti-abortion activists need to "take back the terms 'freedom of choice' and 'reproductive freedom'" and to "emphasize the fact that we were the ones who are really defending the right of women to make an *informed* choice" (quoted in Siegel 2008b, 1676).

This shift is replicated in the tone and narratives advocated by a growing number of American activists. While parts the movement (especially within its absolutist faction) are often accused of being overly punitive, incrementalists insist that the movement must approach pregnant women with compassion in ways that increasingly resemble the nurturant parent tone used by the majority of Canadian activists. For a growing number of activists, "the best interests of the child and the mother are always joined – even if the mother does not initially realize it, and even if she needs a tremendous amount of love and help to see it" (quoted in Siegel 2008a, 1722).

Finally, many of the new narratives deployed by the movement seem to align with those used by Canadian activists. Once again stressing the interrelatedness of the fetus and the women, many suggests that American activists "must insist that the proper frame for the abortion issue is not women's rights versus the unborn's rights, but rather women's *and* children's rights versus the schemes of exploiters *and* profits of the abortion industry" (quoted in Siegel 2008a, 1718). This narrative stresses that when abortions do happen they are coerced, and victimized women do not fully grasp the implication of the procedure.

12.4.2 Differences

If there are some similarities, it also seems clear that there are many important differences in the discourse of the Canadian and American anti-abortion movements. There is no doubt that the traditional portrait continues to accurately describe the dominant strands of the contemporary American movement. Even Reva Siegel, for instance, recognizes that the anti-abortion position continues to be advocated by "the traditional family values coalition (TFV) brokered by the Republican Party in the 1970s and 1980s" and based on a "morality expressly grounded in concerns about sexuality and family roles" (Siegel 2008b, 1684). The movement is still predominantly focused on legislation (even if it is more incremental in nature than in the past), as we have seen with the record number of anti-abortion bills passed in the past decade. It also remains the case that the American movement is still male dominated. In 2004, for example, when President George W. Bush signed the PBA Ban into law, nine white men all over the age of forty surrounded him. Not a single woman was present.

Although the US Supreme Court did use variants of WPAAs to argue in favour of the PBA Ban in *Carhart*, this argument was not one that was used in Congress to pass the bill in the first place nor was it the only, or even most important, consideration in the decision (ibid.). WPAAs are slowly emerging into the mainstream, but American jurists and politicians continue to rely predominantly – and often exclusively – on fetal-centric and religious arguments. This stands in direct contrast to Canadian anti-abortion lawmakers, who resolutely avoid religious appeals in public and use pro-woman argumentation and rhetoric more frequently than fetal-centric ones. Whereas pro-woman discourse is clearly dominant in Canada, Siegel suggests that in the US, it is more of a niche "hybrid discourse that evolved in an effort to argue about the morality of abortion with those outside the ranks of the TVF movement" (ibid., 1686).

The organizational landscape of the two countries also reveals divergent strategies. Whereas the vast majority of national anti-abortion organizations in Canada now strongly employ A-H-W justifications, "pro-woman" framing does not seem to characterize the discourse of most American organizations. Political scientist Melody Rose has found that, while some American anti-abortion organizations (such as the Elliot Institute) rely on the testimonies of women who regret their abortion, other more traditional organizations continue to use old rhetorical strategies that stress fetal personhood. The results of Rose's content analysis of a number of American anti-abortion organizations revealed that "most of the older organizations like [the] National Right to Life [Committee], continue to feature adorable babies and personified fetuses in the marketing materials. In contrast to the messaging of the Elliot Institute ... Focus on the Family, one of the largest pro-family, anti-abortion organizations in the country, shows very little evidence of this frame extension in its messaging" (Rose 2011, 15).

There are a number of reasons that might help explain why A-H-W arguments are more prevalent in Canada than in the US. First, the Canadian anti-abortion movement has had much less success than its American counterpart – something that would make the need for strategic re-orientation potentially more obvious and pressing. Differences in the political saliency of religion between Canada and the US also probably help explain why religion continues to play such an important role in American anti-abortion discourse whereas Canadian discourse has been largely sanitized of religious arguments. The historical context of abortion discourse in Canada is likely also a key factor. In Canada, the abortion debate has consistently been highly medicalized – both because of the unique role that Canadian physicians (such as Henry Morgentaler) played in challenging Canada's abortion laws and because that was the logic that the Supreme Court of Canada used to decide the abortion question in several key cases (e.g., focusing on a health-infused definition of the right to security of the person to strike down abortion laws). In this context, it makes sense, that the Canadian movement would adopt a similar medicalized A-H-W language to counter pro-choice physicians' claims that abortion improves women's health.

This short discussion leaves many questions unanswered. But it is a start, as well as, we hope, an impetus for future research.

PART III

Conclusions and Implications

Chapter 13

Theoretical Implications

In 1990, the abortion issue was still very much a public and political issue in Canada, with both government and private members' bills seeking to recriminalize abortion in various ways. Legislative efforts to restrict abortion were accompanied by a largely male-led discourse that reflected a fetal-centric, "anti-woman," strict father metaphorical tone that painted doctors and other health care professionals as victims, forced to provide the abortions demanded by selfish and irresponsible women. More than twenty-five years later, private members continue to table anti-abortion legislation. But the framing of, and strategy behind, these attempts is very different than it was in earlier years. Rod Bruinooge's Bill C-510, for example, did not seek a general prohibition on abortion but only on procedures he called "coerced abortions" – situations in which women were forced into abortions by partners or other external individuals. Whereas in 1991 Boudria sought to protect doctors from "selfish" women, who were cast as villains, in 2010 Bruinooge's bill was framed entirely as protecting women, who were now cast as victims. Borrowing language that would not be out of place in many feminist analyses, proponents of Bill C-510 argued that such a law was necessary because women face (often subtle) widespread structural coercion that forces them into abortions they do not actually want. In the space of two decades, then, the traditional discourse regarding "abortion coercion" (where women were the selfish villains and medical professionals the coerced victims) had been entirely inverted, with women now being portrayed as the victims of patriarchal abortion coercion and the anti-abortion movement as protectors of women's interests rather than their moral discipliners.

Over the course of this book, we have demonstrated that the continuities and differences highlighted by the Boudria and Bruinooge bills are indicative of a broad and deep evolution of the anti-abortion movement and the advocacy strategies it uses to champion the anti-abortion position, particularly in Canada. These findings suggest a number of wide-ranging empirical, theoretical, and practical insights, which we discuss in the final two chapters. In this chapter, we summarize the key findings of the book (particularly Part II), outline some of the most important empirical and theoretical implications of our analysis, and discuss a number of the methodological implications of our study. We then close the book with a short chapter that focuses on the practical implications of this study for the other side of the abortion debate.

13.1 Our Findings

The essential argument of this book has been that, despite significant continuity in certain areas, the abortion debate – and in particular the various arguments and other rhetorical strategies employed by the anti-abortion movement – has shifted profoundly over time. Part I highlighted this shift by outlining the comparative histories of abortion discourse and politics in Canada, the United States, and, to some degree, the United Kingdom from the early 1800s until the beginning of the twenty-first century. This comparative history showed that, although there have been important similarities between the two countries, there have also been deep differences. Part I demonstrated that the main actors in the abortion debate – as well as the nature of the strategies of persuasion they used – have evolved and changed substantially over time. These findings suggest that older representations of the anti-abortion movement and its discourse might not always be reliable guides for understanding more recent iterations.

Part II offered the results of our detailed analysis of the contemporary anti-abortion movement in Canada and the strategies of persuasion it currently employs. In chapter 7 we asked whether there are any indications that the movement itself has been consciously reconsidering and reformulating its strategies of persuasion. What did we find?

- There is strong evidence to suggest that influential actors in the movement have been consciously debating and revising their strategy and have implemented highly focused, results-oriented strategic plans.
- Although legislative change remains a focus for some actors, many others focus equally, and often more intensely, on the broader task

of changing Canadian "culture," values, and public opinion around abortion.

- The movement has enthusiastically embraced online resources not only to network intensively and build a pan-Canadian anti-abortion movement, but also to reach out directly to Canadians in ways that would have been difficult and costly using traditional communication, including the mainstream media.
- Many actors in the movement believe that today the abortion debate is primarily a communications battle and that it is worth investing deeply in developing innovative, creative, and highly professional communication skills and strategies.
- Important actors in the movement continue to believe in the importance of in-the-street, face-to-face tactics of persuasion but also believe that, for such tactics to be truly effective, they must be approached somewhat differently than they were in the past.

It is possible that not all the major actors in the contemporary anti-abortion movement would agree with all of these points. Indeed, it seems that there are serious strategic debates within the movement and that a variety of players do not necessarily agree with each other's strategic decisions. Overall, however, the evidence suggests that the contemporary anti-abortion movement has been seriously reconsidering its strategic vision and that this has led many actors to update, revise, and hone their approaches.

Chapters 8 through 11 examined the degree to which the actual public advocacy and strategies of persuasion employed by the contemporary Canadian movement differ from those used by previous generations of anti-abortion activists. Chapter 8 began this task by examining the most explicit forms of discursive persuasion: the use of philosophical appeals and explicit argumentation. The traditional portrait of the anti-abortion movement tends to suggest that, philosophically, anti-abortion discourse asserts the authority of, and appeals directly to, religious sources as the grounds for its position. It also portrays anti-abortion discourse as defending its position almost exclusively through reference to fetal-centric arguments (e.g., fetal right to life, the fetus as person, fetuses as feeling pain, and so on). Was this traditional portrait supported in Canadian anti-abortion discourse? We determined the following.

- Although religious institutions seem to continue to provide significant financial and logistical support to the movement and many individuals appear to be motivated by religious commitments, many activists have explicitly expressed concern that religious appeals have had limited success in Canada and can be counterproductive.

- Concerns about religious discourse seem to have been taken seriously by the movement, as, today, the public discourse of the anti-abortion movement in Canada almost entirely eschews appealing to religion.
- Anti-abortion discourse is no longer dominated by fetal-centric arguments; instead, an "abortion-harms-women" (A-H-W) argument (that seeks to argue against abortion by claiming that it harms women in a variety of ways) has become the central argument in contemporary Canadian discourse.
- Contemporary fetal-centric arguments continue to play an important role in anti-abortion discourse (even if they have now been complemented/exceeded by A-H-W arguments), but the content of these arguments has changed significantly in ways that make them more consistent with a general "pro-woman" framing.
- The movement has supported this move towards pro-woman arguments by also (perhaps inadvertently) employing the technique of "visual signalling." The fact that the most visible spokespeople of the movement are increasingly spokeswomen functions to powerfully, and almost subconsciously, reinforce and underline the credibility of the "pro-woman" arguments.

We show that these changes are part of an overall shift towards a much more modern, "pro-woman" positioning that seeks to convince its audience to support an anti-abortion position through quite different strategies of persuasion than those used by earlier iterations of anti-abortion activism.

Chapters 9, 10, and 11 examined anti-abortion discourse more deeply to test whether these arguments and philosophical appeals are reinforced by other, less obvious, rhetorical strategies embedded in contemporary anti-abortion discourse. We found that such rhetorical strategies are used, and are very different from what the traditional portrait would suggest. In particular we found that contemporary anti-abortion discourse:

- employs a variety of frame-extension techniques to reinforce a modern, "pro-woman" message – something that holds the potential of expanding the movement's appeal beyond its traditional base of supporters. In particular, anti-abortion discourse:

o   has attempted to extend its brand identity by presenting itself as the heir to, and ally of, a variety of historical and contemporary progressive social justice movements

o   employs, redefines, and redeploys a variety of traditional "feminist" values such as substantive equality and even "choice" itself to support an anti-abortion position

o   utilizes issue-framing techniques to attempt to establish analogical links between the anti-abortion position and traditional feminist positions such as combating violence against women and sexual violence

o   has added a female-centric epistemology, highly reminiscent of standpoint feminist epistemology, which uses women's testimonials to argue that abortion is harmful for women;

- has embraced a nurturing, compassionate metaphorical tone and dramatically reduced the frequency, visibility, and targets of the traditional punitive, "strict father" tone;
- employs narrative structures that paint women as the victims of abortion rather than as villains.

All of these techniques, we argue, work together to present a coherent, potent, and multilayered image of the anti-abortion movement, and the anti-abortion position, as more progressive and concerned with women than feminism itself – a positioning that is very different than those embodied in the traditional portrait and earlier iterations of Canadian and American anti-abortion discourse.

Finally, chapter 12 sought to offer a brief consideration of the degree to which similar organizational strategies and rhetorical techniques – as well as the overarching "pro-woman" theme – are present in the contemporary US context. Our very preliminary analysis suggests that (a) "pro-woman" rhetoric is present in the American movement (and in fact was pioneered by certain stakeholders of the movement) and (b) it remains a minor (though perhaps growing) voice in the overall American anti-abortion movement. In contrast to Canada, however, "pro-woman" rhetoric seems to be decidedly secondary – a minor strain within a larger movement that remains fairly accurately represented by the traditional portrait. And given the cultural makeup of the anti-abortion movement and the political opportunity structure it faces in the US, it seems unlikely that this will change quickly (although, it is possible that the relatively rapid shift on same-sex marriage over the past several years might encourage anti-abortion strategists to look beyond their traditional social conservative strategies in the future).

13.2 Implications for the Study of Canadian Politics

Our findings hold a number of substantive implications and raise further questions not only for scholars and observers who study abortion politics specifically but also for scholars in a variety of related subfields. Insofar as our study demonstrates that the nature of the contemporary anti-abortion movement in Canada and its communications strategies differ significantly from those of the earlier Canadian and American movements (and to some degree the contemporary American movement), the most obvious implication for academic scholarship on Canadian politics is our substantive finding that the traditional portrait is no longer an accurate representation of the anti-abortion movement. We are not saying that the traditional portrait is irrelevant. Far from it. Classic studies like Brodie, Gavigan, and Jenson's *The Politics of Abortion*, for example, capture the essence of the Morgentaler era of abortion politics in Canada and the traditional portrait remains accurate in many respects in the US. Rather, what we are saying is that the strategies of persuasion used by contemporary Canadian anti-abortion discourse are quite different (reflecting some continuity, significant novelty, and some hybridity) from those used in the 1980s and early 1990s, and that we therefore need an updated portrait.

Scholars who focus primarily on formal electoral and institutional politics in Canada may also find abortion politics – and the shifting strategies of the anti-abortion movement – to be an increasingly relevant area to track. For, if the past several years are any indication, the abortion debate may yet become a political issue that at some point moves from its current peripheral location to something much more visible and actively contested. Despite Harper's refusal to engage on this issue throughout his nearly ten years as prime minister, there are many other potential political allies of the movement who would open it up again if they saw a chance to do so. This seems particularly relevant given that, as this book was going to press, the Conservative Party of Canada was in the beginning stages of a leadership race to determine Harper's replacement. With social conservative MPs like Jason Kenney (who began his political career as an anti-abortion activist in Saskatchewan) in the running, it seems quite possible that the abortion issue will once again re-emerge at the political level. Moreover, the anti-abortion movement has become far more sophisticated and savvy about how to position the issue in ways that might appeal more to mainstream voters. It has become more adept at framing anti-abortion bills in ways that attract much broader attention and support, even in the mainstream media, and it has begun to intensify its efforts to lobby, cultivate, and place staffers and MPs in Parliament. As we have seen with other issues (e.g., same sex marriage in Canada and the US), unexpected events can enable determined political movements to raise the salience of a given issue and challenge the status quo in surprising ways.

13.3 Implications for the Study of Political Movements, Communication, and Ideology

The case of anti-abortion discourse also holds a variety of implications for the study of Canadian political movements, political communications, and ideology. Our findings are a reminder that, despite the fact that many observers tend to view them as homogeneous and slow to change, many "conservative" political and social movements are as fragmented, evolving, diverse, and multi-vocal as other social and political movements (more akin to rhizomatic grassroots assemblages than arboreal root and branch structures, to use a Deleuzian metaphor). Our analysis has revealed that, within what looked like a fairly united and static anti-abortion movement, there was significant evolution and change over time (in terms of the public face and voice of the movement overall). Moreover, there are important contemporary strategic and discursive differences between different types of actors (e.g., MPs versus bloggers) and even between different actors of the same type (e.g., between the Canadian Centre for Bio-ethical Research's graphic, fetal-centric approach and those of most of other Canadian organizations).

Our findings also demonstrate, however, that analysing a movement with an eye to its potential internal diversity does not make it impossible to identify broad common threads and patterns. In the case of contemporary anti-abortion discourse, our study has clearly demonstrated that, despite the diversity of the actors, goals, and strategies of persuasion, there are many common trends across the discourse of the movement as a whole. One of the reasons we can say this with confidence is that we ensured that our research design assumed neither unity nor diversity but rather allowed the empirical evidence to decide the question. This approach underlines the value of being sensitive to both diversity and commonality when studying political movements and their communication strategies more generally.

We also believe that our findings provide a revealing window into what is a much wider trend in contemporary Canadian "conservative" discourse and communication strategies in general: the strategy of co-opting, redefining, and redeploying traditionally "progressive" values, arguments, and rhetorical tropes (elements of which have been examined in Saurette and Gunster 2011 and 2013). In many ways, the instrumental use of "pro-woman" tones is far from new – even with reference to abortion politics. As we saw in chapter 2, a variation of the "protect women" argument was a core element of the American Medical Association's campaign to gain control over, and then ban, abortion in the US in the mid-1800s. That said, it was a rather different argument in a different context. Rather than portraying women as modern, autonomous agents and appropriating feminist critiques of sexual assault and patriarchy, the nineteenth-century version of "protect the women" represented women as fragile objects in need of patriarchal guidance and control, especially by male doctors. In this sense, the "A-H-W" argument is not unprecedented. However, the contemporary version does differ from the historical version in important ways.

Conservatives (and other political perspectives) have employed similar "protect the women" discourses in many other issue areas. "Protecting women," for example, has frequently been a theme used by countless actors to justify war. Historically, this argument has been articulated as one concerned with protecting the women and children of the domestic state. Interestingly, however, a slightly different conservative "protect the women" discourse arose in the US and Canada in the aftermath of 9/11. One of the main discourses used by conservatives to justify the invasion of Iraq and Afghanistan was the idea that it was America's duty to protect women and establish equal rights in those countries (see, e.g., Frum and Perle 2004). What is so interesting about this discourse is that, even though this framing is clearly related to older, more patriarchal versions of the "protect the women" tradition, its focus on the establishment of "women's rights" and freedom from patriarchal forces marks it as quite different – and much closer to the "pro-woman" discourse we have sketched in this book. Similar points could easily be made about the Conservative Party of Canada's framing of their 2014 anti–sex work bill (Bill C-36), in which a strategic "sex-work-harms-women" argument has been fairly effective in dividing the progressive community on the issue. As such, we suspect that the A-H-W argument and the "pro-woman" tone of Canadian anti-abortion discourse may be one example of a more general trend of conservative discourse appropriating and repurposing a variety of feminist tropes and arguments.

Moreover, it may be that Canadian conservatism is somewhat at the forefront of this shift. In contrast to the extremist rhetoric of the Tea Party movement (and much of the Republican Party base), the dominant model of conservative ideology in Canada might be called "cappuccino conservatism" (Saurette and Gunster 2013). It is a version of conservatism that has eliminated many of the rhetorical markers and obvious policy positions of the more socially conservative segment of conservatism (in Canada this could include the anti-immigrant, anti-gay, anti-woman tones that were both implicitly and explicitly part of the Reform Party) and embraced an ideological discourse that resonates more easily with some elements of traditionally progressive frames. Our analysis in this book strengthens this argument, demonstrating that even some of the most socially conservative political movements in Canada are also adopting similar discursive strategies. This, in turn, leaves us with a variety of questions for further research regarding how to study/define conservative ideology and discourse. What is contemporary Canadian conservatism? What are its basic principles and policy positions? How should we understand the rhetorical framing of issues if these seem different than the "principles" conservatives champion elsewhere? How do these dimensions compare to other competing ideologies and discourses? And how should we go about answering these questions?

13.4 Implications for the Study of Religion and Politics in Canada

Our analysis of the anti-abortion movement and its discourse suggests some implications for scholarship that examines the role that religion plays in contemporary politics and political discourse in Canada. Recently, there have been a series of journalistic accounts of the role of religion in contemporary Canadian politics. Marci McDonald (2010), Tom Warner (2010), and Don Martin (2010), for example, have all suggested that, with the rise of Stephen Harper, the Christian right in Canada has been able to exercise a growing influence on Canadian politics and policymaking. According to McDonald, "just as Reagan once provided access and regulatory opening that turned television preachers into political-power brokers in Washington, Harper has done the same in Ottawa, where a small band of conservative Christian activists with ties to his government has won a series of policy and personnel concessions destined to change the Canadian political landscape in ways that will be difficult to reverse" (2010, 6–7). These authors provide evidence that there is a growing body of politicized, religiously oriented actors with increasing influence and access in Ottawa.

Given this evidence, one would expect that the anti-abortion movement would be at the forefront of this trend and be emboldened to use highly religious and polarizing discourse. However, this is not at all what we have found. Instead, the contemporary anti-abortion movement has conspicuously sanitized religious appeals from in its public discourse, employing a variety of other argumentative and rhetorical techniques instead. We have not suggested that religious arguments are entirely absent from the Canadian abortion debate (such references do exist, especially in unsanitized, in-group discussions). We readily acknowledge that religious beliefs have been crucial motivators for many individual activists and that religious institutions have provided critical organizational support for the movement, both historically and today. And our historical sketch in chapter 4 highlighted ways in which the movement and its discourse became increasingly focused on religion in the 1970s and 1980s. There is no question that religion has been an important factor in the abortion debate in Canada and that religious institutions and communities have provided, and continue to provide, essential support to the movement.

However, our research has highlighted several other points that are equally relevant. For example, our historical analysis demonstrates that this "religious" turn is a relatively modern, and circumscribed, phenomenon in the abortion debate in Canada. Neither religious institutions or discourse were central to the efforts to criminalize abortion until the late 1960s. It is equally clear from our analysis that, even if religious institutions and beliefs continue to inspire and help organize the movement, the movement does not employ explicit appeals to religious sources as a central strategy of persuasion today.

Why hasn't religious discourse been more present in the public abortion debate in Canada? Why have we not seen the politicization of abortion as a Christian issue? There are many factors that might account for this discrepancy: lower levels of religiosity and religious politicization in Canada; a political culture that has downplayed public displays and expressions of religion; a historical framing of the abortion debate in medical terms; the specific legal and political history of the process of liberalizing abortion laws; and the "brokerage" nature of party politics in Canada (discussed below).

There are other possible explanations as well. For one, even in the 1960s and 1970s, many anti-abortion activists understood that using religious language could be quite contentious, as it often highlighted doctrinal differences between anti-abortion activists of different faiths. The Catholic Church's decision to keep the anti-abortion movement at arms length in Canada (at least publicly and officially) was thus "both a recurring source of conflict in the movement and a key feature distinguishing Canadian anti-abortion struggles from those in the United States" (Herman 1994, 269; see also Cuneo 1989).

The different institutional structures of the American and Canadian political systems have also had an important impact. As we discuss in the section below, while there are some similarities between American and Canadian political parties, their profoundly different organizational structures make them very different institutions in ways that are important for abortion politics (Farney 2012, 83). In the American context, for instance, members of Congress and senators are much less bound by party discipline and, accordingly, enjoy a great deal of autonomy from their political parties. This gives social movements and lobby groups considerable influence over individual politicians without having to win the support of their larger political party. Lobbyists have strong access to individual politicians, and they can use a "piecemeal" strategy of winning influence over politicians one individual at a time, which allows small, but highly motivated and organized, special interest groups to exert inordinate influence (83). In Canada, where individual politicians are bound by the conventions of party discipline, political parties are much more centralized organizations that consolidate power over both policy and strategy into the hands of party leaders – a context that can significantly reduce the impact of advocacy groups that do not have influence with the leadership, even on issues which are traditionally free votes of conscience (6–7).

These differences have had some influence on the degree to which each country's political culture relates to explicit, public, and politicized religious discourse. In the US, the political structure has allowed evangelical Christians (who only make up 26 per cent of the population) to not only exercise great influence over the Republican Party but also to bring religious appeals into the political mainstream. In Canada, in contrast, the main political parties have predominately operated as "brokerage parties" that have "downplayed divisive issues so as to place themselves in the middle of the political spectrum," something that has created much less space for highly religious and moralized policies and arguments (Farney 2012, 84). According to James Farney, if this has been true in general in Canada, it has also been true for mainstream conservative parties, as they too have largely adopted the mantra that "the personal has not been, and is not now, a suitable topic for partisan organization" (84).

Our study provides further evidence of this distance from religious/moral arguments (for now, at least). For what we have found is that in Canada, while religion is not entirely absent from the political realm, religious groups and perspectives have (so far), even on one of the most potentially contentious social issues, intersected with politics in complicated ways that are different, and much less public, explicit, and influential than in the US. Perhaps equally importantly, our study has shown that when it comes to religion, social movements in Canada have learned that it doesn't pay to trumpet their religious beliefs in public and have chosen to focus on other discursive strategies with more widespread appeal. To say this is not to accuse the anti-abortion movement of having a "hidden agenda" (in fact, the anti-abortion movement is fairly clear about its policy agenda – reducing/banning abortion). Rather, it is simply to note that this movement, like many social and political movements, has learned the basic lessons of modern marketing: that political communications isn't about revealing your innermost essence and personal beliefs; it is about identifying and using the arguments and rhetorical techniques that, with the least amount of work, will make your position resonate with, and ultimately convince, the widest set of people.

In this sense, our analysis highlights the importance of examining contemporary political communication with an understanding of the relationship, and difference, between unsanitized discourse (often unscripted and usually internally focused on members/sympathizers of the movement) and sanitized discourse (usually carefully scripted and focused externally on potential new supporters). One of the important advantages of this conceptual division is that it helps us make sense of characteristics that would otherwise seem deeply contradictory and puzzling (e.g., the simultaneous presence of religious motivation, funding, and some internal discourse alongside the almost complete absence of religious themes in the movement's public discourse).

We have barely scratched the surface of this part of the story. It would be fascinating to use interviews, Freedom of Information requests, surveys, and other methods to trace the financial and logistical support that Catholic school boards in Ontario and other religious and semi-religious groups (e.g., various churches, the Knights of Columbus) provide for the March for Life and other events. It would also be extremely valuable to determine the level and sources of funding for the various actors in the anti-abortion movement. Such data would start to sketch out a more robust picture of how the movement organizes and sustains itself, adding an important and currently almost non-existent dimension to the public portrait of the contemporary anti-abortion movement in Canada.

13.5 Explaining the Shape of Contemporary Anti-abortion Discourse in Canada

Some readers might be interested in the question of why the Canadian anti-abortion movement and its discourse have developed in the way they have over the past several decades. On one hand, the development of certain aspects of the contemporary anti-abortion movement and its rhetorical strategies is not particularly surprising insofar as it mirrors elements that we can see in other social movements. For example, the process of professionalization we are now seeing in the contemporary movement in Canada (the increased sophistication of communications, extensive use of online tools, results-oriented strategic plans) can also be seen in many other advocacy areas (e.g., the LGBTQ movement in North America, the pro-choice movement in the US, international development and human rights organizations). Resource mobilization scholars such as Suzanne Staggenborg (1988; 1999) have argued that in many issue areas there has been a widespread shift in which organizations have transformed from "'classical' movement organizations which rely on the mass mobilization of 'beneficiary' constituents as active participants" towards "'professional' social movement organizations [that] rely primarily on paid leaders and 'conscience' constituents who contribute money and are paper members rather than active participants." Staggenborg sees this trend in the evolution of US pro-choice organizations (she does not examine the anti-abortion movement, in any detail) and argues that it helps explain the professionalization of their advocacy behaviour (Staggenborg 1988, 585). In one sense, then, the professionalization and increasing communications and advocacy sophistication of the anti-abortion movement in Canada is part of, and perhaps partially explained by, a much broader trend in social movements across the Western world.

Even if Canadian anti-abortion organizations and actors have professionalized in certain ways that we see in other movements, however, we are nonetheless left with many questions about why the anti-abortion movement and its discourse have developed in the specific way that they have. Why, for example, did the professionalization of the anti-abortion movement occur relatively recently, rather than in the 1980s or early 1990s? And why, in contrast to the US, has the Canadian movement not undergone this process to the same degree? There are many other "why" questions raised by our findings. Given our focus on the discourse that has framed abortion politics in Canada, perhaps the most important question is why the abortion debate has taken the shape that it has in Canada, as opposed to the US or elsewhere? Why did the previous generation of anti-abortion activists adopt the language they did? To what degree, and why, did contemporary actors consciously decide to change their rhetorical strategies? To what degree are some anti-abortion strategies explained by the nature of federalism in Canada? Or by the specific manner and pace through which change occurred in Canada? Or by unrelated events and currents in the larger conservative movement – for example, the Conservative Party's decision to secure electoral success by forcefully taming the elements that were viewed as more extreme and less acceptable to mainstream Canadians? Or by changes in the broader opportunity structures at play in the Canadian context?

Fully answering these questions would require a different study with different methodologies. But we can certainly speculate, from the perspective of a discourse analysis, as to some factors that might contribute to an explanation of why the Canadian discourse has taken the shape that it has.

Part of what makes contemporary Canadian anti-abortion discourse so different from dominant trends in the US is its tendency to avoid explicit religious appeals and instead speak in much more medicalized terms. What might explain this? Part of the explanation likely involves the historic nature of the abortion debate in Canada. As Brodie suggests, in light of the long history of medicalized discourse in supporting the original criminalization of abortion and "given the institutionalization of the discourse of medicalization in the procedures of the [therapeutic abortion committees] and the courts, challenges to the boundaries of the 'private' and 'public' were less successful in Canada. The result was that efforts to restrict abortion on the basis of specific social or moral strictures failed" (Brodie, Gavigan, and Jenson 1992, 41).

The contemporary avoidance of religious appeals and the willingness to use other frames and arguments might also be explained by the broader trends in Canadian society and political culture regarding politicizing religion. As mentioned above, fewer Canadians than Americans are religious, and those that are, are comparatively less intensely religious. This obviously has an impact on how effective religious discourse is likely to be in influencing public opinion. As Farney suggests, "on the whole, Canadians are more socially liberal than Americans as well as being significantly less religious," which has created "less fertile ground for social conservatives north of the border" (Farney 2012, 10).

However, it is not simply the case that Canadians are less religious. The religious community in Canada is also much less politicized and politically organized than in the US (Farney 2012; Malloy 2013). For these reasons and others, Canadian political culture is much less open (in general) to the use of explicit religious appeals. Clearly some actors in the anti-abortion movement are explicitly aware of the limits created by the relative irreligiosity of Canadians and the resistance of Canadian political culture to religious appeals. Both of these factors, then, help explain why the movement might be increasingly choosing to sanitize its public discourse and employ non-religious modes of argumentation and persuasion instead.

The shape of contemporary Canadian anti-abortion discourse might also be explained by the strategic advantage that a political movement can achieve (in both legal and public opinion settings) by appropriating the winning arguments of the other side. In Canada, the establishment of abortion rights in policy, political, and legal spheres was achieved largely through appeals to women's health and the publicizing of the dangers of illegal abortions, something that stands in fairly stark contrast with the US context, in which privacy rights were the dominant argument. It is thus perhaps not surprising that the Canadian anti-abortion movement has so strongly embraced the A-H-W argument, as it offers the highest likelihood of undermining the very legal ground of abortion rights in Canada. The fact that the apparent neutrality and scientific certainty of medical argumentation allows the anti-abortion movement to dialogue with people who otherwise wouldn't want to broach the subject because of its politicized and polemical nature is another strategic advantage that might help explain its attractiveness.

The institutional context and nature of Canadian parties and electoral politics also help explain why the issue has been much less polarized politically and discursively than it has been in the US. The fact that the first major moment of liberalization, in 1969, was legislative and not judicial (thus eliminating the ability of anti-abortion opponents to challenge the procedural legitimacy of the reform by arguing that the process was being hijacked by unelected judicial activists, as was the case in the US) and was national in scope (meaning that the battle was not fought continuously at both federal and provincial levels) potentially helps explain some of the differences between the US and Canadian context (Farney 2012, 9). And, as mentioned above, the fact that the dominant federal Canadian political parties have been largely "brokerage parties" (i.e., parties that tend to try to appeal to a broad coalition of voters and thus trend towards compromise, moderation, and pragmatism) rather than "ideological parties" (i.e., parties that seek their support by holding close to a more strict set of principles) has also affected what types of anti-abortion discourse would likely be successful. Not only has it meant that parties in Canada have tended to avoid the issue when possible (rather than seeking it out as a wedge issue, as in the US). At a broader level, the nature of the party systems in the US and Canada has placed "social conservatives in subtly different situations in each country," with social conservatives and their discursive trends exercising much less influence in Canada (Farney 2012, 10).

The moderating impact of Canada's brokerage model was strengthened by the fact that, by 1969, Canadian public opinion favoured abortion reform. In 1968, 53 per cent of Canadians favoured easier access, and by the time the Supreme Court of Canada returned the *Morgentaler* decision in 1988, public opinion was strongly in favour of completely decriminalizing abortion, with 69 per cent agreed that the decision to have an abortion should be exclusively between a woman and her doctor (Brodie, Gavigan, and Jenson 1992, 60–61). In these circumstances, an anti-abortion position did not appear to be a winning position to most politicians. Moreover, they felt "most comfortable within the familiar terms of medicalization. 'Letting the doctors decide' meant that the political parties did not have to disturb a delicate balance which had grown up between the massive support in public opinion for legal abortion and the small but vocal group of anti-choice militants" (54). Carefully managing and minimizing (rather than inflaming) the issue thus became the generally preferred policy and discursive option among the political elite.

Finally, given the success and impact of the women's movement – and the profound changes to the role that women now play in society – it is perhaps not surprising that even socially conservative causes, such as the anti-abortion movement, are employing "pro-woman" rhetoric that acknowledges and speaks to, rather than simply rages against, these social shifts. In the US, there is still an active "culture war" dimension to politics, with many groups still seeking to roll back a variety of the social transformations of the past forty years (which certainly helps explain the continued popularity in the US of the strategies associated with the traditional portrait). But this is not at all the case in Canada. Even within conservative circles, the "culture war" perspective has never been remotely as influential or widespread as in the US. In Canada, one might say that any movement that wants to be successful politically can no longer afford to be perceived as "anti-woman." This is perhaps especially true in a context defined not only by an overall political culture that is more progressive than that of the US, but also one in which the Quebec electorate plays an important electoral role and holds such strong views in favour of abortion rights.

13.6 Implications for Gender Studies

Our findings also suggest a variety of implications and further questions for the study of gender and politics. For example, to what degree have similar "protect-the-women" themes existed in other policy debates historically – and to what degree do they do so currently? Why is this shift towards pro-woman themes occurring now? Is it related to other broad cultural transformations in North America around conceptions of gender? Has the political appropriation of "pro-woman" positioning by traditionally conservative causes become easier over the past several decades because of developments within the women's movement and the way in which younger women now experience and conceptualize gender politics? What is the impact of "choice feminism," a perspective that valorizes formal personal and individual choice and rejects the idea that certain value judgments or political perspective are inconsistent with feminism (see Kirkpatrick 2010; Ferguson 2010; Snyder-Hall 2010; Marso 2010; Hirschmann 2010)? Have other self-identified "female empowerment" trends, like female "raunch culture" (Levy 2005), that prioritize individualism over collective forms of action been factors in creating the soil for the anti-abortion inversion of traditionally feminist arguments and values?

To a certain extent, these issues do seem to be at play in the Canadian context. It seems clear, for example, that Canadian culture has experienced a deepening "individualization" of politics. Janine Brodie (2008) argues that there has been an important shift in Canadian politics away from the social liberalism of the 1970s and 1980s (with its receptivity to substantive feminist concerns about structural inequality) towards our contemporary neoliberal era in which both dominant government discourse and policy has erased gender equality as an important and stand-alone issue in need of attention and policy solutions. The work of Miriam Smith (2007) and Alexa DeGagne (2012) might also be taken as suggesting that these political shifts have had significant impacts on the way in which social movements organize and advocate. Their studies have shown, for example, that the advocacy strategies and public discourse of key LGBTQ organizations have responded to this neoliberal context and, in doing so, have further embedded individualist themes in North American political culture.

This more individualist context may help explain certain elements of contemporary anti-abortion discourse. For example, the "post-feminist" tendency to decouple equality discourses from what have traditionally been substantive feminist positions (reproductive rights, pay equity, affirmative action, addressing sexual harassment/assault and domestic violence through a variety of policies including women-only safe spaces) is one aspect of the neoliberal context. It is therefore not surprising that contemporary anti-abortion discourse employs a variety of arguments that resonate with this neoliberal perspective (e.g., demanding that public funding for abortion be abolished to respect taxpayer "choice," breaking the assumed connection between being a woman and supporting abortion rights, attacking feminist groups and the "abortion industry" as special interests and elites).

However, our analysis suggests that contemporary anti-abortion discourse is not framed primarily in neoliberal or "equalist" discourse. Rather, what is so interesting about anti-abortion language is that it actively appropriates and redeploys many traditionally feminist tropes. Its value framing does *not* use a thin concept of equality to challenge feminist positions (something that many libertarian conservatives do, for example, by reducing equality to formal equality before the law). Rather, it uses a thick, substantive concept of equality and structural coercion – one that is literally taken from feminist textbooks and approaches – but redeploys it against the feminist movement and abortion rights advocates. We have found that this is the case for almost all of its rhetorical techniques, including epistemological framing (standpoint perspectives), narrative structure (critiques of gendered structural coercion), and issue framing (abortion analogized with domestic violence). Moreover, alongside some attacks on feminism, many of the most vocal new voices in the anti-abortion movement either admit to having a "complicated" – that is, not merely antithetical – relationship to feminism or actively reclaim the title "feminist" for themselves. Hence the growing visibility of groups like ProWomanProLife in Canada and Feminists for Life in the US.

The trend of conservative groups, and particularly the anti-abortion movement, coopting traditionally feminist discourse suggests at least two major implications for future feminist analysis. The first is linked to the fact that, while the appropriation of progressive and feminist-sounding language by conservative movements is neither entirely new nor unique to the anti-abortion movement,[21] what we are seeing with the contemporary anti-abortion movement is arguably a much more widespread, sophisticated, and concerted use of feminist tropes. For this reason, the anti-abortion movement's use of this positioning may turn out to be more successful than past attempts, particularly in gaining the support of younger women. More generally, it may also be the case that the anti-abortion "pro-woman" framing holds the potential for shaping political behaviour as well as individual subjectivity in ways that extend far beyond the explicitly political realm. The anti-abortion reconceptualization of "women's choices," for example, normalizes certain subject positions for women while delegitimizing others in regards to abortion and other issues. The anti-abortion case, then, highlights the ways in which one of the most prized liberal feminist values (choice) can be turned on its head. Indeed, the anti-abortion example might be a particularly powerful case study that supports the concerns that many critical strains of feminism have expressed about the limits and dangers of those types of feminism that rely too exclusively on "choice" as a founding principle (for instance, the growing literature on "reproductive justice" discussed below).

Second, the increased visibility of women within the anti-abortion movement also holds implications for future scholarship on women and gender in regard to conservative politics. Despite the applied and academic interest in the role of women in formal politics, there has been very little study of the role that women, and constructions of gender, play in conservative movements in Canada. The bulk of the academic study of gender and politics in Canada has tended to focus on a limited number of key areas, examining the level of participation and

---

21 REAL Women of Canada, for instance, has never shied away from invoking the language of women's choices or equality in its defence of conservative gender norms.

representation of women in formal political processes and political parties and determining the causal factors that explain the relative under-representation of women in these domains. Moreover, to the extent that the experiences of women in political movements have been examined, they have tended to be in feminist or other "left-wing" organizations.

As the example of the anti-abortion movement demonstrates, however, the ways that representations of gender and gendered interests are employed and navigated by contemporary conservative movements (particularly the roles that women and women's interests are accorded) are rich areas of inquiry. At a minimum, our analysis of the contemporary anti-abortion movement's appropriation of feminist language and the ways in which anti-abortion women have increasingly become leaders in what was traditionally a male-dominated movement suggests that further study of the role that gender and women play in the Canadian conservative movement more generally is a pressing and fascinating, if almost entirely unexplored, area of study.

13.7 Methodological Implications

Finally, our study underlines two methodological points that we believe are worth briefly discussing. The first is the value of a mixed-method approach to critical discourse analysis. The challenge that traditional, large-scale content analyses often face is that, because they do not undertake close, contextual interpretation of texts, these approaches have a hard time identifying and tracking the subtle rhetorical strategies that are often the engine of the persuasive power of a given discourse. In contrast, the challenge for approaches that employ only close, qualitative readings without any quantitative element is that they often have a heightened risk of selection bias – given the smaller number of texts they examine, the possibility that they have chosen unrepresentative texts is much higher. Moreover, if such approaches do not have a systematic way of tracking the frequency and weight of various rhetorical strategies, they are less able to make reliable judgments about the relative importance of various techniques across a given discourse.

Thus, one of the key methodological implications of our study is the idea that, while a mixed method often requires significantly more up-front research-design work than does traditional qualitative interpretation, and significantly more interpretive work than does traditional content analysis, it allows researchers to capitalize on the advantages of both approaches while avoiding their potential weaknesses.

Close, qualitative readings of our entire data set were necessary for us to unearth and trace a variety of the techniques discussed in this book, such as the framing strategies and the narrative structures. We simply could not have identified and analysed these tropes any other way – and we would have missed a major part of the story had we not employed this type of analysis. On the other hand, it was our systematic coding and quantitative analysis that allowed us to confidently identify the dominance and nature of certain key trends. This aspect of our methodology led us to the findings that challenged the deeply held and widely shared assumptions about the role of religion in anti-abortion discourse, as we were able to discover and measure the surprising degree to which religious appeals are absent from Canadian anti-abortion discourse. The quantitative dimension also allowed us to engage in a much more fruitful conversation with sceptical listeners because it provided us with concrete results that focused our discussions and sharpened both our audiences' questions and our answers.

The second methodological implication of our work is the value of building multiple points and types of triangulation into a research project. In this study, we were confident that a mixed method of critical discourse analysis would unearth many interesting, and often counterintuitive, findings about the rhetorical framing of political issues and values. However, we understood that, like every method, it has certain limitations. The validity of its results depends on the robustness and representativeness of the data set, the consistency of the coding and interpretation, as well as a variety of other factors. Moreover, there are certainly many things that discourse analysis cannot show. On its own, it can't necessarily explain where particular rhetorical techniques came from; why actors decided to use those tropes instead of others; what the "real" motivations of the actors are or what they actually believe; how particular organizations, activists, and advocacy campaigns are funded; or what strategies of persuasion will become dominant in the future.

Of course, any method has a variety of limitations. There are no guarantees that interviewing actors in a controversial political context, for example, will lead to genuine, truthful, and authentic information: there are too many political interests at play. In this sense, social scientific inquiry into contentious social and political movements never produces absolute certainty – there are always margins of error. However, it is our job as researchers to try to reduce those margins as much as possible.

In this context, triangulation can be a key research design technique that helps to strengthen the accuracy of a given study. In our work, we triangulated in several ways. First, even within our mixed method approach, we tried to triangulate our data sets by using many different and unrelated sources of data but also by using very different types of data. Second, again within our mixed method approach, we used multiple interpretive approaches – ranging from classical philosophical analysis to narrative analysis and literary criticism to framing theory – with the idea that if we found similar tendencies with respect to so many different rhetorical techniques, our findings would be much more convincing as a whole. Third, we sought to corroborate these results by going beyond our initial formal data set and examining whether the same tendencies were present in different types of anti-abortion discourse (e.g., in semi-public sites of internal discussion as well as social media sites). Finally, we tested the consistency of our findings by leaving behind discourse analysis and extending our analysis into the naturalistic observation of in-group events.

Ultimately, each of these types of analysis was crucial for our study as each allowed us to better understand certain puzzling dimensions and complicated stories we wouldn't have unearthed if we had performed only discourse analysis. Moreover, as a whole, these various points of triangulation confirmed our results to a degree that would not have been possible using any one method. Thus, beyond the substantive implications outlined in the previous sections, we hope that our study has highlighted the value of employing methodological pluralism and various types of triangulation within a single project.

Chapter 14

Where to Now? Practical Implications for Abortion Rights Advocates

The fact that the anti-abortion movement has profoundly repositioned its discourse in Canada (and to some degree in the United States) means that the contemporary and future context of the abortion debate is now quite different. As a result, it is possible that abortion rights activists may need to hone their organizational and communication strategies if they are to continue to be strong and effective public proponents of their position.

It's easy for abortion activists to love the cheeky and humorous signs that supporters often use to challenge anti-abortion activists and their discourse (the picture reproduced as figure 14.1 was taken on Parliament Hill at the 2012 March for Life). They are playful, catchy, TV-friendly, and, at the same time, communicate a sophisticated critique of anti-abortion discourse in just a few words. Moreover, they play an important role in building a sense of shared community among abortion rights activists and are crucial for keeping their spirits high in what can be stressful situations.

Preaching to the choir (or mugging for the camera) certainly has its place. But there are also limits to what this kind of messaging can achieve, and it can sometimes backfire. These kinds of discursive tactics can easily be used by anti-abortion opponents to stereotype the abortion rights movement as out-of-touch-with-the-mainstream, hipster, radical feminists in ways that support anti-abortion framings (as indeed similar photos were). Moreover, these techniques are not usually the most effective way to reach citizens who might be open to supporting abortion rights but who are much less involved politically or are less invested in the specific issue. To reach these people (who are absolutely crucial for the political success of both the abortion rights

Figure 14.1

Source: Robert Allard (www.allardvividphotography.com)

and anti-abortion movements), tactics other than ones that are aimed at "in-group" supporters are likely more effective. This lesson, above all others, is the one that the anti-abortion movement in Canada seems to have learned.

In this final chapter, we briefly discuss some of the questions and considerations that abortion rights advocates might ponder in response to the growth of "pro-woman" anti-abortion discourse. The first part of this chapter discusses the philosophical question of whether a reproductive justice frame would be a useful supplement to the more traditional approaches used by the abortion rights movement in Canada (a question that is also at the centre of practical debates in women's rights organizations around abortion in other countries, especially in the United States). The second part outlines a dozen concrete suggestions about how the abortion rights movement might respond to the "pro-woman" framing in contemporary anti-abortion discourse. Some abortion rights activists and organizations have already begun to implement these strategies. Others may disagree with some of them. The aim of this chapter is not to settle the question of how the abortion rights movement should or will respond. Rather, it is simply to outline some considerations that various elements of the abortion rights movement are considering or may wish to consider.

14.1 A Reproductive Justice Frame?

One possible implication of the new pro-woman rhetoric of the anti-abortion movement is that abortion rights activists might want to consider developing and popularizing additional arguments and positionings to supplement their dominant "choice" frame. One potentially useful perspective that a variety of abortion rights advocates have been increasingly employing is the frame of "reproductive justice," which has already had an impact on both feminist scholarship and abortion-related activism, particularly in the United States.

Reproductive justice analysis first emerged from analysis and activism by women of colour in the US. One of its key arguments is that various structural conditions contextualize, and ultimately limit, the reality of formal "choice," especially regarding abortion access (see Smith 2005; Luna 2009, 2010, 2011). In contrast to "pro-choice" perspectives, reproductive justice advocates argue that it is not sufficient to simply protect formal choice. Rather, it is necessary to view abortion access in a larger context and, in particular, to forward a vision of justice that highlights the importance of protecting both formal rights (the right to choose to reproduce as well as the right to choose not to reproduce) and fostering structural conditions that give those rights their lived reality. A reproductive justice approach to abortion politics thus places abortion rights "within the context of achieving a spectrum of human rights rather than only privacy to make a decision to legally access abortion" (Luna 2010, 556).

There are several reasons why this perspective would be useful in addressing the "pro-woman" anti-abortion discourse in Canada as well, even though there are limits to the applicability to Canada of the largely American-focused reproductive justice literature. First, the reproductive justice literature – which in Canada has been pioneered by indigenous groups such as the Native Youth Sexual Health Network (Danforth 2010) – reminds abortion rights advocates to acknowledge the reproductive injustices of the past (see McLaren 1990; Wahlsten 1997; Danforth 2010). A reproductive justice framework allows contemporary abortion rights advocates both to condemn historical injustices and identify contemporary injustices – all the while strongly defending the importance of formal and real abortion rights.

Second, a reproductive justice frame also offers resources that might help abortion rights activists find solutions for some of the issues highlighted by contemporary anti-abortion discourse. Take the issue of sex-selective abortion in Canada, for example. The anti-abortion movement asserts that it is a significant problem that demands a solution. The temptation for traditional pro-choice advocates might be to reject the issue entirely and claim that, regardless of the situation, a woman's choice is inviolable. This may not be the only, or even the best, strategy to use to confront the issue in the public sphere, however. Supplementing this argument with a reproductive justice perspective would help highlight the fact that women's choices about abortion are heavily influenced by both the formal right to abortion access *and* the broader cultural and structural context (e.g., socio-cultural attitudes, opportunities available for women more generally, the existence, or lack, of robust systems of support for disadvantaged mothers, and so on). A reproductive justice framework highlights the multitude of informal factors – including views about gender – that influence reproductive preferences. This, in turn, would allow abortion rights advocates to examine the question of sex-preference/selection without reducing it to a question of abortion policy. In particular, a reproductive justice response could enable advocates to:

- acknowledge that systematic gender-biased sex selection is, in principle, problematic;
- properly investigate if the alleged problem actually exists (this is a very big "if" – currently there is no reliable evidence demonstrating that it does exist in North America) and, if so, identify its root causes;
- identify various policy options for addressing sex-selective abortion, if it is indeed an issue;
- challenge, with specific arguments and examples, the idea that banning sex-selective abortion would be successful;

- identify better solutions that address the root causes of such a practice while still unequivocally protecting a woman's right to choose;
- justify and champion their approach publicly so that the anti-abortion movement cannot present its response (i.e., seeking to ban the secondary practice of abortion rather than altering the root causes of gender bias) as the only option.

A reproductive justice framework might also make it easier for abortion rights advocates to strongly condemn all types of reproductive coercion (including cases where women actually are coerced into choosing an abortion against their own preferences) while unequivocally defending abortion access. As we have demonstrated, one of the major frames of contemporary anti-abortion discourse in Canada – especially in the political realm – is that of abortion coercion. Rod Bruinooge's Bill C-510 – named "Roxanne's Law" after Roxanne Fernando, a woman who was killed allegedly for not procuring an abortion – used language that carefully replicated feminist critiques of violence against women to claim that the bill was an attempt to "empower pregnant women to stand up against abortion coercion" (Bruinooge 2010b).

Feminists and abortion right activists were horrified by the murder of Roxanne Fernando. But Bill C-510 put abortion rights activists in the challenging position of having to condemn violence against women and the use of coercion while simultaneously arguing against a law that would create additional punishment for certain types of perpetrators. While these two positions are entirely logical and consistent, they present a communications challenge in the public sphere, as they are complicated and can appear to some as in tension with one another. Here, too, the language of reproductive justice might make it easier to express a nuanced position in an unequivocal and convincing fashion. Such a framework would allow abortion rights activists to (a) strongly assert their condemnation of all types of gendered violence, including all types of reproductive coercion (e.g., birth control sabotage, forced pregnancy, forced abortion, child support default, lack of regulated and affordable child care spaces, and so on); (b) outline a variety of policy solutions to all of these issues in ways that protect a woman's right to choice; and (c) publicly champion these policy solutions to ensure that activists and politicians have clear policy proposals to counter anti-abortion policy suggestions.

There are signs that the abortion rights movement is beginning to adopt these types of arguments. One recent report – released by Planned

Parenthood Ottawa, the Ottawa Coalition to End Violence against Women, Canadians for Choice, and the Canadian Federation for Sexual Health (Marriner 2013) – highlights the importance of fusing advocacy around women's sexual health (including access to contraception and abortion) and feminist advocacy against violence against women. The report introduces the concept of "reproductive coercion" as a potentially important frame that supporters of abortion access might use. While the report speaks primarily to abortion providers, some of its basic ideas might be effective for a broader audience as well.

A third advantage of the reproductive justice framework is that it helps remind abortion rights advocates that, although choice-based arguments in favour of abortion rights are crucial, this frame, like any argument, has its limits and weaknesses. The concept of "choice," of course, has a long history in North American feminist activism, literature, theorization, and mobilization. It is not only a persuasive philosophical argument. It has also been deeply embedded in contemporary North American culture in a variety of ways (including many that are non-feminist), for the value of choice also lies at the heart of mainstream institutions such as the market and democratic political institutions. Choice, therefore, resonates widely and deeply within contemporary North American political culture. Focusing on choice will continue to be an indispensible discursive strategy for abortion rights activists.

At the same time, we suspect that choice alone is likely to be insufficient as a frame for abortion rights activism. A discourse focused only on "choice" obscures and neglects the ways in which systemic inequalities can restrict the exercise of real choice (Danforth 2010). Moreover, as we have begun to see with legislative efforts like Bill C-484 and Bill C-510 in Canada, a rhetoric of "choice" that is void of a structural analysis that considers the wider reality of people's ability to implement their choices inevitably runs the risk of being co-opted by anti-abortion discourse. In this respect, the reproductive justice strategy of linking choice around abortion with other progressive "choices" might allow for increased political mobilization and more persuasive public discourse.

The policy issue of provincial/national childcare programs in Canada provides one of the most politically salient examples of this type of potential linkage. In 2006, Prime Minister Stephen Harper scrapped any immediate possibility of creating an affordable national childcare program in Canada. Citing a respect for "parent's choices," Harper maintained that Canadian women did not want or need a national childcare program. Instead, he insisted that women be able to make their own "choices" when it comes to raising their children (CBC News 2005). Harper's use of the concept of "choice" is illustrative of the fact that formal choice alone can easily be flipped to support a variety of progressive or conservative policy positions.

The progressive response, therefore, must not only mobilize the idea of choice but link it to other values and issues to ensure that it remains a concept and value that supports a progressive agenda. Regarding childcare, progressives have to show that the formal and theoretical choice that conservatives champion means nothing to the many women who cannot find or afford the spots that the market makes "available." By showing that structural conditions actually undermine the real possibility of "choice" for many women – and that a just childcare system would offer real choice to all families that need and want it – progressives can use the idea of choice to make their case. But they have to ensure that they adopt a thick concept of choice that is explicitly and inextricably linked to the concrete structural conditions that define its real impact on people.

This is also true with respect to abortion. Limiting choice to "formal choice" is a position that can potentially be undermined and even co-opted by the anti-abortion movement. By employing a vision of thick substantive choice, a reproductive justice perspective champions a variety of policies that seek to enhance real reproductive choice. Such policies would enhance Canadians' real ability to choose to reproduce (e.g., a national childcare system, funding for in vitro fertilization and other fertility treatments, additional child support for families that need it) as well as their real ability to choose not to reproduce (e.g., not just the right to, but also real access to, safe methods of birth control and abortion). Linking both of these dimensions might be particularly important in an era in which an aging population and declining birth rates have raised serious questions about the sustainability of Canada's economic future and prosperity – something that would connect abortion rights to a series of other policy proposals that might garner wide support in mainstream Canadian society.

The fourth relevant aspect of a reproductive justice perspective is that it makes it much easier to explain to Canadians why we must continue to improve abortion *access*, even almost thirty years after the *Morgentaler* decision. Since the early 1990s, analysing and addressing inequalities of real access has been a main focus of both Canadian academic scholarship and grassroots activism related to abortion rights. Rachael Johnstone (2010), for instance, has traced the impact of the ongoing legislative battle for funded abortion in New Brunswick.

Chris Kaposy (2010) has addressed the lack of abortion providers in Prince Edward Island along with other issues in his deliberations over how to improve abortion access in Canada. Sethna and Doull (2013) have documented the geographical barriers to abortion access throughout Canada. Activism (often by medical providers) in this domain has also been strong. For instance, the Kensington Clinic (Calgary's private abortion clinic) has, in collaboration with the National Abortion Federation Canada (NAF Canada), built a travel fund for low-income women from rural areas who have to travel long distances to access abortion. Abortion clinics have also been able to provide women with low- or no-cost birth control (Komarnicki 2013).

Many Canadians assume that, because abortion is not criminalized, it is easily accessible across Canada and that they therefore do not need to pay much attention to the issue. It has thus been very difficult to build the critical political mass required to pass the type of policies that would address the real structural differences in abortion access across Canada. A reproductive justice perspective could help explain, in ways that speak persuasively to a much broader audience, precisely why equality of access is such an important issue.

Lastly, a reproductive justice framework might also facilitate the reactivation/strengthening of proactive collaborative activism between the abortion rights movement and other social justice movements in Canada. The political linkages between the abortion rights movement and other progressive movements were key to the success of abortion reform in the 1970s and 1980s. As Beth Palmer (2012) argues, the alliances between the labour and abortion rights movements played a central role in winning the battle for the "silent majority," as the support of unions (e.g., passing pro-choice motions at their congresses, helping organize rallies and campaigns, and so on) was crucial in convincing politicians that there was broad popular support for abortion law reform. The support of unions remains important. In 2012, for example, when the anti-abortion movement mobilized an anti-abortion caravan, it was met by strong counter-protests across the country, partially due to the organizing efforts of the Canadian auto union (LifeSiteNews 2012). A reproductive justice frame might potentially help strengthen these alliances by offering language that can help clearly explain why the concerns of labour organizations, anti-poverty activists, organizations that help new Canadians, and even those of medical associations are compatible with a commitment to defending abortion rights and improving real access.

14.2 Organizational and Tactical Implications

While the language of reproductive justice provides the abortion rights activist with a nuanced theoretical framework, there are also many organizational and tactical implications of our analysis for the abortion rights movement in Canada. Here we only note a few things that abortion rights activists might consider, given the changing context.

1. Do not assume that the abortion debate in Canada is closed.

The status quo – that is, full abortion rights regulated by medical standards – is largely accepted in Canada. However, the legal context is not as airtight as it may seem. In addition, as we observed earlier, the political context could potentially become more hospitable to revisiting the debate, depending on the next leader, and future electoral strength, of the Conservative Party of Canada. Moreover, it is important to recognize the potential effectiveness of "pro-woman" anti-abortion arguments, which may resonate more effectively with many Canadians. Thus, rather than assuming that the debate is settled and then suddenly finding themselves in the midst of a crisis, abortion rights activists might want to develop a robust counter-strategy – and the resources to implement it – sooner rather than later.

2. Be prepared to embrace the debate – but embrace it strategically.

It is not uncommon to hear abortion rights advocates in Canada say that there is no need for any debate about abortion policy, arguing that the question of abortion rights was clearly and unequivocally settled by the Supreme Court in the late 1980s. The weakness with this perspective is that it misunderstands the nature of debate in the political and public sphere and, in doing so, runs the risk of giving the anti-abortion movement a significant head start in any future debate.

Because we live in a democracy, and because healthy debate in the public sphere is an essential part of our democratic process, many political issues are never fully settled and remain the subject of continuing debate and contestation – even when a strong consensus in favour of one position or another exists. This means that, for many issues, the political battle is never completely over and there is always a possibility that, if circumstances change, policy or laws that were taken to be unchallengeable and unchangeable might nonetheless be challenged and changed. Abortion rights advocates might prefer that a debate regarding increased limits on abortion access, the legal status of the fetus, or any other number of questions never take place. But they alone cannot decide and guarantee this. That's not how politics works. It is therefore important that even those political and social movements that support policies that reflect the status quo continue to do advocacy work to strengthen public and political support for those policies and laws, and ensure they have an effective plan about how to engage in any future debate.

In doing so, it is important for advocates to develop separate strategies for the different spaces where the debate might be fought. On the issue of abortion, for example, abortion rights advocates might want to argue strongly that there is no need for a discussion of this issue in the formal political realm. They can argue in public against the need for a debate in the House of Commons and provide reasons for why it is unnecessary. Moreover, since political and social movements frequently lobby political allies to convince them to discuss (or not discuss) various policy questions (a process that is foundational to democratic politics), they have every right to speak with political parties and representatives in order to convince them of their view (something which the anti-abortion movement does regularly). In these circumstances, if a majority of our political representatives decide not to debate an issue, they have that right. Actively lobbying politicians to not reopen federal abortion policy is thus an entirely legitimate and important strategy for defenders of abortion rights.

However, when it comes to broader debate in the public sphere, the situation is completely different. Abortion advocates cannot simply disavow the existence of a "debate" by fiat or wish it away by refusing to acknowledge it. Even when a given policy or law has long been viewed as an unquestioned norm, a public debate can re-ignite if enough individuals and organizations with views that differ from the norm have enough resources and a strong enough voice to gain sustained attention in the public realm.

In this context, abortion rights activists might do well to embrace the debate in the public sphere when it does reappear. In fact, rather than viewing it as threat, they might welcome it as a chance to proudly and proactively share a clear and persuasive vision of the importance of abortion rights with their fellow citizens. Rather than a burden, engaging in the debate might be seen as an opportunity to strengthen core values that support abortion rights and to educate Canadians about the importance of supporting abortion rights. At the very least, it might be seen as an opportunity to remind Canadians about why abortion rights matter – especially those who were not present for the major abortion debates thirty years ago and who may not have thought about why they should support abortion rights.

There are many reasons why abortion rights advocates should feel confident in their ability to persuade their fellow Canadians of their point of view. Abortion rights advocates have strong arguments and reasons for their position. They also know that most Canadians agree with them, as polls consistently suggest that a strong majority of Canadians support the idea of legal abortion. Perhaps most encouragingly for abortion rights activists, there is some empirical evidence to suggest that actively discussing and debating the abortion issue actually increases support among Canadians. Forum Research polls undertaken before (February 2012) and after (October 2012) Stephen Woodworth's Motion 312 had been debated and voted on in Parliament revealed that, after six months of debate, public support for abortion rights had actually increased significantly. In February 2012, 51 per cent of those surveyed were in favour of access to abortion under any circumstances and 37 per cent under some circumstances (only 10 per cent were in favour of making it illegal in all circumstances). By October 2012, support for abortion rights had strengthened considerably, with 60 per cent favouring abortion access under any circumstances, 30 per cent supporting it under some circumstances, and only 8 per cent in favour of making it illegal (Forum Research 2012).

The benefit of being willing to engage in the abortion debate has been demonstrated politically as well. In the 2014 election in New Brunswick – a province well known for its resistance to abortion rights – the Liberals' promise to address the existing barriers to abortion access seemed to help them defeat the provincial Conservative government and achieve a strong majority.

Abortion rights advocates should be optimistic, then, about what they can achieve when and if broad public debates over abortion policy break out. But they need to be willing to strongly engage in these debates if they are to achieve these positive results. It should not be taken for granted that abortion rights arguments will naturally appear and define the public debate. In fact, abortion rights activists might be very surprised to find how little their perspective is being covered by the media at crucial moments. We have already discussed, for example, how quickly many observers in the mainstream media supported the idea that Mark Warawa's M-408 should have been debated in the House of Commons. Even if the reasons that most observers gave (Parliamentary norms, concerns about democratic deficit) did not necessarily support the content of the motion itself, one effect was to make the anti-abortion position seem like it had much more mainstream support than it actually did.

This trend was repeated when Justin Trudeau announced in May 2014 that the policy of the federal Liberal Party would henceforth be pro-choice and that all MPs would be expected to vote in accordance with this position in any parliamentary vote with implications regarding abortion. For a variety of reasons, Trudeau was vilified by the vast majority of media commentators and op-ed writers. By our estimate, fewer than 10 per cent of op-ed columns across Canada in the weeks following his first announcement were supportive, with more than 80 per cent being critical of his announcement. Again, many of these op-ed pieces were critical for reasons other than the policy itself – for example, they framed it as an example of Trudeau's "tyrannical" leadership model and his hypocrisy – yet the fact remains that the overall media coverage was very critical of Trudeau's announcement and the new policy (Saurette 2014). Even the New Democratic Party, which strongly supports abortion rights, was a vocal critic of Trudeau's new abortion position. Moreover, there were almost no abortion rights activist voices in the media supporting Trudeau's announcement.

This media imbalance has significant effects. The failure of the abortion rights movement to speak out forcefully in support of this new policy made it appear, in the public sphere, that there was much less support for abortion rights and much more resistance to it than there actually was. The more that this impression gains traction, the easier it is for anti-abortion activists to force the debate into Parliament and gain support for their preferred policies, and the harder it is for abortion rights advocates to defend their preferences. In such situations, simply refusing to debate does not have the effect of negating or downplaying the debate. It actually allows the anti-abortion movement to inflame the issue by making abortion rights policies look much more actively contested than they actually are.

In a context where abortion rights advocates cannot control whether the issue re-emerges for debate in the public sphere, where not engaging has negative consequences, and where evidence suggests public debate actually strengthens Canadians' support for abortion rights – it seems to us that advocates of abortion rights should embrace the public debate when it emerges. They should have faith in the strength of their principles and arguments and proclaim them proudly, confident in the knowledge that their efforts will not just protect the status quo, but may deepen the public's understanding of and support for abortion rights, access, and perhaps even reproductive justice issues more widely.

3. Consider adopting a vocabulary that is larger than simply "women's rights and choices."

Building on some of the work in the reproductive justice literature discussed above, abortion rights advocates might locate abortion rights within a wider set of reproductive justice demands. This would not only construct a perspective that is more difficult for anti-abortion advocates to co-opt. It would also potentially speak to a much wider audience and allow abortion advocates to build a strongly supportive and highly diverse political coalition by bundling a variety of issues together.

4. Develop effective rhetorical counter-strategies for each of the main techniques employed by contemporary anti-abortion discourse.

Almost all effective political discourses have built-in counter-responses that anticipate and challenge their opponents' perspective. Contemporary abortion rights discourse is no different in this. It is important for it to ensure that it has a robust set of responses designed to address the specifics of contemporary anti-abortion discourse. There are some general principles that advocates might keep in mind when developing these responses:

• Do not assume that anti-abortion discourse is homogeneous or univocal. It is more diverse than many observers believe.
• Do not assume that what worked for the abortion rights movement thirty years ago will be sufficient today. While there are some similarities in context, there are some very important differences as well.
• Do not assume that messages and messengers that work well with in-group supporters are the most effective ones for the broader public. Rather, develop a variety of counter-strategies aimed at convincing different target audiences.
• Do not ignore anti-abortion arguments that seem self-evidently contradictory or false. The same arguments that may seem unconvincing or even absurd to those who follow the issue closely can be

very persuasive to those who don't. Therefore, seek to counter all techniques of persuasion.

- Perhaps most importantly, remember that a debate is a very specific social and political practice whose goal is to use a variety of rhetorical strategies in an ethical way to persuade an audience that a particular *position* is the best one. To be successful, you do not have to convince the audience to agree with all the *reasons* that you might personally believe are relevant. Indeed, the very idea that everyone who supports a given policy stance should necessarily share the same reasoning is based on a profound misunderstanding of the nature of modern, pluralist democratic politics. It is normal and completely legitimate that a given policy would be supported by a wide coalition of supporters who may champion it for very different reasons and with reference to quite different values. Even abortion rights activists who share the same policy preferences do not all agree on which are the most important or convincing reasons. As such, it is crucial to focus on crafting and communicating arguments and reasons that will reach and convince different audiences. Sometimes that will mean communicating the values and reasons that are most important to abortion rights activists. Other times it will mean focusing on arguments or values that seem relatively unimportant to the activists themselves but that are crucial to the specific audience with which they are communicating. Recognizing and appropriately responding to this reality is a crucial prerequisite for successful communications today. Using the full suite of argumentative techniques is not "selling out," nor is it engaging in unethical behaviour. It becomes unethical only if the message is untrue.

5. Develop a range of strategies to address abortion-harms-women (A-H-W) arguments.

There are many ways in which the abortion rights movement might counter A-H-W arguments, which, as we have seen, have become increasingly prevalent in the anti-abortion discourse. While the scientific evidence debunking the A-H-W arguments is very clear, it has not been sufficiently popularized and rendered "user-friendly" by the abortion rights movement – allowing the anti-abortion movement to continue to promote these ideas in ways that are persuasive to various audiences. The following are some ideas of what might be done in response.

- Identify the top ten A-H-W claims, identify the "source" studies and data on which they are based, evaluate the credibility of these sources and their research methodology, compare their findings to established scientific consensus, and create an authoritative and easily accessed short guide debunking each claim.
- Contextualize any legitimate risks with reference to other medical procedures, as well as with reference to the risks associated with continuing a pregnancy, in order to demonstrate that the risks and effects of abortion are similar to, or less significant than, those associated with many common medical procedures (and often much less significant than continuing a pregnancy).
- Persuade the Canadian Medical Association (CMA) and provincial associations to publish objective medical perspectives on the relative risks of abortion as a medical procedure compared to other common medical procedures. Persuade medical associations and provincial governments to create objective, informative and authoritative websites that provide the scientific consensus on the safety of abortion as a medical procedure in comparison to other common procedures.
- Highlight the paternalism implicit in the claim that the risks associated with abortion justify taking away women's right to make a choice. Show how this logic infantilizes women and treats them as if they are not able to make their own informed decisions.
- Continue to talk about abortion as a medical decision. Highlight that the best way for women to make these decisions is through conversations with their medical practitioners and supportive family members, partners, and friends. This is not only a well-established and successful frame for defending abortion rights in Canada, it is also one of the best ways normalize and destigmatize the procedure.
- Do not allow the anti-abortion movement to conflate the absence of criminal law regulating abortion with the idea that there is no regulation of abortion in Canada. The anti-abortion movement consistently repeats the idea that Canada is alone in the Western world in having no abortion laws and uses this to suggest that abortion is totally unregulated in Canada. Abortion rights activists need to continue to counter this framing by explaining, again and again, that the practice of abortion is already thoroughly regulated in Canada, but by medical standards instead of criminal laws. Some Canadians may not want to see abortion criminalized but may be tempted

towards this position, particularly with respect to third-trimester abortions, if they sense that there are no regulations at all. Therefore, abortion rights activists have to help Canadians understand that, in fact, the medical community carefully regulates abortion and that this is most appropriate form of oversight.

- Highlight examples of how abortion helps women medically and publicize them repeatedly.
- Develop and publicize macro-analyses of the many health, economic, equity, and rights benefits of safe, legal, publicly funded abortion and compare those outcomes to those in countries with rigid anti-abortion laws. These analyses would be a particularly powerful way to counter anti-abortion defunding campaigns.
- Continue to highlight problems of access (e.g., the percentage of hospitals that provide the procedure, the factors that hamper abortion access) to show that abortion is already hard enough to access, even without recriminalizing it.

6. Develop a range of strategies to counter fetal-centric arguments.

There are a number of ways to effectively challenge fetal-centric arguments, many of which the abortion rights movement has already used but many of which have not been repeated and popularized sufficiently over the last several decades.

- Do not assume that the idea that fetuses do not have legal rights is obvious to all Canadians and is inextricably fixed in law. Assume that this is an ongoing argument and that abortion rights activists must be able to easily and convincingly argue against both new and old renditions of fetal rights arguments.
- Identify several of the most straightforward, easily communicated, and persuasive arguments (moral, not just legal) about why the fetus is not a legal person and why the fetus should not be protected under criminal law and repeat them frequently in the public debate. Underline that abortion is, and should be, regulated by medical standards and practitioners. Highlight both moral and scientific arguments to support the abortion rights position.
- Highlight the fact that any legislation that seeks to limit abortion access creates a profound conflict of interest between fetus and mother and that any law limiting abortion through criminal law invariably privileges fetal rights over those of the mother.

- Clarify the question of third-trimester abortions and turn it into a strength rather than an area of potential weakness. Use existing data (or support new studies) to show how rare this practice is – how few third-trimester abortions actually take place, how few doctors provide this service, and how seriously it is treated and regulated. Explain why access to third-trimester abortions is needed in some cases – it is important not to assume that most Canadians will automatically understand this issue. A modified "In Her Shoes" theme (introduced recently by the American arm of Planned Parenthood) could powerfully demonstrate that there are cases (e.g., when serious, incurable birth defects in a fetus are identified late in the pregnancy; when a woman's health is at risk) in which late-term abortion are necessary, even if these decisions are very difficult for the families involved.

7. Develop a range of strategies to counter the new framing and narrative strategies used by anti-abortion advocates.

Although these techniques are subtle and may appear to some to be unimportant, they are actually crucial to the potential success of the anti-abortion movement. Consequently, abortion rights advocates may wish to consider some of the following ideas:

- Contest the identity rebranding of the anti-abortion movement. Highlight five clear and convincing reasons why the connections the anti-abortion movement claims with progressive movements and/or the analogies it makes between abortion and genocides like the Holocaust are inaccurate. Translate these points into easily understandable visuals and slogans that can be easily publicized at anti-abortion events like the March for Life, Genocide Awareness Projects, choice chains, and so on.
- Employ reproductive justice perspectives to frame the values of choice and equality in a "thick" and relational manner that justifies abortion rights arguments and insulates them from being appropriated by anti-abortion argument.
- Challenge the "abortion as violence against women" framing. Strategies might include framing attempts to restrict abortion as attempts to tie the hands of women, infantilize them, or give their reproductive choices to others. (A play on an earlier Election Ontario get-out-the-vote campaign that featured people whose

mouths had been replaced with other people's mouths might be one possibility.)

- Challenge the anti-abortion narrative and its characters. To counter the idea that they are coerced victims, show that women who make decisions about abortion are strong, empowered women making choices for themselves. Show that abortion providers are caring, committed, and largely female providers of medical services to women in need (perhaps something akin to the medical community's effort to position family doctors) – that is, women helping women. Collect and publicize the stories and realities of abortion providers in Canada (see Shaw 2013).

- Develop counter-strategies to highlight the fact that the Silent No More campaign represents only a small minority of women's experiences and that it has no bearing on the question of abortion rights. In a study published in July 2015, researchers found that the vast majority of women do not regret their abortion: 95 per cent of survey respondents indicated that abortion was the right decision for them (Rocca et al. 2015). It might be important for abortion rights advocates to launch campaigns that publicize findings like these alongside personal stories of women that highlight and concretize the ways in which abortion has been a positive, necessary, and relatively straightforward medical procedure. Another approach might be a humorous campaign that mocks the spurious logic of the Silent No More campaign (e.g., "I regret my first husband – let's ban marriage"; "I regret my hangover – let's ban alcohol"; "I regret becoming a teacher – let's ban schools"; "I regret my vote – let's ban Parliament").

- Regularly celebrate and laud the successes and importance of the abortion rights movement in Canada. The vast majority of Canadians strongly support abortion rights. Remind them explicitly of why it is something worth deeply valuing. Continue to celebrate the historical struggle for abortion rights and the women and men who made it happen. But also celebrate the myriad everyday efforts that people today undertake to expand abortion access and help women in need.

8. Do not actively seek to ban anti-abortion clubs and/or talks in universities.

Unless they engage in slander, libel, hate speech, and so on, anti-abortion groups have a right to express their views at universities.

This does not mean that anti-abortion groups have the right to express themselves in any possible way they might wish to, however. It is clearly within a university's mandate to determine the appropriate location and format for public debates, presentations, and so on. Freedom of speech at a university does not mean the right to show every type of image and say anything, at any volume, with any prop, at any time, in every space. Although this is a complex issue with some grey zones, universities generally (and certainly specifically in relation to this issue) have the right to require that debates (particularly controversial ones) take place at certain times, in certain venues, and in accordance with other rules (including regarding the type of images that can be shown) in order to allow for a productive exchange of ideas, the continued functioning of the university, public safety, and so on. Freedom of expression is not an unlimited right in Canada or the United States – laws related to libel, truth in advertising, hate speech, and a variety of other issues constitutionally limit the right to free expression. While universities should be committed to ensuring the widest possible scope for free speech, they also have the right and duty to ensure that debates, demonstrations, and so on, take place in ways that also take into consideration other concerns.

Given this context, abortion rights activists might choose to lobby the university to ensure that anti-abortion events take place in a certain way and in certain spaces. But they shouldn't seek to ban them. Bans are not just philosophically problematic. They are often bad strategy that allows anti-abortion activists to present themselves as victims and martyrs for free speech and thus to gain sympathy from more of the student body and the general public than they otherwise would have. Bans also call attention to, and help publicize, their message by making the event in question a media sensation – something that is often their goal.

In response to anti-abortion events, then, perhaps the most important thing to do is to nurture and support abortion rights activists on campuses and offer training that will help them to debate openly and proudly and to explain clearly and persuasively why abortion rights and access to abortion are so crucial to a healthy and vibrant society.

9. Cultivate a new generation of abortion rights advocates in a wide
   range of fields.

While there are many talented young abortion rights activists in Canada today, the movement does not have particularly a well-coordinated approach to nurturing, training, supporting, and strengthening the next generation of advocates. There are a variety of things that could be done, however:

- Actively build a network of media-savvy, highly motivated, and well-trained abortion rights and reproductive justice advocates who are willing and able to calmly and convincingly make the case for abortion rights in interviews with the media, in debates with anti-abortion activists, and in conversations with people in the street.
- Create a media strategy and process to ensure that media can easily identify and contact a wide assortment of these well-trained and engaged individuals whenever they are pursuing a story on the abortion debate.
- Do not assume that the people with the most experience are necessarily the best spokespersons for every situation. In some contexts, people with certain attributes and credentials will be more convincing than others, despite having less experience.
- Invest in training to leverage the wide range of activism that already exists. Help students set up specific abortion-rights (or related) clubs in high schools and universities. Engage more deeply with existing clubs that have related mandates (women's/feminist resource centres, progressive clubs like public interest research groups (PIRGs) or LGTBQ clubs) to see whether they might also focus on abortion rights and access.
- Invest heavily in certain types of student clubs that are especially important. Medical Students for Choice, for example, might be a particularly important network to invest in, as medical students are not only the abortion providers of tomorrow but also some of the most effective potential spokespeople for abortion rights. Given the credibility that doctors have in the public sphere, their voices hold enormous weight on this issue. Consequently, medical students may well be some of the most obvious leaders of the future abortion rights movement. It might also be worthwhile developing similar clubs in other professional schools (e.g., a Canadian version of Law Students for Reproductive Justice).
- Investigate how abortion is being taught in medical schools and develop a strategy to make it more normalized in the curriculum and to make it easier for interested medical students and residents to pursue an elective in it. This is particularly important as there is so little mandatory training regarding abortion in medical schools in Canada (few of Canada's seventeen medical schools cover abortion in more detail

than one lecture and more than a third of them do not include abortion in mandatory lectures at all) and because it is often very difficult for new doctors to find a clinic that has space to train them (Groen 2015).

10. Develop a strategy to counter anti-abortion street-level organizing.

Given that the anti-abortion movement is increasingly using new street-level tactics beyond protesting in front of clinics, it might be worthwhile for the abortion rights movement to strengthen their capacity to meet and contest these tactics. The following are some possible tactics:

- Develop counter-materials (especially counter-visuals) that would be effective against, for example, the graphic imagery of the Canadian Centre for Bio-ethical Reform (CCBR). Make these widely and easily available for abortion rights activists and groups and encourage them to use them at anti-abortion events (e.g., have groups in every city ready to go out and politely, but firmly, present the other side of the story wherever the CCBR's "choice chains" or Genocide Awareness Projects projects appear).
- Encourage individuals to go out and voice their support for abortion rights when they see anti-abortion protesters at the offices of members of Parliament or close to clinics. Encourage them to write/ call their MPs and/or newspapers and media outlets to express their views when questions of abortion policy are covered.
- Train abortion rights activists to be able to make their case calmly, politely, and convincingly. Remind them that the point is not to convince the anti-abortion activists (this will never happen) but rather to convince the audiences that are watching – audiences that often have a negative response to an aggressive posture on the part of activists.
- Encourage a broad diversity of women to speak out in public about their personal experiences with abortion. It is important that all types of women are represented, and having women who are already mothers, or are visibly pregnant, speak out in support of abortion access is crucial. By (rightfully) placing abortion within the larger realm of reproductive justice, abortion rights advocates can highlight how abortion is not only for women who are not ready to be mothers, but also for women who are already mothers. Presenting motherhood and abortion access as compatible positions could be a potentially powerful frame.
- Consider the role that fathers and other male allies can play in street-level organizing.

11. Network broadly and proactively with other groups and link re-
    productive justice issues with other progressive agendas.

Although the abortion rights movement has traditionally had close
ties to other Canadian progressive movements, it might be worth
enhancing these connections. For example, given the large-scale success and influence of Quebec feminist and progressive organizations in
protecting and enhancing abortion rights and access in Quebec (Quebec has 50 per cent of all abortion centres in Canada despite having
less than 25 per cent of Canada's population), it would be valuable for
English-Canadian groups to network closely with them and learn from
their best practices and successes. Even simply hearing about what
Québécois activists believe is possible might inspire abortion rights
activists elsewhere in Canada. This applies as much to ideas about the
delivery of abortion services and access as it does to political messaging, activism, and other organizational efforts.

The contemporary labour movement should also be a natural and
proactive partner. Given the importance of women to unions and the
labour movement, and the central importance of a wide range of reproductive justice questions to women in the workforce, a reproductive
justice approach would allow the abortion rights movement and the
labour movement to work in concert on a variety of causes, including abortion rights, maternity and parental benefits, fertility issues, and
childcare. Given its history of progressive organizing, another potential
ally might be the queer movement.

Abortion rights advocates may also wish to cultivate links with more
established and conventional groups. These might include the CMA
(whose members continue to have an interest in not being targeted
by abortion laws), the Canadian Bar Association (whose interest in
human rights and constitutional law likely means that most members
support the abortion rights position), and even business groups like
the Conference Board of Canada (whose members have an interest in
ensuring a strong workforce and thus might be convinced to support
abortion rights should the debate emerge). Having powerful allies was
a key part of ensuring abortion liberalization historically and might be
important in the future as well.

12. Research and publicize the infrastructure of the anti-abortion
    movement.

Finally, the abortion rights movement might take a page from the political realm and undertake some opposition research and publicize the results. Currently, it is very difficult to know precisely how much and what types of support religious groups offer in regard to the funding and logistical organization of the anti-abortion movement. However, there is some evidence to suggest it remains substantial. Moreover, as discussed previously, media outlets have reported that publicly funded schools (such as some Catholic schools and school boards in Ontario) provide or facilitate funding, organizational assistance, and in-kind support for the movement (e.g., busing students to anti-abortion rallies). Determining the degree to which this support exists and asking Canadian citizens whether they support the use of public funds and resources for this type of political advocacy might be worthwhile.

These are just a few potential strategic implications for the abortion right movement that flow from our findings. Of course, a variety of abortion rights groups and advocates have already begun to implement many aspects of these potential strategies. Our point is not that changes in anti-abortion discourse require abortion rights activism to radically reinvent their own strategies. The abortion rights movement has achieved enormous success in Canada. The vast majority of the Canadian population believes that abortion is a medical decision that should be undertaken by a woman in consultation with her doctor, and abortion is regulated by the Canadian medical community, not by federal criminal law. Thus, even if there are serious gaps in abortion access in Canada, the abortion rights movement is in a much more advantageous position than the anti-abortion movement.

That said, the fact that the contemporary anti-abortion movement in Canada is increasingly sophisticated and strategic – and is using a variety of new tactics in its attempt to reignite abortion politics in Canada – should remind abortion rights activists that this is not a closed issue. In such a context, it may be necessary to once again actively invest in helping Canadians remember why it is so important to protect and enhance abortion and other reproductive justice rights in Canada.

Acknowledgments

One of the true pleasures of doing collaborative research is that it turns what is often an isolating process involving thousands of hours wrestling with your own thoughts into something much more engaging and dynamic. At its best, researching and writing collaboratively is a conversation that leads to much richer, more surprising, and more robust hypotheses and conclusions than would have resulted from working alone. Even more importantly, it allows you to offload the tasks you like the least and gives you someone else to blame for any mistakes. Happily, we have loved working together for all these reasons and many more. So we'd like to start by thanking each other. Kelly – you're great! It has been inspiring to see your commitment to these issues, thought provoking to discuss these questions with you, and an all around pleasure to work with you! Well thanks, Paul. You're great too! It certainly wasn't a short process. But researching and writing with you helped me see many dimensions that I wouldn't have seen on my own and definitely made the research and writing process a lot more enjoyable!

It should go without saying that our work is also much stronger as a result of both the support and the critical questions and constructive feedback that so many people have provided over the past few years. First off, heartfelt thanks to two budding scholars – Allysa Olding and Mary Lilly – for providing stellar research assistance as well as an extraordinary eye for copy editing (something that neither of us even remotely possesses). In addition, we'd like to thank everyone who invited us to talk, listened to our ideas and evidence, and then helped us think about them in different ways and taught us things we didn't know. We will no doubt have forgotten some people that belong on this list (sorry!), but at a minimum thanks to: Andrew Biro and his colleagues at Acadia University; Karin Galldin and Kathryn Trevenen at the University of Ottawa; Tracy Penny Light, Shannon Stettner, the participants at both the 2014 PEI conference and the 2013 Congress book workshop; the *Canadian Journal of Political Science* and its anonymous reviewers for commenting on and publishing an article outlining some of our early ideas; the members of the CPSA's 2014 John McMenemy's Prize jury for honouring our article with that award; Trevor Harrison and the audience at the 2013 Parkland's Institute annual conference; Linda Trimble, Shannon Sampert, Shane Gunster, and other panel and audience participants at CPSA conferences over the years; Dawn Fowler, Angel Foster, and the other participants at the Canadian sessions at the 2013 and 2014 National Abortion Federation conferences; the incredibly inspiring women of the Centre de Santé des Femmes de Montréal and the Comité de Vigilance (particularly Anne-Marie Messier, Isabelle Tardiff, Audrey Gonin, and Magaly Pirotte); and finally, the many friends and colleagues who read and discussed portions of this material with us, especially Kathryn Trevenen, Leslie Robertson, Susan Spronk, Emilie Cameron, Fred Chabot, Laura Janara, Celia Posyniak, Suzanne Morris, Janice Gordon, Jessica Shaw, Beth Palmer, Dominique Masson, and all those we have forgotten to mention by name.

A special thank you goes out to the anonymous reviewers of the book. It is not a small request to ask someone to take the time to carefully read a long manuscript. And it takes real skill as a reviewer to give feedback that not only highlights the ways that the book could be improved but also energizes the authors' desire to make those changes. We have been very fortunate to have had several reviewers who went well beyond the call and offered both enthusiastic support and extremely perceptive constructive feedback that helped us to significantly improve (but also lengthen – so blame them for that!) the manuscript. We are very grateful both for their effort and for the quality of their suggestions.

Our editor, Daniel Quinlan, also deserves a more-than-appreciative shout-out from us. He was enthusiastic about this project from the first day when we pitched it to him as a short 150-page book. To his enduring credit, he remained just as enthusiastic as it morphed into a much longer and broader book. Not only did he effectively and successfully run the book throughout the procedural gauntlet that is academic publishing, he also read the entire manuscript at various points, offered valuable content and structural suggestions, and was always willing to chat and brainstorm with us. Thanks Daniel – a pleasure as always. Also, thanks to copy editor Barbara Tessman, who saved us from more than a few of the typos and inconsistencies that inevitably populate a book of this length.

We would also like to acknowledge the financial support that we have received to help us undertake this research. In particular, thanks to SSHRC's ASPP, Standard Grants, and Doctoral Fellowship programs, as well as to the Faculty of Social Sciences at the University of Ottawa, for providing financial support to us at various points over the course of this project.

Finally, we'd also like to individually thank a few people who have supported each of us throughout the process.

For Kelly: Thanks to all of the women in my life who are caring, independent, and fiercely smart and who love and encourage other women everyday. To Xav, for teaching me patience and supporting me in every way possible – you're my favourite human and you make me better. To my original fam, for supporting this "alleged" book from the beginning. To Janice – your influence runs deep throughout this project. From such a young age you taught me the importance of loving and trusting women and I have built my life and research around those teachings. I could not be luckier than to have you as my mom. To Jack, my first and most loyal editor – you taught me how to write and how to argue (two of my favourite things). Thank you for always pushing me to be smarter, clearer, and better. To Chuck and Ken – for all your sarcastic words of support, for not ever letting me take myself seriously, and for showing me the importance of smart and loving men.

To Alison, the strongest and most generous friend any person could ask for – you have made Ottawa my home, and life is always better when you are near. To two of my best friends, Hilary and Randi – your strength and ferocity inspires me and you have both taught me about the way friendship can transform into family. To Jon, who first brought me to this topic and provided me with a never-ending supply of relevant articles. To all the amazing women at the Kensington Clinic. To my patient and supportive officemates, Josh, Ben, Poul, and Mohamad. To my colleagues and fellow graduate students at University of Ottawa, who all make me smarter everyday. To Professor Luc Turgeon for showing me that I am actually a Canadianist after all. And to my PhD advisor and co-author Paul – you deserve to be thanked twice. Thank you for teaching me what it means to think and speak with confidence and showing me what kind of academic (and tennis player) I want to be.

For Paul: To start with, thanks to the community that is Ottawa. Like most cities, Ottawa is a pretty odd and fascinating place when you get to know it. It is filled with interesting nooks and crannies, people, and experiences. It pulses with politics at all levels. The fact that I love these aspects of the city probably means that I choose the right profession and discipline. Even so, I wouldn't feel half as warmly towards Ottawa if it weren't also part of the bilingualism, multiculturalism, and natural beauty of the Outaouais region. More than a few of the key ideas in this book have emerged while listening to music at the Black Sheep Inn, biking or running deep into Val-des-Monts, or pausing mid-ski for a wine and fondue break in one of the log cabins in the Gatineau Park. It is a rare luxury to live in a place where in fifteen minutes you can go from the joys of intellectual debate in a vibrant urban space to the very different pleasures of losing yourself (or, for that matter, continuing intellectual debate) in undisturbed nature. I am very thankful for that.

To my colleagues and students at the School of Political Studies (as well as at the APUO) at the University of Ottawa. Almost a decade and another book ago, having just arrived in Ottawa, I wrote that the School was an ideal incubator for the final stages of my first book. Over the past ten years, the School has grown enormously – as has my appreciation for my colleagues, friends, and students. Their collegiality and ideas have created a fascinating and eclectic stew in which the entirety of this book has marinated. And that is not just a mixed metaphor. What is there to say about a group of people whom I not only enjoy chatting with in the corridors of work, but with whom I also regularly enjoy good food, play and listen to music, joke, tease and laugh, learn from, and fight to protect the intellectual and pedagogical integrity of the university? The fact that I am not only proud to be a member of the School (even during our most drawn out departmental meetings!) but also count my colleagues as friends who help make Ottawa the home I love says it all.

To several deeply valued research collaborators and mentors, who are first and foremost also irreplaceable and very dear friends. Your influence runs deep throughout this book, even if you can't see it directly. Kathryn, Shane, Henrik – I wouldn't have considered co-writing this book if I hadn't already experienced the laughter, intellectual stimulation, and deep fulfilment that has come from working with you on earlier (and, I hope, future) projects. Moreover, everything I write – and probably will ever write – bears the mark of Bill Connolly and Jane Bennett. You remain, even now, twenty years after we first met, my foundational intellectual touchstones.

Finally, and most importantly, to the many members of my family (my parents and their partners, Marc, Jacqui, Gus, Arden, Kathleen, Jon, KT, LR, RéRé, Flix, Pablo, Anna, Emma, Lily, Brenda, Neville, the Toronto Friesens, the Calgary Saurettes, and, of course, Kenzie and Stuart) and to my irrepressible friends who are too numerous to mention individually even though they each deserve that and far more. You have helped make me who I am today. You have supported my belief that scholarship like this is important. You have allowed me to do it with passion and intensity. But most importantly, you are the reason I greet every day with a smile. You remind me of the joys of life beyond that of the mind and pen. Of revelling in the splendour of the great outdoors. Of the I'm-a-five-year-old-kid-at-recess bliss I get from jumping on a bike, kayak, surfboard, skis, skates, or snowshoes. Of the always surprising zen that comes from running around chasing bouncing balls of various sizes, frisbees, and dogs. Of the hilarity and sublimity of being a mobile jungle gym/library/cafeteria for all of the amazing kids in my life. Of the uplifting and thought-provoking power of music (a special hey-ho to my fellow band mates in the Dustbowl Daddies). Of the nourishing energy of breaking bread together. Of the fact that we are stronger and happier together – both politically and personally. Each day you remind me to embrace the overflowing abundance of life and to be grateful for every minute of it. One can give no greater gift. Thank you.

Glossary of Key Legal and Political Events, Organizations, and Individuals

This synthetic glossary offers short descriptions of the most important abortion-related legal rulings, political events and policies, organizations, and individuals that have been discussed in this book. It is divided into three main sections:

- A1 covers legislation, policies, and legal decisions.
- A2 covers organizations and campaigns.
- A3 covers individuals.

Each section is further divided on a geographic basis, with subsections for Canada, the US, and the UK, where applicable.

A1. Legislation, Policy, Legal Decisions

A1.1 CANADA

Badgley Report on the Abortion Law. In 1977, the Badgley Committee – which was established by the federal government to assess the effects of Canada's abortion law (section 251 of the Criminal Code) – submitted its report. Its recommendations did not directly address the legal standing of abortion, focusing instead on promoting better family planning to reduce the number of unwanted pregnancies. However, the report's main conclusion was that abortion services were not being delivered as required in Canada.

Bill C-43, An Act Respecting Abortion. Bill C-43 was tabled by Brian Mulroney's Progressive Conservative government in 1989. Following the

Supreme Court's ruling that Canada's abortion laws were unconstitutional, Bill C-43 was intended to place abortion back in the Criminal Code and to ban all abortions unless a doctor ruled a woman's life or health would be threatened. Anyone found in violation of the law (doctors or women) could be sentenced to up to two years in prison. The bill was passed by the House of Commons but was blocked by the Senate.

Bill C-484, An Unborn Victims of Crime Act. Tabled by Conservative MP Ken Epp in November 2007, the bill sought to protect fetuses from third-party attacks. The bill passed second reading but died when a federal election was called in September 2008.

Bill C-510, An Act to Prevent Coercion of Pregnant Women to Abort (Roxanne's Law). Tabled in April 2010 by Conservative MP Rod Bruinooge, the bill sought to criminalize "coerced abortions." It was voted down by Parliament.

Bill C-537, Protection of Conscience Rights in the Medical Profession. Tabled in April 2008 by Conservative MP Maurice Vellacott, the bill sought to protect physicians from performing medical procedures that violated their religious or personal beliefs (such as euthanasia and abortion). Vellacott had previously introduced several similar bills, all of which were voted down by Parliament.

Borowski v. Canada, **1989.** A Supreme Court of Canada decision that declined to rule on whether the fetus had a right-to-life under sections 7 and 15 of the Charter of Rights and Freedoms, arguing that the court had already ruled on this matter in *R v. Morgentaler.*

Canadian Charter of Rights and Freedoms, 1982. A bill of rights that is part of the Constitution Act, 1982. It has provided grounds for litigation for both abortion rights and anti-abortion activists.

Criminal Law Amendment Act, 1968–9. An omnibus bill, tabled by Pierre Trudeau's Liberal government, that introduced major reforms to the Criminal Code of Canada. It decriminalized contraception and abortion in Canada for the first time.

Morgentaler v. The Queen, **1975.** A Supreme Court of Canada decision in which Dr. Henry Morgentaler unsuccessfully challenged Canada's abortion law (section 251 of the Criminal Code).

Motion 312. Tabled by Conservative MP Stephen Woodworth in March 2012, it advocated the creation of a parliamentary committee that would examine if the Criminal Code definition of "human beings" should include fetuses. It was voted down by Parliament.

Motion 408. Tabled by Conservative MP Mark Warawa in September 2012 and argued in Parliament in March 2013, the motion sought to condemn the practice of sex-selective abortion in Canada. The committee studying the motion deemed it non-votable, arguing that the issue was one of health care delivery and therefore fell under provincial jurisdiction. The motion was never debated in the House of Commons.

R. v. Morgentaler, **1988**. The landmark Supreme Court of Canada case that struck down Canada's abortion law (section 251 of the Criminal Code), ruling that it violated a women's right to security under section 7 of the Charter of Rights and Freedoms.

Royal Commission on the Status of Women. A royal commission established by Prime Minister Lester B. Pearson in 1967 that recommended steps that might be taken by the federal government to ensure equal opportunity for Canadian women. Its report, published in 1970, recommended that Canada's abortion law be amended to allow abortion by a qualified medical practitioner on the sole request of any woman who had been pregnant for twelve weeks or less.

Section 251 of the Criminal Code of Canada. After the decriminalization of abortion in 1969, section 251 was introduced as Canada's new abortion law and remained in force until 1988, when it was struck down by *R. v. Morgentaler*. Section 251 authorized abortion performed in an accredited hospital with permission from a therapeutic abortion committee (TAC).

"Sense of the House": The Parliamentary Abortion Debate of 1988. In July 1988, five months after *R v. Morgentaler*, Brian Mulroney's Progressive Conservative government sought "a sense of the House," which would guide it in formulating future abortion legislation. This approach allowed MPs from both sides of the abortion debate to air their views and to introduce their own amendments to the government's resolution. The debate in the House of Commons took place from 26 to 28 July 1988. In the end, no clear consensus on a new abortion law was reached.

Standing Committee on Health and Welfare. A Commons committee established by Justice Minister Pierre Trudeau in 1967 to look at the effects of illegal abortion on Canadian women and society. Hearings took place over five months, and included over a hundred briefs and testimonials, the majority of which favoured a change to abortion law.

Therapeutic abortion committees (TACs). Governed by section 251 of the Criminal Code, TACs, which consisted of at least three doctors appointed by a hospital board, determined whether the continuation of the pregnancy would, or would be likely to, endanger the life or health of the pregnant woman. The agreement of a TAC was necessary if a woman was to secure a therapeutic abortion in Canada between 1969 and 1988.

Tremblay v. Daigle, **1989**. A Supreme Court of Canada decision that found that a fetus has no legal status as a person in Canada.

A1.2 United Kingdom

Abortion Act, 1967. This act legalized abortion by registered practitioners until twenty-eight weeks of pregnancy. In 1990, the act was revised, reducing the time limit to twenty-four weeks.

Abortion Law Reform Association (ALRA). A former advocacy organization that was founded in 1936 to advocate for the legalization of abortion. It was a key actor in the enactment of the Abortion Act of 1967. In 2003, ALRA amalgamated with the National Abortion Campaign to form the organization Abortion Rights.

Bourne Decision, **1938**. Dr. Aleck Bourne was prosecuted for having performed an abortion on a fourteen-year-old victim of rape. As British law allowed abortion before twenty-eight weeks when the woman's mental or physical health was in danger, he was acquitted by a jury after only forty minutes of deliberation. This precedent created a slight opening in abortion access in the UK.

Lord Ellenborough's Act, 1803. An act aimed at clarifying abortion law. The act, also known as the Malicious Shooting or Stabbing Act, prohibited any person from performing or causing an abortion. The punishment for performing, or attempting to perform, an abortion "post-quickening" was the death penalty.

Lord Lansdowne's Act, 1828. *See* **Offences against the Person Act**.

Offences against the Person Act (OAPA), 1828, and amendments. The 1828 act, also known as Lord Lansdowne's Act, consolidated a number of individual statutes (concerning crimes against persons) into a single act, which included laws against post-quickening abortions. Amendments in 1837 eliminated the death penalty for abortion but intensified other types of punishment for performing abortions. This amendment is notable for eliminating the historical distinction between pre- and post-quickening abortions. The 1861 amendments made pregnant women seeking an abortion guilty of a crime.

A1.3 United States

Affordable Health Care for America Act (AHCAA). Colloquially termed "Obamacare," the AHCAA is health care reform legislation championed by President Barack Obama in 2008 with the goal of extending basic health coverage to all Americans. The AHCAA restricts abortion coverage for any insurance plan in which federal funds are used. It was passed into law as the Patient Protection and Affordable Care Act in March 2010.

Commonwealth v. Isaiah Bangs, **1812**. The first American judicial decision regarding abortion. A young woman named Lucy Hollman willingly took a substance that induced a miscarriage. The case centred around her partner, Isaiah Bangs, who was accused of giving her the substance against her will and committing an abortion. The court found Bangs not guilty because a miscarriage could not be considered an abortion if it occurred before the point of quickening.

Comstock Act, 1873. An extension of the Post Office Act – a law that prohibited the distribution of lewd materials, abortifacients, and contraceptive devices through the US Postal Service. The Comstock Laws continued to regulate the distribution of abortion- and contraception-related information and products until the 1930s.

Doe v. Bolton, **1973**. Along with *Roe v. Wade*, the case that led to widespread legalization of abortion across the US. In *Bolton*, after being denied an abortion by a TAC in Georgia, Doe took her case to the US District Court, arguing that the TAC's denial infringed her constitutional right to privacy. While the court ruled that the restrictions placed around abortion in Georgia were unconstitutional (abortions were legal only in cases of rape and fetal deformity and if a woman's life was in imminent danger), it upheld both the TAC approval process and the residential requirement sections of the law. Doe successfully appealed the decision to the US Supreme Court in 1973.

Eisenstadt v. Baird, **1972**. The US Supreme Court case that established the right of unmarried people to possess and use contraception on the same basis as married people (the rights of married people having been established in 1965 by *Griswold v. Connecticut*).

Freedom of Access to Clinic Entrances (FACE) Act, 1994. A US law signed by President Bill Clinton that was meant to curb anti-abortion blockades in front of abortion clinics, a strategy that was popular throughout the late 1980s and early 1990s. It prohibits the blocking of a person's (or a car's) access to a facility.

Gonzales v. Carhart, **2007**. A US Supreme Court decision that upheld the legality of the 2003 Partial-Birth Abortion Act, ruling that the ban did not interfere with the "undue burden standard" set out in *Casey*. The decision is notable because it signalled a shift in Supreme Court jurisprudence towards a restriction of abortion rights.

Griswold v. Connecticut, **1965**. A US Supreme Court decision that ruled that the Constitution protected a right to privacy. The case involved a Connecticut law that banned the use of contraceptives. *Griswold* invalidated the law on the grounds that it violated a marital right to privacy, a right that was later extended to non-married persons as a result of the 1972 case *Eisenstadt v. Baird*.

Harris v. McRae, **1980**. A US Supreme Court decision that upheld the Hyde Amendment and ruled that a pregnant woman's right to privacy did not mean that Medicaid had to fund abortion.

Hyde Amendment, 1976–7. The first anti-abortion victory following the legalization of abortion in 1973, the amendment bans the use of federal money to fund abortion.

Partial-Birth Abortion Act, 2003. Signed by President George W. Bush in November 2003, the act prohibits physicians from performing late-term abortions using what the act calls "partial-birth abortion" (what the medical literature calls "intact dilation and extraction"). It is notable because it is the first abortion ban not to include an exemption based on the woman's health and to directly target medical professionals.

Planned Parenthood of Southeastern Pennsylvania v. Robert P. Casey et al., **1992**. A US Supreme Court decision dealing with the constitutionality of several Pennsylvania state regulations that limited abortion access. While *Casey* upheld the constitutional right to abortion, it altered the standards under which states could restrict that right, creating a new standard for the adjudication of future abortion restrictions (the "undue burden standard").

Roe v. Wade, **1973**. Along with *Doe v. Bolton*, the case that led to the widespread legalization of abortion throughout the US. *Roe v. Wade* began in 1970 in Texas, where a pregnant woman, "Jane Roe," sued Dallas county prosecutor Henry Wade in an attempt to prevent him from enforcing Texas's abortion law, which banned all abortions except to save the life of a pregnant woman. The District Court of Texas found the abortion law to be constitutional; however, Roe successfully challenged the District Court's decision in the US Supreme Court. Together, *Roe v. Wade* and *Doe v. Bolten* established a constitutional right to abortion, leading to the nullification of nearly every law against abortion across the country.

Stenberg v. Carhart, **2000**. A US Supreme Court decision that overturned a Nebraska ban on "partial-birth abortions" for not having an exemption relating to the woman's health or life. The Supreme Court argued that the law violated the due process clause, as outlined in the *Roe* and *Casey* decisions. This decision would be overturned by *Gonzales v. Carhart* in 2007.

Stupak-Pitts Amendment, 2010. An amendment to the Affordable Health Care for America Act (AHCAA) stipulating that the "public option" of the AHCAA would not fund abortions. In exchange for votes that would ensure the passage of the act by Congress, President Obama agreed to the amendment. Although the Stupak-Pitt Amendment was not originally in the version of AHCAA passed by the Senate, Obama issued an executive order banning the use of federal money to fund abortion under the act.

TRAP bills. Bills targeted at the regulation of abortion providers (TRAP) are state regulations that apply only to abortion clinics. They often create standards that are difficult or impossible to implement and are primarily aimed at shutting down abortion clinics. There are two general types of TRAP bills: those that enact barriers for individual abortion providers (e.g., hospital admission requirements) and structural regulation of clinics themselves.

Unborn Victims of Violence Act, 2004. Colloquially known as "Laci and Conner's Law," after a pregnant woman (Laci Peterson) who was murdered by her husband – the bill was championed in part by the American anti-abortion organization the National Right to Life Committee. The bill made it a separate federal crime to kill or harm an "unborn child" during an attack on a pregnant woman. It was signed into law by George W. Bush in 2004.

***Webster v. Reproductive Health Services*, 1989**. A US Supreme Court decision upholding a Missouri law that heavily restricted the use of state funds, facilities, and employees in the delivery of abortion care. It largely overturned the trimester system of abortion regulation, as outlined in *Roe*, replacing it with the "undue burden standard."

A2. Civil Society Organizations and Campaigns

A2.1 CANADA

Abortion Rights Coalition of Canada (ARCC). An organization founded in 2005, and based out of Vancouver, that engages in national advocacy around improving abortion access in Canada. ARCC is run by activist Joyce Arthur.

Abortion Caravan. In 1970, the Vancouver Women's Caucus organized a caravan to raise awareness about abortion rights. It travelled from Vancouver to Ottawa, picking up abortion rights supporters along the way. In Ottawa, it held two days of demonstrations, culminating in thirty women chaining themselves to the parliamentary gallery in the House of Commons.

Alliance for Life. Founded in 1968, the group was one of the most vocal Canadian anti-abortion groups to protest the legalization of abortion in 1969. In 1972, the group would work with Toronto Right to Life to form the Coalition for Life.

Alliance for Life Ontario (AFLO). Established in 1989 to serve as the educational arm of the anti-abortion movement in Canada. Its advocacy includes the development and distribution of anti-abortion materials, the development of Ontario-wide media campaigns, and the facilitation of conferences and local symposiums.

Association for Reformed Political Action (ARPA). A national political organization, founded in 2007, whose mission is to assist Reformed Christians to become more politically active and to forward a biblical perspective in the political realm. It is explicitly anti-abortion.

Campaign Life. Founded in 1978, an anti-abortion group that engaged in political action, protesting section 251 of the Criminal Code of Canada. In 1986, Campaign Life would merge with the Coalition for Life to form Campaign Life Coalition.

Campaign Life Coalition (CLC). Created in 1986, CLC was the result of the merger between anti-abortion groups Coalition for Life and Campaign Life. Its activities primarily revolve around education, youth training, and political advocacy. The CLC is the primary organizer of the Annual March for Life on Parliament Hill.

Canadian Association for the Repeal of the Abortion Law (CARAL). A coalition of abortion rights activists formed in 1974 to protest the incarceration of Dr. Henry Morgentaler. After the Morgentaler decision, the group was renamed the Canadian Abortion Rights Action League. Throughout the 1980s and early 1990s, CARAL, which had local chapters across Canada and over 18,000 members, was active in opposing restrictions on abortion access (section 251 of the Criminal Code). CARAL disbanded in 2004.

Canadian Bar Association (CBA). An organization, founded in 1896, that represents Canadian lawyers, judges, notaries, law teachers, and law students from across Canada. It was a key actor in the decriminalization of abortion in 1969.

Canadian Conference of Catholic Bishops. The national assembly of the bishops of Canada, originally founded in 1948, the group was a vocal opponent of the decriminalization of abortion.

Canadian Centre for Bio-ethical Reform (CCBR). An offshoot of the American Center for Bio-ethical Reform (CBR). Founded in 2001 and based out of Calgary, the CCBR engages in a range of anti-abortion advocacy, including advocacy training, leafleting, interviews, debates, and public demonstrations.

Canadians for Choice (CFC). A pro-choice organization formed in 2002 that advocates for abortion rights in Canada. Its primary activities include researching the accessibility of abortion care in Canada. In 2014, it merged with Canadian Federation for Sexual Health (formerly Planned Parenthood Canada) and Action Canada for Population and Development to form Action Canada for Sexual Health and Rights.

Canadian Medical Association (CMA). An organization, founded in 1967, that represents more than 83,000 physicians in Canada. The CMA was a key actor in the decriminalization of abortion in 1969.

Choose Life Canada. Founded in 1985 by evangelical preacher Ken Campbell following the 1984 acquittal of Dr. Henry Morgentaler. The office of Choose Life Canada was situated next door to Morgentaler's Toronto abortion

clinic and was primarily involved in the picketing of Ontario abortion clinics throughout the 1980s.

Coalition for Life Canada. Created in 1973 as a sister organization to Alliance for Life and Toronto Right to Life, this group was a vocal opponent of
Canada's abortion law throughout the 1970s. It also represented the more
militant and religious sect of the anti-abortion movement of that period. In
1986, it would join with Campaign Life to create Campaign Life Coalition.

deVeber Institute. Founded in 1982 as the Human Life Research Institute, this
is an anti-abortion research group based in Toronto. Its mandate is to con-
duct research and publish studies relating to the impact of biotechnological
advances on family and society. The majority of its research focuses on the
effects of abortion.

Evangelical Fellowship of Canada (EFC). A national parachute association of
church denominations, educational institutions, and local church congregations. Formed in 1964, the EFC advocates for public policy issues that
concern the evangelical community; this includes lobbying against legal
abortion. The EFC publishes *Faith Today*, one of the few explicitly evangelical magazines in Canada.

Genocide Awareness Project (GAP). An anti-abortion display that is tempo-
rarily installed at different locations (e.g., busy intersections, university and
college campuses) across the United States and Canada. The displays are
graphic in nature and often analogize abortion with events like the Holocaust by parralleling graphic images of fetuses with images of genocide.
The GAP is produced by the Center for Bio-ethical Reform (CBR) and its
Canadian counterpart (the CCBR).

Humanist Fellowship of Montreal. A national not-for-profit group founded
in 1968 that promoted the separation of religion from public policy and
education in Canada. The group, now called Humanist Canada, supports
reproductive choice, and Dr. Henry Morgentaler was its first president.

Institute of Marriage and Family Canada (IMFC). The research arm of Focus
on the Family Canada. Founded in 2006 and based in Ottawa, its primary
activities involve research and advocacy on family-related issues in Canada.
The IMFC's executive director, Andrea Mrozek, is a leading anti-abortion
activist and founder of the blog ProWomanProLife.

Knights of Columbus. The world's largest Catholic fraternal service organization, with chapters in countries all over the world, including Canada. The
Knights are active participants in the organization and funding of the Annual March for Life in Ottawa.

LifeCanada (LC). An anti-abortion organization formed in 2000 to operate
as a national association of local and provincial anti-abortion educational

groups across Canada. In collaboration with its member groups, LC conducts polling, implements media campaigns, and develops educational resources.

March for Life. Anti-abortion marches held annually in many countries, including Canada, the US, France, and the Czech Republic. The first March for Life in Canada was in 1998. In 2014, it was estimated that 12,000 anti-abortion protestors from across Ontario participated in the march on Parliament Hill in Ottawa. The Canadian March for Life is organized by the CLC.

National Abortion Federation Canada (NAF Canada). The Canadian arm of the American National Abortion Federation.

National Campus Life Network (NCLN). A national organization that trains, organizes, and supports anti-abortion postsecondary students across Canada, working to promote the anti-abortion message on campuses. It was founded in 1997 by a group of forty postsecondary students.

ProWomanProLife (PWPL). An anti-abortion blog, founded in 2007 by Andrea Mrozek, that comprises exclusively female bloggers who represent a spectrum of anti-abortion beliefs.

REAL Women of Canada. A national organization, founded in 1983, that characterizes itself as a "pro-family conservative women's movement" (REAL Women of Canada n.d.). REAL Women holds an explicitly anti-abortion position and opposes legal abortion in Canada.

Signal Hill (SH). An anti-abortion organization based in British Columbia and formed in 2008, its activities primarily involve improving youth engagement with the anti-abortion movement through media and educational programs. It is a vocal proponent of adopting a "gentler approach" to anti-abortion advocacy (McDonald 2010, 119).

Silent No More Canada. The Canadian chapter of the Silent No More Campaign, which is based in the US. The Canadian branch was formed in 2002.

The New Abortion Caravan. Taking up the strategy of the Abortion Caravan of 1970, this anti-abortion group drove from Vancouver to Ottawa in 2012, stopping in towns and cities along the way. Its display of graphic imagery of aborted fetuses was intended to convince Canadians to oppose legal abortion.

Toronto Right to Life Association (TRL). An anti-abortion organization founded in 1971, and based in Toronto, that engages in political advocacy and education.

Vancouver Women's Caucus (VWC). A short-lived abortion rights organization that existed between 1968 and 1971. Its main purpose was to organize the 1970 Abortion Caravan.

We Need a Law. A campaign, organized by the ARPA, devoted to lobbying in favour of legislation restricting abortion in Canada.

A2.2 United States

40 Days for Life Campaign. An anti-abortion campaign, founded in the US in 2004. It is now active in various cities in North America, Europe, and Australia, where campaigns are managed by local volunteers

Abortion Counseling Service of Women's Liberation. *See* **Jane Collective**.

American Birth Control League (ABCL). Founded in 1921 by birth control activist Margaret Sanger, the league campaigned to reform restrictive contraception laws and opened medically supervised reproductive health clinics for the poor.

American Law Institute (ALI). Founded in 1923, with a mission to reduce the uncertainty around and complexity of US common law. On the abortion issue, ALI argued for a unified federal law (rather than a state-by-state patchwork) and published a reformed "model" criminal code in 1959 that advocated the relaxing of limitations on women attaining abortions.

American Medical Association (AMA). Founded in 1847, the AMA is the largest association of physicians and medical students in the US. It was a key stakeholder in criminalizing abortion throughout the second half the nineteenth century. Currently, the AMA does not reject the medical practice of abortion if it is performed under circumstances that do not violate the law.

Americans United for Life (AUL). Formed in 1971, AUL works through legal avenues and advocates legislative reform to eliminate legal abortion in the US. In 2011, it released a prototype "Women's Ultrasound Right to Know Act: Model Legislation and Policy Guide," which has help guide states in implementing TRAP bills throughout the country.

Association for the Study of Abortion (ASA). An organization, founded in 1964 and comprised primarily of legal and medical professionals, whose primary role was to educate the public on the topic of abortion rights by providing speakers for public events and media appearances. Two of the founding member – Larry Lader and Lonny Myers – would go on to form NARAL.

Center for Bio-ethical Reform (CBR). An anti-abortion organization founded in 1990 that focuses primarily on political advocacy. It is particularly well-known for it use, and philosophical defence, of graphic imagery and controversial tactics designed to engage the general public on the topic of abortion.

Concerned Women for America (CWA). An organization founded in 1979 by Beverly Diego, the wife of an evangelical minister, in the belief that Christian women were not being included in discussions about women's rights. CWA opposes legal abortion largely from a religious perspective, believing in the sanctity of human life from conception to natural death.

Eagle Forum. An explicitly Christian organization, founded in 1972 and led by Phyllis Schlafly, that advocates for a return to traditional values and education. The group actively opposes legal abortion and any public funding of abortion care.

Feminists for Life. A nonpartisan organization founded in 1972 that declares itself to be feminist, nonsectarian, and anti-abortion.

Jane Collective. Formally named the Abortion Counseling Service of Women's Liberation, the Jane Collective operated from 1969 to 1973 to address the scarcity of doctors willing to perform safe abortions prior to its legalization in 1973. Members of the collective learned how to perform abortions themselves and began offering the service. It is estimated that the Jane Collective performed over 11,000 illegal abortions (Rose 2008).

LifeSiteNews. An anti-abortion news site that covers abortion-related news internationally (with a particular focus on the US and Canada). John Westen launched the site in 1997 to counter a perceived pro-choice bias in mainstream media coverage. The Canadian branch of LifeSiteNews is operated by the CLC.

National Abortion Federation (NAF). A professional association of abortion providers in North America. Established in the US in 1977 through the merger of the National Association of Abortion Facilities (NAAF) and the National Abortion Council (NAC), NAF offers training and services to abortion providers, as well as information about abortion and referral services to women. Originally an American organization, it now has chapters in Canada, Australia, and Mexico.

National Association for the Repeal of Abortion Laws (NARAL). An organization, founded in 1969 by Larry Lader and Lonny Myers, that works as a lobby group opposing abortion restrictions throughout the US. The organization lobbies Congress and works with state affiliates.

National Organization for Women (NOW). A women's rights group founded in 1967 and one of the first feminist groups to explicitly demand the repeal of abortion legislation in the US. It is currently the largest organization of feminist activists in the US, with hundreds of thousands of members and more than 500 affiliates. NOW continues to advocate against abortion restrictions in the US.

National Right to Life Committee (NRLC). An anti-abortion organization founded in 1968 by the National Conference of Catholic Bishops, it is the oldest and largest national anti-abortion organization in the US, with affiliates in all 50 states and over 3,000 local chapters. The group works through education and lobbying to restrict abortion rights and access across the country.

Operation Rescue. A fundamentalist Christian anti-abortion organization, founded in 1986 by Randall Terry. Operation Rescue has largely been credited with pioneering and popularizing highly confrontational social protest and direct action in the anti-abortion movement. It now operates under the name Operation Save America.

Silent No More Awareness. A campaign that compiles and publicizes stories of women who regret their abortions. Formed in 2002 by cofounders Janet Morana (executive director for Priests for Life) and Georgette Forney (president of Anglicans for Life), the campaign is intended to counter the discourse that abortion care benefits women. As of 2014, the Silent No More Awareness campaign has chapters in seventeen countries, including Canada.

Society for Humane Abortion (SHA). Founded in 1962 as the Citizens Committee for Humane Abortion Laws, this organization became one of the first groups to openly use a women's rights discourse to argue in favour of abortion rights. Throughout the 1960s, the SHA rejected many proposed bills that would have liberalized abortion access, arguing that such proposals gave physicians a disproportionate control over women's reproductive choices.

A3. Individuals

A3.1 CANADA

Arthur, Joyce. A Canadian abortion rights activist and the founder and executive director of the Abortion Rights Coalition of Canada (ARCC).

Bergeron, Veronique. An anti-abortion blogger at ProWomanProLife.

Borowski, Joe. A Canadian politician and anti-abortion activist. From 1969 to 1971, Borowski served as a cabinet minister in Manitoba's NDP government. Borowski sought to have the courts declare abortion a violation of the fetus's right to life under the Canadian Charter of Rights and Freedoms. In 1989, the Supreme Court of Canada refused to hear Borowski's appeal because the abortion law had already been struck down by the *Morgentaler* decision the previous year.

Boudria, Don. A Liberal MP from 1984 to 2005, he held several cabinet positions and served as Deputy Liberal House Leader. He was a vocal opponent of abortion and tabled six private members' bills seeking to recriminalize abortion.

Bruinooge, Rod. A Conservative MP from 2006–2015, he is a vocal opponent of legal abortion and tabled a private member's bill that sought to ban coerced abortion in Canada.

Byfield, Joanne. Former president of the anti-abortion organization LifeCanada.

Epp, Ken. A Conservative MP from 2004 to 2008 and a vocal opponent of legal abortion. In 2007 he tabled private member's bill C-484 (the Unborn Victims of Crime Act), which sought to amend the Criminal Code to include additional charges for injuring or causing the death of a fetus while committing another offence.

Fainman, Jack. An obstetrician and abortion provider who was shot in his Winnipeg home in 1997 by a suspected anti-abortion activist. While he survived the attack, it did end his medical career.

Gibbons, Linda. An anti-abortion activist who has spent significant time in jail after being found guilty of trespassing and violating injunctions that protect abortion clinics from having anti-abortion protesters directly block access and harass patients.

Golob, Alissa. A Canadian anti-abortion activist and the youth coordinator for Campaign Life Coalition (CLC).

Gray, Stephanie. A Canadian anti-abortion activist and co-founder and former executive director of the Canadian Centre for Bio-ethical Reform (CCBR).

Harper, Stephen. The Conservative prime minister from February 2006 to November 2015. While he stated unequivocally that abortion would not be recriminalized under his leadership, he also refused to fund abortion care abroad as part of his international maternal health policy.

Hughes, James. An anti-abortion activist and the national president of Campaign Life Coalition (CLC).

Jeffs, Jakki. An anti-abortion activist and the executive director of Alliance for Life Ontario.

Kay, Barbara. A long-time columnist for the *National Post* who writes on the topic of abortion policy.

Koop, James. An American anti-abortion activist and terrorist who was convicted of the murder of Dr. Barnett Slepian, an American obstetrician and abortion provider. It has been speculated that Koop committed attacks on other abortion providers in Rochester, New York, and three Canadian cities. He was a suspect in the shooting of Dr. Jack Fainman.

Morgentaler, Henry. A Canadian physician, abortion provider, and abortion rights activist. Throughout the 1970s and 1980s, Dr. Morgentaler committed safe abortions across Canada in defiance of Canada's abortion law (section 251 of the Criminal Code). The first doctor in North America to use vacuum aspiration, he opened twenty abortion clinics across Canada and trained more than 100 abortion providers throughout his career. Morgentaler successfully challenged the constitutionality of section 251 in the Supreme Court of Canada in *R v. Morgentaler* in 1988.

Mrozek, Andrea. The executive director of the Institute of Marriage and Family (IMFC), a vocal anti-abortion activist, and founder of the blog ProWomanProLife (PWPL).

Mulroney, Brian. Progressive Conservative prime minister from September 1984 to June 1993. In 1991, following the *Morgentaler* decision, Mulroney tabled Bill C-43, legislation that, while recriminalizing abortion, was largely viewed as an attempted compromise.

Pellerin, Brigitte. A founding member of the anti-abortion blog ProWomanProLife.

Romalis, Garson. An abortion provider in British Columbia, he was shot (in 1994) and stabbed (in 2000) by anti-abortion activists. He survived both attacks.

Richmond, Rebecca. An anti-abortion activist and the executive director of National Campus Life Network (NCLC).

Schouten, Mike. An anti-abortion activist and director of the We Need a Law campaign.

Schutten, Andre. General legal counsel with the Association for Reformed Political Action (ARPA) since 2011. He is a vocal anti-abortion activist and speaker.

Short, Hugh. A Hamilton-based obstetrician and abortion provider who was shot by an anti-abortion activist in 1995 while watching television in his home. He survived the attack.

Sonier, Faye. Legal counsel for the Evangelical Fellowship of Canada (EFC) and a regular blogger at the anti-abortion blog ProWomanProLife (PWPL).

Stowe, Emily. The first female doctor to practise medicine in Canada. In 1879, she was charged with performing a pre-quickening abortion for a young teenager whom Stowe claimed was suicidal as a result of her pregnancy. She was eventually acquitted, largely due to lack of evidence.

Szabo, Paul. A Liberal MP from 1993 to 2011 and a vocal opponent of legal abortion.

Tremblay, Jean-Guy. In 1989, Tremblay successfully obtained an injunction preventing his former girlfriend Chantal Daigle from terminating her pregnancy. In an unprecedented decision, the Quebec Court of Appeal upheld the injunction by a margin of 3–2. The decision was overturned by the Supreme Court in *Tremblay v. Daigle* (also in 1989).

Trudeau, Pierre. Liberal prime minister from April 1968 to June 1979 and from March 1980 to June 1984. He was a supporter of abortion rights and decriminalized the practice of abortion in Canada in 1969 by way of an omnibus bill.

Van Maren, Jonathon. An organizer, speaker, and current executive director for the Canadian Center for the Bio-ethical Reform (CCBR).

Vellacott, Maurice. A Conservative MP since 1997, he is a vocal opponent of legal abortion and has tabled six anti-abortion private member's bills throughout his career.

Walberg, Rebecca. An anti-abortion blogger for ProWomanProLife (PWPL).

Warawa, Mark. A Conservative MP since 2004, he is a vocal opponent of legal abortion. In 2012, he tabled Motion 408, which sought to condemn the practice of sex-selective abortion in Canada.

Westen, John Henry. The founder and president of LifeSite News.

Woodworth, Stephen. A Conservative MP from 2008 to 2015, he is a vocal anti-abortion advocate and participates regularly in anti-abortion protests and activities. In 2012, Woodworth introduced Motion 312, which proposed the formation of a parliamentary committee to examine whether the Criminal Code definition of "human being" should include fetuses. The motion was defeated following its second reading.

Zaleski, Tanya. An anti-abortion blogger for ProWomanProLife (PWPL).

A3.2 United States

Bachman, Michelle. A Republican member of the House of Representatives since 2007. She is a supporter of the Tea Party Movement and a vocal opponent of abortion rights. Her involvement with the anti-abortion movement dates back to the 1970s.

Cunningham, Gregg. The founder of the Center for Bio-ethical Reform.

Gunn, David. An American abortion provider who was assassinated by an anti-abortion activist and terrorist in 1993. He was subject of "wanted"-style posters distributed by Operation Rescue.

Palin, Sarah. The governor of Alaska from 2006 to 2009 and the Republican vice-presidential nominee in the 2008 election. She is a vocal opponent of abortion rights, even in cases of rape and incest, and a member of the organization Feminists for Life.

Perry, Rick. The governor of Texas from 2000 to 2015. He has been key in dramatically reducing the accessibility of abortion in Texas and opposes abortion in all cases, including rape and incest.

Sanger, Margaret. A birth control activist, sex educator, and nurse. She was a key actor in the legalization of birth control in the US and established organizations that would eventually evolve into Planned Parenthood. While she was a vocal supporter of legal contraception – and is often considered a pioneer of the reproductive rights movement in the US – she remained publicly opposed to abortion.

Santorum, Rick. A US senator from 1995 to 2007. He ran for the 2012 Republican Party presidential nomination, finishing second to Mitt Romney. He is a vocal and active opponent of legal abortion.

Storer, Horatio. A physician of obstetrics and gynaecology and vocal opponent of abortion in the US from the late 1850s to the 1910s. His influence contributed to the widespread criminalization of abortion in the second half of the nineteenth century.

Terry, Randall. Founder and president of Operation Rescue.

Tiller, George. An abortion provider and former director of Women's Health Care Services, one of the only three clinics to offer late-term abortions in the US. Throughout his career, Tiller was the frequent target of anti-abortion violence. He was assassinated in 2009 by anti-abortion activist and terrorist Scott Roeder.

Historical Timeline – Abortion Politics in the United Kingdom, Canada, and the United States

The chart below is an overview of some of the key abortion-related political and legal events and contexts in the United Kingdom, Canada, and the United States since 1800. The shading represents the comparative intensity of the formal, legal limitations on access to abortion during each period. Lighter shading signals less intense/widespread legal and political restrictions to abortion access; darker shading signals more intense/widespread legal and political restrictions.

	UK	Canada	US
Pre-1800	- Loose regulation by common law - Abortion legal pre-quickening - Laws punished providers, not pregnant women - Rarely prosecuted - Not politicized, no debate	- Same as UK	- Similar to UK
1800-1850	- Politicization of debate at elite level- 1803 Lord Ellenborough's Act, 1828 and 1837 OAPA explicitly criminalize abortion, intensify punishments	- Slight political debate at elite level - Most colonies adopt versions of UK laws	- Legal/legislative context similar to UK pre-1800 - Incipient politicization of debate, after 1830 some states start to codify common law norms into statutes - AMA founded 1847

	UK	Canada	US
1850–1900	- Updated 1861 OAPA includes life imprisonment as potential punishment; for first time criminalizes women seeking abortions - Widespread illegal abortion	- Little political debate - Canadian federal government largely adopts 1861 UK OAPA - Widespread illegal abortion	- Dr Horatio Storer advocates anti-abortion policy, AMA agrees in 1857 - AMA actively lobbies for criminalization - Wave of anti-abortion laws - 40 states criminalize abortion, 1860–1880 - Federal Comstock Act, 1873 - By 1900, abortion is illegal in every US state - Widespread illegal abortion
1900–1940	- Costs of widespread illegal abortion increasingly clear - Groups push for legal reform (ARLA report, 1936) - 1938 Bourne decision; 1939 Birkett committee pushes for legal reform on basis of women's health	- Widespread illegal abortion - Costs of illegal abortion becoming clear but virtually no public debate on abortion - Limited debate re: birth control	- Abortion prohibited in all US states - Little political contestation of abortion policy - Widespread illegal abortion - Fight to liberalize of birth control gains momentum
1940–1960	- Issue disappears during Second World War and aftermath - Widespread illegal abortion continues - Private members' bills, medical associations, organizations like Protestant churches build political pressure - In practice, some increase in access	- Widespread illegal abortion - Very limited public debate on abortion until 1959 Chatelaine article sparked some conversation	- Widespread illegal abortion - Abortion policy becomes increasingly contested - Small number of physicians form TACs to use narrow legal medical exceptions to provide abortion access - ALI begins to push for liberalized abortion laws, publishes model legislation, lobbies
1960–1980	- Parliamentary medical advisory committee formed, recommends reformed legislation - Abortion Act, 1967 liberalizes abortion access up to 28 weeks if 2 doctors judge pregnancy a	- Ontario chief coroner calls public inquest into deaths from illegal abortions - CBA and CMA recommend substantial legal reform; Parliament holds hearings - Trudeau's 1969 Omnibus Reform Bill	- Abortion highly politicized - Vocal feminist groups (e.g., NARAL, NOW) expose costs of illegal abortions, demand rights - AMA liberalizes policy, 1967 - By 1969, 10 states adopt ALI model legislation - Abortion laws eventually ruled unconstitutional

	UK	Canada	US
	risk to women's physical or mental health	includes s. 251 legalizing abortion under TAC system - Growing feminist critique of s. 251 and TAC system; Abortion Caravan 1970 - 1977 Badgley Report highlights problems with s. 251 - Morgentaler challenges s. 251 by opening non-TAC abortion clinics, is prosecuted multiple times - Emergence of vocal anti-abortion movement	in series of legal cases: *Griswold* (1965) strikes down parts of Comstock laws; *Eisenstadt* (1972) extends *Griswold* to non-married couples; *Roe* (1973) and (*Doe*) 1973 strike down abortion bans in first trimester as unconstitutional and rule that second trimester limits permitted only on grounds of protecting women's health - Religious right and modern anti-abortion movement emerges - Hyde Amendment, 1976, bans federal funding of abortion; renewed annually
1980-2000	- Revised Abortion Act, 1990 reduces access to 24 weeks but expands and clarifies list of acceptable reasons (essentially creating full access to abortion until 24 weeks) - Little politicization of the issue, stable status quo	- Legal battle intensifies; culminates in Supreme Court of Canada striking down s. 251 (*Morgentaler*,1988) and ruling that fetuses not covered by Charter rights (*Daigle*, 1989) - Mulroney's Bill C-43 (1991) proposes to recriminalize abortion, passes House of Commons, defeated in Senate - Status quo: abortion no longer criminally prohibited; access to abortion regulated by medical providers according to provincial medical standards; in practice, access to abortion during first and second trimesters. However, almost	- Hyper-politicization in state, federal, legal, civil society contexts - Rising political influence of religious right - Proliferation of mainstream anti-abortion advocacy organizations - Emergence of extremist anti-abortion organizations (e.g., Operation Rescue blockades of abortion clinics) and anti-abortion terrorism (assassination of medical providers, bombings of abortion clinics, etc.) - Increasing anti-abortion legislation (e.g., laws regarding informed consent, mandatory waiting periods, ultrasound viewings, parental consent, state scripted mandatory counselling, etc.) - *Roe* eroded by series of Supreme Court decisions – *Webster* (1989) erodes Roe trimester protection

	UK	Canada	US
		no third trimester abortions performed in Canada - Dozens of anti-abortion private members' bills in 1990s; none pass - Largely de-politicized, little public debate	and introduces "undue burden standard"; *Casey* (1992) allows state laws re pre-abortion counselling, informed consent, waiting periods, fetal personhood
2000-2015	- Little politicization of the issue, stable status quo	- Little public or Parliamentary debate 2000–10 - Anti-abortion movement begins to rebuild capacity and intensify (first March for Life in 1998, CCBR founded 2001, PWPL founded 2007) - Increased politicization (Motions 312, 408) and media attention in 2010+ - Harper says Conservative government won't reopen abortion (2011); Liberal leader Justin Trudeau states official Liberal policy pro-choice (2014)	- Hyper-politicization of debate in state, federal, legal, and civil society contexts - Explosion of anti-abortion legislation/policy at state and federal level (e.g., abortion bans; TRAP bills; defunding policies; waiting periods; etc.) - *Roe* abortion rights further eroded by Supreme Court decisions – *Stenberg* (2000) allows states to ban PBAs as long exceptions for women's health exist; *Gonzales* (2007) allows states to ban all PBAs without health exceptions; *McCullen v. Coakley* (2014) strikes down abortion clinics' buffer zone

Historical Timeline – Abortion Discourse in Canada and the United States

The chart below is an overview of some of the key characteristics of the discourse defining the abortion debate in Canada and the United States since 1800. The shading represents the comparative intensity of the formal, legal limitations on access to abortion during each period, as outlined in the historical timeline in Appendix B. Lighter shading signals less intense/widespread legal and political restrictions to abortion access; darker shading signals greater restrictions.

	Canada	US
Pre-1800	- Abortion rarely discussed in public forums; largely non-politicized	- Abortion rarely discussed in public forums; largely non-politicized
1800-1850	- Early anti-abortion laws forwarded by the medical community; largely framed around scientific construction of fetus as a person - Abortion represented as dangerous/life-threatening for pregnant women - Pregnant women often represented as naive and ignorant and in need of protecting	- Early anti-abortion laws forwarded by medical community; largely framed as necessary to protect women from dangerous (and racialized) abortionists and midwives. - Pregnant women often represented as naive and ignorant and in need of protecting
1850-1900	- Increase in anti-abortion legislation and public discourse - Anti-abortion arguments framed around medical concerns over dangers of abortion and maternal mortality; medical/scientific	- Abortion becomes more obvious social reality; gains public attention; increased debate - Women considering abortion increasingly represented as immoral/irresponsible

Canada	US
concerns for fetal life; and professional concern about unprofessional practices	- Public anti-abortion arguments largely avoid overtly religious/moralized language and instead grounded in scientific/medical rationales - Emergence of racialized anti-abortion discourse portraying US as under threat of immigrant take-over
1900–1940 - Voices in favour of contraception and abortion slowly grow - Discourse in favour of abortion and contraception reform largely framed using medical grounds (e.g., widespread dangers and disastrous health outcomes due to illegal abortions)	- Rise of political movement in favour of liberalization of contraception - Birth control largely framed as working-class issue, employing the language of responsible "family planning" - Radical branches of pro-contraception movement introduce more explicitly feminist arguments in favour of legal contraception - Simultaneous emergence of eugenics arguments in favour of liberalization of birth control
1940–1960 - Emergence of stronger pro-contraception movement, largely mirroring that of US - Birth control reform discourse stresses social, economic, and feminist dimensions of reproductive choice and costs of illegal contraception - Emergence into mainstream of some early abortion reform arguments, largely framed around importance of providing abortion for "under-privileged" women and (to some degree) medical arguments (e.g., disastrous health outcomes of illegal abortions)	- Strong push in favour of abortion reform - Abortion reform position primarily framed around arguments regarding women's health; early abortion reformers still accept idea that abortion is morally ambiguous act - Narrative of dangerous "back alley abortion" emerges, stressing physical and psychological harm of clandestine abortion - Anti-abortion advocates develop "pro-life heritage tale" placing opposition to abortion in narrative of social progress; such advocates present themselves and their arguments as morally/ culturally superior
1960–1980 - Movement in favour of abortion reform emerges in early 1960s, largely led by elites (CMA, CBA) - Early abortion reform movement employs heavily medicalized discourse stressing maternal health benefits of legal, accessible abortion - Medicalized discourse accompanied by arguments about women's rights	- As 1960s progress, discourse in favour of abortion reform shifts and expands away from women's health arguments towards rights/equality/choice arguments - Arguments about need to end clandestine abortion morph into constitutional demands for repeal of anti-abortion laws based on bodily integrity and rights-based arguments

	Canada	US
	and bodily integrity, but downplayed at first by policymakers and opinion leaders - Grassroots, feminist pro-choice discourse foregrounding women's rights; reproductive choice and bodily integrity increasingly prominent from late 1960s as women's movement engages publicly and vigorously on issue - Anti-abortion discourse counters new abortion reform discourse by stressing fetal personhood and arguing legal abortion will lead Canada to moral decay - Anti-abortion discourse largely downplays religion in the formulation of public arguments; focuses on scientific construction of fetal right to life	- "Right to privacy" arguments define legal campaign for abortion reform, culminating in the *Roe v. Wade* and *Doe v. Bolton* Supreme Court decisions striking down all state abortion bans as unconstitutional - Immediately after *Roe*, anti-abortion movement focuses on defunding abortion care, invoking arguments around taxpayer "discrimination" and "choice." Countered by pro-funding discourse arguing that defunding is dangerous for low-income women - Anti-abortion advocates adopt increasingly fetal-centric, highly moralized, religious discourse - Women seeking abortion increasingly represented as selfish and morally incapable of making responsible decisions about their reproductive lives
1980-2000	- Evangelicals increasingly influence anti-abortion movement and its public arguments - Canadian anti-abortion movement not able to make inroads into mainstream politics - Anti-abortion discourse varied and diverse but largely revolves around (1) fetal-personhood arguments; (2) religiously driven discourse arguing that abortion will lead to the downfall of society; and (3) increasingly confrontational and moralizing discourse with anti-woman tone and arguments - Abortion rights activists increasingly make medical, equality, and rights-based arguments in favour of legal abortion - Growing anti-abortion movement of 1980s links issue to other women's liberation issues (e.g., child care, equal pay, etc.)	- Intensification and increasing dominance of explicitly religious frame and discourse in anti-abortion movement - Anti-abortion discourse increasingly aggressive as influence of groups like Operation Rescue increase; anti-abortion terrorism peaks in 1980s and early 1990s - "Rescue mission" emerges as key mode of framing anti-abortion activism; supported by religious, fetal-centric, anti-woman discourse centred on fundamentalist reading of Bible - Given nature of legal argumentation and court decisions, anti-abortion legal discourse largely avoids religion and tends to frame its arguments around fetal personhood and, to some degree, women's health - Abortion rights activists continue to frame position with reference to women's health, rights and choice, and bodily integrity

	Canada	US
2000–2015	- Enactment of the Canadian Charter of Rights and Freedoms (particularly s.7) creates legal opportunities for right-based arguments that both abortion rights and anti-abortion activists use in legal arguments and public discourse - In public realm, anti-abortion discourse becomes increasingly aggressive, religious, and anti-woman (e.g., Borowski) - Anti-abortion lawmakers oppose legal abortion on grounds of fetal right to life; all bills fail; little public debate inspired by discourse or parliamentary bills - Conscience clauses, defunding campaigns, and abortion-harms-women arguments define much contemporary anti-abortion activism	- Fetal personhood arguments and religious framing continue to dominate discourse of anti-abortion movement in public debate - Arguments framing abortion as dangerous to women's physical and psychological health find legal traction, particularly at state level

References

Abbreviations

AFLO   Alliance for Life Ontario
ARCC   Abortion Right Coalition Canada
ARPA   Canada Association for Reformed Political Action Canada
CCBR   Canadian Centre for Bio-ethical Reform
CLC   Campaign Life Coalition
EFC   Evangelical Fellowship of Canada
LC   LifeCanada
NAF   National Abortion Federation
NARAL   National Association for the Repeal of Abortion Laws
NCLN   National Campus Life Network
PWPL   ProWomanProLife
SH   Signal Hill
TRL   Toronto Right to Life

Court Cases

Borowski v. Canada (Attorney General), [1989] 1 S.C.R. 342
Commonwealth v. Isaiah Bangs (1812), 9 Mass. 387
Doe v. Bolton (1973), 410 U.S. 179
Eisenstadt v. Baird (1972), 405 U.S. 438
Gardner v. Massachusetts (1938), 305 U.S. 559
Gonzales v. Carhart (2007), 550 U.S. 124
Griswold v. Connecticut (1965), 381 U.S. 479
Harris v. McRae (1980), 448 U.S. 297
Meyer v. Nebraska (1923), 262 U.S. 390

Morgentaler v. The Queen, [1976] 1 S.C.R. 616

Planned Parenthood of Southeastern Pennsylvania v. Robert P. Casey et al. (1992), 505 U.S. 833

R. v Morgentaler, [1988] 1 S.C.R. 30

R. v. Oakes, [1986] 1 S.C.R. 103

Roe v. Wade (1973), 410 U.S. 113

Stenberg v. Carhart (2000), 530 U.S. 914

Tileston v. Ullman (1943), 318 U.S. 44

Tremblay v. Daigle, [1989] 2 S.C.R. 530

United States v. One Package of Japanese Pessaries (1936), 86 F.2d 737

United States v. Vuitch (1971), 402 U.S. 62

Webster v. Reproductive Health Services (1989), 492 U.S. 490

Other Sources

40 Days for Life. 2014. "40 Days for Life 2014 Campaign Report." http://40daysforlife.com/report/2014report.pdf.

40 Days for Life. n.d. "About 40 Days for Life." http://40daysforlife.com/about.cfm?selected=mission.

Abortion Act [UK]. 1967. C. 87. http://www.legislation.gov.uk/ukpga/1967/87/section/1.

Abortion Rights. 2013. "History of Abortion Law in the UK." http://www.abortionrights.org.uk/index.php/media-and-resource-centre/abortion-law/275.

Acevedo, Zoila. 1979. "Abortion in Early America." *Women and Health* 4(2): 159–67. http://dx.doi.org/10.1300/J013v04n02_05.

Ackerman, Bruce. 1991. *We the People*. Volume 1. *Foundations*. Cambridge: Harvard University Press.

AFLO. 2010a. "Did You Know?"

AFLO. 2010b. "Men and Abortion."

AFLO. 2010c. "The Trauma of Abortion."

AFLO. n.d. "Contact us." http://allianceforlife.org/contact-us.

American Law Institute. n.d. "ALI Overview: Creation." http://www.ali.org/index.cfm?fuseaction=about.creation.

Americans United for Life. 2011. "Women's Ultrasound Right to Know Act: Model Legislation and Policy Guide for the 2011 Legislative Year." http://www.aul.org/wp-content/uploads/2010/12/Ultrasound-Requirement-2011-LG-_2_.pdf.

Annas, George J. 2010. "The Real Pro-Life Stance: Health Care Reform and Abortion Funding." *New England Journal of Medicine* 362(16): 2558–63 e56. http://dx.doi.org/10.1056/NEJMp1003944.

ARCC. 2012. "Anti-Choice Private Member's Bills and Motion Introduced in Canada since 1987." *Abortion Right Coalition of Canada*. http://www.arcc-cdac.ca/presentations/anti-bills.html.

Arendt, Hannah. 1958. *The Human Condition*. Chicago: University of Chicago Press.

Aristotle. 1992. *The Art of Rhetoric*. New York: Penguin Classics.

ARPA Canada. 2007. "About Us." http://arpacanada.ca/about-arpa/about-arpa.

ARPA Canada. 2013. "Reformed Pro-Life Prayer Service and Training Session." March for Life Event, Jubilee Church of Ottawa, Ottawa, ON. 9 April.

Arthur, Joyce. 1999. "Abortion in Canada: History, Law, and Access." *Pro-Choice Action Network*. http://www. prochoiceactionnetwork-canada. org/articles/canada.html.

Arthur, Joyce. 2003. "Special Report: Where Is the Anti-choice Movement Headed?" *Pro-Choice Press* (Summer). http://www.prochoiceactionnetwork-canada.org/prochoicepress/03summer.shtml.

Arthur, Joyce. 2011. "Why Abortion Care Must Be Fully Funded." 20 October. http://www.arcc-cdac.ca/action/abortion-funding.html.

Asian Communities for Reproductive Justice. 2005. "A New Vision for Advancing Our Movement for Reproductive Health, Reproductive Rights, and Reproductive Justice." http://strongfamiliesmovement.org/assets/docs/ACRJ-A-New-Vision.pdf.

Atlantic Wire. 2012. "The Most Offensive Words from the Akin Episode Didn't Come from Akin." 22 August. http://www.theatlanticwire.com/politics/2012/08/most-offensive-words-akin-episode-didnt-come-akin/56064/.

Auld, Alison. 2014. "With Abortion Clinic Closed, N.B. Women Turn as Far as Maine and Montreal." *Globe and Mail*, 3 November. http://www.theglobeandmail.com/life/health-and-fitness/health/with-abortion-clinic-closed-nb-women-turn-as-far-as-maine-and-montreal/article21422621/.

Backhouse, Constance. 1991. "The Celebrated Abortion Trial of Dr. Emily Stowe, Toronto, 1879." *Canadian Bulletin of Medical History/Bulletin canadien d'histoire de la médecine* 8(1): 159–87.

Basset, Laura. 2013a. "Anti-Abortion Laws Take Dramatic Toll On Clinics Nationwide." *Huffington Post*, 26 August. http://www.huffingtonpost.com/2013/08/26/abortion-clinic-closures_n_3804529.html.

Basset, Laura. 2013b. "Paul Ryan Cosposors New Fetal Personhood Bill." *Huffington Post*, 9 January. http://www.huffingtonpost.com/2013/01/09/paul-ryan-personhood-bill_n_2440365.html.

Basset, Laura. 2013c. "Rick Perry Sign Abortion Bill into Law." *Huffington Post*, 18 July. http://www.huffingtonpost.com/2013/07/18/rick-perry-abortion-bill_n_3613158.html.

Basset, Laura. 2014. "Senate Candidate Joni Ernst Endorses Federal Personhood Bill for Fetuses." *Huffington Post*, 16 October. http://www.huffingtonpost.com/2014/10/16/senate-candidate-endorses_n_5997126.html.

Bazelon, Emily. 2007. "Is There a Post-Abortion Syndrome?" *New York Times*, 21 January. http://www.nytimes.com/2007/01/21/magazine/21abortion.t.html?pagewanted=1&_r=1&ei=5088&en=5092fc3344065aec&ex=1327035600&partner=rssnyt&emc=rss&adxnnlx=1190370959-M3NVF8bZOGTDu468IEZo8g.

Beckwith, Francis. 2001. "Taking Abortion Seriously: A Philosophical Critique of the New Anti-Abortion Rhetorical Shift." *Ethics and Medicine* 17(3): 155–66.

Bendery, Jennifer. 2013. "Rick Santorum on Texas Abortion Bill: It's Not Radical, It's Part of a 'Movement of Love.'" *Huffington Post*, 11 July. http://www.huffingtonpost.com/2013/07/11/rick-santorum-texas-abortion-bill_n_3581566.html.

Berlin, Isaiah. 1969. *"Two Concepts of Liberty": Four Essays on Liberty*. Oxford: Oxford University Press.

Bernays, Edward. 2005. *Propaganda*. Brooklyn: Lg Publishing.

Berthiaume, Lee. 2013. "Despite Being in New York, Harper Will Shun UN Podium Again." *National Post*, 13 September. http://news.nationalpost.com/2013/09/20/despite-being-in-new-york-harper-will-shun-un-podium-again.

Blanchard, Dallas. 1994. *The Anti-Abortion Movement and the Rise of the Religious Right*. New York: Twayne Publishers.

Boesveld, Sarah. 2011. "P.E.I. to 'Stay with Status Quo' on Abortions." *National Post*, 23 December. http://news.nationalpost.com/news/canada/p-e-i-to-stay-with-status-quo-on-abortions.

Bordo, Susan. 1993. *Unbearable Weight: Feminism, Western Culture, and the Body*. Berkeley: University of California Press.

Boucher, Joanne. 2004. "The Politics of Abortion and the Commodification of the Fetus." *Studies in Political Economy* 73 (Spring/Summer): 69–88.

Bowen, Kurt. 2004. *Christians in a Secular World: The Canadian Experience*. Montreal: McGill-Queen's University Press.

Brodie, Janine. 2008. "We Are All Equal Now: Contemporary Gender Politics in Canada." *Feminist Theory* 9(2): 145–64. http://dx.doi.org/10.1177/1464700108090408.

Brodie, Janine, Shelley A.M. Gavigan, and Jane Jenson. 1992. *The Politics of Abortion*. Toronto: Oxford University Press.

Brown, Andrew (producer), Evan Grae Davis (director). 2012. *It's a Girl* (documentary). Shadowline Films.

Brown, Wendy. 2006. "American Nightmare: Neoliberalism, Neoconservatism, and De-democratization." *Political Theory* 34(6): 690–714. http://dx.doi.org/10.1177/0090591706293016.

Brownmiller, Susan. 1975. *Against Our Will: Men, Women, and Rape*. New York: Fawcett Books.

Bruinooge, Rod. 2010a. "Roxanne's Law." http://www.roxanneslaw.ca/QuestionsandAnswers.html.

Bruinooge, Rod. 2010b. "Roxanne's Story." http://www.roxanneslaw.ca/Roxanne'sStory.html.

Butler, Judith. 2004. *Undoing Gender*. New York: Routledge.

Calgary 40 Days for Life. 2013. *Facebook page*, 11 October. https://www.facebook.com/257887950923999/photos/a.258739754172152.62087.257887950923999/604484136264377/?type=1&theater.

Calgary 40 Days for Life. n.d. *Facebook page*. https://www.facebook.com/pages/Calgary-40-Days-for-Life/257887950923999.

Canada. 1982. *Constitution Act, 1982*. http://laws-lois.justice.gc.ca/eng/Const/page-15.html. May 11, 2013.

Canada. 1998. *Abortion: Constitutional and Legal Developments*. Law and Government Division. http://publications.gc.ca/Collection-R/LoPBdP/CIR/8910-e.htm.

Canada. House of Commons. 2006. *Debates*, 29 May.

Canada. House of Commons. 2008a. *Debates*, 27 February.

Canada. House of Commons. 2008b. *Debates*, 3 March.

Canada. House of Commons. 2008c. *Debates*, 8 March.

Cassidy, Keith. 1996. "The Right to Life Movement." In *The Politics of Abortion and Birth Control in Historical Perspective*. Edited by Donald Critchlow. University Park, PA: Penn State University Press.

CBC News. 2005. "Tories Promise New Childcare Allowance." 5 December. http://www.cbc.ca/news/canada/tories-promise-new-child-care-allowance-1.525608.

CBC News. 2009a. "Abortion Rights: Significant Moments in Canadian History." 13 January. http://www.cbc.ca/news/canada/story/2009/01/13/f-abortion-timeline.html.

CBC News. 2009b. "Court Hears Appeal in Morgentaler's Fight with N.B. Government." 13 January. http://www.cbc.ca/news/canada/new-brunswick/story/2009/01/13/nb-morgentaler-case.html.

CBC News. 2010. "No Abortion in Canada's G8 Maternal Health Plan." 26 April. http://www.cbc.ca/news/politics/no-abortion-in-canada-s-g8-maternal-health-plan-1.877257.

CBC News. 2011a. "Death Penalty Not on Agenda." 18 January. http://www.cbc.ca/politics/story/2011/01/18/harper-mansbridge-interview-tues.html#ixzz1Bu5SbDCu.

CBC News. 2011b. "Government Apathetic on Abortion, MP Brad Trost Says." 28 September. http://www.cbc.ca/news/politics/story/2011/09/28/pol-trost-reaction-planned-parenthood.html.

CBC News. 2011c. "Harper Says He Won't Reopen the Abortion Debate." 21 April. http://www.cbc.ca/news/politics/canadavotes2011/story/2011/04/21/cv-election-parenthood-042111.html.

CBC News. 2012. "Anti-Abortion Protestors March on Legislature." 10 May. http://www.cbc.ca/news/canada/anti-abortion-protesters-march-on-legislature-1.1244959.

CBC News. 2013a. "Morgentaler's Death Puts N.B. Abortion Lawsuit in Limbo." 30 May. http://www.cbc.ca/news/canada/new-brunswick/morgentaler-s-death-puts-n-b-abortion-lawsuit-in-limbo-1.1369360.

CBC News. 2013b. "P.E.I. Abortion Policy Needs Clarity, Says Group: Group Wants Resolution Stating 'Life Begins at Conception Rescinded.'" 28 January. http://www.cbc.ca/news/canada/prince-edward-island/p-e-i-abortion-policy-needs-clarity-says-group-1.1413174.

CBC News. 2014. "Abortion Service on PEI Would Have Saved Money." 20 October. http://www.cbc.ca/news/canada/prince-edward-island/abortion-service-on-p-e-i-would-have-saved-money-report-1.2803587.

CBC News. 2015. "New Health Centre Opening in Former Morgentaler Clinic." 16 January. http://www.cbc.ca/news/canada/new-brunswick/new-health-centre-opening-in-former-morgentaler-clinic-1.2912283.

CBC Radio. The Current. 2013. "Changing the Language in the Anti-abortion Crusade." 19 April. http://www.cbc.ca/thecurrent/episode/2013/04/19/changing-language-in-the-anti-abortion-crusade/.

CCBR. 2007. "Persecution from Within." http://www.unmaskingchoice.ca/training/classroom/graphic/persecution.

CCBR. 2009. "CCBR: Making Abortion Unthinkable." February/March. http://www.unmaskingchoice.ca/sites/default/files/newsletters/ccbr_2009_february-march.pdf.

CCBR. 2011a. "EndtheKilling: Making Abortion History." http://www.unmaskingchoice.ca/sites/default/files/endthekilling_explained_5.pdf.

CCBR. 2011b. "Social Reform: Part 1 – Canada's Suffragettes." http://www.unmaskingchoice.ca/tag/nellie-mcclung.

CCBR. 2013a. "A Warning to Pro-Lifers." http://www.unmaskingchoice.ca/ sites/default/files/publications/publications_a_warning_to_pro-lifers.pdf.

CCBR. 2013b. "'Choice' Chain." http://www.unmaskingchoice.ca/projects/ choicechain.

CCBR. 2013c. "Do We Need a Law" (podcast). http://www.unmaskingchoice. ca/sites/default/files/etk_podcast_12_-_do_we_need_a_law.mp3.

CCBR. 2013d. "EndtheKilling Postcards." http://www.unmaskingchoice.ca/ endthekilling/postcards.

CCBR. 2013e. "Genocide Awareness Project." http://www.unmaskingchoice. ca/projects/gap.

CCBR. 2013f. "Lesson 12: Challenges Facing the Pro-Life Movement." http:// www.unmaskingchoice.ca/book/export/html/884.

CCBR. 2013g. "Media Coverage." http://www.unmaskingchoice.ca/about/ media.

CCBR. 2013h. "Reforming Our Movement, Reforming Our Culture: How Can Canadian Pro-Lifers Make Abortion Unthinkable in the 21st Century." http://www.unmaskingchoice.ca/sites/default/files/publications/ reforming_our_movement_reforming_our_culture.pdf.

CCBR. 2013i. "Schedule." http://www.unmaskingchoice.ca/about/ schedule.

CCBR. 2013j. "The New Abortion Caravan." http://www.unmaskingchoice. ca/caravan.

CCBR. n.d. "Contest of Wills." http://www.unmaskingchoice.ca/sites/ default/files/publications/publications_the_contest_of_wills.pdf.

Center for Bio-ethical Reform. n.d.-a. "Director Profiles." http://www. abortionno.org/about-cbr/director-profiles/.

Center for Bio-ethical Reform. n.d.-b. "Matthew 28:20." http://www. abortionno.org/matthew-2820/.

Chamberlain, Geoffrey. 2006. "British Maternal Mortality in the 19th and Early 20th Centuries." *Journal of the Royal Society of Medicine* 99(11): 559–63. http://dx.doi.org/10.1258/jrsm.99.11.559.

Chamberlin, Pam. 2006. "Politicized Science: How Anti-Abortion Myths Feed the Christian Right Agenda." *Public Eye* (Summer). http://www.publiceye. org/magazine/v20n2/chamberlain_politicized_science.html.

Charles, Vignetta, Chelsea B. Polis, Srinivas K. Sridhara, and Robert W. Blum. 2008. "Abortion and Long-Term Mental Health Outcomes: A Systematic Review of the Evidence." *Contraception* 78(6): 436–50. http://dx.doi. org/10.1016/j.contraception.2008.07.005.

Cicero. 2001. *Cicero: On Moral Ends*. Edited by Julia Annas. Cambridge: Cambridge University Press.

CLC. 2009a. "Defund Abortion Campaign." http://www.
    campaignlifecoalition.com/index.php?p=Defund&lookUp=true.

CLC. 2009b. "Pastors Corner." http://www.campaignlifecoalition.comfindex.
    php?p=Pastors_Corner.

CLC. 2013a. "40 Days for Life." http://www.campaignlifecoalition.com/
    index.php?p=40_Days_For_Life.

CLC. 2013b. "March for Life." http://www.campaignlifecoalition.com/index.
    php?p=March_For_Life.

CLC. n.d.-a. "Chronology of Laws." http://www.campaignlifecoalition.com/
    index.php?p=Chronology_of_Laws.

CLC. n.d.-b. "Harm to Women." http://www.campaignlifecoalition.com/
    index.php?p=Harm_to_Women.

Columbia University. Mailman School of Public Health. 2013. "Section IV:
    Abortion" (reproductive health module). http://www.columbia.edu/itc/
    hs/pubhealth/modules/reproductiveHealth/abortion.html.

Concerned Women for America. n.d. "About Us." http://www.cwfa.org/
    about/.

Connolly, William. 1993. *The Terms of Political Discourse*. Oxford: Blackwell.

Connolly, William. 2002. *Neuropolitics: Thinking, Culture, Speed*. Minneapolis:
    University of Minnesota Press.

Connolly, William. 2008. *Capitalism and Christianity, American Style*. Durham,
    NC: Duke University Press. http://dx.doi.org/10.1215/9780822381235.

Craine, Patrick. 2012. "Pro-life MP Releases His Own Expose on CTV
    Pregnancy Centre 'investigation.'" *LifeSiteNews*. 1 February. http://www.
    lifesitenews.com/news/pro-life-mp-releases-his-own-expose-on-ctv-
    pregnancy-centre-investigation.

Critchlow, Donald. 1995. *Abortion and Birth Control*. University Park, PA: Penn
    State University Press.

Cross, Pamela. 2009. *Abortion in Canada: Legal but not Accessible*. A
    YWCA discussion paper. http://www.ywcatoronto.org/upload/
    advocacy-2009%20policy%20abortion%20in%20Canada.pdf.

CTV News. 2014. "Group Surpasses Fundraising Goal." 5 August. http://
    atlantic.ctvnews.ca/group-surpasses-fundraising-goal-in-attempt-to-save-
    morgentaler-clinic-1.1947270.

Cuneo, Michael. 1989. *Catholics against the Church: Anti-abortion Protest in
    Toronto*. Toronto: University of Toronto Press.

Condit, Celeste. 1990. *Decoding Abortion Rhetoric: Communicating Social Change*.
    Chicago: University of Illinois Press.

Danforth, Jessica. 2010. "Reproductive Justice – For Real, for Me, for Now."
    http://www.nativeyouthsexualhealth.com/reproductivejustice.pdf.

Dailard, Cynthia. 2004. "Courts Strike 'Partial-Birth' Abortion Ban: Decisions Presage Future Debates." *Guttmacher Report on Public Policy* 7(4): 1–4.

DeGagne, Alexa. 2012. "Queer Bedfellows of Proposition 8: Adopting Social Conservative and Neoliberal Political Rationalities in California's Same-Sex Marriage Fight." *Studies in Social Justice* 7(1): 107–24.

Delacourt, Susan. 2013. *Shopping for Votes: How Politicians Choose Us and We Choose Them*. Toronto: Douglas & McIntyre.

deValk, Alfonse. 1974. *Morality and Law in Canadian Politics: The Abortion Controversy*. Montreal: Palm Publishers.

deVeber Institute for Bioethics and Social Research. 2004, "Women's Health after Abortion: The Medical and Psychological Evidence." 27 January. http://www.deveber.org/text/whealth.html.

Dobbs, Frank. 2010. "Interview: Preston Manning." *UCObserver*. http://www.ucobserver.org/faith/2010/10/preston_manning.

Dubinsky, Karen. 1985. *Lament for a "Patriarchy Lost"?* Feminist Perspectives, no. 1. Ottawa: Canadian Research Institute for the Advancement of Women.

Dworkin, Andrea. 1983. *Right-Wing Women*. New York: Perigee Books.

Dworkin, Ronald. 1986. *Law's Empire*. Cambridge: Harvard University Press.

Dworkin, Ronald. 1996. *Freedom's Law*. Cambridge: Harvard Uuniversity Press.

Eagle Forum. n.d. "Our Mission." http://www.eagleforum.org/misc/descript.html.

Eckholm, Erik. 2011, "Across Country, Lawmakers Push Abortion Curbs." *New York Times*, 21 January. http://www.nytimes.com/2011/01/22/us/politics/22abortion.html?_r=0.

EFC. 2013a. "Board Members." http://www.evangelicalfellowship.ca/board.

EFC. 2013b. "Leadership Team." http://www.evangelicalfellowship.ca/LeadershipTeam.

Ehrenreich, Nancy, ed. 2008. *The Reproductive Rights Reader: Law, Medicine, and the Construction of Motherhood*. New York: New York University Press.

Erdman, Joanna. 2006. "In the Back Alleys of Health Care: Abortion, Equality and Community in Canada." *Emory Law Journal* 56: 1093–156.

Ewen, Stuart. 1996. *PR: A Social History of Spin*. New York: Basic Books.

Fainman, Jack, and Roland Penner. 2011. "A Shot in the Dark." *Free Press* (Winnipeg). 12 November. http://www.winnipegfreepress.com/arts-and-life/entertainment/books/A-shot-in-the-dark-133741193.html.

Fairclough, Norman. 2001. *Language and Power*. New York: Longman.

Faludi, Susan. 1991. *Backlash: The Undeclared War against Women*. New York: Anchor Books.

Farney, James. 2012. *Social Conservatives and Party Politics in Canada and the United States*. Toronto: University of Toronto Press.

Feminists for Life of America. 2013. "Share the Good News: Better than Abortion." http://www.feministsforlife.org/ads.

Ferguson, Michaele. 2010. "Choice Feminism and the Fear of Politics." *Perspectives on Politics* 8(1): 247–53. http://dx.doi.org/10.1017/S1537592709992830.

Fernandez, Manny. 2014. "Abortion Law Pushes Texas Clinics to Close Doors." *New York Times*, 6 March. http://www.nytimes.com/2014/03/07/us/citing-new-texas-rules-abortion-provider-is-shutting-last-clinics-in-2-regions.html.

Ferree, Myra, William Gamson, Jurgen Gerhards, and Dieter Rucht. 2002. *Shaping Abortion Discourse: Democracy and the Public Sphere in Germany and the United States.* New York: Cambridge University Press.

Filipovic, Jill. 2013. "How the Right Plays with Murder: The Antiabortion Movement's Cycle of Violence." *Salon*, 10 September. http://www.salon.com/2013/09/10/how_the_right_plays_with_murder_the_anti_abortion_movements_cycle_of_violence.

Finkelman, Paul, and Melvin Urofsky. 2003. *Landmark Decisions of the United States Supreme Court.* Washington, DC: CQ Press.

Fiske, John. 1982. *Introduction to Communication Studies.* New York: Routledge. http://dx.doi.org/10.4324/9780203323212.

Flanagan, Tom. 2012. "Landing the Big One: Political Science in the Pursuit of Power." WSSR Graduate Student Workshop, Concordia University, Montreal QC. 7 May.

Flyvbjerg, Bent. 2001. *Making Social Science Matter: Why Social Inquiry Fails and How It Can Succeed Again.* Cambridge: Cambridge University Press. http://dx.doi.org/10.1017/CBO9780511810503.

Forum Research. 2012. "Six-in-Ten Believe Abortion Should Be Legal in all Circumstances." 29 October. https://www.forumresearch.com/forms/News%20Archives/News%20Releases/15628_Canada-wide_-_Abortion_Issues_%28Forum_Research%29_%2820121029%29.pdf.

Foucault, Michel. 1972. *The Archeology of Knowledge.* New York: Vintage Books.

Fox News. 2004. "Senate Passes Unborn Victim Bill." 26 March. http://www.foxnews.com/story/2004/03/26/senate-passes-unborn-victims-bill/.

Francome, Colin. 2004. *Abortion in the USA and the UK.* Aldershot, UK: Ashgate Publishing.

Friedan, Betty. 1963. *The Feminine Mystique.* New York: W.W. Norton and Company.

Friedman, Thomas L. 2012. "Why I Am Pro-life." *New York Times*, 29 October. http://www.nytimes.com/2012/10/28/opinion/sunday/friedman-why-i-am-pro-life.html.

Frum, David, and Richard Perle. 2004. *An End to Evil: How to Win the War on Terror*. New York: Random House Digital.

Fuszara, Malgorzata. 1991. "Legal Regulation of Abortion in Poland." *Signs* 17(1): 117–28. http://dx.doi.org/10.1086/494716.

Gagnon, Lysiane. 2010. "A Distinctly Quebec View on Abortion." *Globe and Mail*, 31 May. http://www.theglobeandmail.com/commentary/a-distinctly-quebec-view-on-abortion/article4321007.

Gallup. 2011. "Americans Still Split Along 'Pro-choice,' 'Pro-life' Lines." 23 May. http://www.gallup.com/poll/147734/americans-split-along-pro-choice-pro-life-lines.aspx.

Gallup. n.d. "Abortion." http://www.gallup.com/poll/1576/abortion.aspx.

Gee, Graham. 2007. "Regulating Abortion in the United States after Gonzales v Carhart." *Modern Law Review* 70(6): 979–92. http://dx.doi.org/10.1111/j.1468-2230.2007.00673.x.

Gerson, Jen. 2015. "With Social Conservatism Seemingly Spent as a Political Force, Its Adherents Forced to Rethink Their Strategy." *National Post*, 2 January.

Gilmartin, Mary, and Allen White. 2011. "Interrogating Medical Tourism: Ireland, Abortion and Mobility Rights." *Signs* 36(2): 275–80. http://dx.doi.org/10.1086/655907.

Ginsburg, Faye. 1989. *Contested Lives: The Abortion Debate in and American Community*. Los Angeles: University of California Press.

Gitlin, Todd. 1980. *The Whole World Is Watching: Mass Media in the Making and Unmaking of the New Left*. Berkeley: University of California Press.

Gladwell, Malcolm. 2007. *Blink: The Power of Thinking without Thinking*. New York: Back Bay Books.

Global News. 2013. "Young Pro-lifers Shun Harper as Rally Moves to Ottawa." 9 March. http://globalnews.ca/news/549204/young-pro-lifers-shun-harper-as-rally-comes-to-ottawa/.

Goffman, Erving. 1974. *Frame Analysis: An Essay on the Organization of Experience*. Cambridge: Harvard University Press.

Gold, Rachel Benson, and Elizabeth Nash. 2012. "Troubling Trend: More States Hostile to Abortion Rights as Middle Ground Shrinks." *Guttmacher Policy Review* 15(1): 14–19. http://www.guttmacher.org/pubs/gpr/15/1/gpr150114.html.

Gold, Rachel Benson, and Elizabeth Nash. 2013. "TRAP Laws Gain Political Traction While Abortion Clinics – and the Women They Serve – Pay the Price." *Guttmacher Policy Review* 16(2). http://www.guttmacher.org/pubs/gpr/16/2/gpr160207.html.

Golob, Alissa. Twitter post. 29 March 2013. https://twitter.com/alissagolob.

Golob, Alissa. Twitter post. 13 June 2013. https://twitter.com/alissagolob.

Golob, Alissa. Twitter post. 19 August 2013. https://twitter.com/alissagolob/
status/369677567554367489/photo/1.

Gonin, Audrey, Véronique Pronovost, and Mélissa Blais. 2014. "Enjeux éthiques
de l'intervention auprès de femmes vivant une grossesse imprévue au
Québec." *Fédération du Québec pour le planning des naissances.* Montreal. www.
fqpn.qc.ca/?attachment_id=2478.

Gordon, Kelly, Paul Saurette, and Kathryn Trevenen. 2012. "From Jezebel to
Snow White: The Shifting Representations of Women in Canadian Anti-
abortion Discourse." Paper presented to a meeting of the Canadian Political
Science Association, Edmonton, AB.

Gramsci, Antonio. 1971. *Selections from the Prison Notebooks.* Trans. G. Smith
and Q. Hoard. New York: International Publishers.

Gray, Stephanie. 2011. "Abortion: The Great Debate Dialoguing Persuasively."
Paper presented to the Pro-Life World Congress, Costa Rica. http://www.
unmaskingchoice.ca/sites/default/files/publications/costa_rica_pro_life_
world_congress.pdf.

Grimes, Andrea. 2013. "Texas Lawmakers Propose TRAP Bill That Could
Eliminate All but Five Providers in State." *RH Reality Check,* 13 February.
http://rhrealitycheck.org/article/2013/02/13/texas-lawmakers-propose-
trap-bill-that-could-eliminate-all-but-five-providers-in-state/.

Groen, Danielle. 2015. "When It Comes to Abortion, Do Medical Schools Need
to Smarten Up?" *Chateleine,* 21 January. http://www.chatelaine.com/living/
features-living/abortion-education-canada-medical-schools-smarten-up/.

Grubb, Andrew. 1990. "Abortion Law: An English Perspective." *Law, Medicine
& Health Care* 146(18): 649–73.

Guion, Lisa, David Diehl, and Debra McDonald. 2002. *Triangulation:
Establishing the Validity of Qualitative Studies.* Gainesville: Florida
Department of Family, Youth, and Community Sciences.

Guttmacher Institute. 2000. "Rights without Access: Revisiting Public Funding
of Abortion for Poor Women." *Gutttmacher Report on Public Policy* 3(2).
www.guttmacher.org/pubs/tgr/03/2/gr030208.html.

Guttmacher Institute. 2013a. "Laws Affecting Reproductive Health and
Rights: 2012 State Policy Review." http://www.guttmacher.org/
statecenter/updates/2012/statetrends42012.html.

Guttmacher Institute. 2013b. "Overview of Abortion Laws." 1 October. http://
www.guttmacher.org/statecenter/spibs/spib_OAL.pdf.

Guttmacher Institute. 2013c. "State Funding of Abortion Under Medicaid." 1
October. http://www.guttmacher.org/statecenter/spibs/spib_SFAM.pdf.

Guttmacher Institute. 2013d. "State-Level Assault on Abortion Rights
Continues in First Half of 2013." 8 July. http://www.guttmacher.org/
media/inthenews/2013/07/08.

Guttmacher Institute. 2015. "State Policies in Brief as of January 1, 2015: Overview of Abortion Laws." 1 January. http://www.guttmacher.org/statecenter/spibs/spib_OAL.pdf.

Habermas, Jurgen, and William Rehg. 1998. *Between Facts and Norms: Contributions to a Discourse Theory of Law and Demoncracy.* Cambridge: MIT Press.

Halfmann, Drew. 2011. *Doctors and Demonstrators: How Political Institutions Shape Abortion Law in the United States, Britain, and Canada.* Chicago: University of Chicago Press. http://dx.doi.org/10.7208/chicago/9780226313443.001.0001.

Hall, Stuart. 1997. *Representation: Cultural Representations and Signifying Practices.* London: Sage Publications.

Haraway, Donna. 1998. "Situated Knowledges: The Science Question in Feminism and the Privilege of Partial Perspective." *Feminist Studies* 14(3): 575–99.

Harding, Sandra. 1986. *The Science Question in Feminism.* Ithaca, NY: Cornell University Press.

Hartsock, Nancy. 1998. *The Feminist Standpoint Revisited and Other Essays.* Boulder, CO: Westview Press.

Hasham, Alyshah. 2012. "Catholic Teachers under Fire for Promoting Pro-life Motion to Students." *Toronto Star*, 23 April. http://www.thestar.com/news/gta/2012/04/23/catholic_teachers_under_fire_for_promoting_prolife_motion_to_students.html.

Haussman, Melissa. 2001. "Of Rights and Power: Canadian Federal Abortion Policy, 1969–1991." In *Women's Movements and the Democratic State.* Edited by D. Stetson. New York: Oxford University Press. http://dx.doi.org/10.1093/0199242666.003.0004.

Haussman, Melissa. 2005. *Abortion Politics in North America.* Boulder, CO: Lynne Rienner Publishers.

Hassman, Melissa. 2013. *Reproductive Rights and the State: Getting the Birth Control, RU-486, Morning-After Pills and the Gardasil Vaccine to the US Market.* Santa Barbara, CA: Praeger.

Hayer, Barbara. 1979. "Abortion." *Signs* 5(2): 307–23. http://dx.doi.org/10.1086/493710.

Health Canada. 2012. "First Nation Health Status Report." http://publications.gc.ca/collections/collection_2013/sc-hc/H26-4-2012-eng.pdf.

Health PEI. 2014. "About Us." http://www.healthpei.ca/aboutus.

Herman, Didi. 1994. "The Christian Right and the Politics of Morality in Canada." *Parliamentary Affair* 47(2): 268–79.

Herring, Mark. 2003. *The Pro-Life/Choice Debate.* Westport, CT: Greenwood Press.

Hindell, K., and M. Simms. 1968. "How the Abortion Lobby Worked." *Political Quarterly* 39(3): 269–82. http://dx.doi.org/10.1111/j.1467-923X.1968. tb00267.x.

Hirschmann, Nancy. 2010. "Choosing Betrayal." *Perspectives on Politics* 8(1): 271–78. http://dx.doi.org/10.1017/S1537592709992866.

Hoggan, James. 2009. *Climate Cover-up: The Crusade to Deny Global Warming.* Vancouver: Greystone Books.

Holmes, Melissa, Heidi Resnick, Dean Kilpatrick, and Connie Best. 1996. "Rape-Related Pregnancy: Estimates and Descriptive Characteristics from a National Sample of Women." *American Journal of Obstetrics and Gynecology* 175(2): 320–25. http://dx.doi.org/10.1016/S0002-9378(96)70141-2.

hooks, bell. 1981. *Ain't I a Woman: Black Women and Feminism.* Boston: South End Press.

Hopkins, N., S. Reicher, and J. Saleem. 1996. "Constructing Women's Psychological Health in Anti-abortion Rhetoric." *Sociological Review* 44(3): 539–64.

Hudes, Sammy., 2014. "Abortion Group Outraged after PEI Premier Dismisses Plan to Bring in Doctors from Out of province." *National Post*, 27 May. http://news.nationalpost.com/2014/05/27/abortion-group-outraged-after-p-e-i-premier-dismisses-plan-to-bring-in-doctors-from-out-of-province/.

Hudson, Natalie. 2004. "The Contraception Misconception." *LifeSiteNews.* http://www.lifesitenews.com/ldn/2004_docs/contraceptionmisconception.htm.

Huffington Post. 2012. "Rick Santorum on Opposition to Abortion in Cases of Rape: Make the Best Out of a Bad Situation." 23 January. http://www.huffingtonpost.com/2012/01/23/rick-santorum-abortion-rape_n_1224624.html.

Huffington Post Canada. 2012. "Mark Warawa's Motion 408 Aimed at Condemning Sex-Selection Abortion." 27 September. http://www.huffingtonpost.ca/2012/09/27/mark-warawa-motion-408-abortion_n_1920769.html.

Huffington Post Canada. 2013. "Pap Tests Ontario: Women Protest Changes to Funding for Cancer Test." 29 February. http://www.huffingtonpost.ca/2013/02/28/pap-tests-ontario_n_2783738.html.

Interim. n.d. "Pro-life Parliamentarians and Their Bills and Motions." http://www.theinterim.com/wp-content/uploads/2011/05/ProlifeBillsandmotions.pdf.

Jaco, Charles. 2012. "Jaco Report: Full Interview with Todd Akin." *Fox 2 Now. KTVI.* 19 August. http://fox2now.com/2012/08/19/the-jaco-report-august-19-2012/.

Jalsevac, John. 2009. "Outspoken MP Slams Canada's 'Abortion Regime.'"
    LifeSiteNews. 27 November. http://www.lifesitenews.com/news/archive//
    ldn/2009/nov/09112704.
Jelen, Ted, and Marthe Chandler, eds. 1994. *Abortion Politics in the United States
    and Canada.* Westport, CT: Praeger.
Jelen, Ted, and Clyde Wilcox. 2003. "Causes and Consequences
    of Public Attitudes toward Abortion: A Review and Research
    Agenda." *Political Research Quarterly* 56(4): 489–500. http://dx.doi.
    org/10.1177/106591290305600410.
Johnson, Luke. 2012. "Mitt Romney: Todd Aikin Rape Comment Are 'Insulting,
    Inexcusable.'" *Huffington Post.* 20 October. http://www.huffingtonpost.
    com/2012/08/20/mitt-romney-rape-pregnant_n_1810811.html.
Johnstone, Rachael. 2010. "Framing Reproductive Rights: The Politics of
    Abortion Access and Citizenship in a Post-Morgentaler Era." Paper
    presented at a meeting of the Canadian Political Science Association.
Joyce, Theodore, Stanley Henshaw, Amanda Dennis, Lawrence Finer, and Kelly
    Blanchard. 2009. "The Impact of State Mandatory Counseling and Waiting
    Period Laws on Abortion: A Literature Review." *Guttmacher Institute.* http://
    dspace.cigilibrary.org/jspui/bitstream/123456789/24036/1/Impact%20
    of%20state%20mandatory%20counseling%20and%20waiting%20period%20
    laws%20on%20abortion.pdf?1.
Kahneman, Daniel. 2011. *Thinking, Fast and Slow.* Toronto: Farrar, Straus and
    Giroux.
Kaposy, Chris. 2010. "Improving Abortion Access in Canada." *Health Care
    Analysis* 18(1): 17–34. http://dx.doi.org/10.1007/s10728-008-0101-0.
Kay, Barbara. 2009. "Women Deserve Better Than Abortion." *National Post,*
    4 February. http://oped.ca/National-Post/barbara-kay-women-deserve-
    better-than-abortion.
Kellough, Gail. 1996. *Aborting Law: An Exploration of the Politics of Motherhood
    and Medicine.* Toronto: University of Toronto Press.
Kennedy, Mark. 2004. "New Poll Shows Most Canadian Support Abortion –
    with Some Restrictions." *National Post.* 7 April. http://news.nationalpost.
    com/2012/07/04/new-poll-shows-most-canadians-support-abortion-with-
    some-restrictions.
Keown, John. 2002. *Abortion, Doctors and the Law: Some Aspects of the Legal
    Regulation of Abortion in England from 1803 to 1982.* Cambridge: Cambridge
    University Press.
King, Leslie, and Gina Husting. 2003. "Anti-Abortion Activism in the US
    and France: Comparing Opportunity Environment of Rescue Tactics."
    Mobilization: An International Quarterly 8(3): 297–312.

Kirkpatrick, Jennet. 2010. "Introduction: Selling Out? Solidarity and Choice in the American Feminist Movement." Symposium. *Perspectives on Politics* 8(1): 241–45. http://dx.doi.org/10.1017/S1537592709992829.

Knights of Columbus. 2013. "Canadian March for Life." 10 May. http://www.kofc.org/en/news/releases/detail/canada_mfl2013.html.

Komarnicki, Jamie. 2013. "Low-Cost Birth Control Available Again at Clinics." *Calgary Herald*, 7 May. http://www.calgaryherald.com/health/cost+birth+control+available+again+clinics/8345684/story.html.

Kuhn, Thomas S. 1962. *The Structure of Scientific Revolutions*. Chicago: University of Chicago Press.

Lake, Randall. 1986. "The Metaethical Framework of Anti-Abortion Rhetoric." *Signs* 11(3): 478–99. http://dx.doi.org/10.1086/494252.

Lakoff, George. 1987. *Women, Fire, and Dangerous Things: What Categories Reveal about the Mind*. Chicago: University of Chicago Press. http://dx.doi.org/10.7208/chicago/9780226471013.001.0001.

Lakoff, George. 1996. *Moral Politics: How Liberals and Conservatives Think*. Chicago: University of Chicago Press.

Lakoff, George. 2009. *The Political Mind: A Cognitive Scientist's Guide to Your Brain and Its Politics*. New York: Penguin Books.

Lakoff, George, and Mark Johnson. 2003. *Metaphors We Live By*. Chicago: University of Chicago Press. http://dx.doi.org/10.7208/chicago/9780226470993.001.0001.

LC. 2002. "Abortion May Cause Increased Mortality." 28 August. http://www.lifecanada.org/html/abortion/postabortion/mortality.htm.

LC. 2003. "15 Years of Choice?" 27 January. http://www.lifecanada.org/html/abortion/topical/fifteen_years.htm.

LC. 2010a. "Our Mission." http://www.lifecanada.org/who-we-are/mission.

LC. 2010b. "Time for a Fresh Look at the Medical and Psychological Risks of Abortion on Women." http://www.lifecanada.org/html/abortion/postabortion/risks.html.

LC. 2012. "Who We Are." http://www.lifecanada.org/who-we-are.

Leavy, Zad, and Jerome Kummer. 1962. "Criminal Abortion, Human Hardship and Unyielding Laws." *Southern California Law Review* 35: 123–218.

Lewis, Charles. 2010. "Outspoken Evangelical Isn't Afraid to Get into Scraps." *National Post*, 5 November. http://life.nationalpost.com/2010/11/05/outspoken-evangelical-isnt-afraid-to-get-into-scraps/.

Lewis, Charles. 2011. "Serial Abortion Clinic Protester, Linda Gibbdon, Back in Jail." *National Post*, 9 August. http://life.nationalpost.com/2011/08/09/serial-abortion-clinic-protester-linda-gibbons-back-in-jail.

Levy, Ariel. 2005. *Female Chauvinist Pigs: Women and the Rise of Raunch Culture.* New York: Free Press.

LifeSiteNews. 2003."Canadian March for Life Draws 3,500 – Majority Youth." 15 May. http://www.lifesitenews.com/news/archive/ldn/2003/may/03051501.

LifeSiteNews. 2012. "Canadian Auto Workers Union Battles 'New Abortion Caravan' Pro-life Campaign." 11 June. http://www.lifesitenews.com/news/canadian-auto-workers-union-battles-new-abortion-caravan-pro-life-campaign/.

Lorde, Audre. 2003. "The Master's Tools Will Never Dismantle the Master's House." In *Feminist Postcolonial Theory: A Reader.* Edited by R. Lewis and S. Miller. New York: Routledge.

Luluquisin, Clarissa. 2013a. Twitter post, 29 September, 7:13am. http://twitter.com/clarlulu.

Luluquisin, Clarissa. 2013b. Twitter post, 29 September, 09:10am. http://twitter.com/clarlulu.

Luna, Zakiya T. 2009. "From Rights to Justice: Women of Color Changing the Face of US Reproductive Rights Organizing." *Societies without Borders* (4): 343–65. http://dx.doi.org/10.1163/187188609X12492771031618.

Luna, Zakiya T. 2010. "Marching toward Reproductive Justice: Coalitional (Re) Framing of the March for Women's Lives." *Sociological Inquiry* 80(4): 554–78. http://dx.doi.org/10.1111/j.1475-682X.2010.00349.x.

Luna, Zakiya T. 2011. "'The Phrase of the Day': Examining Contexts and Co-optation of Reproductive Justice Activism in the Women's Movement." *Research in Social Movements, Conflicts and Change* 32: 219–46. http://dx.doi.org/10.1108/S0163-786X(2011)0000032013.

Luntz, Frank. 2007. *Words That Work: It's Not What You Say, It's What People Hear.* New York: Hyperion Books.

MacKinnon, Catharine. 1987. *Feminism Unmodified: Discourses on Life and Law.* Cambridge: Harvard University Press.

MacKinnon, Catharine. 1989. *Toward a Feminist Theory of the State.* Cambridge: Harvard University Press.

MacKinnon, Catharine. 1996. "Not a Moral Issue." In *Application of Feminist Legal Theory to Women's Lives: Sex, Violence, Work and Reproduction.* Edited by K. Weisberg. Philadelphia: Temple University Press.

Major, Brenda, Mark Appelbaum, Linda Beckman, Mary Ann Dutton, Nancy Felipe Russo, and Carolyn West. 2009. "Abortion and Mental Health: Evaluating the Evidence." *American Psychologist* 64(9): 863–90. http://dx.doi.org/10.1037/a0017497.

Malloy, Jonathan. 2013. "The Relationship between the Conservative Party of Canada and Evangelicals and Social Conservatives." In *Conservatism in*

Canada. Edited by James Farney and David Rayside. Toronto: University of Toronto Press, 184–208.

Manning, Preston. 2009. "Navigating the Faith/Political Interface." *C2C Journal*, 19 June. http://c2cjournal.ca/2009/06/navigating-the-faithpolitical-interface/.

Marmon, Sharon, and Howard Palley. 1986. "The Decade after *Roe versus Wade*: Ideology, Political Cleavage, and the Policy Process." *Research in Politics and Society* 2: 181–209.

Marriner, Sunny. 2013. *Bridging Services for Women: Coordinating a Community Response to Violence against Women and Sexual and Reproductive Health*. Ottawa: Planned Parenthood Ottawa, Ottawa Coalition to End Violence against Women, Canadians for Choice, Canadian Federation for Sexual Health. http://www.ppottawa.ca/cms/upload/dir/ppo/Documents/Bridging%20Services%20For%20Women.Final.PubReady.pdf.

Marso, Lorie. 2010. "Feminism's Quest for Common Desires." *Perspectives on Politics* 8(1): 263–69. http://dx.doi.org/10.1017/S1537592709992854.

Martin, Lawrence. 2010. *Harperland*. Toronto: Penguin Canada.

Marx, Karl. 1844. "On the Jewish Question." In *Marx/Engels Collected Works*. Vol. 3. London: Lawrence and Wishart.

Mathie, William. 1986. "Reason, Revelation and Liberal Justice." *Canadian Journal of Political Science* 19 (03): 443–66. http://dx.doi.org/10.1017/S0008423900054512.

McAdam, Doug, Sidney Tarrow, and Charles Tilly. 2001. *Dynamics of Contention*. Cambridge: Cambridge University Press. http://dx.doi.org/10.1017/CBO9780511805431.

McCarthy, John, and Mayer Zald. 1977. "Resource Mobilization and Social Movements: A Partial Theory." *American Journal of Sociology* 82(6): 1212–41. http://dx.doi.org/10.1086/226464.

McDonald, Marci. 2010. *The Armageddon Factor*. Toronto: Random House.

McLaren, Angus. 1990. *Our Own Master Race: Eugenics in Canada, 1885–1945*. Toronto: McClelland and Stewart.

McLaren, Angus, and Arlene Tigar McLaren. 1997. *The Bedroom and the State*. Oxford: Oxford University Press.

McMahon, Tamsin. 2011. "PEI Abortion Ban Challenged by New Pro-Choice Movement." *National Post*, 16 November. http://news.nationalpost.com/2011/11/16/p-e-i-abortion-ban-challenged-by-new-pro-choice-movement.

Mendelsohn, Matthew, and Richard Nadeau. 1997. "The Religious Cleavage and the Media in Canada." *Canadian Journal of Political Science* 30(1): 129–46. http://dx.doi.org/10.1017/S0008423900014967.

Meyer, David, and Suzanne Staggenborg. 1996. "Movements, Countermovements, and the Structure of Political Opportunity." *American Journal of Sociology* 101(6): 1628–60. http://dx.doi. org/10.1086/230869.

Mickleburgh, Rod. 2014. "Garson Romalis Risked His Life to Perform Abortions." *Globe and Mail*, 21 February. http://www.theglobeandmail. com/news/british-columbia/garson-romalis-risked-his-life-to-perform-abortions/article17052093/?page=all.

Mitchinson, Wendy. 1998. "Agency, Diversity, and Constraints: Women and Their Physicians, Canada, 1850–1950." In *The Politics of Women's Health: Exploring Agency and Autonomy.* Edited by S. Sherwin. Philadelphia: Temple University Press.

Mohanty, Chandra. 2003. *Feminism without Borders: Decolonizing Theory, Practicing Solidarity.* Durham, NC: Duke University Press. http://dx.doi. org/10.1215/9780822384649.

Mohr, James C. 1978. *Abortion in America: The Origin and Evolution of National Policy, 1800–1900.* New York: Columbia University Press.

Montopoli, Brian. 2010. "Sarah Palin: I Understand the Temptation to Have an Abortion." *CBSNews*, May. http://www.cbsnews.com/8301-503544_162-20005002-503544.html.

Mooney, Chris. 2004. "Research and Destroy: How the Religious Right Promotes Its Own 'Experts' to Combat Mainstream Science." *Washington Monthly*, October. http://www.washingtonmonthly.com/ features/2004/0410.mooney.html.

Morton, Frederick Lee. 1992. *Morgentaler vs. Borowski.* Toronto: McClelland and Stewart.

Morton, Frederick Lee, and Avril Allen. 2001. "Feminists and the Courts." *Canadian Journal of Political Science* 34: 55–84.

Morton, Frederick Lee, and Rainer Knopff. 2000. *The Charter Revolution and the Court Party.* Toronto: University of Toronto Press.

Muldoon, Maureen. 1991. *The Abortion Debate in the United States and Canada.* New York: Garland Publishing.

NAF. n.d-a. "Access to Abortion in Canada: Abortion Coverage by Region." National Abortion Federation Website. http://www.nafcanada.org/access-region.html.

NAF. n.d-b. "History of Violence." http://prochoice.org/education-and-advocacy/violence/.

NAF. n.d-c. "Public Funding for Abortion: Medicaid and the Hyde Amendment." http://prochoice.org/education-and-advocacy/about-abortion/abortion-facts/.

NARAL. 2015. "'Personhood' Measures: Extreme and Dangerous Attempts to Ban Abortion." 1 January. http://www.prochoiceamerica.org/media/fact-sheets/abortion-personhood.pdf.

National Right to Life Committee. n.d.-a. "About NRLC." http://www.nrlc.org/about/.

National Right to Life Committee. n.d.-b. "Mission Statement." http://www.nrlc.org/about/mission.

NCLN. Twitter post. 28 September 2013a. 19:07. https://twitter.com/NCLN.

NCLN. Twitter post. 28 September 2013b. 19:16. https://twitter.com/NCLN.

NCLN. Twitter post. 28 September 2013c. 19:18. https://twitter.com/NCLN.

NCLN. Twitter post. 28 September 2013d. 19:26. https://twitter.com/NCLN.

NCLN. Twitter post. 29 September 2013a. 09:53. https://twitter.com/NCLN.

NCLN. Twitter post. 29 September 2013b. 09.45. https://twitter.com/NCLN.

NCLN. n.d. "About." http://www.ncln.ca/about.

Newman, Alex. 2011. "Young, Female and Pro-Life." *Faith Today* (May/June): 18–21.

Newman, Alex. 2013. "Why Is It Hard to Talk about Abortion in Canada." *Faith Today* (May/June): 18–22.

Oldfield, Duane M. 1996. *The Right and the Righteous: The Christian Right Confronts the Republican Party.* Lanham, MD: Rowman and Littlefield.

OnTheIssues. 2013a. "Michelle Bachmann on Abortion." 24 June. http://www.ontheissues.org/house/Michele_Bachmann_Abortion.htm.

OnTheIssues. 2013b. "Paul Ryan on Abortion." 25 June. http://www.ontheissues.org/house/Paul_Ryan_Abortion.htm.

Palmer, Beth. 2012. "Choices and Compromises: The Abortion Movement in Canada, 1969–1988." PhD dissertation, York University.

Pan, Z., and G.M. Kosicki. 1993. "Framing Annalysis: An Approach to News Discourse." *Political Communication* 10(1): 55–75. http://dx.doi.org/10.1080/10584609.1993.9962963.

Perrault, Martine, and Linda Cardinal. 1996. "Le droit au choix et le choix du droit: l'expérience de L'Ontario Coalition for Abortion Clinics et the jugement *Morgentaler*." *Canadian Journal of Political Science* 29: 244–67.

Pieklo, Jessica. 2014. "TRAP Laws and the 'Emptying of *Roe*.'" *Reality Check*, 14 April. http://rhrealitycheck.org/article/2014/04/14/trap-laws-emptying-roe/.

Planned Parenthood. 2013. "In Her Shoes." http://www.ppaction.org/site/PageServer?pagename=pp_ppol_notinhershoes#.UaS75-scuHk.

PWPL. 2007. "The Story." http://www.prowomanprolife.org/the-story/.

PWPL. 2008. "The Plan." http://www.prowomanprolife.org/the-plan/.

PWPL. 5 January 2008. "The Question Nobody Is Asking." http://www.prowomanprolife.org/2008/01/05/the-question-nobodys-asking/.

PWPL. 4 February 2008. "Why I'm Prowomanprolife." http://www. prowomanprolife.org/2008/02/04/why-im-prowomanprolife/.

PWPL. 20 February 2008. "Revolution in Reverse." www.prowomanprolife. org/2008/02/20/a-revolution-in-reverse.

PWPL. 23 February 2008a. "How Can It Be Right if It Feels So Wrong?" http://www.prowomanprolife.org/2008/02/23/how-can-it-be-right-if-it-feels-so-wrong/.

PWPL. 23 February 2008b. "The Ultimate Goal." http://www. prowomanprolife.org/2008/02/23/the-ultimate-goal/.

PWPL. 18 March 2008. "A Woman's Right to Choose." http://www. prowomanprolife.org/2008/03/18/a-womans-right-to-choose/.

PWPL. 20 March 2008. "Can We Talk? Honestly I Mean." http://www. prowomanprolife.org/2008/03/10/can-we-talk-honestly-i-mean/.

PWPL. 17 April 2008. "Planned Parenthood – In the Influencing Business." http://www.prowomanprolife.org/2009/04/17/planned-parenthood-in-the-influencing-business/.

PWPL. 6 May 2008. "The Wrong Side of History." http://www. prowomanprolife.org/2008/05/06/the-wrong-side-of-history/.

PWPL. 13 May 2008. "What Fits in Mother Russia." http://www. prowomanprolife.org/2008/05/13/what-fits-in-mother-russia/.

PWPL. 14 May 2008. "They're Playing Politics Again." http://www. prowomanprolife.org/2008/05/14/they%E2%80%99re-playing-politics-again/.

PWPL. 15 May 2008. "This Pro-abortion Culture Brought to You By." http://www.prowomanprolife.org/2008/05/15/this-pro-abortion-culture-is-brought-to-you-by/.

PWPL. 20 May 2008. "A Lesson in Prevention." http://www. prowomanprolife.org/2008/05/20/a-lesson-in-prevention/.

PWPL. 26 May 2008. "The Pink Elephant." http://www.prowomanprolife. org/2008/05/26/the-pink-elephant/.

PWPL. 1 June 2008. "From Andrea with Love." http://www. prowomanprolife.org/2008/06/01/from-andrea-with-love/.

PWPL. 2 June 2008. "A Tempest in a Teacup." http://www.prowomanprolife. org/2008/06/02/a-tempest-in-a-teacup/.

PWPL. 3 July 2008. "A Callous Sort of Canada." http://www. prowomanprolife.org/2008/07/03/a-callous-sort-of-canada/.

PWPL. 11 July 2008. "Morgentaler Never Forced a Woman to Have an Abortion." http://www.prowomanprolife.org/2008/07/11/morgentaler-never-forced-a-woman-to-have-an-abortion/.

PWPL. 13 July 2008. "About the Strategy." http://www.prowomanprolife. org/2008/07/13/about-the-strategy/.

PWPL. 17 July 2008. "Yeah Good Question." http://www.prowomanprolife.org/2008/07/17/yeah-good-question/.

PWPL. 19 July 2008. "I Blame Rampant Individualism." http://www.prowomanprolife.org/2008/07/19/i-blame-rampant-individualism/.

PWPL. 16 September 2008. "The Uneasy Conscience of Feminism." http://www.prowomanprolife.org/2008/09/16/the-uneasy-conscience-of-feminism/.

PWPL. 1 October 2008. "Palin and Pro-life Consistency." http://www.prowomanprolife.org/2008/10/01/palin-and-pro-life-consistency/.

PWPL. 10 October 2008. "The Abortion Distortion." http://www.prowomanprolife.org/2008/10/10/the-abortion-distortion/.

PWPL. 11 October 2008. "Now He's a 'Catalyst for Change.'" http://www.prowomanprolife.org/2008/10/11/now-hes-a-catalyst-for-change/.

PWPL. 21 October 2008. "Why Imagine, This Is Real Life." http://www.prowomanprolife.org/2008/10/21/why-imagine-this-is-real-life/.

PWPL. 22 October 2008. "Suicides on the Rise." http://www.prowomanprolife.org/2008/10/22/suicides-on-the-rise/.

PWPL. 5 November 2008. "Never Again?" http://www.prowomanprolife.org/2008/11/05/never-again/.

PWPL. 13 November 2008. "Where Is Freedom of Choice When You Really Need It, Part II." http://www.prowomanprolife.org/2008/11/13/where-is-freedom-of-choice-when-you-really-need-it-part-ii/.

PWPL. 18 November 2008. "Canada without Abortion. By Choice." http://www.prowomanprolife.org/2008/11/18/canada-without-abortion-by-choice/.18 april18.

PWPL. 3 December 2008. "Conversation with the Previous Generation." http://www.prowomanprolife.org/2008/12/03/conversation-with-the-previous-generation/.

PWPL. 11 December 2008. "It's Gonna Take Time." http://www.prowomanprolife.org/2008/12/11/its-gonna-take-time/.

PWPL. 28 December 2008. "Name That Author." http://www.prowomanprolife.org/2008/12/28/name-that-author/.

PWPL. 31 December 2008. "And Speaking of Extinct." http://www.prowomanprolife.org/2008/12/31/and-speaking-of-extinct/.

PWPL. 3 January 2009. "My Nomination for Canadian of the Year." http://www.prowomanprolife.org/2009/01/03/my-nomination-for-canadian-of-the-year/.

PWPL. 18 January 2009. "Gaaaack! Huckabee Calls Abortion Slavery." http://www.prowomanprolife.org/2008/01/18/gaaaack-huckabee-calls-abortion-slavery/.

PWPL. 11 February 2009. "The Debate Rages On." http://www.
prowomanprolife.org/2009/02/11/the-debate-rages-on/.

PWPL. 16 February 2009. "Sweden, Home of 'Gender Equity.'" http://www.
prowomanprolife.org/2009/02/16/sweden-home-of-gender-equity/.

PWPL. 8 March 2009. "I Have a Dream, a Song to Sing." http://www.
prowomanprolife.org/2009/03/08/i-have-a-dream-a-song-to-sing/.

PWPL. 9 March 2009. "When You Work in an Abortion Clinic." http://www.
prowomanprolife.org/2009/03/04/when-you-work-in-an-abortion-clinic/.

PWPL. 27 March 2009. "PWPL in the Citizen." http://www.prowomanprolife.
org/2009/03/27/pwpl-in-the-citizen/.

PWPL. 17 April 2009. "Planned Parenthood – in the Influencing Business."
http://www.prowomanprolife.org/2009/04/17/planned-parenthood-in-
the-influencing-business/.

PWPL. 18 April 2009. "New Study: Abortions Cause Relationship Problems."
http://www.prowomanprolife.org/2009/04/18/new-study-abortions-
cause-relationship-problems/.

PWPL. 20 April 2009. "Choice Pushers." http://www.prowomanprolife.
org/2009/04/20/choice-pushers/.

PWPL. 29 April 2009. "Make a Statement without Saying a Word." http://
www.prowomanprolife.org/2009/04/29/make-a-statement-without-
saying-a-word/.

PWPL. 13 May 2009. "Canada's Future or Rather Its Present." http://www.
prowomanprolife.org/2009/05/13/canadas-future-or-rather-its-present/.

PWPL. 14 May 2009. "A Fight We Can't Lose." http://www.prowomanprolife.
org/2009/05/14/a-fight-we-cant-lose/.

PWPL. 21 May 2009. "A Pro-life Movement for the New Millennium." http://
www.prowomanprolife.org/2009/05/21/a-pro-life-movement-for-the-new-
millennium/.

PWPL. 13 June 2009. "I Knew She Was onto Something." http://www.
prowomanprolife.org/2009/06/13/i-knew-she-was-onto-something/.

PWPL. 17 July 2009. "When Logic Replaces Sancitity of Life." http://www.
prowomanprolife.org/2009/07/27/when-logic-replaces-sanctity-of-life/.

PWPL. 19 June 2009. "Running Low in the Sympathy Department." http://
www.prowomanprolife.org/2009/06/19/running-low-in-the-sympathy-
department/.

PWPL. 28 July 2009. "New Study Shows Higher Risk of Breast Cancer after
Abortion." http://www.prowomanprolife.org/2009/07/28/new-study-
shows-higher-risk-of-breast-cancer-after-abortion/.

PWPL. 5 August 2009. "Abortion and Domestic Violence." http://www.
prowomanprolife.org/2009/08/05/domestic-violence-and-abortion/.

PWPL. 10 September 2009. "This Is the One Thing I Would Change above All Others." http://www.prowomanprolife.org/2009/09/10/this-is-the-one-thing-i-would-change-above-all-others/.

PWPL. 16 April 2010. "Are Women Coerced into Abortion in Canada?" http://www.prowomanprolife.org/2010/04/16/are-women-coerced-into-abortions-in-canada/.

PWPL. 18 May 2010. "The Abortion Distortion Part 145,367." http://www.prowomanprolife.org/2010/05/18/the-abortion-distortion-part-145367/.

PWPL. 2 November 2010. "Not Surprising to Readers of This Blog." http://www.prowomanprolife.org/2009/11/02/not-surprising-to-readers-of-this-blog/.

PWPL. 11 April 2013. "Page One News." http://www.prowomanprolife.org/2013/04/11/page-one-news/.

PWPL. 25 April 2013. "I'm a Mother-to-Be." http://www.prowomanprolife.org/2013/04/25/im-a-mother-to-be/.

PWPL. 25 May 2013. "Stephanie Gray in the National Post." http://www.prowomanprolife.org/2013/05/25/stephanie-gray-in-national-post/.

PWPL. 4 July 2013. "'Hoes before Embryos' and Pro-choice Messaging Tactics." http://www.prowomanprolife.org/2013/07/04/hoes-before-embryos-and-pro-choice-messaging-tactics/.

PWPL. 16 August 2013. "How Popular Do You Think This Man Is?" http://www.prowomanprolife.org/2013/08/16/how-popular-do-you-think-this-man-is/.

Rauhala, Ann. 1987. "Abortions More Difficult to Obtain, Groups Say Women Must Travel, Borrow for Procedure." *Globe and Mail*, 30 January, p. A1.

Razack, Sherene. 2004. *Darks Threat and White Knights: The Somalia Affair, Peacekeeping, and the New Imperialism*. Toronto: University of Toronto Press.

REAL Women of Canada. n.d. "About Us." http://www.realwomenofcanada.ca/about-us/.

Reagan, Leslie. 1996. *When Abortion Was a Crime*. Berkeley: University of California Press.

Reardon, David C. 1987. *Aborted Women, Silent No More*. Chicago: Loyola University Press.

Reed, James. 1978. *From Private Vice to Public Virtue: The Birth Control Movement and American Society since 1830*. New York: Basic Books.

Reid, Gail. 2011. "Pro-Life and Positive." *Faith Today* (May/June): 7. http://digital.faithtoday.ca/faithtoday/20110506/?pg=7#pg7.

Reitman, Janet. 2014. "The Stealth War on Abortion." *Rolling Stone*, 15 January. http://www.rollingstone.com/politics/news/the-stealth-war-on-abortion-20140115.

Revie, Linda. 2006. "More Than Just Boots! The Eugenic and Commercial Concerns behind A.R. Kauffman's Birth Controlling Activities." *Canadian Bulletin of Medical History* 23(1): 119–43.

Richardson, Chinué Turner, and Elizabeth Nash. 2006. "Misinformed Consent: The Medical Accuracy of State-Developed Abortion Counseling Materials." *Guttmacher Policy Review* 9(4): 6–11.

Risen, James, and Judy Thomas. 1998. *Wrath of Angels: The American Abortion War*. New York: Basic Books.

Rocca, Corrine, Katrina Kimport, Sarah Roberts, Heather Gould, John Neuhaus, and Diana Foster. 2015. "Decision Rightness and Emotional Responses to Abortion in the United States: A Longitudinal Study." *PloSone* 10(7): e0128832.

Rose, Melody. 2008. *Abortion: A Documentary and Reference Guide*. Westport, CT: Greenwood.

Rose, Melody. 2011. "Pro-Life, Pro-Woman? Frame Extension in the American Antiabortion Movement." *Journal of Women, Politics and Policy* 32(1): 1–27. http://dx.doi.org/10.1080/1554477X.2011.537565.

Saletan, William. 2004. *Bearing Right: How Conservatives Won the Abortion War*. Los Angeles: University of California Press.

Samuels, Dorothy. 2011. "Where Abortion Rights Are Disappearing." *New York Times*, 24 September. http://www.nytimes.com/2011/09/25/opinion/sunday/where-abortion-rights-are-disappearing.html.

Sanger, Alexander. 2004. *Beyond Choice: Reproductive Freedom in the 21st Century*. Cambridge: Perseus Books.

Sanger, Margeret. 1921. "The Eugenic Value of Birth Control Propaganda." *Birth Control Review* 5(10): 1–10.

Sanneh, Kelefa. 2014. "The Intensity Gap: Can a Pro-Life Platform Win Elections?" *New Yorker*, 27 October. http://www.newyorker.com/magazine/2014/10/27/intensity-gap?utm_source=tny&utm_campaign=generalsocial&utm_medium=facebook&mbid=social_facebook.

Saurette, Paul. 2013. "Conservative MP Mark Warawa's Motion 408 Is about Abortion, Not Free Speech." *Toronto Star*, 3 April. http://www.thestar.com/opinion/commentary/2013/04/03/conservative_mp_mark_warawas_motion_408_is_about_abortion_not_free_speech.html.

Saurette, Paul. 2014. "Critics of Trudeau's Abortion Stance Are Missing the Point." *Toronto Star*, 27 May. http://www.thestar.com/opinion/commentary/2014/05/27/critics_of_trudeaus_abortion_stance_are_missing_the_point.html.

Saurette, Paul, and Kelly Gordon. 2013. "Arguing Abortion: The New Anti-Abortion Discourse in Canada." *Canadian Journal of Political Science* 46(1): 157–85. http://dx.doi.org/10.1017/S0008423913000176.

Saurette, Paul, and Shane Gunster. 2011. "Ears Wide Shut: Epistemological Populism, Argutainment and Canadian Conservative Talk Radio." *Canadian Journal of Political Science* 44 (1): 195–218. http://dx.doi.org/10.1017/S0008423910001095.

Saurette, Paul, and Shane Gunster. 2013. "Canada's Conservative Ideological Infrastructure: Brewing a Cup of Cappuccism Conservatism." In *Tax Is Not a Four-letter Word*. Edited by S. Himelfarb and J. Himelfarb, 227–66. Waterloo, ON: Wilfrid Laurier University Press.

Schutten, Andre. 2013. "Pro-Life 101." Speech delivered at St. Patrick's Basilica, Ottawa, ON, 9 May.

Sethna, Christabelle, and Marion Doull. 2013. "Spatial Disparities and Travel to Freestanding Abortion Clinics in Canada." *Women's Studies International Forum* 38: 52–62. http://dx.doi.org/10.1016/j.wsif.2013.02.001.

SH, 2010a. "Psychological Effects." https://www.thesignalhill.com/options/after-abortion-health/psychological-effects-of-abortion.

SH, 2010b. "Physical Effects of Abortion." https://www.thesignalhill.com/options/after-abortion-health/physical-effects-of-abortion.

SH. n.d. "Take Control: Informed Choice." https://www.youtube.com/watch?v=nNqU6EbuOt8&list=PL321EEFF3D1533E12&index=15.

Sharpe, Robert Joel. 2003. *Brian Dickson: A Judge's Journey*. Toronto: University of Toronto Press.

Shaw, Jessica. 2006. "Reality Check: A Close Look at Accessing Abortion Services in Canadian Hospitals." *Canadian for Choice*. http://www.canadiansforchoice.ca/report_english.pdf.

Shaw, Jessica. 2013. "Full-Spectrum Reproductive Justice: The Affinity of Abortion Rights and Birth Activism." *Studies in Social Justice* 7(1): 143–59.

Siegel, Reva. 2007. "The New Politics of Abortion: An Equality Analysis of Woman-Protective Abortion Restriction." *University of Illinois Law Review* (3): 991–1065.

Siegel, Reva. 2008a. "Dignity and the Politics of Protection: Abortion Restrictions under Casey/Carhart." *Yale Law Journal* 117(8): 1694–1800. http://dx.doi.org/10.2307/20454694.

Siegel, Reva. 2008b. "The Right's Reasons: Constitutional Conflict and the Spread of Woman-Protective Antiabortion Argument." *Duke Law Journal* 57(6): 1641–92.

Siegel, Reva, and Sarah Blustain. 2006. "Mommy Dearest?" *American Prospect* 17(10): 22–6.

Silent No More. 2010a. "About us." www.silentnomoreawareness.org.

Silent No More. 2010b. "Testimonials." http://www.silentnomoreawareness.org/testimonies/.

Smith, Andrea. 2005. "Beyond Pro-Choice Versus Pro-Life: Women of Color and Reproductive Justice." *National Women's Studies Association Journal* 17(1): 119–40.

Smith, Joanna. 2010. "A Helping Hand, Far from Home, in a Time of Need." *Toronto Star*, 31 May. http://www.thestar.com/news/canada/2010/05/31/a_helping_hand_far_from_home_in_a_time_of_need.html.

Smith, Miriam. 2007. "Queering Public Policy." In *Critical Policy Studies*. Edited by M. Orsini and Miriam Smith. Vancouver: UBC Press.

Snow, David, and Robert Benford. 1988. "Ideology, Frame Resonance and Participant Mobilization." *International Social Movement Research* 1: 197–217.

Snow, David, and Robert Benford. 1992. "Master Frames and Cycles of Protest." In *Frontiers in Social Movement Theory*. Edited by A.D. Morris and C.M. Mueller. New Haven, CT: Yale University Press.

Snow, David, and Robert Benford. 2000. "Framing Processes and Social Movements: An Overview and Assessment." *Annual Review of Sociology* 26: 611–39.

Snow, David, E. Burke Rochford, Jr., Steven K. Worden, and Robert D. Benford. 1986. "Frame Alignment Processes, Micromobilization, and Movement Participation." *American Sociological Review* 51(4): 464–81.

Snyder-Hall, R. Claire. 2010. "Third-Wave Feminism and the Defense of 'Choice.'" *Perspectives on Politics* 8(1): 255–61. http://dx.doi.org/10.1017/S1537592709992842.

Soloman, Andrew. 2013. "Medical Progress, Social Progress, and Legal Regression." *New Yorker*, 13 April. http://www.newyorker.com/online/blogs/newsdesk/2013/04/north-dakota-abortion-bill-politics-disabilities-health.html.

Staggenborg, Suzanne. 1988. "The Consequences of Professionalization and Formalization in the Pro-choice Movement." *American Sociological Review* 53(4): 585–605. http://dx.doi.org/10.2307/2095851.

Staggenborg, Suzanne. 1999. "The Consequences of Professionalization and Formalization in the Pro-Choice Movement." In *Waves of Protest: Social Movements Since the Sixties*. Edited by J. Freeman and V. Johnson. Lanham, MD: Rowman and Littlefield.

Steel, David. 2004. "We Need to Rethink My Abortion Law." *Manchester Guardian*, 6 July. http://www.guardian.co.uk/politics/2004/jul/06/society.health.

Steiner, Mark. 2006. *The Rhetoric of Operation Rescue*. New York: T. T. and Clark.

Stettner, Shannon. 2012. "'He Is Still Unwanted': Women's Assertions of Authority over Abortion in Letters to the Royal Commission on the Status of Women in Canada." *Canadian Bulletin of Medical History* 29(1): 151–71.

Stone, Laura. 2013a. "Young Pro-Lifers Shun Harper as Rally Comes to Ottawa." *Global News*, 9 May. http://globalnews.ca/news/549204/young-pro-lifers-shun-harper-as-rally-comes-to-ottawa/.

Stone, Laura. 2013b. "Ottawa Catholic Schools Paid $3,000 to Send Students to Pro-life Rally." *Global News*, 10 May. http://globalnews.ca/news/552626/ottawa-catholic-schools-paid-3000-to-send-students-to-pro-life-rally.

Storer, Horatio. 1868. *Criminal Abortion: Its Nature, Its Evidence, Its Law*. Boston: Little Brown.

Strauss, Leo. 2002. *Introduction to Political Philosophy*. New York: Scholarly Book Services.

Stromp, Stanley. 2013. "Mulroney-Era Cabinet Documents Reveal Struggle to Replace Abortion Law Thrown Out by Court." *Toronto Star*, 7 November. http://www.thestar.com/news/canada/2013/11/17/mulroneyera_cabinet_documents_reveal_struggle_to_replace_abortion_law_thrown_out_by_court.html.

Sunstein, Cass. 1993. *Democracy and the Problem of Free Speech*. New York: Free Press.

Swaine, John. 2012. "US Election: Mitt Romney Met Todd Akin Doctor Jack Willke during 2012 Campaign." *Telegraph* (UK), 22 August. http://www.telegraph.co.uk/news/worldnews/us-election/9493653/US-election-Mitt-Romney-met-Todd-Akin-doctor-John-Willke-during-2012-campaign.html.

Talaga, Tanya. 2011. "Hudak Admits to Once Supporting Anti-abortion Petition." *Toronto Star*, 19 July. http://www.thestar.com/news/canada/2011/07/19/hudak_admits_to_once_supporting_antiabortion_petition.html.

Tatalovich, Raymond. 1997. *The Politics of Abortion in the United States and Canada*. New York: M.W. Sharpe.

Thomas, W.D. 1977. "The Badgley Report on Abortion Law." *Canadian Medical Association Journal* 116(9): 966.

Tietze, Christopher, and Stanley K. Henshaw. 1986. *Induced Abortion: A World Review*. New York: Guttmacher Institute.

Tilly, Charles, and Sidney Tarrow. 2006. *Contentious Politics*. Boulder, CO: Paradigm Publishers.

TRL. 2006. "Toronto Group Launches Campaign." 10 July. http://righttolifetoronto.org/index.php?id=26.

TRL. 2010a. "Abortion Statistics." http://www.righttolife.to/key-life-issues/abortion/statistics.

TRL. 2010b. "A List of Major Psychological Sequelae of Abortion." http://www.righttolife.to/wp-content/uploads/2010/02/psychological-effects-of-abortion.pdf.

TRL. 2012. "Student Club Manual: Your Guide to Starting and Maintaining a High School Pro-Life Club." http://www.vivere.info/PDF/StudentClubManual.pdf.

Valenza, Charles. 1985. "Was Margaret Sanger a Racist?" *Family Planning Perspectives* 17(1): 44–46.

Vanderburgh Right to Life. 2009. "Speech by Sarah Palin." http://www.youtube.com/watch?v=AJTM04kGxv0.

Van Dyken, Ruth. n.d. "From Criminal Law to Political Watchdog, Andre Schutten Stands on Guard for You." *Christian Renewal*. http://crmag.com/politicalwatchdog.

VanMaren, Jonathon. n.d. "Abortion Advocate: Graphics Work." http://www.unmaskingchoice.ca/sites/default/files/publications/abortion_advocates_say_graphics_work.pdf.

Vellacott, Maurice. 2005. "Violence No More." 11 May. http://www.mauricevellacott.ca/maurice.html.

Vellacott, Maurice. 2008. "Niece of Martin Luther King Jr Says Abortion is the Civil Rights Movement of the 21st Century." 7 May. http://www.mauricevellacott.ca/2003%20MV%20Speaks/May%207,%202008%20-%20PPLC%20press%20conf%20press%20release.pdf.

Vellacott, Maurice. 2009. "Vellacott Condemns Saskatoon Doctors for Promoting a Climate for Less Abortion." 20 November. http://www.mauricevellacott.ca/2003%20MV%20Speaks/November%2020,%202009%20-%20Vellacott%20commends%20Saskatoon%20doctors%20for%20promoting%20a%20climate%20for%20less%20abortion.pdf.

Vellacott, Maurice. 2010a. "AAPLOG Responds to Joyce Arthur." 5 March. http://www.mauricevellacott.com/Newsroom/March%205,%202010%20-%20AAPLOG%20letter%20re.%20Joyce%20Arthur%20assertions%20on%20abortion.pdf.

Vellacott, Maurice. 2010b. "Letter to Vellacott and Trost." 5 March. http://www.mauricevellacott.ca/2003%20MV%20Speaks/March%205,%202010%20-%20AAPLOG%20letter%20re.%20Joyce%20Arthur%20assertions%20on%20abortion.pdf.

Wahlsten, Douglas. 1997. "Leilani Muir versus the Philosopher King: Eugenics on Trial in Alberta." *Genetica* 99(2–3): 185–98. http://dx.doi.org/10.1007/BF02259522.

Warawa, Mark. 2012. "MP Mark Warawa Introduces Motion to Condemn Discrimination against Females via Sex-Selective Pregnancy Termination." 27 September. http://www.markwarawa.com/media_/mark_in_the_news/mp-mark-warawa-introduces-motion-to-condemn-discrimination-against-females-via-sex-selective-pregnancy-termination.

Warawa, Mark. 2013. "Protect Girls: Stop Gendercide." http://www.markwarawa.com/stop-gendercide/.

Warner, Tom. 2010. *Losing Control: Canada's Social Conservatives in the Age of Rights*. Toronto: Between the Lines.

Warren, Mary Anne. 1985. *Gendercide: The Implications of Sex Selection*. Lanham, MD: Rowman and Littlefield.

We Need a Law. n.d. "About: Can It happen?" http://weneedalaw.ca/about/can-it-happen.

Westen, Drew. 1985. *Self and Society*. Cambridge: Cambridge University Press. http://dx.doi.org/10.1017/CBO9780511598418.

Westen, Drew. 2007. *The Political Brain: The Role of Emotion in Deciding the Fate of the Nation*. New York: Public Affairs.

Williams, Daniel. 2010. *God's Own Party: The Making of the Christian Right*. New York: Oxford University Press.

Willke, John. 1978. *Sex Education in the Classroom?* Cincinnati: Hayes Publishing.

Wilson, Joshua. 2013. *The Street Level Politics of Abortion*. Stanford: Stanford University Press.

Wodak, Ruth, and Michael Meyer. 2009. *Methods of Critical Discourse Analysis*. 2nd ed. London: Sage.

Wong, Beth. 2012, "Jason Kenny Would Reopen Abortion Debate: Pro-Life MP." *Vancouver Observer*, 27 September. http://www.vancouverobserver.com/politics/jason-kenney-would-re-open-debate-abortion-pro-life-mp.

Wood, Jennifer. 2005. "In Whose Name? Crime Victim Policy and the Punishing Power of Protection." *National Women's Studies Association Journal* 17(3): 1–17. http://dx.doi.org/10.1353/nwsa.2005.0076.

Wood, Mary Anne, and Lisa Bolin Hawkins. 1980. "State Regulation of Late Abortion and the Physician's Duty of Care to the Viable Fetus." *Missouri Law Review* 45: 394.

Woodworth, Stephen. 2012a. "Motion 312: 1st Hour of Debate." 26 April. http://www.stephenwoodworth.ca/speeches/motion-312-1st-hour-of-debate.

Woodworth, Stephen. 2012b. "Motion 312: Full Text." http://stephenwoodworth.ca/motion-312/motion-312-full-text.

Wu, Fanda, and Joyce Arthur. 2010. "A Survey of Anti-Choice Protesting Activity at Canadian Abortion Clinics." http://www.arcc-cdac.ca/presentations/ARCC-survey-protest-activity.pdf.

Yeoman, Barry. 2001. "The Quiet War on Abortion." *Mother Jones* (September/October). http://www.motherjones.com/politics/2001/09/quiet-war-abortion.

Youngman, Nicole. 2003. "When Frame Extension Fails: Operation Rescue and the 'Triple Gates of Hell' in Orlando." *Jounal of Contemporary Ethnography* 32(15): 521–54.

Index

40 Days for Life Campaign, 8, 178–81, 377
abortifacients, 44–5, 99
Abortion Act of 1967, 98
Abortion Caravan, 106–7, 121, 175, 373
abortion-harms-women anti-abortion arguments: general, xv, xvii, 32, 198–208, 217, 269, 294, 318, 350; harm to personal life, 206, 208; physical/medical harm, 199–200, 206–10; psychological harm, 199, 206–10, 299–300, 306
Abortion Law Reform Association (ALRA), 97–8, 370
Abortion Rights Coalition Canada (ARCC), 6, 16, 373
Affordable Health Care for America Act (AHCAA), 88, 370
Akin, Todd, xii, 293, 303
Alliance for Life, 109, 373
Alliance for Life Ontario (AFLO), 169, 206, 209, 259, 261, 286–7, 373
Ambrose, Rona, 9
American Birth Control League, 48, 377
American Law Institute (ALI), 51–2, 57, 377

American Medical Association (AMA), 39–46, 49, 52–4, 60, 63, 79, 153, 377
Americans United for Life (AUL), 167, 306, 377
anti-abortion arguments: abortion-harms-men, 200, 202; abortion-harms-society, 200, 202; anti-woman, xiii–xvii, 12–16, 39, 43, 67, 76, 91, 109, 114, 116, 133, 138, 143, 155–6, 189, 210–13, 230, 234, 270, 273, 276, 283, 287, 293, 297–8, 303, 305, 315, 323, 333; fetal personhood, 15, 43, 68, 75–6, 82, 94, 114–15, 125, 130, 137–8, 143, 147, 155, 200–6, 216–18, 220, 253, 292, 300, 311; religious, xvii, 14, 23, 26–7, 65–8, 72, 91, 109, 113, 138–9, 151–3, 189, 191–7, 202, 206, 294–5, 309, 311, 318, 323–6, 328–9, 335; wrong side of history, 200, 202. See also civil rights: anti-abortion arguments/language; abortion-harms-women anti-abortion arguments; pro-woman rhetoric
anti-abortion violence, xvii, 13, 15, 77–9, 91, 134–6, 151, 154–5, 183, 298

Arendt, Hannah, 18
Association for Reformed Political
  Action (ARPA): organization 24,
  162, 166–7, 170, 191, 193, 195, 215,
  373; We Need a Law campaign,
  162–3, 166–8, 376. *See also* Shouten,
  Mike; Schutten, Andre
Association for the Study of
  Abortion (ASA), 58, 377

Bachmann, Michelle, 293
Badgley Report, 107–8, 367
Bergeron, Veronique, 234,
  255–8, 275, 280, 379. *See also*
  ProWomanProLife blog
Berlin, Isaiah, 223
bill C-43, 9, 132–4, 367
bill C-275, 138
bill C-484, 9, 24, 147, 169, 218, 253,
  282, 342, 368. *See also* unborn
  victims acts
bill C-510, 9, 24, 143, 169, 282, 286,
  315, 341–2, 368. *See also* Fernando,
  Roxanne
bill C-537, 9, 368
bill S-7, 139
bill S-16, 137–8
Birkett Commission, 98
Birthright (clinic), 109
Borowski, Joe, 129–30, 156, 271, 286,
  379. See also *Borowski v. Canada*
Borowski v. Canada, 129–30. *See also*
  Borowski, Joe
Boudria, Don, 137, 215, 379
Bourne, Aleck, 97–8, 370. See also
  Bourne decision
Bourne decision, 97–8, 370. *See also*
  Bourne, Aleck
Breitkreuz, Garry, 142
brokerage politics, 324–5, 330

Bruinooge, Rod, 24, 143, 215, 241,
  279, 282, 286, 288–9
Bush, George W., 79, 83, 146, 310

Campaign Life Coalition (CLC), xi,
  24, 109–10, 142, 179, 191, 193–5,
  205–6, 215, 218, 238, 259, 374. *See
  also* Golob, Alissa
Campbell, Ken, 110
Canadian Abortion Rights Action
  League (CARAL), 107, 120, 374
Canadian Bar Association (CBA),
  102–3, 374
Canadian Birth Control League, 100
Canadian Centre for Bioethical
  Reform (CCBR): choice chains,
  294, 353, 357; end the killing
  campaign, 182–4; genocide
  awareness project (GAP),
  175–6, 236, 294, 353, 357, 375;
  organization, xv, 24, 163–87,
  194–6, 214, 216–17, 220, 235–6,
  241, 248–50, 284, 294, 357, 374. *See
  also* Centre for Bioethical Reform;
  Gray, Stephanie; Van Maren,
  Jonathon
Canadian Conference of Catholic
  Bishops, 69, 104, 108–9, 374
Canadian Federation for Sexual
  Health, 342, 374
Canadian Medical Association
  (CMA), 102–4, 351, 358, 374
Canadian politics, 113, 320, 323–5
Canadians for Choice, 274
cappuccino conservatism, 323
Catholicism: Catholic Church, 109,
  325, Catholic schools, 215, 326,
  359; views on abortion, 16, 46,
  50, 69, 91, 108–16, 134, 193–4, 305.
  See also Canadian Conference

of Catholic Bishops; Catholics for Free Choice; Knights of Columbus

Catholics for Free Choice, 69

Center for Bioethical Reform (CBR): Matthew 28:20 materials, 294–5; organization, 235, 294–5, 377

Chatelaine magazine, 101–2

choice (language of), xvii–xviii, 49, 56–7, 62–9, 126–7, 147, 150, 242, 245, 249–53, 309–10, 319, 331–40, 342–9, 351, 353

Choose Life Canada, 110, 374

Christian reconstructionism, 75

Christian right: Canada, 111–13, 115, 323; US, 65, 68–79, 91, 154. *See also* Catholicism; religion

civil rights: anti-abortion arguments/language, 111, 236, 294–5; anti-abortion activists, 113–16; movement, 56, 71, 154, 236–7

Clinton, Bill, 78, 83

Coalition for Life, 109, 111, 375

Committee on Criminal Abortion, 41

Commonwealth v. Isaiah Bangs, 38, 370

Comstock Act, 45, 48–9, 371

Concerned Women for America, 293, 377

Conference Board of Canada, 358

Connolly, William, 18, 223–4, 247

Conservative Party of Canada, 11, 113, 149, 237, 244, 288, 322–6, 330, 345

Criminal Law Amendment (1969), 101, 105, 108

critical discourse analysis (CDA), 25–7, 334–7

culture wars, 70, 202, 207, 284, 331

discourse: approach to, 17–21; sanitized vs. unsanitized, 49–50, 197, 309, 311, 324–6. *See also* critical discourse analysis; framing; narrative; rebranding

Doe v. Bolton, 59–64, 77, 91, 149–50, 371

Dworkin, Andrea, 265, 273

Eisenstadt v. Baird, 59, 371

Elliot Institute, 300, 308, 311

Emergency Organization for the Defense of Unborn Life, 104

Epp, Jake, 112

Epp, Ken, 24, 147, 218, 253, 282, 368, 380

Evangelical Fellowship Canada (EFC), 24, 174, 191–5, 213–15, 375

Faludi, Susan, 13–14, 73–7, 273, 279, 288

family heritage anti-abortion activists, 113–16

feminism, 115, 210, 230, 245–6, 250, 254–6, 258, 261–2, 265–6, 270, 283, 287, 319, 331–3

Feminists for Life of America, 304

Fernando, Roxanne, 24, 282, 341, 368. *See also* bill C–510

Flanagan, Tom, 197

Focus on the Family Canada, 23, 311, 375. *See also* Institute of Marriage and Family

framing: epistemological framing, 26, 264–70; issue framing, 26, 32–3, 253–64; rhetorical strategy, xvi, 19, 21, 26, 32–3, 222–45, 251–5, 257–64, 268, 270, 282, 294, 319–20; values framing, 26, 32–3, 245–53

Freedom of Access to Clinic Entrances Act (FACE Act), 78, 154, 371

Gardner v. Massachusetts, 48
Gibbons, Linda, 155, 179, 380
Gladwell, Malcolm, 228, 403
Golob, Alissa, 215, 218, 238, 259, 380.
    See also Campaign Life Coalition
Gonzales v. Carthart, 83–4, 295, 307,
    310, 371
Gray, Stephanie, 168, 177, 184, 213,
    214, 250, 294
Griswold v. Connecticut, 48, 58–9,
    61–2, 371
Guttmacher Institute, 5, 85

Haidasz, Stanley, 138–9
Harper, Stephen, 6, 9–11, 113,
    149, 170, 175, 182, 242, 320, 323,
    342–3, 380
Harris v. McRae, 87, 371
Hyde Amendment, 66–8, 72, 79,
    87–8, 91, 148, 372

implicit association test, 228
informed consent: arguments,
    199, 251, 255, 300; legislation,
    81–2
Institute of Marriage and Family
    Canada (IMFC), 24, 214, 375

Jane Collective, 57, 377–8

Kahneman, Daniel, 226–9
Kay, Barbara, 176, 198, 212, 380
Kenney, Jason, 9–10, 320–1
Kensington Clinic, 344
Knights of Columbus, 109,
    326–7, 375

labour movement, 121, 358
Lader, Larry, 58, 377
Lakoff, George, 18, 33, 272–6

Liberal Party of Canada, 7, 24,
    149, 348
LifeCanada, 23, 172, 191, 215,
    252, 375
LifesiteNews, xi, xiii, 172, 191,
    274, 378
Littlejon, Reggie, xiv
Lord Ellenborough Act, 93–4, 117, 370
Lord Lansdowne's Act. *See* Offences
    against the Person Act

Manning, Preston, 192, 211, 236
Manning Centre, 10, 197
March for Life, xi–xvi, 8, 25, 161, 167,
    172–3, 194–6, 215, 240, 242, 263,
    270, 327, 337, 353, 374, 376
March for Life Youth Conference,
    xiv–xv, 161, 172–3, 193
Martin, Keith, 138
Medicaid, 87–8
medicalized discourse, 43, 46, 51,
    54–7, 63, 97–8, 102–3, 106, 108,
    110, 117, 125, 127, 153–6, 300,
    311–12, 328
methodological reliability, 27–31
Meyer v. Nebraska, 61
moral majority, 112
Morgentaler, Henry, 104, 107, 118,
    123–9, 380
Morgentaler v. The Queen, 118–19
motion 312, 9–10, 138, 167, 217,
    236–7, 241, 347, 368
motion 408, 6, 9, 143, 167, 171, 218,
    242–3, 261–2, 348, 368
motion 523, 142
Mrozek, Andrea, 23, 169, 171, 177,
    192, 212–14, 240–1, 251, 254, 257,
    267, 279–80, 289–90, 309, 381. *See
    also* Institute of Marriage and
    Family; ProWomenProLife blog

Mulroney, Brian, 8, 112, 126, 128, 132, 381
Myers, Lonny, 58, 377

narrative (rhetorical strategy), xvii, 19–21, 26, 30, 33, 53–5, 68–9, 101, 121–2, 254–9, 269–71, 277–91, 310, 319, 332, 335–6, 353–4
National Abortion Federation (NAF) Canada, 140, 344, 376
National Association for the Repeal of Abortion Laws (NARAL), 58, 373
National Campus Life Network (NCLN), 24, 165–6, 173, 186–8, 214, 376
National Council of Women, 107
National Organization for Women (NOW): NOW bill of rights, 58; organization, 58, 378
National Right to Life Committee (NRLC), 147, 293, 297, 303, 378
negative liberty, 223–5
networks of association, 53, 222, 227–34
new (anti-)abortion caravan, 344, 376
New Brunswick, 6–7, 92, 94–5, 140–1, 148, 343–4
New Left, 121
nurturant parent tone, 21, 33, 271–7, 310

Offences against the Person Act, 94, 370
Operation Rescue, 13, 71–9, 91, 112, 134, 152, 155, 297, 379
Operation Save America, 79, 379
Ottawa Coalition to End Violence against Women, 342
Ouellet, Marc, 22

Palin, Sarah, 189–90, 290, 292–3, 304, 382
Pankiw, Jim, 142
Partial Birth Abortion Ban (PBA Ban), 83, 295, 371–2
patriarchy, 256–8, 282, 322
Paul, Alice, 248, 260
Pellerin, Brigette, 23, 191–2, 214, 381
Perry, Rick, 303
Petrasek, Grace, 115. *See also* REAL Women
Planned Parenthood, 47, 266, 353
Planned Parenthood of Southeastern Pennsylvania v. Robert P. Casey et al., 81–3, 86, 89, 91, 296–7, 371–2
positive liberty, 223–4
post-abortion syndrome (PAS), 209–10, 240, 299
pre/post quickening distinction, 39–41, 93, 145
Prince Edward Island (PEI), 6, 92, 140, 148, 200, 344
Pro-Life World Congress, 184
ProWomanProLife (PWPL) blog, 22–4, 168–71, 174, 177, 191–2, 199, 205, 213–14, 238, 240–1, 247, 251, 255–8, 267–9, 275–80, 283–91, 309, 376
pro-woman rhetoric, xiii–xviii, 32–3, 181, 184, 200, 212, 218, 220–1, 233, 238, 243, 245, 248, 254–5, 270–1, 277, 283–4, 288–9, 292–311, 318–19, 322, 330–3, 338–9, 345

Quebec, 22, 107, 119–20, 131–2, 139, 240, 331, 358

REAL Women, 115, 376
Reardon, David, 209, 300, 308–9

rebranding, xvii, 213, 222, 231–2,
244, 353
Reform Party, 113, 149, 236, 323
Reid, Gail, 199
religion, xvii, 14, 23, 26–7, 65–9, 72,
91, 109, 113, 138–9, 151–3, 189,
191–7, 202, 206, 294–5, 309, 311,
318, 323–6, 329, 335
Renaissance Canada Ministry, 110
repetition (rhetorical strategy), 206–11
Report on Criminal Abortion, 41
reproductive justice, 250, 333,
338–45, 349, 353, 356–9
Republican Party / Grand Old Party
(GOP), 4, 70–1, 77, 148, 293, 310,
323, 325
Resolution 17, 140
revivalist Catholic anti-abortion
activists, 113–16, 134
rights: arguments/language, viii, 54,
56, 58, 62–4, 82–4, 86, 104–6, 108,
111, 118–19, 126–32, 143, 147, 190,
198–9, 213, 217, 233, 247, 253–5,
300–3, 308–9; Charter rights,
122–5, 130–2, 137; fetal rights,
xiii, 129–32, 147, 181, 352; human
rights, 168, 232–8, 327, 339; LGBT
issues, 238, 327, 332; privacy
rights, 58–63, 68, 80, 83, 87, 150,
329, 339; right to security, 124, 150,
213, 369; women's rights, 14, 54,
57, 82–3, 86, 104, 126, 143, 199, 213,
218, 233, 247–8, 253–5, 259, 300,
303–4, 308, 349. See also civil rights
Rilseston v. Ullman, 48
Roe v. Wade, 4–5, 59–61, 65, 71, 79–80,
85, 90–1, 250, 268, 296, 372
Romalis, Garson, 135, 381
Romney, Mitt, xi, 4–5, 303
Roxanne's Law. See bill C-510

Royal Commission on the Status of
Women (RCSW), 102, 369
R. v. Morgentaler, 6–8, 11, 92, 118,
120, 123–6, 129–30, 137, 140–1,
143, 149–50, 164, 166, 250, 270,
330, 343, 369
R. v. Oakes (Oakes Test), 122–5
Ryan, Paul, 295

Sanger, Margaret, 47–50, 56, 58–9,
100, 382
Santorum, Rick, 147, 190, 293, 303, 383
Schouten, Mike, 167–8, 381. See also
Association for Reformed Political
Action
Schutten, Andre, 170, 195–6, 381.
See also Association for Reformed
Political Action
section 7, 122–6, 129
section 251 (Criminal Code), 105–7,
118–19, 123–6, 129, 133, 150, 369.
See also therapeutic abortion
committees
Signal Hill, 23, 169, 203, 215, 255,
268, 286–7, 376
Silent No More campaign, 169, 177,
268–70, 299, 354, 376
Society for Humane Abortion (SHA),
57, 379
Sonier, Faye, 23, 174, 213–14, 381.
See also ProWomanProLife blog
standpoint epistemology, xviii,
264–9, 319, 332
Steckle, Paul, 137
Stenberg v. Carthart, 83
Stephen, Alexander Maitland, 100
stereotypes, 228–30, 260, 272, 275
Storer, Horatio, 41, 43–4, 63, 152,
383. See also American Medical
Association

strict father tone, 21, 33, 271–80, 315, 319
Stupak-Pitts Amendment, 88, 372
Summerhill, Louise, 109
Susan B. Anthony List, 293, 304
system 1 and 2 thinking, 229–30
Szabo, Paul, 24, 381

Tea Party, 79, 323
therapeutic abortion committees (TACs), 51–2, 60–1, 67–9, 77–8, 105–9, 114–16, 119, 125, 131, 369. See also *R. v. Morgentaler*; section 251
Toronto Right to Life (TRL), 165–6, 187, 209–10, 259, 267, 285–6, 376
traditional portrait: in Canada, xvii, 14–17, 153–6, 159–63, 166, 170, 180–1, 182, 186, 188–92, 196, 198, 199–200, 216–18, 220, 243, 254, 271, 274–5, 279, 284, 291, 317–20, 331; in United States, xii, xviii, 12–13, 15, 31–2, 67, 152–6, 292–7, 301, 310, 319, 331. See also anti-abortion arguments; religion
TRAP bills, 85–7, 90, 148, 252–4, 306–7, 372
triangulation, 27, 29–31, 335–6
TRL/NCLN High School Student Club Manual, 165, 187, 214
Trudeau, Justin, 7, 149, 348
Trudeau, Pierre, 101, 103, 105, 120, 368

unborn victims acts, 24, 146–7, 218, 282, 368, 373
UN Declaration of Human Rights, 237

undue burden standard, 80–1, 89, 297
United States v. One Package of Japanese Pessaries, 48

Vancouver Women's Caucus, 106, 121, 168, 376. See also Abortion Caravan
Van Loen, Peter, 9
Van Maren, Jonathon, 168, 175, 381. See also Canadian Centre for Bioethical Reform
Vellacott, Maurice, 24, 139, 179, 207–8, 237, 252, 259, 287, 382

Walberg, Rebecca, 191, 288–9, 382. See also ProWomanProLife blog
Wappel, Tom, 138
Warawa, Mark, 6, 9–10, 143, 167, 169, 171, 218, 242, 261–4, 348, 382
Webster v. Reproductive Health Services, 79–82, 89, 91, 373
Westen, Drew, 18, 211, 227–32, 236, 244, 277–8
Westen, John Henry, 172, 382. See also Lifesite News
Willke, John C., xi–xv, 76–7, 302–3, 308
Women's International League for Peace and Freedom, 100
women's "right to know" acts, 142, 306
Woodworth, Stephen, 9–10, 138, 167, 217, 236–7, 241–2, 347, 382

Zaleski, Tanya, 210, 240, 274, 382. See also ProWomanProLife blog